FILMED IN SUPERMARIONATION

STEPHEN LA RIVIÈRE

network

Published by
Network Distributing Limited,
19-20 Berghem Mews,
Blythe Road,
London, W14 0HN
networkonair.com

Book design and typesetting by Martin Cater
Cover design and chapter introduction graphics by Justin T. Lee

First printing 2009
Second printing (new edition) 2014

ISBN 978-0-9929766-0-6

Editor: Anita Jackson

Printed in Hong Kong

With grateful thanks to the following people for the help and time given in the preparation of this book: Gerry Anderson, Sylvia Anderson, Betty Anderson, Mary Anderson, Dee Anderson, Jamie Anderson, Joy Anderson, Bob Bell, Ed Bishop, John Blundall, John Bluthal, Martin Bower, Denise Bryer, Steve Camden, Chris Cassell, Mike Clark, Victoria Clarke, Brian Cobby, Thomas Cock, Simon Coward, Terry Curtis, Chris Dale, Barry and Annette, Davies, Kevin Jon Davies, Theo de Klerk, Sam Denham, Mike Dennison, Robert Easton, Leo Eaton, David Elliott, Richard Farrell at Andersonic, Gary Files, Catherine Ford, Andrew Foxley, Alex J Geairns, Peter and Anna George, Pauline Gitter, David Graham, Cy Grant, Keith Grant, Graydon Gould, Richard Gunner, Douglas Hamilton, Rob Hammond, Simon Harries, Bill Harris, Dave Hicks, Ken Holt, Islet Park Residents' Association, Anita Jackson, Bill James, John Jelly, Brian Johnson, Osamu Kishikawa, Julian Knott, David Lane, Brian La Rivière, Julia and Joy Laurey, Shaqui Le Vesconte, Rosalind Lloyd, Alistair Lock, Doug Luke, Julien Lugrin, Francis Matthews, Liz Morgan, Gerry O'Riordan, Andy and Helen Rolfe, Nicholas Parsons, Alan Pattillo, Alan Perry, Nicole Pilcher, Laura Demetriades at Protyres Slough, Arthur Provis, Jill Raymond, John Read, Shane Rimmer, Desmond Saunders, Alan Shubrook, Ernest 'Plugg' Shutt, Judith Shutt, Slough Library, Slough Observer, Boyd Skinner, Rosemary Anne Sisson, Andrew Swann, John and Jean Taylor, David Taylor, Anthony Taylor, Dave Thornhill, Peter Thornley, Ralph Titterton, Leigh Took, Chris Trice, Mike Trim, Ken Turner, Mary Turner, Simon Wickes, Keith Wilson, Shaun Whittacker-Cook, White Waltham Aerodrome, Victoria Williams, Roger Woodburn, Martin and Hugh Woodhouse, Satoko Yamaguchi, Matt Zimmerman (and anyone else I might have forgotten…).

Also, extra special thanks to Tim Beddows for indulging just about every whim I've had on this project ("I want to blow up Bray Studios…"), Susan Buck for providing a secret base to retire to, and to Geraldine Donaldson for putting up with it all.

Dedicated to:
Andrew Smith and Justin Lee – for being my supportive co-pilots on this tough, challenging and amazing journey. Thank you.

CONTENTS

David and wife, Averil, at the the Royal Television Society Awards.

FOREWORD

In 2002, a seventeen-year-old student telephoned to ask for an interview about my work on Gerry Anderson's puppet films. This interview, together with others from those involved in making the programmes, was part of a website that he wanted to develop. The results of the interviews were very good and I contacted the student, Stephen La Rivière, and suggested that he write a book about the making of the various puppet shows. "No," said Stephen, "I want to make films"...

And so he did and, indeed, has made some very good documentaries. The first film, *Full Boost Vertical*, was about the making of *Supercar* and again Stephen wanted to interview me. I had just come out of hospital and was recovering from a heart-bypass operation, but felt that I would be okay to do this. After *five* hours of being interviewed I was exhausted. However, Stephen hadn't finished with me yet... I was driven to the old studio at Slough where we met up with old friends and puppet colleagues; Mary Turner, Roger Woodburn and cameraman John Read. We carried out another gruelling three hours of filming with us reminiscing about the days of long ago...

...In spite of this, Stephen and I remain good friends...!

In 2008, Stephen finally decided to write this book. He spent a great deal of time researching the facts, looking through newspapers, books, paperwork, old film archives and, *most importantly*, talking to those who made the films. This first edition was published in 2009.

Last year, Stephen decided to turn the book into a brilliant new documentary-film of the same name for cinema and television, rounding up the old team again for further interviews and quizzing us about things we'd long since forgotten. Over the course of doing this he has managed to gather even more information about those far-off days and, as a result, he has been able to update and republish this book in a super new format.

It's hard to believe that after fifty years the interest in the puppet shows is as strong as ever. And for fans old and new, here is the book that tells the real story of those enjoyable years and how it all happened...

David Elliott, June 2014

Director, Editor and Production Supervisor at A.P. Films 1957 – 1966

(*The Adventures of Twizzle* to *Thunderbirds*)

The ADVENTURES of TWIZZLE

TORCHY the BATTERY BOY

•1957-1958•

HOW IT BEGAN 1

The Adventures of Twizzle, and Torchy the Battery Boy

"They are all most keen and enthusiastic to make these the best puppet films ever made. I too feel that this is a wonderful opportunity, and may well be the beginning of something big!"

Puppeteer, Joy Laurey, August 16th 1957

PART-TIME TYPIST for local Film Studios
Afternoons. – Telephone Maidenhead 140

The advertisement placed by 'local film studios' in the *Maidenhead Advertiser* on August 17th 1956 attracted little attention. Sandwiched between larger adverts for the Canadian Red Cross Hospital in Taplow, British Filters in Maidenhead and an advert promoting sexual inequality by proclaiming, 'Men with Ambition Required', it would have been easy to overlook this notice among the multitude of classifieds for other companies.

"You do realise you'll be working with five men?" the first telephone applicant was asked. "That won't be a problem," she replied. A short time later a second applicant called and succeeded in making a strong impression. "She sounds really nice," enthused one of the directors, deciding to employ her and no doubt hoping that her typing skills were adequate. The first applicant was promptly forgotten, both by the company and by history. Such is fate…

The second applicant faced a strenuous walk up the steep hill, with lush fields to the right and red brick cottages lining both sides of the road, protected from the bright sunlight by trees in full leaf. She arrived at Stockwells, a small cul-de-sac on Berry Hill, Taplow, and came to the large, dilapidated old house that was home to the modest film studios of the ad, namely, Pentagon Films. She paused for a moment to check it was the right place, wondering what awaited her inside a building so imposing but also so obviously neglected. Undeterred, she stepped up to the house, knocked at the door and waited to be greeted.

Her name was Sylvia Thamm.

Vandervell Products Lt
COX GREEN MAIDENHEAD
Telephone 2801.

LEDGER CLERK, Experienced female required, aged 23/40. Hours 9 a.m.—5.30 p.m., 5-day week.—Telephone Maidenhead 2275, Ext. 1, or write the Secretary, C.W.C. Equipment Ltd., Kings Grove, Maidenhead.

OPPORTUNITY FOR YOUNG MAN having completed National Service, as Co. Clerk in Company operating modern system of Standard Costing. Every encouragement given to suitable candidate.—Apply to Assistant Secretary, British Filters Ltd., Cox Green. Maidenhead 4144.

PART-TIME TYPIST for local Film Studios Afternoons.—Telephone Maidenhead 140.

SECRETARY/SHORTHAND TYPIST required for Matron's Office. Must be capable of working on own initiative. Salary within scale £175—£500 per annum according to age. Applications, stating age and experience with names and addresses of two referees, to Secretary, Canadian Red Cross Memorial Hospital, Taplow.

SECRETARY/SHORTHAND TYPIST required to fill responsible vacancy in Estate Director's department of property company. Work of varied and interesting nature. Age 21-35. Hours 9—5.30. Every fourth Saturday morning working.—Apply Slough Estates Ltd., Bedford Avenue, Trading Estate, Slough. Telephone Slough 20303.

SECRETARY to Chief Engineer required. —Apply Ronald Trist & Co. Ltd., Bath Rd., Slough.

SHORTHAND TYPIST required.—Apply Ronald Trist & Co. Ltd., Bath Rd., Slough.

SHORTHAND TYPIST required by local agricultural engineers.—Telephone Maidenhead 372.

THE MIDLAND BANK has a vacancy in Maidenhead/Slough/Windsor area for a young lady Clerk aged 16-20. Applicants should be single and of a good educational standard. Non-contributory pension scheme; annually progressive salary scale according to age. £215 per annum at 16, £250 per

2604

FILM PRODUCERS.

PENTAGON FILMS LTD.
(T.V., instructional, industrial, educational & short feature films, animated, diagram & cartoon), Stockwells, Berry hill, Taplow. Phone, Maidenhead 140 & 2160

• • •

"I saw this ad, and it said 'film company'. I've always been a great film person. So when I saw that I thought, 'Ah – I'd be interested in that'," remembers Sylvia. "They didn't give too much information. When I got to the top of the hill – Berry Hill, Taplow – outside Maidenhead, I thought, 'I can't see anything that looks like a studio here.' And I walked away and walked back again. And then I saw this old house. Beautiful old house. Well, it had been. It was like something out of a Hollywood movie. Everything looked ramshackle, but it had once been a fantastic building. I walked up to the door, knocked – nothing at all. And then I begin to get worried. I think, 'What are they doing here? I don't like this.' I started to walk away and thought, 'Why did I bother?' As I got to the gate I saw a movement in one of the upstairs windows. And I thought, 'Oh my god, someone's in there.' So my first instinct was to go, and then I thought, 'Well, that wouldn't be very nice.' I went back to the door and the door creaked open and there was a very nice man, quite small, very serious, who I later learned was one of the chiefs of the company. Anyway, we went up some stairs and we went to a big board room. I felt as if I was at an audition or something, and I'm saying to myself inside, 'I'm not going to stay here.' They were questioning me as if I was getting this top job. And I thought, 'Little do you know that I'm never going to come

Left, above: "I saw this ad..." situations vacant column, Maidenhead Advertiser, August 17th, 1956. Below: Small ad for Pentagon films.

back!' So off I went. 'My god I've got out of that!' Two days later I got a phone call – urgent phone call – and they said, 'Please, when can you start? We're in a lot of trouble – we've got something coming.' Whereas before they were saying, 'Oh, we'll let you know.' So that's how it all started…"

When Sylvia joined the group of 'five men' in mid-1956, Pentagon was a fledgling company formed in March that year. It was the result of a collaboration between a group of film-makers previously employed by another production company, Polytechnic Films.

Established after the war in 1946 by E Smith Morris, a camera engineer known almost universally to friends as 'Smithy', Polytechnic specialised in *Instructional, industrial, educational & short features, animated, diagram & cartoon* films.[1] The company operated out of a dilapidated house in Taplow, in the shadow of several major film studios including Bray, Denham and of course Pinewood, which was to be found on the outskirts of neighbouring town, Slough.

Polytechnic was approached in 1955 by Pete Collins, a theatrical agent, to produce a series called *Pete's Freaks*, a show that would feature unlikely freakish stunts and off-beat characters from across Europe. Gerry Anderson, a 26-year-old film and dubbing editor, was hired to direct the series, despite having no previous experience as a director. Anderson remembers: "He (Collins) said, 'I want a show called *Pete's Freaks.*' I said, 'That sounds like a brand of biscuits!'" Taken aback by this off-the-wall observation, and realising that Peek Freans' biscuits might pop into other minds, Collins revised his title. When the series was commissioned, it sounded less like a tabloid headline and was called *You've Never Seen This.* Throughout the next few months Anderson and his crew put out feelers across Europe in search of bizarre and intriguing, if generally pointless, talents. The throng of contributors included a cyclist who claimed to be able to ride at 109 miles per hour, a woman who created clothes from dogs' hair, a restaurant that ignored tradition (in the pre-fast food world at least) by making customers feel unwelcome and deliberately serving inedible food, not to mention a man who lived in a bottle for a year. The shoot was fraught with difficulties and with the sort of make-or-break situations that can lead to arguments between collaborators or forge closer bonds. In this case, Anderson and his cameraman, Arthur Provis, overcame the odds and formed a close friendship.

"We did three trips out to Europe and it was a nightmare to shoot," remembers Arthur. "Pete Collins had been an alcoholic. He used to be so careful about what he ate. He even used to smell fruit salads to make sure there was no alcohol in them."

In spite of this vigilance, there were occasional relapses. "During one of the trips he disappeared for days. Gerry and I literally held the show together."

Gerry's first wife, Betty, recalls Gerry's account of the problematic shoot vividly. "Early in the production of the series, Gerry

---

1 Listing from Maidenhead services directory 1955.

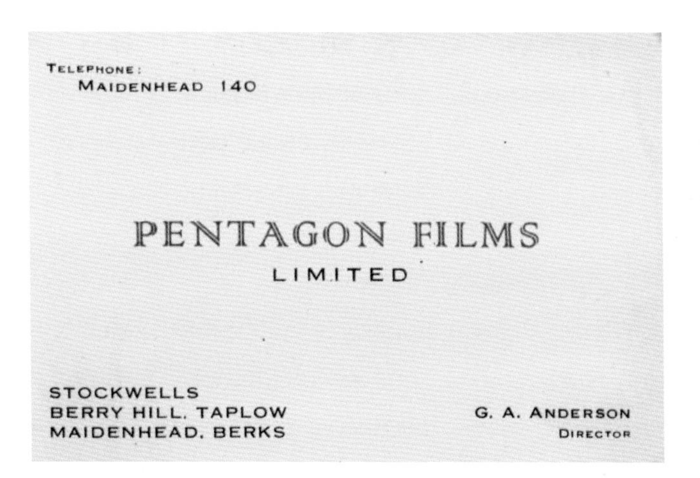
TELEPHONE:
MAIDENHEAD 140

PENTAGON FILMS
LIMITED

STOCKWELLS
BERRY HILL, TAPLOW
MAIDENHEAD, BERKS

G. A. ANDERSON
DIRECTOR

went away to film and I was expecting him to be away about 3 weeks. However, it was only about a week later, he arrived unexpectedly and I was shocked to see him home so soon. I asked him what happened and this is what he said: The guy who was supposedly the producer was expected to come out a day or so after the crew, but he didn't turn up. He was coming with the money. We're talking cash. They didn't know what to do. They had virtually no more money to carry on and they went to where he was going to be staying, which was quite a nice little hotel, nothing too posh. Then Gerry said that one of the crew said, 'I'll tell you what. I wonder if this guy went to the place next door by mistake.' So they went to this place next door and he was there, but he was absolutely drunk out of his mind. He had to be taken to hospital, and he'd blown most of the money. Gerry said they're not sure how he'd managed to get rid of so much. He said, 'We had to come home because we didn't have the money to carry on filming.'"

Pete Collins had christened his show well. *You've Never Seen This* turned out to be a very apt title because most viewers had no opportunity to see it. Despite securing a sale to Associated Redifussion, only a few instalments are known to have been broadcast, in late 1955.[2]

Collins' antics came at a price, though. Polytechnic's backers removed their funding support for the company. "Pentagon went to wall over this," says Arthur.[3]

Following *You've Never Seen This* four members of Polytechnic decided to establish a new company, specialising in the same type of business, but also hoping to capitalise on the recent formation of Independent Television. Together with Gerry Anderson,

---

2 At the time of writing, three editions are known to have been broadcast. It is possible that others were shown as unscheduled filler material.

3 Arthur, Gerry and Betty remember that Polytechnic went bust. However, according to Companies House the company dissolved in 1968. It seems more likely that the company was dormant after 1955.

Arthur Provis and Red Ferderer (sound recordist on *You've Never Seen This*), Smith Morris, the owner of Polytechnic, formed a new company with finance provided by Douglas Dobbs. "We called ourselves Pentagon Films because there were five of us," says Provis, providing the logical explanation. "And we were initially based at Red's house in Walton-on-Thames." Shortly afterwards, the Pentagon team decided to move back to Polytechnic's former home in Berry Hill. "The house was big and had a little film studio so it was good for us, but the place was riddled with dry rot."

September 1955 saw the not-altogether welcome arrival of commercial television in the United Kingdom. Launched in the 1930s, the interruption of broadcasts during the war had severely curtailed television's success with the masses, but the 1950s saw the medium come into its own. Coverage of the Queen's coronation in 1953 secured the TV screen a place in many living rooms throughout the land. At a time when the publication of George Orwell's novel *Nineteen Eighty-Four* was relatively fresh in the mind, it is not surprising that these 'telescreens' were viewed by some as the first step towards the dystopian world of 'Big Brother', as depicted by Orwell, and that the medium struggled to win over its detractors. Indeed, there was deep disquiet about the social acceptability of owning a television. Was this picture-box just a mind-numbing toy suitable for the stupid and semi-literate? "People who drop their aitches are now putting them on their roofs," remarked one indignant (and snobbish) commentator, referring to the H-shaped aerials appearing throughout Britain. If the British Broadcasting Corporation, with its lofty ideals, was viewed with such suspicion for venturing into television, it seemed inevitable that the advent of commercial television would rouse a storm of protest. Lord Reith, Director General of the BBC, a man passionately committed to public interest broadcasting free from political and commercial paymasters, was furious. He was not one to mince his words: "Somebody introduced smallpox, bubonic plague and the Black Death. Somebody is minded now to introduce sponsored broadcasting." Television had one other problem: few people understood it and even fewer had a vision for developing it. To many executives, television was at worst merely radio with pictures and, at best, an electronic method of saving people the effort of going to the theatre to watch a performance.

1954 had seen the founding of the Independent Television Authority, a body formed to oversee the development of Independent Television. It was charged with dividing the UK into three franchise areas, otherwise known as 'regions'. These franchises (London, the Midlands and the North) were initially awarded to four broadcasters for the launch[4] – Associated British Cinemas (ABC), Associated

---

4. Weekdays and weekends were separate and awarded independently. For instance, ATV had the Midlands on weekdays and London on weekends.

Opposite, left: Gerry's business card. Right: 'Twicicles as nicicles': Pentagon's first tangle with marionettes.

TeleVision (ATV), Associated-Rediffusion, and Granada. Together they made Independent Television (ITV), the first rival to the BBC and the UK's first commercial television station. Unlike the BBC, funded through the licence fee paid by every household in possession of a television set, ITV was subsidised by sponsored advertisements. Scottish Television's Roy Thompson would later famously describe an ITV franchise as "a licence to print money."

Pentagon benefited from this untapped market and attracted a number of high profile commissions, including Anadin and Kellogg's Rice Crispies, and produced commercials for a variety of everyday objects. "We made adverts for all sorts of things," says Arthur Provis. "Beer, cigarettes etc. We didn't do too badly." It was the commission from Kellogg's, however, that inadvertently changed the lives of Anderson and Provis forever.

Amongst the schedules in ITV's inaugural month, there was a new puppet show for children, *The Adventures of Noddy*, based on the Enid Blyton books. In 1955, Kellogg's purchased the rights to use Noddy in commercials, and was soon ready to commission adverts featuring him. Kellogg's approached Pentagon in 1956 to produce the commercials, using the original puppets from the series with puppeteer Peter Hayes. "This Noddy puppet was operated around the (cereal) pack. We were quite impressed with this," says Arthur Provis. "Gerry said, 'Why don't we make a film with puppets? We can make our actors instead of renting them.' Which we all thought was funny."

Pentagon had another experience with puppets when they produced a 15-minute, colour cinema film called *Here Comes Kandy*. Although Gerry and Arthur aren't credited, many of the names on the on the end titles were frequent collaborators with Pentagon Films, some of whom went on to become future collaborators with A.P. Films.

These puppet encounters brought Pentagon to the attention of marketing executive, Suzanne Warner, and prolific romantic novelist, Roberta Leigh, who had developed an idea for a children's television series entitled *The Adventures of Twizzle*.

In *The Stage and Television Today* in 1964, Roberta talked about securing her commission: "I didn't know one end of the camera from another when John McMillan (Associated Rediffusion executive) gave me my very first start with *The Adventures of Twizzle*. I sent him a manuscript; he loved it, told me to make a film, and put the money up for it. I blithely said, 'Yes,' because I was quite determined to do it and I wanted to see my characters come alive."

"A woman called Roberta Leigh turned up one day with 52 scripts for a series called *Twizzle*," says Gerry Anderson. "She asked us if we'd like to do them and we said, 'Yes!' Then she said they were with puppets and I nearly vomited on the floor."

By the time Leigh and Warner approached Pentagon, Anderson and Provis had grown disillusioned with their other partners and had decided to take the risky step of going it alone in the notoriously precarious business of film-making. "We'd already

made up our minds to leave when Roberta came along," says Arthur. "Gerry and I told her we were leaving and that we were interested in producing the films."

The two friends left Pentagon in the summer of 1957[5] and promptly incorporated a new company, eventually settling on the name A.P. Films – Anderson Provis Films – although it was not unknown for both directors to forget this even-handed title and refer to it as either 'Anderson Productions' or 'Arthur Provis Films' respectively!

Roberta was keen to get the series underway quickly and, after a number of meetings at her house in Hampstead, a contract was drawn up between the newly-founded A.P. Films and her quirkily named company, Banty Books Productions. Leigh drove a hard bargain, wanting 52 fifteen-minute episodes, with the first films to be ready for transmission in November 1957. Aware that the turn-around time would be crippling, Anderson and Provis had no choice but to accept the commission and its meagre budget of around £450 per episode. Gerry Anderson confesses that he had optimistic visions of himself as a sort of Stephen Spielberg of the time. So, the reality seemed grim: "There I was making puppet films, but we needed the money, so we took them on."

Before a frame of film could be exposed, the first task for the company was to find a suitable space to make the series. Eventually

5. Contrary to popular belief, Pentagon Films did *not* go into liquidation in 1957. It continued operating after Gerry and Arthur left, and was finally dissolved in 1968 along with Polytechnic.

Above: "Miss Havisham's wedding feast" – Islet Park's gothic exterior and, right, inside.

they settled on Islet Park House, a pseudo-gothic Victorian mansion situated on the banks of the River Thames in Maidenhead, a few miles from their previous offices at Berry Hill. The secluded mansion, which managed to look ornate and impressive by day, but evoke the feeling of a haunted house by night, had obviously seen better days and was surrounded by an immense amount of overgrown foliage in serious need of a gardener. Puppeteer Roger Woodburn, who joined the company a little later, remembers: "I invited a friend there from the North, and he said it was a bit like some time in the '20s or '30s there'd been a wild party, and everyone had died and no-one had bothered to clear up; it was a bit like Miss Havisham's wedding feast. There were two or three grand limousines. They were derelict, with plants growing through them. You'd go through the undergrowth and find a statue of Diana at an angle. Very spooky."

To help them with their new venture, Anderson and Provis engaged three other staff. Unhappy at their old company, Pentagon Films, Sylvia Thamm left to assist the new company at Islet Park. Arthur Provis recruited two former colleagues – Reg Hill, an artist and carpenter who had recently been working in special effects, and John Read, an experienced rostrum cameraman. Such was their dedication that Read, Hill and Thamm were awarded directorships and shareholdings during production of *Twizzle*.

To construct the miniature protagonists, Anderson approached Joy Laurey, a respected puppeteer known for her puppet creation, Mr Turnip, in the children's television series *Whirligig*. "I had a letter out of the blue from Gerry Anderson asking me to lunch in London to discuss making some puppets for a film," Joy recalls. "I'd never heard of Gerry Anderson, but he had heard of me through The Puppet Guild. Apparently, Gerry had also approached other puppeteers and seen their puppets but decided on me. I think it was on the strength of Mr Turnip, which I'd been doing on TV for about nine years. He was a puppet with a lot of movement and had mobile eyes."[6]

Gerry Anderson explains: "I contacted a puppeteer and she came along with this papier mâché puppet with a very rough face; eyes were painted, mouth was painted – it didn't open – and it had thick carpet thread to control the puppet. Then she said, 'What you do is get a sheet of hardboard, I stand behind it and on the hardboard you paint a little scene like a garden, a few props and a fork, spade, a couple of flower pots, and I lean over the top and I perform with the puppet, and you film it.' Well, of course, I couldn't see how we could make a television series like that!" "We hadn't got any idea about making puppets or shooting puppets. It wasn't in our ambition at all," says Sylvia.

Traditionally, puppets come from a theatrical background, and in the 1950s even puppets that had graduated to the television screen still maintained their theatricality. Lacking affinity with puppetry traditions and approaching potential problems with the

---

6. All Joy Laurey quotations are from an interview by Christine Glanville and Rowena White. Contemporary correspondence is supplied by Joy herself.

mindset of film-makers, Anderson and Provis began devising a way to make these puppets work for film. "We approached making the series like we were shooting a proper film," says Arthur. "We thought OK, this is very simplistic stuff to do. But as we're doing it we might just as well make it as well as we could," states Sylvia.

With hindsight, it can be seen that the desire to make true feature films was the driving force behind advancing the sophistication of the puppet stars. Gerry, particularly, was quite embarrassed that he might be perceived as someone who simply fiddled with puppets. Instead of traditional locked-off camera shots, filmed against a two-dimensional flat, as favoured by the staid world of 1950s puppet television, it was decided that *these* puppets should be given the same treatment as their human counterparts, with long-shots, close-ups, etc., in a three-dimensional set. To film in this manner, though, required moving the puppeteers from their traditional operating position, behind the flats, to a bridge high off the ground, allowing the camera and lights full access to their subjects.

With the permission of the tolerant owner, Mrs Whitworth, the five team members – Anderson, Provis, Hill, Read and Thamm – began adapting the premises to suit their specific needs. The chief additions and alterations were to the ballroom, which doubled as a small studio space. A freestanding bridge (constructed from Dexion) was installed, allowing the puppeteers to operate the marionettes from approximately six feet above floor level. Joy Laurey says: "I had no input on that at all. I was just confronted by this thing like the Forth Bridge. There was a point when they got a bit worried, as it started to sag if more than two people were on it at once. They didn't seem to know if it was really safe, but as long as they could clip their lights onto it and hang scenery from it, it was okay. It was a Meccano nightmare, the bridge." Roger Woodburn exclaims: "It was hell for the puppeteers! You had to bend over slightly or you'd hit your head on the ornate plaster ceiling!" Fellow puppeteer Mary Turner, who joined A.P. Films in 1958, also remembers how uncomfortable the bridge was: "The puppeteers' bridge had a well in the middle, so that we could just about stand upright under the ceiling. We then had to step up to lean against the rail, bend our backs, and work the puppets. The well was a handy place to lie down while a shot was being discussed by the crew below – as long as you kept alert enough to appear when needed!"

Rooms directly above the ballroom were converted into cutting rooms, and attic rooms were leased as makeshift bed-sits for the overworked crew to retire to. "Islet Park was a bit like a hotel," says editor David Elliott. "I had two rooms for editing with a couple of benches and a Moviola." Elliott had originally worked as Gerry Anderson's assistant dubbing editor on two films in the early 1950s – *Appointment in London* and *They Who Dare*. In the long, dark hours in the cutting rooms, Elliott formed a close friendship with Gerry and subsequently with his first wife, Betty Anderson, and so was an obvious choice to edit the forthcoming puppet pictures, initially at Anglo-Scottish Pictures in Addlestone, and then at Islet

Park once all the equipment had been installed.

A contract dated August 19th 1957 details that Joy Laurey and her company, The Laurey Puppet Company, were hired to produce the puppets for the series, free of charge, and to operate them for £25 per day, beginning at 8:30 and ending at 18:00, for no less than four days a week. Puppets were to be completed in time for filming to begin on September 1st 1957. The contract stipulated that The Laurey Puppet Company would provide 'competent operators', and they came in the form of Murray Clark and Christine Glanville. For Christine, it was to be the beginning of a working association with Gerry Anderson that would last for forty years.

On August 16th, Joy Laurey wrote to Christine:

> *The films are now going to be shot in a wonderful Studio located in the ballroom of a country mansion near Maidenhead. I have met the director, camera-man and art director (a girl) and they are all most likeable. They are all most keen and enthusiastic to make these the best puppet films ever made in this country. I too feel that this is a wonderful opportunity, and may well be the beginning of something big!*
>
> *As we will be working with long strings from an overhead bridge, it will only be feasible for us to rehearse on the actual set. The first (or pilot) film is not too complicated, and there will be adequate opportunities for us to rehearse in the ordinary way as we go along, but as both the puppets and surroundings will be new, I think it would be a great help if wee* (sic) *three (you, Murray and I) spent Saturday 30th Sept.[7] down at Maidenhead, feeling our way round, and trying out things generally, if this day is convenient.[...]*
>
> *Incidentally, one of the characters is a very lovable cat who keeps falling over his paws. Directly I saw him (the drawing that is) I thought of you and wondered if you would make him your particular 'baby' for the series.*

While the puppets were built by Joy, costumes and props were a more family affair. "I used to make the clothes for *Twizzle* and the little beds and wardrobes and chairs and things," says Betty. "I used to do the models for them at that time. Quite a few actually. Little rugs and things. What I hadn't realised, because I'd never done anything like that before – I trained as a dressmaker, that's what I was – that for films things had to be such an exact way. Especially if you're doing something for puppets. You don't want the wardrobe so big or so small. It has to be in line with the puppets. So that's where I was involved. Because we had so little money to make the film it was a money saving exercise. Gerry said, 'Have a go,' and I did. And it worked out very successfully." Reflecting on her oft-forgotten contribution to the early success of A.P. Films, Betty says, "I was involved in the part where we were hard up and always short of money."

Although Roberta Leigh had engaged A.P. Films because

---

7. As production started in early September, we can safely assume Joy means August. However, August 30th 1957 was a Friday. Therefore, it seems likely that Joy in fact meant August 31st , which was a Saturday.

she lacked the necessary film-making experience, this did not deter her from intervening in her role as producer. "Roberta Leigh was very much a guiding influence during the pilot," says Laurey. "She thought it was just a case of saying what was wanted and 'boom', that was it. Of course, it's not quite like that. Everyone was new and didn't know what to expect."

Leigh regularly visited the studio to keep up to date with the progress of the series, and contributed a number of songs for the show. She, or her friend Leslie Clair, would hum or sing the songs while recording them onto a tape which she would then pass over to future A.P. Films stalwart, Barry Gray, to arrange and record. "'She's got something,' Barry used to say," remembers Provis. "And he was right. We all used to hum the bloody tunes all day." Like the members of A.P. Films, Gray also had his work cut out, sometimes recording as many as sixteen songs in a nine-hour day.

Fully crewed, the killer schedule was initiated. Production could now begin on the series, as Arthur Provis remembers: "We worked so hard. We worked at least twelve hours a day. Gerry worked twenty to get the series ready. I worked twelve. To begin with, the scripts were impossible; we had to re-write them, because of the limits with puppets. I mean, they can't do anything. If anyone tells you they can walk, forget it, they can't!"

This comment is backed up by Joy Laurey, who wrote again to Christine Glanville on August 27th, days before filming commenced, stating:

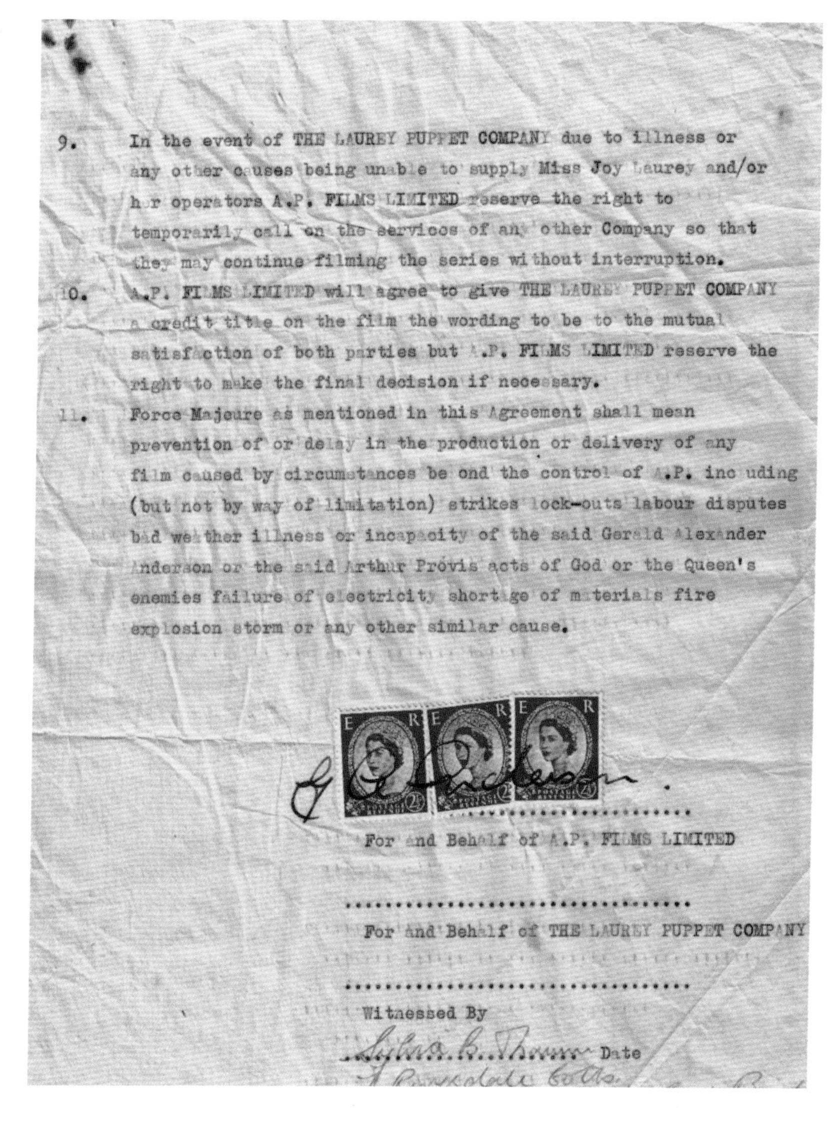

9. In the event of THE LAUREY PUPPET COMPANY due to illness or any other causes being unable to supply Miss Joy Laurey and/or her operators A.P. FILMS LIMITED reserve the right to temporarily call on the services of any other Company so that they may continue filming the series without interruption.

10. A.P. FILMS LIMITED will agree to give THE LAUREY PUPPET COMPANY a credit title on the film the wording to be to the mutual satisfaction of both parties but A.P. FILMS LIMITED reserve the right to make the final decision if necessary.

11. Force Majeure as mentioned in this Agreement shall mean prevention of or delay in the production or delivery of any film caused by circumstances beyond the control of A.P. including (but not by way of limitation) strikes lock-outs labour disputes bad weather illness or incapacity of the said Gerald Alexander Anderson or the said Arthur Provis acts of God or the Queen's enemies failure of electricity shortage of materials fire explosion storm or any other similar cause.

....
For and Behalf of A.P. FILMS LIMITED

....
For and Behalf of THE LAUREY PUPPET COMPANY

....
Witnessed By

.... Date

Page from Joy Laurey's contract, signed by Sylvia.

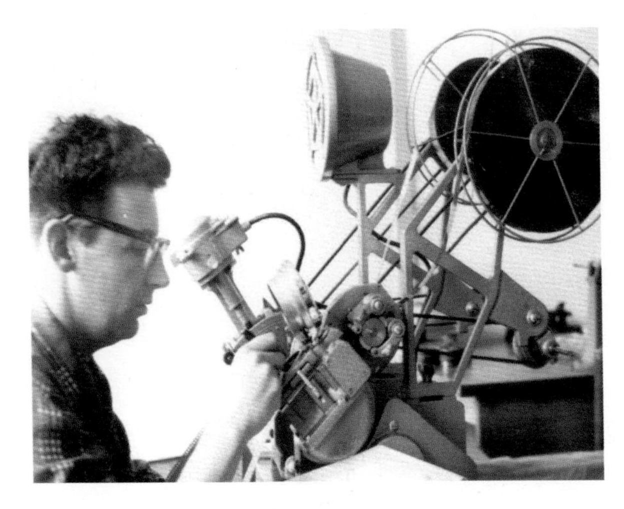

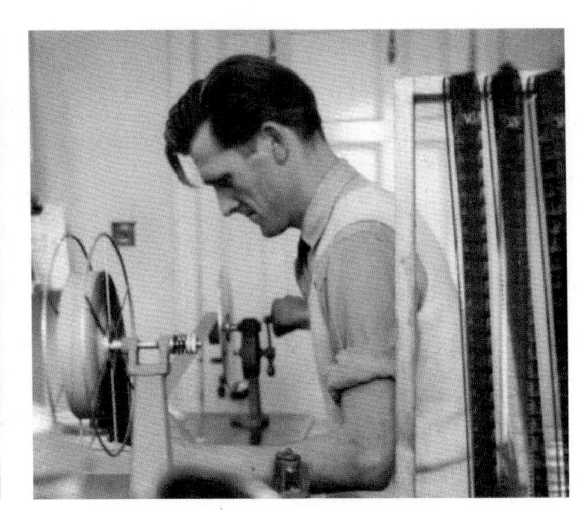

Here is a provisional script for the 'Pilot' to give you some idea of the type of characters etc. Don't worry too much about the seemingly impossible moments – I am seeing to it that they are either resolved or cut out of the final shooting script!

Slight change of schedule – rehearsal day will now be Monday September 2nd, instead of Saturday. I personally am very relieved as it may mean that the paint on the faces is likely to be dry! […]

Needless to say – I am extremely 'up to my eyes' at the moment, but I am extremely pleased with the puppets that have emerged to date. […] P.S. Please treat this script as confidential at the moment as the whole project has not yet been released to the press.

"I was very worried about Twizzle's unbalanced shape," says Joy, who made the puppets based on illustrations supplied by Roberta Leigh. "It was almost impossible. He had spindly legs, a fat tummy, and a very big head which was very difficult to manipulate. He was also required to double or treble in height, and no one could work out how to do this. I suggested two puppets, one with telescopic limbs for the trick sequences, from which we could cut away to a puppet which had the ability to move and walk normally. There was no way – that I could work out – that a telescopic marionette would have the facility of actually walking.

"A lot of the puppets were difficult to manipulate because they were the wrong shape. Never before had I made a puppet that I hadn't designed myself, and of course, the strings were excruciatingly long. I remember we had awful problems with the cat, and Christine came to the rescue. After the pilot we remade him."

It wasn't just the puppeteers having problems with the wires:

"I got a call from Humphries Film Labs,"[8] recalls David Elliott. "They said that I needed to come up and look at an episode because the rushes were scratched. This caused quite a lot of concern and we thought that we'd have to reshoot, until I saw a copy and realised that the scratches were in fact the strings!"

Before the marionettes could appear before the cameras, it was necessary to record dialogue tracks, which the puppeteers would react and respond to when performing.

Remembering their only other experience with puppets, Anderson and Provis hired the voice of Noddy himself, actress Denise Bryer. Bryer, who provided the purring tones of Footso as well as other subsidiary characters, specialised in voice-overs, preferring the anonymity of the microphone and rarely appearing on film. "She was absolutely the best voice artist we had," Arthur Provis enthuses. "When she played the cat she used to climb on chairs, climb on tables – just like a cat! She used to miaow. Absolutely brilliant! Everyone was in awe of her." "Eartha Kitt!" exclaims David Elliott. "That's what I'll always remember Denise for. Singing as Eartha Kitt for a song she did for the cat." Denise has a clear recollection of this: "I'm Footso the Cat...," she sings. "Funny how these things stay with you," she laughs. The role of Twizzle himself was undertaken by actress Nancy Nevinson, while male voices fell to Frank Duncan.

Aiming to film one episode a day, many of the crew worked round the clock, becoming full-time residents of the imposing mansion in order to get the initial episodes ready in time. The series was shot on 35mm black and white stock, with Arthur Provis and John Read acting as cameramen, whilst Reg Hill designed, constructed and painted the sets in greyscale[9], with the assistance of part-time apprentice Derek Meddings. Sylvia had by now graduated from being a humble part-time secretary to working, full-time, ostensibly on secretarial and continuity duties, but clearly becoming influential in other important ways.

The Adventures of Twizzle concerns the escapades of a toy called Twizzle who is capable of extending, or 'twizzling', his arms and legs. At the beginning of the first episode we are shown an illuminated shop window on a dark evening. "Have you ever heard of a Twizzle toy?" we are asked by the narrator. "You haven't? Well, That's because there's only one of them." Passing through the window into the shop, we are introduced to Twizzle,

---

8. A.P. Films / Century 21 had their films processed by three laboratories over their puppet career. Humphries for *Twizzle* and *Torchy*, Kays for *Supercar* and *Fireball XL5*, and Rank for *Four Feather Falls* and every one of their colour shows.

9. *The Adventures of Twizzle* was the only APF series where the sets were painted greyscale. The subsequent shows had sets and costumes in colour. Christine Glanville recalled in 1996 that her mother, who helped make the costumes in the early days, would use a panglass given to her by Reg Hill, which she would look through to gauge how certain colours would appear in black and white, before she used the fabric.

Opposite: David Elliott and Gordon Davie, in the cutting room at Islet Park.

a very expensive toy which costs two shillings and six pence. A short while later, a horrible, spoilt little girl enters the shop and harangues the elderly shop keeper into selling Twizzle to her for two shillings. Terrified of being sold to the little girl, Twizzle hides in a jack-in-the-box until the dead of night, when he runs away from the shop. After walking for hours, Twizzle meets a cat called Footso. "I ran away from a house where I lived because the children were always laughing at my big paws," Footso mews pathetically. Finding themselves outcasts, Twizzle and Footso befriend each other, and the rest of series follows this unlikely pair as they face the perils and pleasures of life.

"It was terrible!" exclaims Arthur Provis. "We really didn't have enough money or time and it wasn't very good." When viewed through time's rear-view mirror, and taking into account 1950s television as a whole, it can be seen that Arthur's criticisms are, in fact, rather harsh. *Twizzle*'s nearest television counterpart, *Noddy*, is far less sophisticated, merely showing puppets dangled against a 2-D backdrop, with a locked-off camera. *Twizzle*, in comparison, features tracking shots, interesting lighting, a mixture of two and three-dimensional sets, and is undoubtedly head and shoulders above its rival.

The Adventures of Twizzle was successfully completed and delivered on time, with production wrapping in January 1958. The first episode, *Twizzle and Footso*, was transmitted on November 13th 1957, and launched APF into the world of television.[10] This one known surviving episode provides an interesting portal back into the world of 1950s television where life appears to be much simpler. The show's innocence and whimsical style is a world away from, not only the children's programming of today, but from A.P. Films' own output of just a few years later. For all its faults, *The Adventures*

10. It also launched their international television careers as the series was sold to other countries. One episode secured the front cover of the *New Zealand Listener* listings magazine.

Above: Twizzle, Footso and friends as seen on screen.

of Twizzle was a pioneering exercise for A.P. Films, and laid solid foundations for what would be just around the corner.

APF celebrated the completion of their first commission with a party in January 1958. It marked the beginning of the relationship between Gerry and the company secretary, Sylvia Thamm. Gerry and Betty would separate in 1959.

• • •

With their first production successfully in the can, the assembled team disbanded (except for David Elliott, who continued editing the remaining films for a couple of months), leaving the original five to contemplate the future. There was enough money left to continue paying their lease on Islet Park for a short while, but the money would not sustain them long with wages to pay as well. Roberta made it clear that she had a new idea she wanted to pursue, but the finance would have to be secured first. With no immediate commissions, Anderson, Provis, Read, Hill and Thamm found themselves looking for outside work. "We all took jobs to see us through the quiet time," says Provis. "I went to Anglo-Scottish Pictures to make commercials. Reg worked on *The Adventures of Robin Hood* at Nettlefold Studios.[11] [12] We put our earnings into the kitty and only took out what we needed. Some of us needed more than others. But that didn't matter."

During this quiet time, Gerry Anderson was invited by an old colleague of his, Frank Sherwin Green, to come and direct an episode of the filmed television series *Martin Kane – Private Investigator*, a cut-price detective series with William Gargan in the lead role. Anderson directed two episodes – *The Film Studio Story,* which he was credited for, and *The Museum Story* which he took over, uncredited, when the original director, John Kalvin, became unwell. On the first production, in another twist of fate, Anderson met a young actor called David Graham, who would soon become a staple voice in many of APF's future productions.

Roberta Leigh returned to meet with the APF partners a short time later, to discuss production of a new series: *Torchy the Battery Boy*. Leigh had managed to secure limited finance, and APF were commissioned to produce five 'pilot' episodes.

Torchy was visibly a more ambitious production. Though not on par with later shows from the APF stable, it is a significantly more sophisticated programme than its predecessor. Roberta Leigh blithely took credit for the mounting complexity of the films in 1964: "We did *Twizzle* in the old way, with one or two sets, the camera staying in one place and the puppets just walking on and walking off. But I was the very first person in this country to visualise puppet films being made in terms of live action filming, and that's the way we did our second series, *Torchy* – with 20 set-

---

11. Renamed Walton Studios by this time after Sapphire Films took over the studios.

12. Sylvia Thamm also did a stint on *The Adventures of Robin Hood* as a continuity girl. It was there that she met Alan Perry, who joined APF as a Clapper / Loader in 1960.

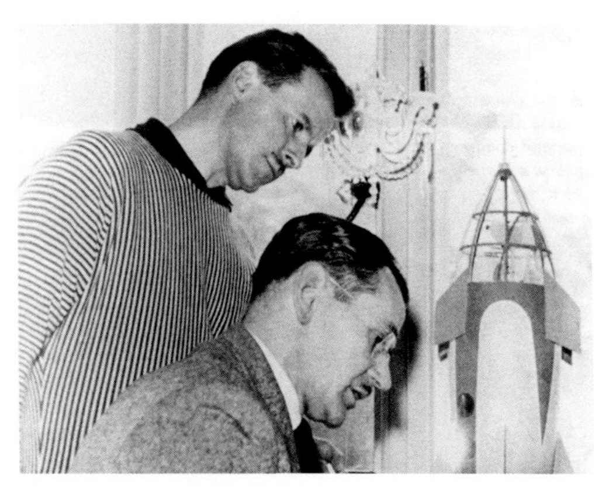
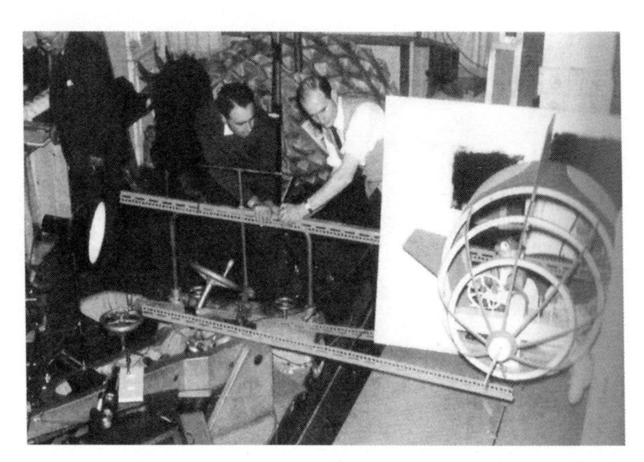

ups of the same scene, every scene shot from a different angle so we could intercut."[13]

In *Torchy*, cardboard cut-out backdrops have largely been replaced by three-dimensional sets, while the puppets have a slightly more sophisticated construction of plastic wood, rather than papier mâché. The puppets, which were built by Christine Glanville in her father's garage, feature the very beginning of a hint of what would evolve into the lip-sync mechanism, with each puppet now equipped with a moveable lip, albeit operated by a string.[14] To accommodate the moveable lip, a space had to be made under the lip for it to sink into when open, and then a soft material was required to fit across the gap to disguise the cavity, without restricting the mouth movement. When on the look-out for a suitable material, it was Christine's father who was nominated to go out and purchase as many varieties of condom as possible! His efforts were in vain: thin, soft leather was eventually used.

Christine had inherited the position of chief puppeteer on the series, after Joy Laurey had decided to take on other work. To assist her, and Murray Clark who also stayed, Christine enlisted the services of a young puppeteer by the name of Mary Turner. Mary recalls her introduction to the company: "I was interviewed at Roberta's house, along with other puppeteers, by her, Gerry and Arthur. Having passed the interview, most of the puppet making was done by Christine at her home, so during the preparation period, I was assisting Reg in the art department, cutting out leaves for trees, etc."

13. *The Stage and Television Today* (1964)

14. Some of the *Twizzle* puppets had some sort of flap that was supposed to represent a mouth. However, they were never very successful and the *Torchy* puppets are much closer to what would eventually become a Supermarionation puppet.

Above, L-R: Mary Turner and Christine Glanville pressed against the ceiling at Islet Park / Bob Bell and Reg Hill with Torchy's rocket / Arthur and Gerry prepare the rocket for filming.

Torchy the Battery Boy is definitely from the same mould as *Twizzle*, in that it is another twee children's adventure from the pen of Roberta Leigh, although with APF hitting their stride in the world of puppet films, the show succeeds in being less static than *Twizzle*.

The first episode begins in the garden of Mr Bumbledrop, a kindly old man who lets children play in his garden. One day, his beloved dog, Pom-Pom, is accidentally swept into the sky when a gust of wind catches the kite that he is dutifully holding on to. Devastated at the loss of his animal companion, Mr Bumbledrop builds himself a new focus for his affection – a toy grandson called Torchy, who has a magic lamp on his head. Torchy uses his magic lamp to locate Pom-Pom in the world of Topsy-Turvy Land and sets off in a rocket built by Mr Bumbledrop to rescue his dog. The rest of the series concerns the adventures of Torchy and his friends on Earth and in Topsy-Turvy land. It is a difficult task to look at the series through contemporary eyes (and indeed to describe its set-up!) without extrapolating from the then-innocent elements an unintentionally seedier side to the series. This is not helped by several lines of dialogue, most notably the aged Mr Bumbledrop's exclamation: "I'll make a toy boy!"

Production on the first episode took ten days, and by August 1958 the five pilot episodes had been shot.[15] Once again, the crew were laid off until Roberta confirmed her order for an additional 21 episodes. During September 1958, Gerry, Sylvia, and John Read worked at Islet Park on *Further Up the Creek*, a film starring David Tomlinson and Frankie Howerd. David Elliott was employed on the picture as a dubbing editor by Bill Lenny, and when someone was needed to do the post-syncing, Elliott suggested Anderson. Initially working from Shepperton, Gerry eventually took the work back to Islet Park where he, John and Sylvia put in long hours fitting the post-sync to the film. Sylvia explains: "In the late fifties, when sound equipment was not as sophisticated as it is today, there would often be poor sound quality on location, which meant that a sound-track would require re-recording in a sound-proofed studio. Now, Frankie Howerd was a brilliant artist, but quite hopeless at re-voicing his own dialogue, because, as an instinctive performer, he rarely repeated a line or an intonation in exactly the same way. His mouth movement, therefore, often failed to match the newly recorded dialogue. As most of the film had been re-recorded, we spent hours on it; it was a nightmare crash-course in film editing techniques for me and one I shall never forget."[16]

During September, Roberta returned with the much-needed commission. With no other work in the offing, APF once again accepted a contract from Leigh, though this time under more favourable terms with a budget of £27,000 for the series agreed on – a large budgetary increase on *Twizzle* for under half the number of episodes!

---

15. The version of events recounted here differs quite severely from the accepted story about APF's early days. In the version usually printed, it is claimed that APF was in operation for six months and on the verge of bankruptcy when *The Adventures of Twizzle* was commissioned. However, contemporary diary sources and contracts made available for this book, show that this version is inaccurate and that it was between *Twizzle* and *Torchy* that the directors were forced to take on other jobs to keep the company afloat.

16. *From My Fab Years*, Sylvia Anderson (2007).

On October 14th 1958, two months after production had finished on the first five films, a new contract was drawn up stipulating the requirements for the remainder of the series. This contract laid out details such as the payment schedule, the need to deliver three films every month beginning in January 1959, and that all films should be delivered by July of that year.

Now used to the trials of working with puppets, A.P. Films created each 15-minute adventure at great speed, working not dissimilarly to their established shooting methods on *Twizzle*. Construction went on in the ballroom and greenhouse; filming was carried out exclusively in the ballroom, and the rushes were passed upstairs to one of the bedrooms for editing.

The bedrooms were also home to the dialogue recording sessions. Birmingham-based husband and wife sound engineers John and Jean Taylor produced their recordings in the unlikely setting, using some much needed ingenuity. "We weren't allowed to tamper with the rooms," says John. "We acoustically treated the room by putting blankets up on the wall." At regular intervals, the new voice cast consisting of Olwyn Griffiths, Patricia Somerset, Jill Raymond and Kenneth Connor, would assemble to record the next set of episodes. Jill Raymond speaks of the recording sessions fondly. "What I remember clearly was how primitive the set-up was. They found a really small room for the recordings and it was actually draped with sheets.

"Kenneth Connor had a very dirty mind. His big chance came when I played Flopsy the Ragdoll, because her stuffing kept falling out and then she wanted the stuffing put back again." Lines innocently given to Ragdoll such as, 'I do hope Pilliwig can find something soft and woolly to stuff inside me,' did not help the situation. "He couldn't really be restrained," continues Jill. "It did make the recordings tricky, but it also made them a lot of fun!"

Roger Woodburn speaks of the 'primitive set-up' with great warmth. "It was a real cottage industry. Everybody did everything, I remember. I used to get out of bed, get dressed, go down two flights of stairs and still arrive in the studio late for work! We had a turkey and cooked it in a 5,000ft film can. We worked right up to Christmas Eve – no long Christmas break, just two days. It sounds like, 'By-gum we used to have it hard back then.' But I still think, 'They used to pay me for having all that fun!'"

The team, once again, worked day and night to produce the films in the very cosy environment of Islet Park. "Sometimes things were a little cosier than they should have been!" notes Gerry with a wry smile. David Elliott is a little less delicate about the situation. "Islet Park should have rocked with all the activity going on!"

As with *The Adventures of Twizzle*, Roberta Leigh kept a firm grip on production and was a frequent visitor to the studio. However, as Mary Turner recalls, the crew didn't always find Roberta endearing: "We were all working late one evening, when

Opposite, above: Flooding at Islet Park, winter 1958. Below, right: Arthur Provis checks the camera. Left: Roberta Leigh in Fruitown.

Roberta arrived with her chauffeur. We were all starving. Roberta got the message and sent her chauffeur out for food. He came back with a large bar of chocolate, which Roberta proceeded to break up, giving everyone a piece! It didn't go down very well!"

Whilst A.P. Films didn't work through famine, they certainly did through flood. In late 1958, the Thames Valley region experienced particularly high levels of rainfall. The cold weather caused a lot of the water to freeze and, as the temperature started to rise, the ice began to thaw. It wasn't long before the Thames had burst its banks; Islet Park was surrounded by water. "Christ, that was marvellous!" exclaims David Elliott. "Well, it wasn't marvellous, but I mean the way that everyone got through it."

"We came out on a Friday night," says Roger Woodburn. "We'd finished filming and everybody was going home for the night when someone ran in and said, 'The driveway! It's flooded! It's all underwater!' On the Monday, it was even worse. Where I worked, and where the sets were built, was like an old conservatory. We built a jetty, loaded up the punt with all the sets and everything, and brought them over to the main house. It was quite an adventure!"

Puppeteer Mary Turner continues: "The house was built up, so the house itself wasn't flooded. I remember Roger lying back in the punt, strumming away on his guitar. You could hear the music across the water."

Despite being ahead of schedule, APF couldn't allow the flood to interrupt filming. The water eventually subsided, with the series still on course and with no casualties, despite a potentially disastrous incident where Roger Woodburn found himself being swept away by the fierce current. Fortunately, a nearby tree proved to be his salvation and injury, or worse, was averted.

The flood wasn't the only bit of colour in those fraught days, as Roger Woodburn recalls of puppeteer Murray Clark: "Murray was a bit of a fantasist. He had a letterhead printed in seven colours, but he didn't have a company; a bit of a Walter Mitty. He was a frustrated disc jockey. Up in the flat he had a turntable, a real lash-up, and he used to play music into the studio – not when we were shooting, but when we were preparing. We had this music whether we liked it or not. It was just like having a radio station. Finally when he was fired, he stormed back to his room and suddenly the speaker went 'Boing!' and crashed into bits." Murray, in his blind fury, had tugged at a cable running into his bedroom, forgetting the speaker attached to the other end. He decamped from Islet Park that day, leaving Roger the sole occupant of his flat. Roger continues: "I remember Gerry asking if he could share my flat. It was at the time he was leaving his first wife for Sylvia and needed accommodation. It was a very strange arrangement."

Murray did leave a lasting legacy, though, as Mary Turner explains: "Because the puppet strings were so long, and to keep them from getting slack and tangled, a pole about seven feet long with hooks at the top to carry the control was invented, to transport the puppets from their storage area to the bridge. By the time I arrived, the rod had acquired the name 'Murrayprodder', because, apparently, its other purpose was to wake Mr Clark when he was sleeping on the bridge! After his departure, its name from then on, and for every other series, was the 'prodder'. Future puppeteers often asked where the name came from."

By the beginning of 1959, APF was well ahead of schedule. So much so that in January the company's accountants, the firm of Jaz W. Elliott, Station Road, Ilford, wrote to Barry Gray, the musical arranger, and asked for a temporary loan of £1,000 to assist the financing of the series.

> *"[…] Before the series commenced we prepared a budget showing the anticipated expenditure week by week, and the finance which will be required. The expenditure for the first ten weeks was anticipated to be £10,613; the actual expenditure, which we calculated when we called on the company yesterday, came to £10,614. We enclose a schedule showing how this is made up, so that you will see that the Company is keeping very closely to its budget. On the other hand, the production of the films has exceeded expectations; at the moment nine have been completed, whereas six only were anticipated and it appears that the series will be finished some weeks earlier than expected. […]"*

It seems that A.P. Films' efficiency had worked against them; they found themselves unable to request a further sum of money from Roberta ahead of the next scheduled payment, as to do so would force them to admit that they had managed to produce nine episodes

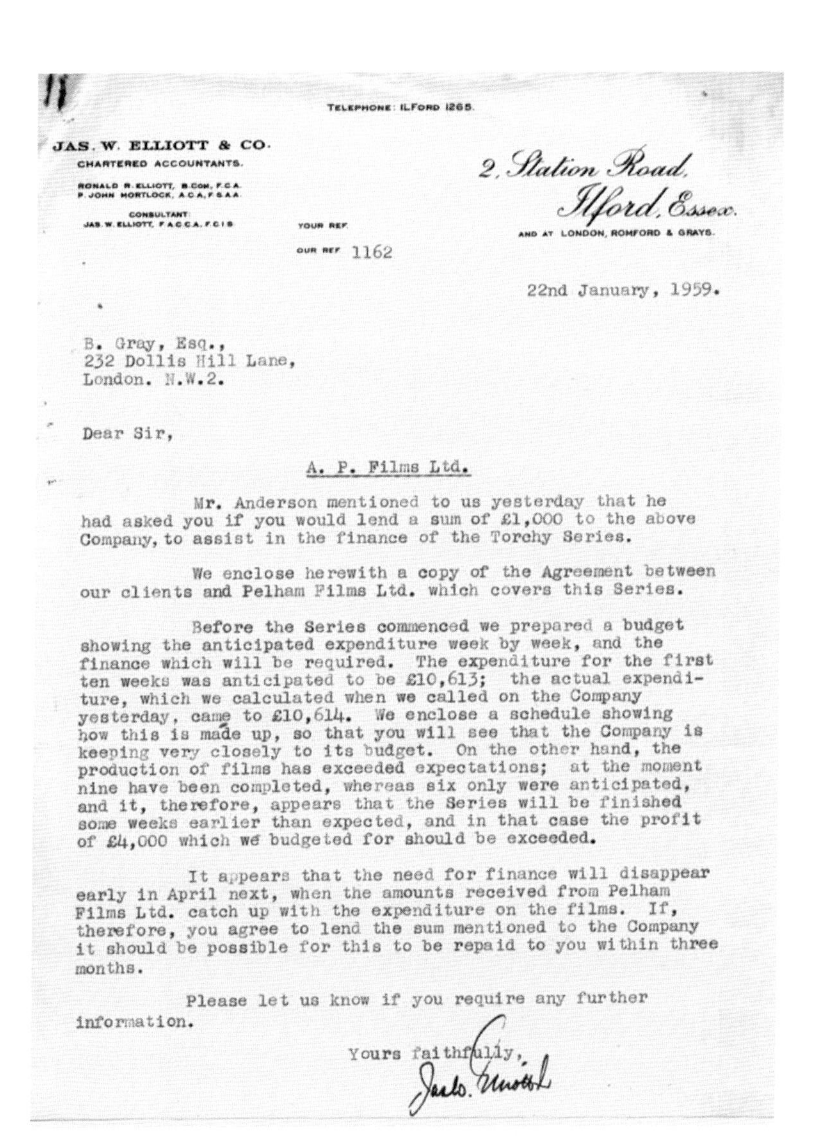

TELEPHONE: ILFORD 1265.

JAS. W. ELLIOTT & CO.
CHARTERED ACCOUNTANTS.

RONALD R. ELLIOTT, B.COM., F.C.A.
P. JOHN MORTLOCK, A.C.A., F.S.A.A.

CONSULTANT:
JAS. W. ELLIOTT, F.A.C.C.A., F.C.I.S.

2, Station Road,
Ilford, Essex.

AND AT LONDON, ROMFORD & GRAYS.

YOUR REF.

OUR REF. 1162

22nd January, 1959.

B. Gray, Esq.,
232 Dollis Hill Lane,
London. N.W.2.

Dear Sir,

A. P. Films Ltd.

Mr. Anderson mentioned to us yesterday that he had asked you if you would lend a sum of £1,000 to the above Company, to assist in the finance of the Torchy Series.

We enclose herewith a copy of the Agreement between our clients and Pelham Films Ltd. which covers this Series.

Before the Series commenced we prepared a budget showing the anticipated expenditure week by week, and the finance which will be required. The expenditure for the first ten weeks was anticipated to be £10,613; the actual expenditure, which we calculated when we called on the Company yesterday, came to £10,614. We enclose a schedule showing how this is made up, so that you will see that the Company is keeping very closely to its budget. On the other hand, the production of films has exceeded expectations; at the moment nine have been completed, whereas six only were anticipated, and it, therefore, appears that the Series will be finished some weeks earlier than expected, and in that case the profit of £4,000 which we budgeted for should be exceeded.

It appears that the need for finance will disappear early in April next, when the amounts received from Pelham Films Ltd. catch up with the expenditure on the films. If, therefore, you agree to lend the sum mentioned to the Company it should be possible for this to be repaid to you within three months.

Please let us know if you require any further information.

Yours faithfully,

Letter from AP Films' accountants requesting a loan of £1000 from musical arranger Barry Gray.

for the cost of six! Barry Gray, despite having been introduced to APF by Roberta, bailed the company out.

Torchy holds the unlikely distinction of marking the beginning of APF's Special Effects pedigree. Gerry Anderson explains: "There was a rocket taking off outside a thatched cottage where Torchy lived. John Read and Reg Hill spent the whole afternoon wiring up hundreds and hundreds of sparklers. Then we went out to have dinner, and we came back and we were all ready to do this big shot, and they explained to me that I had two wires. 'On action, Gerry, touch the two wires, the sparklers will all ignite and overhead the special effects guy will pull it up on a pulley.' I touched the two wires and nothing happened. 'Cut.' 'Turnover.' Touched the two wires. Nothing happened. I was getting worried because it was a major shot for us. On my right hand side, there was an ornate pillar and in the pillar were two 10 Amp plugs – two brass holes. This time, I stuck the two wires straight into the mains. There was an enormous flash, so bright that I couldn't see for a moment. All the sparklers ignited, there was lots of smoke and everyone was shouting and hollering. They pulled it out of shot and we'd made our first special effects shot. A bit amateurish, but we finally got it."

The twenty-six episodes were delivered ahead of schedule in March 1959. Roberta was once again delighted with the work done by A.P. Films and immediately asked them to produce a second series. A.P. Films declined. The discovery that Leigh had organised things so that she received a disproportionate chunk of the profits did not endear her to Gerry and his colleagues.

In the London ITV region, *Torchy the Battery Boy* arrived on television a mere three days before the premiere of the next APF television production... one without Roberta Leigh's name on it.

FOUR FEATHER FALLS

•1959•

TWO GUN TEX OF TEXAS 2

Four Feather Falls

By the end of 1958, A.P. Films was ensconced in the fantasy lands of *Torchy the Battery Boy*, where toys could come to life, rockets could be built overnight using household materials, and where oversized fruit made particularly novel housing for the characters. These adventures were being produced under the strict guidance of children's author and romantic novelist, Roberta Leigh. However, unknown to Leigh, A.P. Films were also playing in another land with magical properties.

Over the course of a year working with the team, composer Barry Gray had developed a keen interest in this unlikely crew trying to bring puppets to life in a mansion in Maidenhead and so, when it came to an idea of his own, he talked to APF about it instead of Roberta, despite his continuing allegiance to her.

After arousing their interest, Barry scribbled out very rough outlines and a basic synopsis of a pilot episode for a puppet western series entitled *Two Gun Tex Tucker*, which featured law-man of Spelltown – Tex Tucker; his fat assistant – Buster; the town handy-man – Slim Jim; and the general store owner – Jake Jollymop, who was also assigned the position of series storyteller. This idea was developed with a few more scribbles into *Two Gun Tex of Texas*:

> *Four Feather Falls Kansas. A small, yet happy western town with a touch of magic about it, due to a certain strange happening in the time of the early settlers, from which the town got its name. The main places of interest and action are the Main Street, Sherriff's Office and Jail, and the General Store.*
>
> *The hero of the town* (is) *commonly known as Two Gun Tex of Texas, from where he originally came. […]*
>
> *His outstanding characteristic is his two silver guns in there* (sic) *bright red holsters. He can bring down two thrown flying nickels at one double draw and has never been known to miss. Some say this is due to magic […]*

Jake Jollymop metamorphosed into Timothy Twinkle and new additions included Tex's dog and horse, Rusty and Snowy; Martha Lollipop the owner of the general store and town gossip, and her assistant Red Feather, leader of an Indian tribe that she had found and rescued. There was also a host of other characters,

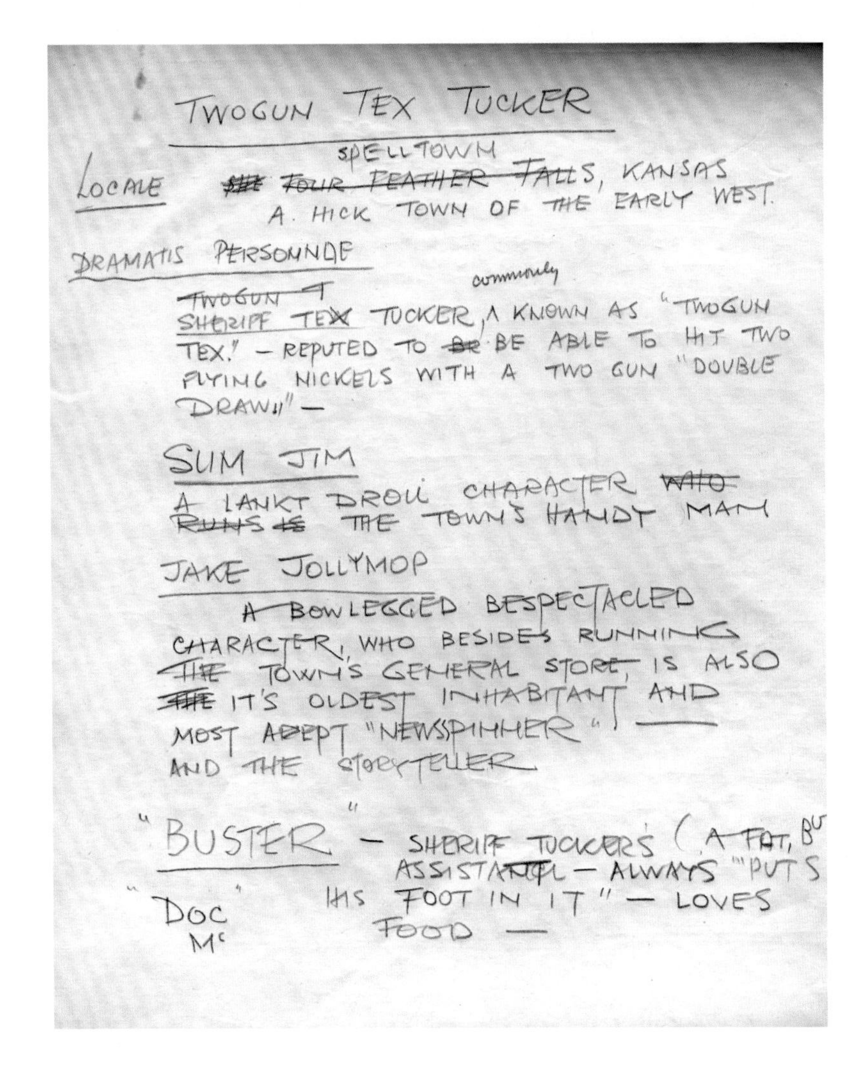
TWOGUN TEX TUCKER

LOCALE ~~FOUR FEATHER FALLS~~ SPELLTOWN, KANSAS
A HICK TOWN OF THE EARLY WEST.

DRAMATIS PERSONNAE

~~TWOGUN~~ SHERIFF TEX TUCKER, commonly KNOWN AS "TWOGUN TEX." – REPUTED TO BE ABLE TO HIT TWO FLYING NICKELS WITH A TWO GUN "DOUBLE DRAW!" –

SLIM JIM
A LANKY DROLL CHARACTER ~~WHO RUNS IS~~ THE TOWN'S HANDY MAN

JAKE JOLLYMOP
~~A~~ BOWLEGGED BESPECTACLED CHARACTER, WHO BESIDES RUNNING ~~THE~~ TOWN'S GENERAL STORE, IS ALSO ~~THE~~ IT'S OLDEST INHABITANT AND MOST ADEPT "NEWSSPINNER" — AND THE STORYTELLER

"BUSTER" – SHERIFF TUCKER'S (A FAT, BU ASSISTANT – ALWAYS "PUTS HIS FOOT IN IT" – LOVES FOOD –

"DOC" Mc

Above: Page from an early outline for *Four Feather Falls*

including Little Jake – Timothy Twinkle's grandson, and Jock the Doc, the resident doctor. These ideas were in turn refined, and a short-lived title, *The Sheriff of Four Feather Falls,* preceded the final transformation into a series of 15-minute adventures entitled *Four Feather Falls*.

Set in the fictional town of the same name, *Four Feather Falls* begins with wandering Tex Tucker (accompanied by Rocky, his horse, and Dusty, his dog) finding a little lost Indian boy, Makooya, and embarking on a small mission to return the boy to his tribe. Tex is rewarded for his efforts by Makooya's father, Big Chief Kalamakooya, with four magic feathers which, as described in the opening titles for 38 of the 39 episodes, "...enable Tex's dog and horse to speak[1] and for his guns to fire without him even touching them!" (Viewers would, perhaps, have been disappointed to discover that it was not magic that made Tex's guns fire, but two wires attached to a bike's handlebars). The rest of the series largely concerns Tex upholding the law in Four Feather Falls against the dastardly, but frequently inept villains who try to upset its quaint, peaceful lifestyle, and follows the lives of the town's inhabitants, including Grampa Twink (elderly resident of *Four Feather Falls* and part-time storyteller), Little Jake (Twink's grandson), Ma Jones (general store proprietor), Dan Morse (telegraph operator), Doc Haggerty (Doctor) and Slim Jim (owner of the saloon). Despite being unique in APF's catalogue of independent programming, in

1. One of the earliest ideas stated that Tex had actually taught his horse to speak.

that it features no 'sci-fi', it does introduce a couple of elements that would become a staple of APF's forthcoming shows, notably: handsome heroes with chiselled features (except maybe *Supercar*'s poor Mike Mercury); and a comedy duo of inept villains represented here by Mexican bandits Pedro and Fernando, who would pave the way for Masterspy and Zarin, Harper and Judd (*Supercar*), Mr and Mrs Space Spy (*Fireball XL5*) and perhaps most memorably Titan and X20 (*Stingray*).

On May 11th 1959, G. E. Marsh, the company's Production Manager wrote to Barry from their offices at Islet Park stating: *"I wish to confirm our understanding regarding your original story idea for the "Four Feather Falls" puppet film series.*

In consideration of the sum of £100, –, –,[2] *all rights in any form of the original script and idea which you originally conceived are hereby conceded to A.P. Films Limited."*

Of all the people to work with A.P. Films, Barry Gray is one of the most fondly remembered by cast and crew. "There is no doubt that Barry Gray made an enormous contribution to our Supermarionation successes and we were very fortunate to have known and enjoyed his enormous talent," says Sylvia Anderson. *Four Feather Falls* Director, Alan Pattillo, also remembers Barry warmly: "He was an enchanting character, he was very 'North Country', very talented, he had a great feeling for melody and dramatic moments, and his scoring of the episodes was always bang on."

2. The dashes and commas here indicate spaces left to add shillings and pence.

Barry Gray at work on a score for *Thunderbirds*.

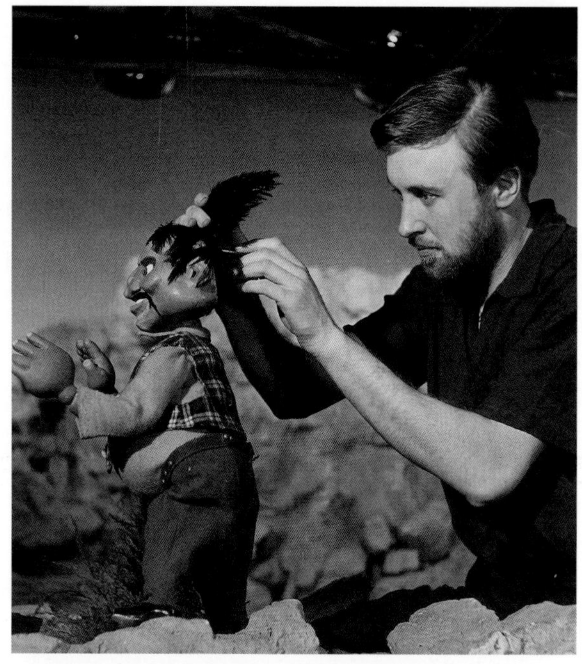

ELEGRAPH
OFFICE
HOTEL

Born in 1908, Barry Gray was blessed with a prolific career as a composer and arranger, and for a time had been Vera Lynn's Musical Director. However, the success of the future APF shows, for which he composed and arranged the music, genuinely took Barry by surprise. He used his new found wealth to indulge his hobby of expensive cars, as Alan Pattillo remembers: "He bought a *very* expensive car (a Facel Vega), but he was very anxious that his mother didn't find out about it, because she regarded it as a great expense. So he would drive from our studios to the underground car park in Hyde Park, and park his expensive car there. He would then move across to another aisle and crawl into an old banger which he would then park outside the family home!"

Barry was clearly fond of the APF crew, and was happy to help Gerry Anderson, who had been planning to escape from Roberta Leigh for some time.

"I was their secret weapon!" laughs Roger Woodburn, who in November 1958, after being spotted on a television talent show, was engaged by the company to carve bodies for the new *Four Feather Falls* puppets. He remembers vividly getting the job. Following the talent show he accompanied his parents on a drive around the West Country. Finding the impromptu holiday boring, Roger leapt on a train back home. "I got home and the mail was on the mat and there was a letter that was addressed to me and it was from a company called A.P. Films saying they were desperately trying to find puppeteers and was I interested? I rushed to the phone and they unfortunately said the job had gone because they'd been waiting for a week and I hadn't replied. In my first bit of initiative ever I said, 'Well, I happen to be coming to London anyway on business. Perhaps I could come and see you?' They said, 'Yes, fine. We're always interested in puppeteers.' So the following day I got a train to London. I got off the train and went to a phone box at Euston and phoned them up and they said, 'Right, where are you?' I said, 'I'm in a phone box in Euston.' They said, 'Stay there! Don't let anyone else in. We'll call you back!' And I waited and waited and waited. And finally they phoned back and said, 'How much money have you got? Can you afford a train fare to Maidenhead? Get in a taxi to Paddington and we'll reimburse you. Get to Maidenhead and we'll meet you at the station.' They didn't tell me why. It was an hour of heart in the mouth stuff wondering what was happening. I finally arrived in Maidenhead, and was met by a guy in a car who whisked me away to a funny old house called Islet Park. It was all very suspect – it didn't feel right! He told me the story that they had been making a television series called *Torchy the Battery Boy* and wanted to start a new series called *Four Feather Falls* and they needed someone to make the puppets before they finished the old series so that they could have

Opposite: "I was their secret weapon!" Roger Woodburn at work on *Four Feather Falls*.

a quick change over when production finished. I was hired for six weeks to make the puppets."

Having managed to produce so many episodes of *Torchy* on a smaller budget than initially projected, A.P. Films found themselves in a position to finance the production of their own pilot episode. Fearful, perhaps unnecessarily, that Roberta would cancel her contract with APF, losing them a much needed commission if she got wind of the new venture, all development was kept under wraps.

"I never met her, but she was a bit like the Wicked Witch of the West," says Roger Woodburn. "The very mention of the words 'Roberta Leigh' and the blood would drain out of everyone's faces. I was hired to get *Four Feather Falls* ready, and I was told Roberta Leigh mustn't know about this. I was working in the conservatory with the carpenters. We had an old field telephone in an olive green box. Open the top and it would go to the house – the lines were strung through the trees. One day it went 'ding-a-ling-a-ling-a-ling!' I picked it up and there was a 'Get out of there! Fast! Roberta's on her way up!' She came in a limo up the drive and she saw me and cross-examined Gerry. 'Who was that boy I saw?' 'Oh he's the gardener!' One day I was working as a puppeteer and she turned up – they bundled me out in a blanket out the back!"

Embarrassment at making puppet films lingered, but these new puppets were a radical departure from their *Twizzle* and *Torchy* counterparts.

The strings were actually no longer technically strings, as they were now specially drawn from ultra thin tungsten steel. Keen to remove all evidence that these were marionettes, the search was on for the thinnest wire possible. *The wire suppliers, P. Ormiston and Sons Ltd. of Ealing, have been able to introduce a special type of "three thou."*[3] *wire with a chemically-applied matt surface to minimise studio lighting reflections,* reported *The Stage and Television Today* three years later, in 1962. Whilst these wires weren't entirely invisible, their visual impact could be reduced through anti-flare and powder paints. Unfortunately, there was a price to pay for low visibility. "They used to etch the wires to make them black, which made them very brittle," says Roger Woodburn. On a crew under pressure to stick to a rigid timetable, snapped wires were an unwelcome, frequent, occurrence.

The biggest innovation, though, was that for the first time these puppets could 'talk'.

"It was originally done by hand," says Roger Woodburn, referring to the manual lip-movements employed on *Torchy*. "Gerry, who had been an editor, had terrible trouble with the synching because the trouble with humans (when operating puppets) is that you start behind and catch up. It's not like the sync was always out by 10 frames or 4 frames. It was different every time. People caught up, but it was difficult to edit. So that's when the electronic idea came in."

"Gerry was always talking about making things better," says John Taylor, the Birmingham-based sound engineer who, with his wife, was responsible for the recording of all the dialogue tracks and

3. Eye wires were 'three-thou'. All supporting wires were 'five-thou'.

sound effects. "We said that we might be able to help him develop the lip-sync unit. Experiments were done and my partner Charles Hollick, together with Roland Wright, came up with the lip-sync mechanism."

"There was a tape playback deck, and the impulses went out through the puppet wires and down to the puppet's head, and this would operate a solenoid which would move the mouth open and closed," explains cameraman Julien Lugrin who joined the company in late 1960.

The first wiring diagram for the 'Electronic Natterer' Mark 1 was produced on December 28th 1958, and drew on the same basic scientific principal as an audio meter. The sound from the tape would be converted into electrical impulses, but instead of operating a needle measuring the volume of sound, it would cause an electromagnet to open and close. When installed inside the head, the electromagnet when active would force open the lower lip, and when inactive a small return spring would cause the lip to close. With certain adjustments, it was possible to alter the sensitivity of the unit, meaning that when working efficiently, the puppet's lip should open and close on every syllable uttered. The system was described in 1962, by *The Stage and Television Today* thus:

> *To Charles Hollick and Roland Wright is due a great deal of credit for this entirely British and novel TV lip-sync system.*
>
> *Up to four figures can be made to speak at once. Hence the 4-channel natterer.*

John Taylor (left) and Charles Hollick (right) work on the lip-synch unit they designed.

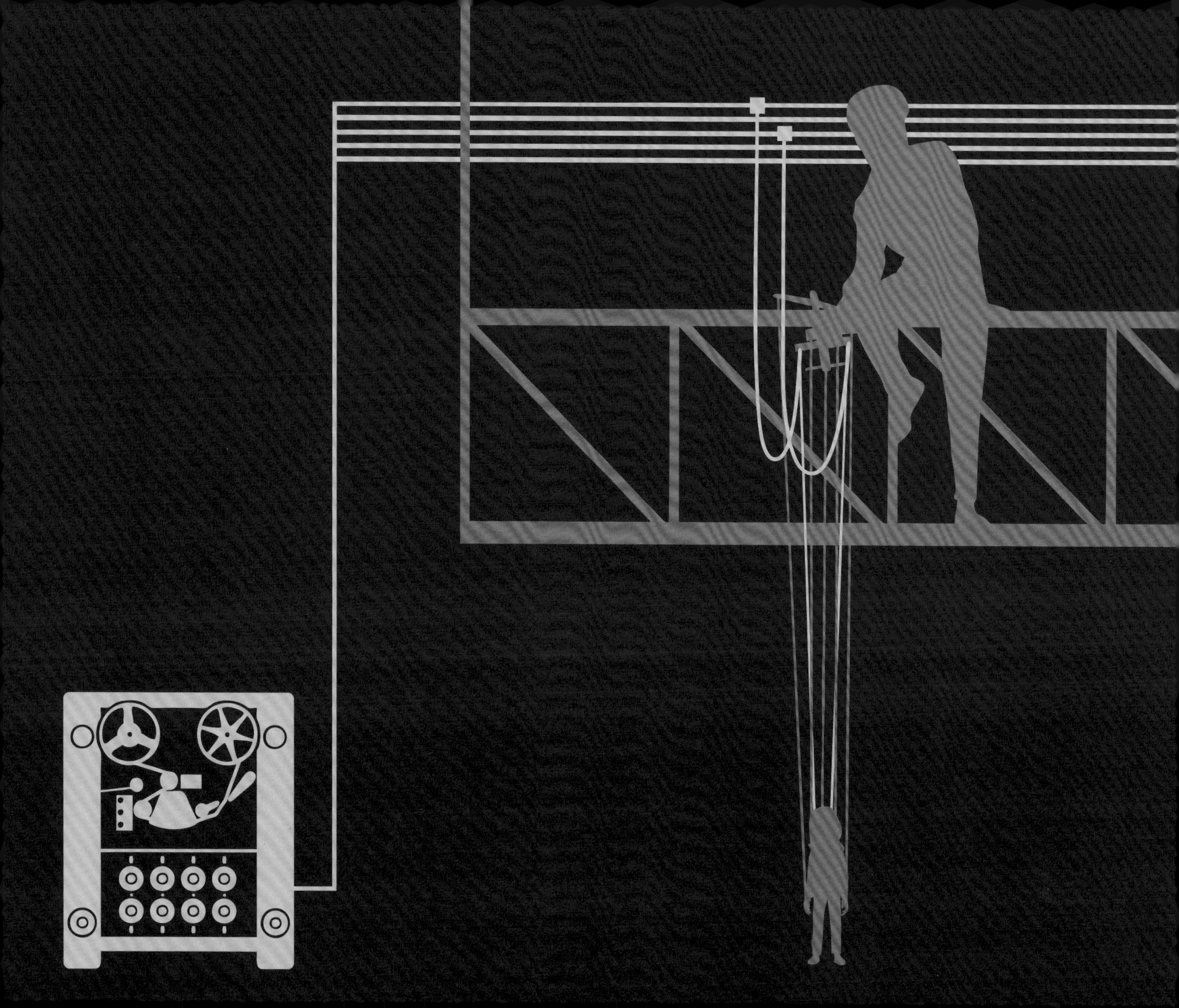

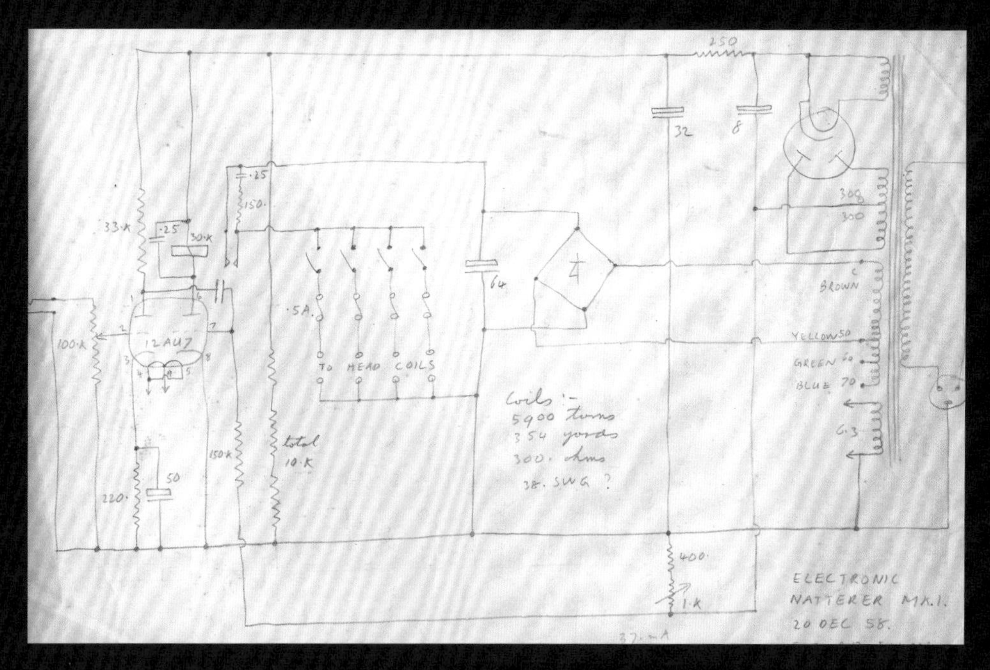

Making the Marionettes Speak

The incoming speech signals at J1 are amplified to the required level in part A of V1, under the control of VR1. The signals are then applied via C4 to part B of V, working as an anode-bend rectifier. The working point of the valve characteristic curve is controlled by VR2, which regulates the standing negative bias on V1 B grid. By suitable adjustment of V R 1 and V R 2 each separate syllable produces a unidirectional pulse of current in the coil of RL 1. The contacts of RL1 complete the circuit from a DC power supply to the lip magnet coil in the puppets head. The lip will therefore move in synchronism with the applied speech signals. The length of time for which the mouth remains open per syllable is controlled by the setting of VR 2, and careful adjustment of the latter can produce a high degree of naturalness. The diagram shows the connections for one puppet only. When more than one puppet is to be operated, further stages similar to V1 can be added as required, all working from the same incoming signals and from a common power supply. The operator controls which puppet is to 'speak' by closing the appropriate selector switch SW 1(A), (B), (C), etc.,

(Original diagram by Roland Wright, Hollick & Taylor)

Cables control figures' movements and also take the 0-50-volt pulses (DC) which operate the lips through solenoids. An ingenious part of the Hollick and Anderson circuitry is "retention", a delay-line effect, which keeps the lips open for a varying time after the pulse has "blipped" so that the mouths stay open for longer "Ah" sounds and shut quickly for short vowels.

There is a bias control on the natterer panel to regulate this light and shade of lip movement."[4]

The implementation of this new system meant a radical overhaul of the way that the marionettes were constructed. Puppeteer Mary Turner describes in detail the difficult process for building the skulls for the new Super-marionettes: "The *Torchy* heads were in wood in a traditional way and made by Christine Glanville and her family. They were hollowed out to a certain extent in order to accommodate the moving eyes and mouth. At this time, the mouth was operated by the puppeteer. By the next series, *Four Feather Falls*, experiments had been done with solenoids to be able to move the mouth mechanically, which meant the head needed to be made with a thin shell to leave more room for the solenoid, along with a more sophisticated eye bracket. This was very difficult to do in wood. The answer was fibreglass resin, which was being used in boatbuilding at that time.

"Puppeteers had to find out solutions of working with this unfamiliar substance to achieve a hollow head. One of the few mould-making materials available at that time which was flexible was a rubber named Vinamold. Clay was the most suitable modelling material to use, as the rubber had to be poured hot, but the clay had to be kept damp until finished, otherwise it shrank and became distorted if allowed to dry out. Vinamold came in a block as a semi-hard opaque dark red jelly – it was rather slimy to touch. It was cut into chunks and heated in its own special double-sided electric pot to liquidise it. It was probably an oil-based product and the smell from it while heating was so bad that it was best not to be in the room at the time.

"The clay head was modelled on a 1 inch wood rod. It was then suspended horizontally face up, ready for moulding in a square wooden box with the top open, with at least a 1 ½ inch space between it and the box. The heated rubber was poured in from the top and left to cool back to its original state. The wood was then broken away leaving a square block of rubber entirely encasing the head. A sharp blade was used to cut the rubber in half, so that one part was the face, and the other was the back of the head. The clay was scooped out so as to be left with two negative halves. Two or three layers of resin and fibreglass material were painted in to build a thin shell inside of these.

"When the fibreglass halves were hardened and taken out of the Vinamold, the face had to have considerable work done on it before being joined to the back. Eye openings, the lower lip, and a

4. According to www.telegoons.org , puppeteer Ronald Field devised his own electronic lip-sync unit in the late 50s that may have pre-dated APF's system. The system, which was patented in 1962, also involved the use of a solenoid and was installed in the Telegoon puppets.

semi-circular section underneath the lip were cut out. The next job was to join the lip back into the mouth with hinges at the corners so that it could open and shut. There was also a lever put on the back of the lip which would be worked by the solenoid mounted inside. Teeth were put in, and the painted wooden eyeballs were fixed onto brackets and put in their sockets.

"The two halves of the head were joined together using the fibreglass as a glue. The surface of the face was carefully sanded in order to prepare for a very fine finish.

"To get inside the completed head, a section was cut out of the back. Then it was a case of juggling with the eye mechanisms and mouth solenoid in the cramped space to get them fixed and working. When this was done, there was a semi-circular gap under the lip which allowed the mouth to move. The best material to fill

Above, left: Christine Glanville and Mary Turner carry out trepanning. Right: Mary at work painting a puppet.

the gap, which needed to be flexible and match the fibreglass shell, proved to be a very soft chamois leather which was moulded to the surface of the fibreglass. This took time, skill, trial and error to get it right.

"Painting was the next job. The first undercoat usually showed up some irregularities that had to be smoothed out. The final coat was stippled on so as not to show any brush marks. Putting on the hair was a very time consuming process as it had to be done gradually by sticking layer upon layer onto the head in small pieces, then combed, cut and styled.

"Silicone rubber, which could be used for mould-making, came into use sometime after *Four Feather Falls*. As it was cold-cure, plasticine could be used for modelling the heads. It was easier to get a good and more detailed finished on the surface and it did not dry out like clay did."

Despite Anderson's desire to produce increasingly realistic puppet shows, it was the size of the solenoid that meant it would be several years before he could achieve his ultimate goal of creating the first perfectly proportioned marionette. The actual proportions of the puppets led to problems for Reg Hill, and later Bob Bell, in the art department: set-pieces and props (most of which had to be crafted in-house) needed to be scaled to either the oversized heads and hands, or the slightly more realistically proportioned bodies. In the end, a 'mix and match' routine was established, where items such as chairs would be in scale with the bodies, whilst items that would be handled by the puppets, such as cups, would be in the larger scale of the heads.

While Roger Woodburn and Jack Whitehead carved the bodies, the heads and hands were made by Christine Glanville (Tex Tucker, Dusty, Dan Morse, Makooya, Kalamakooya, Pedro and Fernando) and Mary Turner (Doc Haggerty, Rocky, Slim Jim, Ma Jones, Grandpa Twink and Little Jake). Guest characters, or 'revamps', as they were known, were made from plasticine, sculpted onto a blank shell. Revamps were particularly vulnerable, as the wires could slice an unfortunate puppet's nose off, if not careful!

"I tried experimenting with hands made with some sort of rubber, of which there wasn't much available at that time," says Mary Turner. "Unfortunately, the bendable copper wire I put inside rotted the rubber in no time, so they were not usable. The future (wooden) ones after *Four Feather Falls* (for *Supercar* and *Fireball XL5*) were made by an outside company from our carvings."

With the sets and puppets completed, and *Torchy* coming to the end of production, it was time for A.P. Films to notify Roberta that they would not be taking any further commissions. "I think there was some bitterness," says Sylvia. "There was an attitude of, 'I've given you my best stories and now you're competing.' It was a shock to her that we weren't going to carry on with these umpteen things that she wanted us to do. We knew that they would always remain the same because of the cost and they were *her* stories. So we realised that if we stayed on with her we were just digging ourselves a hole. We realised we could do better – but it would cost more money. She wasn't interested in it being better quality – just the fact her name was up there. She was quite shocked that these impoverished filmmakers were saying, 'No thanks. We don't want to do anymore.' I think her ego suffered on that. But I suppose we owe her a debt really. We'd never have got into puppetry if it hadn't been for Roberta Leigh."

The separation also caused friction between the founding partners Gerry Anderson and Arthur Provis. "Roberta asked us to make another series of *Torchy,* and Gerry didn't want to do it. I didn't understand him turning down 26 episodes when we could have done both. I told him he could do *Four Feather Falls* and I'd do *Torchy*, but he wouldn't have it," says a bewildered Arthur.

Torchy the Battery Boy was completed three months ahead of the July 1st 1959 delivery date, which had been specified in the contract between APF and Pelham Films in October 1958. Roberta took ownership of the puppets, sets, etc., and a further 26 episodes of *Torchy* began filming at British Pathe under the stewardship of Vivian Milroy.

In March 1959, production began on the pilot episode of *Four Feather Falls*, *How it Began*, at Islet Park. With puppets and sets ready to be wheeled straight out onto the floor at the conclusion of *Torchy*, the only thing left to organise was the casting of the voices. For Dusty the dog, Rocky the horse, and bandit Pedro, Kenneth Connor's services were once again engaged following

Carry on, cowboy – Kenneth Connor and Pedro.

his performance as Mr. Bumbledrop in *Torchy*. For Ma Jones, Little Jake, Makooya and the full repertory of female and child voices, Denise Bryer was contracted as she had been deemed so successful in *The Adventures of Twizzle*. Recalling his brief stint on *Martin Kane, Private Investigator,* Gerry remembered actor David Graham, and cast him as Pedro's intellectually challenged sidekick, Fernando. This left only the part of Sheriff Tex Tucker to cast. The answer came one day when Gerry was at Denise Bryer's home. "Denise was reading for Gerry, and Gerry was doing the part of Tex Tucker. He was stumbling along a bit and I asked if I could be of any assistance," says Nicholas Parsons, who at the time was Denise's husband. "I read a few lines and he said, 'We've got our Tex Tucker!'" Gerry remembers: "I thought he was the last person in the world to play an American cowboy, but in fact he was very good. Nicholas is a good friend, so I know he won't mind me saying this, but he used to drive me barmy! We'd finish a take and he'd say, 'Is that OK, Gerry?' 'Yes.' 'I don't mind doing it again!' I used to find that very trying!"

With Nicholas on board to provide Tex Tucker's speaking voice, the next task was to secure the services of his singing voice. "I suggested we use a singer called Michael Holliday who sounded exactly like Bing Crosby," says Arthur Provis. Holliday was a successful, British-born crooner in the 1950s whose career had unofficially begun when he won a talent contest in Liverpool. He won a second contest when serving in the Navy, and this inspired him to earn a living by singing. In the mid-50s he was signed up by EMI and by 1959, when Gerry approached him, he was enjoying a relatively successful career. Cautiously, APF hired Holliday to sing one song for the pilot film in March 1959. Following their commission for a full series, they re-engaged the singer in early May. The contract stipulated, amongst other things, that:

1. *The Artiste will record on or about the 20th May 1959 four songs written and composed by the composer for use on the sound track of a series of television films entitled "Four Feather Falls"*
2. *In consideration of the sum of £400 to be paid by the Producers to the Artiste as aforesaid the Artiste grants the Producers the unrestricted right to use the recordings in connection with up to 52 films in the series throughout the world.*
3. *The Composer hereby grants to the Artiste the right to publish the four songs referred to in para.1 and the song "Two Gun Tex" recorded by the Artiste in fulfilment of a contract between the Artiste and the Producers dated the 10th*

Opposite: Tex Tucker learns his lines, with a little assistance from Nicholas Parsons.

March 1959 and to record the said five songs on gramophone records.

And perhaps most importantly:

4. *The Company agrees to give the Artiste screen credit to occupy not less than 60% of the screen space.*

As agreed Holliday returned to record another four songs[5], which he did at the Gate Studios in Elstree. The recording day got off to a bad start when an alarming breakdown in communication meant Holliday travelled to Shepperton Studios instead. This concerned the producers greatly, as they were worried that the star who had cost them so much was not going to appear. Fortunately, Holliday realised his mistake and the recording went ahead as planned.

Holliday's final hit was recorded in 1960, the first year in a decade which would see a rapid decline in the popularity of his type of music. After battling with depression, Michael Holliday committed suicide at the age of 34 in 1963.

Sinking so much money into the pilot film was a major gamble for A.P. Films. They had burnt the bridge with their only customer and so it was imperative to make the pilot film as impressive as possible. Roger Woodburn recalls the night before shooting commenced. "Reg said, 'Oh my god. We need this saddle for a close up and it needs to look good.' He had a photograph in a *National Geographic* of a Mexican rodeo cowboy doing rope tricks. And there was a white palomino horse with this guy standing on its back doing rope tricks and the saddle was magnificent. It was incredible. He said, 'It needs to look like that.' I said, 'Well, I'll have a go at it.' He was very off-hand but he didn't have any alternative. Everybody went and left the studio and I spent the night on my own just with the sound of the lights cooling down – ping ping. I sat in the ballroom at Islet Park for the whole night making the saddle. I made it all in balsa wood, then covered it in leather. The night went and I was so in my element – I couldn't believe they were going to pay me for this! Next thing I knew it was seven in the morning. Door opened and people were coming in with cups of coffee. Reg came in and he was obviously impressed and it had got him out of trouble. Although Reg would never show it that night probably ensured I stayed employed."

Things moved at a great pace for A.P. Films at this time. Mrs Whitworth, the owner of Islet Park, played a key part in securing APF their next commission. "The lady who ran Islet Park said, 'Meet my friend Stuart Levy at Anglo Amalgamated,'" recalls Arthur Provis.

Sylvia continues the story in her book, *My Fab Years*: "Gerry informed us that important visitors would be looking around the studio. They came from a company called Anglo Amalgamated which our switchboard operator always amused us by calling 'Anglo

---

5. The five songs were: *Four Feather Falls*, *Two Gun Tex of Texas*, *The Rick-Rick-a-Rackety-Train*, *Happy Hearts and Friendly Faces* and *The Phantom Rider*. *Four Feather Falls* was the first song to be recorded and is sung by Tex in *How it Began*. The end titles to that episode would have been added later when *Two Gun Tex of Texas* had been recorded.

Mealgamated.' They made typical B-movies on modest budgets – and it showed. The partners Nat Cohen and Stuart Levy were well known in Wardour Street at the time. Stuart Levy was recently widowed and, I would guess, in late middle age. Anyway, I duly showed them around and they seemed impressed, but I do not remember either having a great deal to say, or obviously making a stunning impression. The next day, however, Stuart Levy phoned Gerry and asked to see him urgently in his office. We were all thrilled, imagining that he wanted to discuss a film or work of some sort. [...] It transpired though, that Levy was attracted to me and wanted to meet me again. Could Gerry arrange it? I am ashamed to say that we took advantage of his interest [...]"

On April 15th 1959, Gerry wrote to Barry Gray regarding various issues, including the rights to the series and noted: *There is, of course, still the £100 to be paid to you for the original idea and I will let you have a letter of agreement along with the cheque as soon as the main series agreement with Anglo is signed.* A further handwritten note at the bottom states: *P.S. S Levy is hoping for a decision within next 24 hrs.*

Stuart Levy swiftly contacted APF, saying that Anglo Amalgamated would be financing the series; however, it seems that he had not consulted Nat Cohen who was not so enthusiastic and notified Gerry that his partner had acted in haste. Gerry comments in his biography[6]: "I told Nat a white lie and said that Stuart had promised me. Looking back on it, Stuart was a nice guy and I think he had said yes because he could see how desperate I was. I think even Nat felt a little guilty about this, so he spoke to Granada and got them to finance it." Granada viewed the pilot and gave APF an immediate commission for a further thirty-eight 15-minute episodes of *Four Feather Falls*.

APF had to mobilise quickly to get into production and with the news of their new commission, Mrs Whitworth offered to sell Islet Park to the company. Gerry and Arthur once again held conflicting views, and this was another disagreement that weakened their increasingly fragile business relationship. Although Gerry was in favour of buying the premises, he ultimately conceded to Arthur, who argued that having turned down the 26 *Torchy* pictures, they were in no position to start purchasing property. Arthur was evidently looking to the past with his cautious, even pessimistic, assessment of their financial position, while Gerry optimistically looked forward to profits that the new Granada commission would generate.

In April of that year, APF gave notice to Mrs Whitworth and by June the company was established at its new base – a warehouse on Ipswich Road on the Slough Trading Estate. Staff members travelled back and forth the few miles between the old and new bases in their own cars to help transport equipment. "I was in the car with my assistant Gordon Davie," says David Elliott, smiling, "and we'd stopped at the traffic lights. Gerry and Arthur were in a car next to us. I was so busy giving Gerry the two-fingered salute that I drove

6. *What Made Thunderbirds Go – The Authorised Biography of Gerry Anderson,* by Simon Archer and Marcus Hearn (2002)

Above, L-R: Tex, Rocky and Dusty / Walter Brennan on strings – Grandpa Twink / An early example of APF special effects.

Below, left: David Graham in full flight as Fernando / Nicholas Parsons and Kenneth Connor on set with Tex, Rocky and Dusty.

Above, left: The 'Murrayprodder' in action. Right: Michael Holliday strums Tex Tucker's tiny guitar.

Below, L-R: A selection of characters from *Four Feather Falls*.

straight into the back of a lorry! Gerry thought it was so funny that he offered to pay for the damage." Elliott also remembers one unlikely piece of 'equipment' that they needed to dispose of: "A grass snake was purchased for *Four Feather Falls* and painted by Reg Hill to look like a rattle snake. When we were in the middle of transferring the studio to Slough, I was helping Reg to clear out at Islet Park and Reg said, 'What shall we do with the snake?' I suggested that we let it go in the long grass in the wooded area in the grounds. Reg and I often wondered if anybody saw it and if it scared them!"

In around eight weeks weeks, APF had finished one series, filmed the pilot for a new series, received a full commission and had moved lock, stock and barrel to new, bigger (although slightly less glamorous) premises. There was no doubt the company was going from strength to strength.

"It all got a bit more like a factory when we moved to Ipswich Road," says Roger Woodburn. "It was probably more practical, but something went when we moved from Islet Park." The set-up was certainly more organised. One end of the studio housed a number of small partitioned offices, in addition to the cutting rooms, while the remainder of the studio was given over to the shooting stages. An annex, running the length of the building, was home to the darkroom, and the workshop where the puppets and sets would be constructed.

The central feature of the studio was the construction of a Dexion bridge, fixed to the ceiling. Sets were then built on moveable rostrums. The bridge was lined with miniature gallows, so that the puppets could be hung up in order to give the puppeteers' aching arms a rest. Puppeteer Judith Shutt, who came to A.P. Films in 1962, remembers the weight of the characters: "The puppets weighed quite a bit. I came down from the bridge one lunchtime and stood on a rusty nail at the bottom. So, I had to go for a tetanus injection in Slough at what they called 'dressing stations'. The area was full of factories, so they had these places with a nurse. She gave me a test jab and then I had to wait half an hour to wait to see if I had a reaction. When she came to do my main injection, I had to have one in each arm, she said, 'Good god girl! You've got arms like navvies!' I was quite thin, but the muscles in my arm were very, very strong. I was very upset about it at the time!"

One of the earliest problems, and subsequently innovations, came about as a result of the bridge. Usually, a puppet's strings would be no more than a foot or two long, meaning the operator would have very direct control. However, when suspended near the ceiling, isolated from the puppet by several feet of wire, the puppeteers found they had significantly less control over their charges. A movement that would be very sharp and direct at the end of two foot strings would be less so at the end of five. "There was this amazing delay between the operator moving the control and the puppet reacting," says Roger. Another issue was that the operators were unable to see the eyelines of the puppets from so far away. Christine Glanville explained in 1995: "The thing was, we could only see the tops of their heads. We couldn't see where their

noses were so we couldn't tell where they were looking. It was very difficult to get eyelines." Clearly it wouldn't do to have a puppet excitedly describing the dramatic action visible through a window when staring at a blank wall!

Initially mirrors were experimented with, but these caused problems with light reflections on the set. The answer to the problem came in the form of a chance visit to the new Slough studio made by a keen salesman, who demonstrated an early form of closed-circuit video camera. Quickly realising the potential of this gadget, a camera was bought and fitted to the eyepiece of the Arriflex film camera viewfinder. By looking down the viewfinder, where traditionally the cameraman would look, the video camera was able to see what the film camera was shooting and relay the image back to a monitor. As a result, the entire crew, including the puppeteers, could see exactly what was being shot. For the benefit of the puppeteers, who would be working the opposite way to everyone else, facing the crew, the image was reversed.

Roger Woodburn recalls the trials of working with the new system: "It was inherently unreliable. Halfway through a magic take, the picture would start to roll – the vertical hold would go and then

Above, left: Puppeteers on the Dexion bridge and, right, the bridge seen above the puppet set.

Sylvia chats with David Elliott between set-ups.

it would come back. All the cables were suspect. It did add to the workload tremendously, but in the long run it certainly helped. The coverage it gave was also unreliable. Arthur was doing the (camera) operating and he wanted to look through the camera, but all he had was a monitor on a bracket on the side of the camera. The monitors were very poor – it was a very crude video system. It wasn't high definition and it also gave lots of vignetteing because it was basically a camera looking through the viewfinder, without any purpose-built optics which you now have. Therefore it was very difficult to see the edge of the frame, particularly on wide angle lenses. You'd just have a hotspot in the middle. So, regularly when we were watching rushes there'd be a stage-hand leaning on the broom on the side of the frame watching the puppets, or somebody sitting on the edge of frame operating some string or nylon thread which extended out of the picture. I was a downstairs puppeteer. As far as Arthur was concerned, I was out of the picture. Then when we saw the rushes, sure enough, there was my hand or my knees or my nose which he hadn't seen, so this caused a lot of friction and arguments - that together with the time lost; everyone sitting around in the studio unable to do anything because the picture was unviewable; it was just squiggles all over the monitor while they waited for some electronics boffin to arrive from somewhere who would come in with a screwdriver and tweak it. The analogue video tube inside was very susceptible to being overexposed. Like staring at the sun. On one occasion an electrician was moving a lamp. John (Read) asked for it to be swung around. The light went straight into the lens of the camera and that was it. The camera was completely finished.

"I felt Arthur was very conservative, with a small 'c', in his views of new technology," continues Roger. "It was hard work and I understand his frustration. At that time, usually the director would say, 'Was that good?' and the cameraman just said, 'Yes', but the director didn't know where anyone was in the frame. It's standard stuff now whether you make films in Hollywood or films in Bangladesh – they're all using video-assist."

The most striking departure from Islet Park methods was the addition of a raised booth at one end of the building, looking down onto the studio floor. One side of the booth was home to Reg Hill, who would draught his designs whilst being able to observe proceedings, and the other side contained the tape deck and lip-sync unit, and a monitor showing the output of the Pye camera mounted in the Arriflex viewfinder. From here, the theory was that the director would be able to observe the action and, via a microphone linked to loudspeakers on the floor, direct the action. In his biography, *What Made Thunderbirds Go*,[7] Gerry recalls: "We were very short of space, but I was nevertheless anxious to be up to date. With a sense of drama, I imagined the scene of a television director looking through a glass screen to the studio floor below." The set-up was described by *The Stage and Television Today* in 1961: *At the far*

---

7. *What Made Thunderbirds Go – The Authorised Gerry Anderson Biography* by Simon Archer and Marcus Hearn (2002)

end of the studio is the control-room. The director is here instead of being on the set. He can see everything that is happening not only through the glass panel but on a television screen.

The TV is on a closed circuit and comes direct from the camera photographing the scene. The director, therefore, sees exactly what will be shown on screen when the films are televised. There are further TV screens in all parts of the studio.

The producer, Gerry Anderson, can watch what is going on from his executive office.[8] *The puppeteers up on their six-foot high gantry, have one in front of them so that they can watch the camera angles instead of only looking down on the puppets.*

Although the theory sounded exciting and modern, the reality was often unpredictable and frustrating so it's not surprising that it strained the patience of certain members of the crew.

"I never liked the booth," says Alan Pattillo, who joined the series as an editor before graduating to the role of director. Alan remembers with amusement David Elliott proclaiming with a sense of mischievous irony: "'It's marvellous. You speak into the microphone and they obey!'"

Alas, it was never that simple.

Roger Woodburn is more specific in his criticisms. "Gerry had this square view of the world which was this monitor which told him *that's* what it is, but not what was happening just outside that monitor. And of course it was open to abuse because what people used to do was just pan the camera off onto a brick wall. And he'd be raging up there because all he could see was a bit of brick and a fire bucket, and he couldn't see anything else other than what he could see through the window, but there were so many lights in the way... I used to think to myself, 'Just come out – come out. If you come down onto the studio floor, you'll understand immediately why we're not shooting.' He used to be shouting, 'Why, why, why aren't we turning? We've only shot two seconds today!' As I said, if only he'd come out onto the studio floor and had a look he'd have found out what it was. He used to say, 'That puppet's mouth isn't moving properly.' It was either too much sensitivity so it would say, 'hell-ll-ll-ll-oo ho-oo-ow ar-are you to-d-d-d-day,' or else it was the other way and it used to go, 'hellohowareyoutoday' and you had to find this optimum. A lot could be done from the lip-sync room, but inevitably some of it had to be done as adjustments inside the head, and to do the adjustments the wig had to come off and the back of the head had to be opened up and a lot of tweaking done. Then you had to say, 'Run the test again,' and he used to look at the monitor and he'd say, 'No – more' or 'Less'. So what you used to do was just stand in front of the camera, so your backside was in front of the lens, and count to fifty. 'One, two, three, four, five, six, seveneightnineten,' and then you'd stand away again and go, 'Try that!' and he'd go, 'That's much better!' and we'd carry on. It was pure emperor's new clothes."

---

8. The ability to watch the filming from across the studio remained a feature until they closed in 1969.

The reality is, that isolating the director from the action, was common in television studios at that time as they were a completely different working environment. A director would be responsible for creating a play for television, with up to four video cameras working simultaneously to capture the action, from a range of angles. By selecting the shots the director was, in effect, producing a final edited programme in real time. Therefore, it was felt that the director could better instruct the technicians from a separate vantage point, where he could follow the output of the various cameras without interrupting the shooting. Film, on the other hand, is a completely different medium, where each shot is individually lit and filmed and is inevitably a much longer process, particularly as much creative work is done after filming, when editing decisions must be made. A 30-minute television play could be captured in real-time, whereas a filmed half hour could take in excess of two weeks to complete. By solving one set of problems, Gerry had inadvertently found himself trying to tailor television techniques to suit film, and it was not a comfortable fit.

Roger remembers further frustration with the puppets: "Puppets, inevitably, during the course of operating used to get tied up in knots, and to start with you used to have to ask the camera technicians to sort it out. It was like asking Godzilla to do brain surgery – CRACK! 'Oh it seems to have come off!' So I became a downstairs puppeteer so that arms that were twisted the wrong way, etc., could be sorted."

"Stay right where you are!" David Elliott gives orders.

All these difficulties came to a head in October 1959 when Arthur Provis resigned his directorship of the company and relinquished his shares. "I put Arthur and Gerry as a bit like the ant and grasshopper," says Roger Woodburn. "Gerry was destined to go somewhere and had ideas and ambitions and Arthur was a bit, 'Oh, that's new. Not sure about that.' It actually worked very well; the two of them made a good equilibrium. As things got more successful the difficulties between them got greater." Anderson says of Provis: "Arthur, while a delightful man and a brilliant cameraman, was a great worrier who didn't share my belief in investing in the future expansion of the company. I wanted to push forward and he wanted to take things more steadily."

A contract dated October 12th 1959 specifies the terms of Arthur's withdrawal from the company. The financial details of this 'divorce' are interesting:

> *Mr. Provis shall sell the Company his Thirty shares in Company and the Company shall pay Mr. Provis therefor* (sic) *the sum of* *THREE THOUSAND POUNDS* *to be as follows:*
>
> *(a)* *TWO THOUSAND POUNDS* *on or before the execution of this deed.*
>
> *(b)* *FIVE HUNDRED POUNDS* *to be satisfied by the transfer to Mr. Provis of the ownership of a Ford Anglia car Index No. 899 GBH and the Company agrees to see that such change of ownership is properly registered.*
>
> *(c) The balance of* *FIVE HUNDRED POUNDS* *to be paid to Mr. Provis by twelve monthly instalments of* *FORTY-ONE POUNDS THIRTEEN SHILLINGS AND FOUR PENCE* *each the first of such instalments to be paid on First Day of January One Thousand Nine Hundred and Sixty and each subsequent payment on the first of each month.*

In addition to this, Arthur was awarded a 5% share of the profits in *Four Feather Falls*, as well as receiving assurances that he would no longer be held accountable for any actions of the company, including indemnity against …*any claim in respect of rent or breach of agreement under a Lease dated Fifth June One thousand nine hundred and fifty nine and made by Slough Estates Ltd.* amongst other potential breaches.

Arthur Provis signed away his rights to the future development of the company for what probably appeared a large sum of money, but the phenomenal successes which followed make this seem, in retrospect, a pittance. Fortunately, Arthur has no regrets. He continued his career in puppets, joining forces with Roberta Leigh. The company was now left with four directors: Gerry Anderson (the managing director), John Read, Reg Hill and Sylvia Thamm. Sylvia was not merely the managing director's girlfriend: she was a hard-working member of the company who had persuaded her mother to invest in the company in its early days. Although her experience in film was minimal compared to the other directors, she managed to increase her list of duties to include editing the dialogue tapes.

The crew agree that cheerfulness and conviviality pervaded the studios at this time, but it is not surprising that, working in such claustrophobic conditions, the usually happy atmosphere was broken by odd moments of friction. "I was asked one evening by Arthur Provis to a pub to have a drink," says Roger Woodburn. "Fine, went along. Turned out to be a pitch. Tried to get me to join his new company. I said no, I didn't want to. The next morning Gerry hauled me up about it. He knew I'd been to the pub and he knew who I'd seen, and he wanted to know what I'd been doing. I'd gone there with another guy called Jack Whitehead, who was a woodcarver at the studio. I was quite young and just assumed I'd been hauled up in front of the boss and that was it, but Jack was very, very angry that in his private time, after shooting, he'd gone to a pub in Taplow or Cookham, met and had a beer with a guy who happened to offer him a job and it had got back to Gerry and he knew what had been offered! If it had been now, I'd have felt equally angry as it was a bit *Nineteen Eighty-Four*."

These moments of tension, however, were fortunately a rare exception rather than the norm, and many members of the team who worked on *Four Feather Falls* cite this as being the happiest time at the studios; a time when they were starting to break new ground, before they were a successful factory line – a time when essentially they were a group of mates who came together to make fun puppet films. "I'd been told as a lad that you didn't enjoy work. You get paid for it and have fun after. Yet here I was, playing with puppets, having an absolute ball, and at the end of the week they pay you money as well!" says Roger Woodburn with a broad smile, clearly nostalgic for those heady days of long ago. David Elliott concurs: "*Four Feather Falls* really was my happiest time at the studios. I thought it was a great little series. Everyone really pulled together to get it done, no matter how much overtime – days, nights, weekends. When we were getting ready for the pilot episode, my wife, who was heavily pregnant at the time, came all the way up to the studio to help make the hay bales. It was such a team effort. An absolute joy to make."

Filming continued through the remainder of 1959 until April 1960 when all 39 episodes were in the can. During this time, Gerry relieved himself of part of his workload and shared directorial duties (until this point he had directed every episode since the beginning of *Twizzle)*, with first David Elliott and then Alan Pattillo, who would both alternate in the cutting rooms and on the stages. "I remember watching the rushes in the viewing theatre. No sound of course, but I fell in love with these puppets," says Alan Pattillo. David Elliott recalls his promotion: "I'd been doing the lip-sync on some of *Four Feather Falls* and so Gerry and I spent a lot of time in the booth together. We'd always discuss the shots and chat about ideas for each episode. Gerry came into me one day and said that he'd like me to start directing, as he had so much to do and that he couldn't continue to direct every episode himself. I said that I'd rather wait until after my wife had given birth to our first child. However, he persuaded me and I went onto the stage to do my first episode

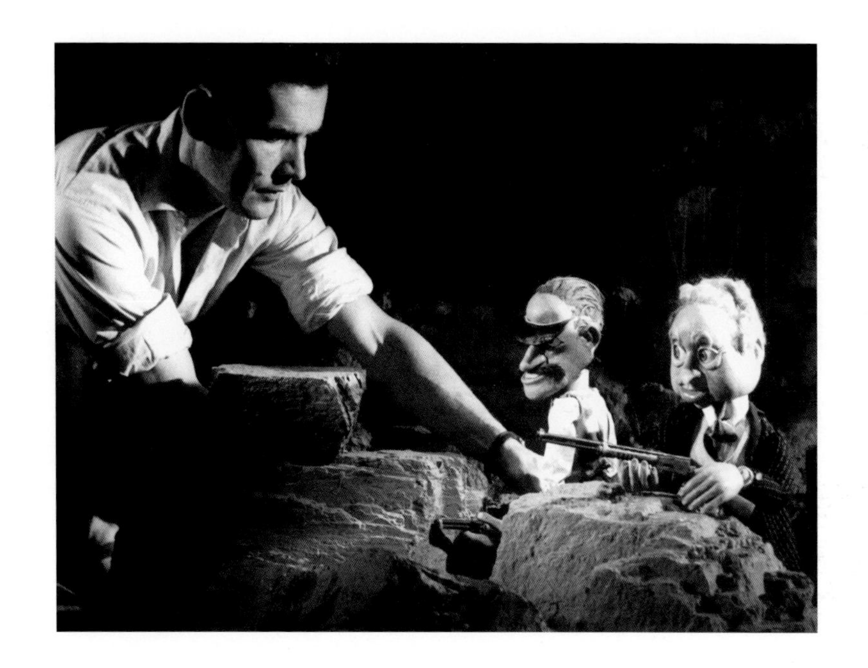

(*Trapped*). We'd literally just finished shooting, when I got a call saying that my wife was giving birth. I jumped into the car and got from Slough to Harrow in just twenty minutes!"

David has other fond memories: "As it was a western series, obviously there was no shortage of weapons, which was great fun. We used to have these little arrows that Roger Woodburn would blow through a blowpipe, which was a bit hit and miss. Once he fired and the arrow lodged itself in a puppet's eye! I remember Gerry showing a visitor around once and as they stepped out of the booth, Gerry said to this bloke, 'We also have our own intercom system.' They both looked up and there was the speaker full of arrows. 'Obviously they don't like everything the Director says!' said Gerry smiling.

"The production manager, Jim Marsh, and I went to the bank to get the wages; he and I had been for a drink beforehand and he had with him the full scale revolver from the series. He took the gun into the bank and stuck it over the counter and said, 'Give us the money!' 'You've had a good lunch boys. I can smell the beer from here!' the cashier said. Nowadays you'd get shot for that!" David has no shortage of stories involving weapons: "The person who wore the guns in the live-action shots was Gordon Davie (assistant

Above, left: John Read sets up a gunfight. Right: Bob Bell in the props store.

editor). One of the shots I dreamt up was a duel. I had Gordon in the foreground and a puppet in the background. The gun had a blank. Gordon tried to do a fast draw and dropped the gun and everyone dived down in case it went off! We re-set and did the shot and Gordon fired. Even though it was just a blank, which can still be dangerous, it took the puppet off its strings! Interestingly, putting live action shots in, like hands picking things up, became a feature of many of the shows we did after *Four Feather Falls*." Alan Pattillo recalls the technique of live-action inserts: "You would have a shot of a puppet leaning forward, very painfully, to pick something up. Then, you would cut to a human hand. I don't think it ever convinced the audience, but that was part of the charm. It was almost real, but not quite."[9]

David continues about live action shots: "We went to film some live-action inserts, at Burnham Beeches, of a knife being thrown and sticking into a tree, as well as a shot of a gun out being pulled out of a holster. We were doing this and all of a sudden a little man appeared with a shotgun which was taller than him. He said, 'What are you doing here? Have you got permission?' 'No, do we need permission? What's the problem?' 'A lady saw you when she was going by, playing around with knife and guns.' We then turned around and about 100 yards away were a few coppers! We promptly pleaded guilty and left!"

---

9. In the early Supermarionation shows, the hand artist (a member of the crew) would wear a rubber glove to give the appearance of being a puppet hand. From *Stingray* onwards, the use of a glove was abandoned.

David Elliott wasn't the only member of the crew to find himself in trouble at Burnham Beeches. Art Assistant Bob Bell managed to get himself arrested after breaking local conservation laws by taking twigs for set dressing! Roger Woodburn remembers Bob Bell with affection: "Bob was of the generation that had literally come of age when war broke out. When the war finished, many men of that age had no jobs to return to and hadn't learnt a trade." Bob Bell was in his late 30s when he joined APF during *Torchy,* after working as a matte painter at Shepperton studios. "He was always grateful to Gerry for the opportunity he gave him to excel," smiles Roger. "Bob was the first person I really got to know, other than the two girls I was working with," continues Roger. "I remember the first time I heard him speak. Sylvia said to someone, 'You're completely gormless!' then she said, 'I wonder what that means?' Bob popped up from behind a set and said, 'It's a medical term – it means without gorms!' I thought, 'I'm gonna like this guy.'

"He was trying to get some lumps of coal piled up in a little heap to look like some rocks in the prairies," continues Roger. "Coal looks wonderful because it looks like strata in miniature. Gerry was getting very cross with him on the intercom. 'For goodness sake, hurry up!' Bob couldn't get these coals to balance right and we were losing time, and Gerry was getting more and more frustrated. Secretly, Bob had got these lumps of foam rubber that were exactly the same colour as the coal and when Gerry said, 'For goodness sake, hurry up!' again Bob jumped up and said, 'Oh for God's sake!'

and he took these lumps of rubber and he threw them straight at the glass and the whole control room disappeared under the desk, and the rubber went 'boing!' and bounced off the glass. There was a moment's silence. Nothing happened. Then, slowly, they came up peering over the desk." David Elliott continues: "Gerry did see the funny side of the joke though. He had to. Everyone else did!"

Roger has lots of stories about Bob. "There was a scene in the main street of the town at night. On the windows, which were tracing paper, they wanted silhouettes of lots of things going on. Bob and I were both given the job of lying on the floor behind the set with cardboard cutouts of cowboys with big hats and holding them there jiggling them about. We had to wait while they were lighting. 'OK, We're going to do a take. OK Jiggle!' And we were jiggling away, the two of us side by side. 'Cut, cut, cut. We're going again, just wait.' And then there was a lot of mumbling, we couldn't hear the other side. Then Bob turned to me and he said, 'Do you realise there are men out now in the North Sea trawling for fish. Battling with the elements. And what are we doing? We've got two cardboard cowboys and we're jiggling them about. Do you consider that a job worth doing?' Then we had the giggles and then next thing you know someone was screaming, 'We're running! ACTION!' 'Mm? What? Oh!' Jiggle, jiggle, jiggle."

Four Feather Falls was opened to the public in February 1960 and attracted a lot of media attention. "It had a great deal of charm and it did very well. It got the front cover of the *TV Times*," says Gerry. The show's success even translated into a modest run of merchandise including an annual (written by Sylvia), a board game and a comic strip. At this stage, APF had little involvement with tie-in products and had no inkling of the merchandising empire that would rise from their studios over the next few years.

The final episode of *Four Feather Falls* was filmed in April 1960, and a few weeks later David Elliott delivered the last print to Basil Litchfield of Granada Television. With a well-regarded success on their hands, A.P. Films enthusiastically awaited the commission for a second run of episodes. "We really were so thrilled with it and we thought, 'We've really got it here now'," says Sylvia. "So we just waited, as so many people have to do in our business, for the phone to ring. And when it doesn't ring it's not a very good sign. Money was running out now. Finally we phoned. And they said, 'It was lovely. We really enjoyed it. But thank you very much. I don't think we need any more.'"

SUPERCAR

•1960•

SUPERCAR

FULL BOOST VERTICAL! 3

Supercar

As *Four Feather Falls* was winding down in early 1960, APF received a call from the agent representing actor Kenneth Connor. He informed the studio that he had a young writer on his books by the name of Hugh Woodhouse, and enquired as to whether they would be interested in meeting him. [1]

A meeting was arranged and Hugh was invited to submit some story proposals for *Four Feather Falls*, before subsequently being commissioned to write two stories, *Safe as Houses* and *Fancy Shooting*. At the time, Woodhouse was under contract to the BBC as a staff writer, working in a caravan outside the new, partly-constructed Television Centre in Shepherd's Bush. In order to avoid alerting his employers to a potential breach of contract (his ran until mid-1960), Hugh asked to be credited under his brother's name, Martin Woodhouse.

It was over the course of a general chat that the conversation between Gerry Anderson and Hugh turned to the subject of what would be next. It was then that Gerry and Reg Hill presented their new idea, as Hugh explains: "Gerry Anderson had this idea for a super-car, which could go along the surface at amazing speed, could fly, could go underwater, could do most of the things that James Bond later did. This was a fifteen-minuter, with the pilot, Mike Mercury – a good clean, all-American guy, his rather freckled side-kick – a kid called Jimmy and, of course, for merchandising, a woolly animal which was Mitch the Monkey."

Hugh continues: "If you consider, and I'm not just saying this because they were invented by Gerry Anderson, that there were three characters – Mike Mercury, Jimmy and Mitch… You ain't got a lot of dialogue going with those three. So we brought in Doctor Beaker, who was a character."

Hugh expands on this point: "Gerry Anderson had one

---

1. APF was on the look-out for new writers, when Jill Allgood departed after nine scripts for *Four Feather Falls*. Although her scripts were the last produced, Hugh Woodhouse recalls that he wrote the final two scripts commissioned for the series. These two, *Safe as Houses* and *Fancy Shooting* seem to have been produced as episodes 34 and 36 (out of 39) respectively. Mary Turner remembers Jill Allgood: "Jill Allgood was a BBC producer on Childrens' TV in the early days at White City. On alternate Saturdays she had a magazine-type programme. A fellow puppeteer introduced my mother to her and she invited us on a few times with our own puppets. When a new head of Childrens' TV was appointed, as so often happens, the woman brought her own people in and Jill was out of a job. At some point, she was writing for a radio show with Bebe Daniels and Ben Lyon. It was a few years later when Gerry was looking for writers for *Four Feather Falls* that I suggested her. Eventually she fell out with Gerry. She was rather a strong character."

fifteen-minuter, Martin and Hugh Woodhouse[2] had another fifteen-minuter which was called *Beaker's Bureau*[3], which was, to be perfectly honest, a pinch from *Professor Branestawm*. We worked out *Beaker's Bureau* around a sort of scientific investigation of the baddies. So *we'd* got that, Gerry Anderson had got *Supercar* and we put the two together, with Martin and Hugh adding in the villain, who was called Masterspy, and his obviously inefficient sidekick – you have to have an inefficient sidekick! – called Zarin, so we came up with this thirty-minute format."

The premise of *Supercar* was very straight-forward. However, as Gerry Anderson explains, the idea for such an amazing vehicle wasn't just for the benefit of exciting story-telling: "As we progressed with the puppet shows, we managed to get them to do more or less what we wanted – or with cinematic tricks make them *look* as though they did what we wanted. The thing we couldn't get them to do was to walk. Of course, as Sam Goldwyn once said, 'movies must move,' and so we came up with the idea of Supercar. The whole point was that all the characters could sit in Supercar and it could fly around at great speed, could drive along the road, land on water, go under water, and therefore we got the movement into the film, without the puppets having to walk."

2. Martin and Hugh Woodhouse always refer to their partnership in the third person.

3. *Beaker's Bureau* had been developed with another format called *Roderick Rumble* for the BBC when Hugh was a staff writer. The BBC showed no interest and so Hugh presented the concept to APF.

Between Gerry, Reg, Martin and Hugh (and no doubt with the odd suggestion from other crew members), the format was whittled and reworked until the two concepts of *Supercar* and *Beaker's Bureau* dovetailed smoothly. The characters are beautiful in their comic-book simplicity: the hero (fearless test-pilot Mike Mercury); the child – for young viewers to identify with (Jimmy Gibson); the nutty-professors (Doctor Beaker and Professor Popkiss); the cuddly loveable animal (Mitch); and the villain, complete with bumbling sidekick (Masterspy and Zarin).

APF were experiencing a heady euphoria in the early months of 1960; they had survived in the difficult world of independent film-making for nearly three years, and their first independent venture, *Four Feather Falls*, had been extremely well received. Indeed, in the week the show premiered in February 1960, a greatly coveted accolade for artistic endeavour came their way: they captured the front page of the ITV listings magazine, *TV Times*. What made this even more special was that they had succeeded in getting this unexpected prize position when competing with a new puppet television series premiering that week in the London region[4]: their own *Torchy the Battery Boy*, which must have pleased them greatly (and Roberta Leigh less so). That week's edition carried a double-page spread about both shows, although the author seems to be unaware that they were made by the same company. Whilst on one page Roberta Leigh

4. Certain other regions first screened *Torchy* in 1959.

condemns violence in children's shows ("I deplore violence of the knifing-killing sort. Children, being imitators, may then want to rush about with knives or shout, 'Drop dead'"), writing on the adjoining page, W.O. Court ignores the ethics of the magic guns and enthuses about the new technological marvel:

> *Striking effects and new techniques in the art of puppetry are promised in* Four Feather Falls*, a series about a Wild West town of that name which starts next Thursday. Each 15-minute show is shot in the same way as a feature film, using elaborate sets and location shooting.*
>
> *An electronic device – I am told it has never been used before in puppetry – ensures that the puppets' lips are synchronised with the voices [...]*

As APF had hoped, the ability of the marionettes to 'speak' was a major selling point for the series. Of course, not everyone agreed: Roberta Leigh later told *The Stage and Television Today* in 1963: "It is all too easy to turn a puppet into a mechanical doll with dozens of gimmicks, but my puppets aren't dolls." Fortunately, her views were the exception rather than the rule.

However, the excitement of their new success was overshadowed with daunting news almost immediately. Granada's response to the new series had been so favourable that, before *Four Feather Falls* had even broadcast in February 1960, APF presented the channel with their new idea. A beautifully illustrated, spiral-bound brochure was produced by Reg Hill for *Supercar*,

Above: Ipswich Road studios - the inspiration for Black Rock laboratory?

Below: Some of the team around the time of production on *Supercar*.

featuring an array of dazzling paintings of concepts for the series. It was rushed over to Granada who would shortly show *Four Feather Falls,* not only to great acclaim, but also to great financial advantage as they had succeeded in securing a Network transmission (all ITV regions bought and transmitted the show simultaneously). However, Granada declined to invest in the new idea and, furthermore, they wanted no further episodes of *Four Feather Falls*. Thirty-nine episodes of A.P. Films' unique style of programming were more for than enough for them it seemed. Aware that they would need to find a new investor, APF took advantage of a triple-page spread granted to the puppet western in *The Stage and Television Today* in the week of the first episode and placed the following advert: *FOUR FEATHER FALLS was devised and produced by A.P. FILMS LTD at their new studios in Slough. NOW! An entirely NEW SERIES, based on a fresh and exciting subject, using this highly successful technique is available. For further information ring SLOUGH 21370*

Production concluded on *Four Feather Falls* in April 1960 and, once again, APF found itself scrabbling around for work in order to pay the bills. The first job came from close to home, via *Four Feather Falls* voice artist Nicholas Parsons. In December 1959, Parsons had written and starred in three commercials for Blue Cars Travel Agency. These adverts were well-received and, in March 1960, Ken Fox, Managing Director of Blue Cars, summoned him in again to discuss producing another three promos. Encouraged by the previous three, Parsons had formed D.N. Productions and saw this second batch of commercials (which he co-wrote with David Ellis) as a chance to cement his place in the advertising industry. In 1984, Nicholas Parsons explained the story: "I went up with some ideas (to see Ken Fox) and the one he chose was this very off-beat and funny one. There had never been a funny commercial on television. I knew we were sticking our neck out and I never thought he'd have the guts to back it up. But he said, 'Yes, we'll do it.'

"I went to Gerry and said, 'I've got this contract.' I think the figure was three and a half thousand pounds – which was peanuts then – to make three commercials and an advertising film. Gerry had just heard from Granada that *Four Feather Falls* was not to continue, so he was in a state of flux and looking for any little bit of extra cash. I wanted to establish my production company and I said, 'Gerry, I'll share the cash with you.'

"He worked at a loss, I worked at a loss, but I wanted to establish my production company, hoping to break into the world of making commercials. I had a very talented wife who could do absolutely any voice at all, so she did it for love."

The advertisements were shot at Ipswich Road in May 1960, following a quick upgrade to the sound-proofing of the studio. As sound recording was never necessary at the factory, the building echoed and allowed in all sorts of extraneous noise from the extremely busy A4 that ran outside. Finances would certainly not run to expensive foam for sound-proofing, but, in true cottage-industry style, John Read improvised. He purchased 1,500 egg-boxes and

Mike Mercury and co dangle in front of some of the 1,500 egg boxes bought by John Read as soundproofing.

fixed them to the walls. Three commercials were shot, all featuring Nicholas Parsons and Denise Bryer: *Germans* – a female German spy is awarded the Iron Cross for discovering Blue Cars; *Gambler* – a suicidal gambler decides not to kill himself after realising that a Blue Cars holiday will make his life worth living again; and *Martians* – two Martians observing that the sudden flurry of activity on earth is caused by people visiting Blue Cars.

The adverts were edited and delivered to the delighted clients who also took delivery of a 15-minute 'Ad-mag' featuring Parsons and Arthur Haynes which had also been filmed at Ipswich Road. Preparations were then made for the production of the advertising film they had been contracted for. This would take members of the A.P. Films crew across Europe to France, Switzerland, Austria, Italy, Yugoslavia, Spain and Denmark. With a miniscule budget, it was inevitable that (much to Gerry's regret) a number of staff had to be released until a new commission was found. This was not a great surprise to the crew though, as it had become the norm for staff to be laid-off at the end of each series and offered re-employment when the next project came along.

At around the time these advertisements were being made, Gerry's long-cherished wish to produce live-action features came a step closer, giving him hope that he would not always be seen as a puppet specialist. Nat Cohen and Stuart Levy of Anglo Amalgamated, who had previously introduced Gerry to Granada, asked APF if they would like to produce a 'B' movie or 'second feature' for them. "In those days it was called a B-movie," explains Gerry. "You'd go to the cinema and you'd have a big movie and you'd have a B-movie."

A screenplay entitled *Crossroads to Crime* was commissioned from scriptwriter Alun Falconer, and a budget set at £16,500, with filming taking place during June 1960 in and around Slough. Anderson's hopes of becoming a big movie producer soon began to unravel as shooting commenced. "Christ, it was awful!" cringes David Elliott, who both edited the picture and directed some of the 'second unit' material. "I don't really want to remember it!" says Sylvia. "Quite honestly we felt it was a bit beneath us! We were doing all these fantastic things that no one else had done and now we come to this little bit of a low grade thing."

The wafer-thin plot is a tedious affair concerning the planned theft of £20,000 worth of ingots, and is remembered with dread by anyone who worked on the production. Filming took a little over two weeks in total, and this haste is reflected in the finished product, which is more than a little rough around the edges. Despite one journal generously describing the film as a 'modest little thriller,'[5] audiences were sparse and most viewers seem to have responded with yawns.

Although the film was a disaster, it is remembered with great amusement by David Elliott. "There was a commercial at the time for Strand cigarettes with a very tough looking guy in a Mackintosh standing by a lamp-post in the dark. The slogan was 'You're never

---

5. From *Monthly Film Bulletin.* (1960)

Above, top left: Ray Soni, John Read and Mary Turner at an APF party. Right: The puppeteers gather for a group shot.
Below, left: Julien Lugrin with Mike and Mitch. Right: Alan Pattillo and lip-sync operator John Drake.

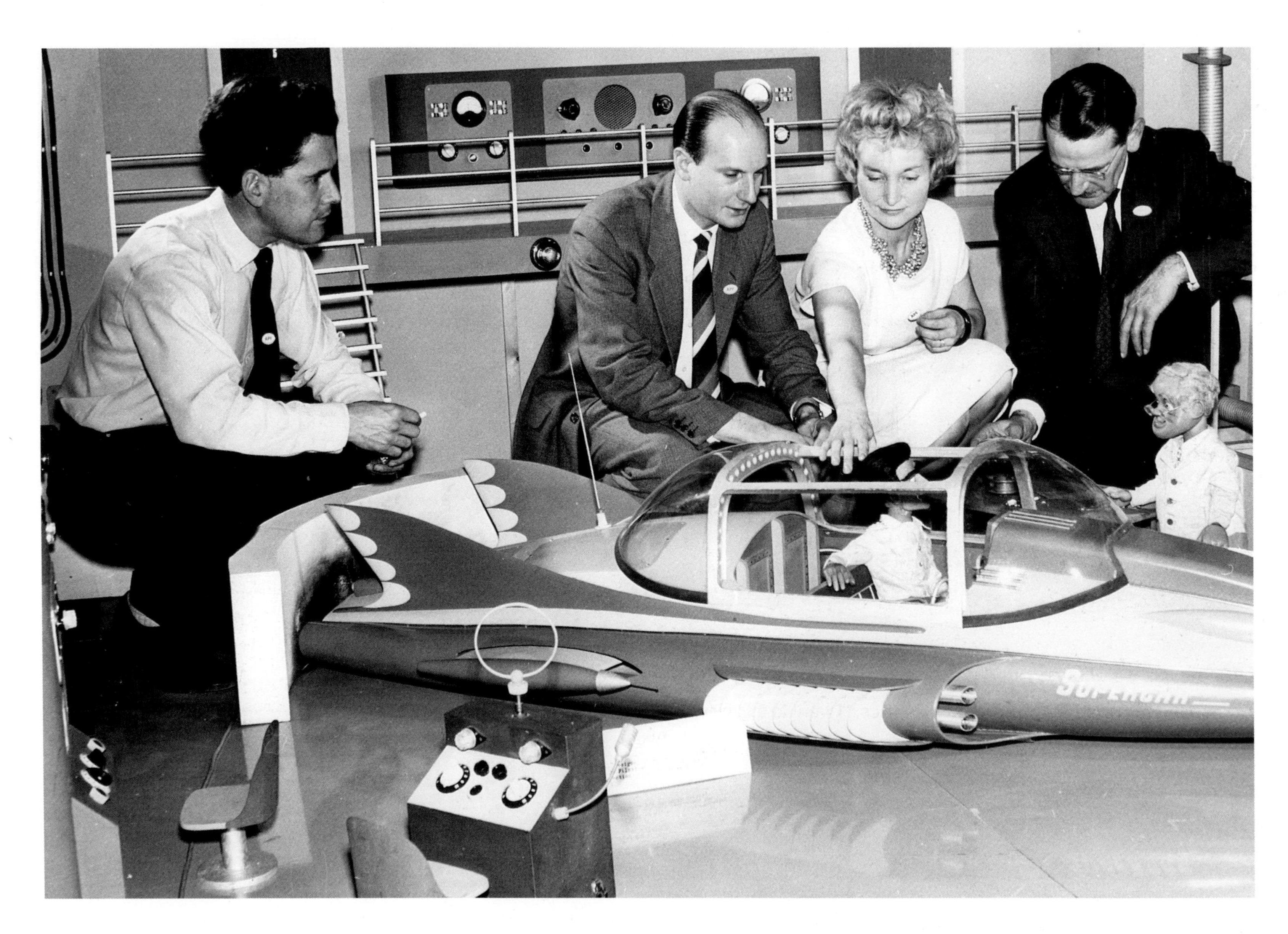

John Read, Gerry, Sylvia, and Reg Hill in the Supercar laboratory.

alone with a Strand.' Anyway, we hired the same actor (Terence Brooks) for his tough-guy image and I said to him, 'Right, in the shot, you're on the tailboard of the lorry and I want you to jump off.' He looked at me and said in the most effeminate voice, 'Oooh, I couldn't do *that*. Much too high!' It was only three feet and the lorry wasn't even moving! So I had to put on his coat and do the stunt myself! By the time we got to Burnham Beeches to film a scene with George Murcell lurking behind a tree going, 'pssst – mate – in 'ere,' Sylvia and I were standing on the opposite side of the road just wetting ourselves with laughter!"

Gerry Anderson picks up the story: "Eventually the film was finished and I took it along to the distributors, Nat Cohen and Stuart Levy. We sat and watched the picture and when the end titles played out, I waited for them to say something. There was total silence… Eventually Nat Cohen turned around and said, 'I'll say this much, Gerry. I've seen worse.'"

The judgement came as a cruel blow to Gerry, even though he knew very well that the film was not a great work of art. Actor David Graham had his own encounter with the critics. "I went to this cinema in Kilburn and I sat squirming through this film. It wasn't good. It just wasn't good. It was so bad it became a classic possibly! As I got up to go a voice behind me said, 'What a fucking awful picture!'"

Crossroads to Crime promptly disappeared after its brief spell at the cinema and has only been saved from total obscurity by the fact that it came from the illustrious studio that later produced *Thunderbirds*. From a historical point of view, it does have something to interest the enthusiast, as it grants the viewer a brief glimpse of the interior of A.P. Films' Ipswich Road studios, which featured as the gang's warehouse.

Following filming of *Crossroads to Crime*, some of the crew, including John Read and Bob Bell, departed for their Eupropean tour with Nicholas Parsons for the Blue Cars Ad-mag programme, leaving Gerry and the remaining team to consider their options. Money was burning up rapidly and, as no company can run on thin air, the directors decided to pull the plug. A call was put out to the equally miserable crew in Switzerland, who themselves had overspent and exhausted their funds, to inform them of the decision to liquidate the company. The crew returned to base with the film unfinished.[6]

While attempting to console themselves and mulling over limited options at their studios in July[7] 1960, an old friend and

---

6. Mary Turner recalls how the Blue Cars Ad-mag was finished: "To save money, John (Read) went later as a one-man crew with Nicholas to Spain. John told the tale of trudging up a hill after Nicholas while he carried all the camera gear to shoot a scene. He got all set up, turned around and there was Nicholas waving to him from another hill, shouting that it was better from there. In the high temperature, John was not too pleased!"

7. July 1960 is a best guess, as Barry Gray had a contract issued to him on August 10th 1960 pertaining to music for *Supercar*. Given the time needed for pre-production, plus the shooting of the back projection plates (the aerial photography was done over several sessions) it seems likely that A.P. Films would have had a minimum of a month to prepare for the first episode to be filmed in September. Fortunately, from then on, it is easier to work out the rotation of episodes due to diary sources.

colleague, Frank Sherwin Green, called the studio. "Frank Sherwin Green, who used to give us work, was a fantastic character," says Sylvia. "When we were at our wits end he'd say, 'Oh come on. Let's have a drink.' Anyway, Frank Green rang and I said, 'Frank, we're looking for work.' He said, 'What do you mean?' I said, 'We're looking for work.' He said, 'Well that's ridiculous.' He said, 'I'm coming in tonight to see you.' So he came in and we were all sitting around miserable and weary and we told him the whole story."

Anderson picks up the story: "We told him that we were going bust. He said, 'You can't do this Gerry. I mean, look you've got a control room here – you actually built it with your own hands. You've got bridges for the puppets and you've got a projector and BP (back projection).' He said, 'I can't bear the thought of you closing down. I've got a friend called Connery Chappell and he knows Lew Grade. I'll have a word and see if I can get you a meeting.'" True to his word, Green picked up the phone to Connery Chappell, who at that time was working on the pilot of the new ITC filmed series *Ghost Squad.*

In 1960, Lew Grade was one of the most powerful men in the entertainment business. Louis Winogradsky (shortened to Lew Grad, but settling on Lew Grade after a misspelling on an advert) arrived in England at the age of five in 1911, an immigrant from Tomak, South Crimea. By the 1920s, he was a professional dancer, and when he entered the World Charleston Championships he won a contract to dance in cabaret. It was through his cabaret work that Grade met agent Joe Collins, and when Grade was forced to retire from dancing after developing water on the knee, he joined Collins at his agency, first as an employee and then as a partner. After falling out with Collins he formed his own agency with his brother, Leslie.

In 1954, Grade's attention was drawn to an advert in *The Times* for applications to become a commercial broadcaster on the proposed Independent Television Network. Grade, and a consortium of other big names in the theatrical industry, formed the Independent Television Programme Company Ltd (ITP) and entered their application: it was refused. It was felt that to award such a collection of powerful names one of the few available franchises would strengthen their monopoly in the entertainment business. However, one of ITP's rivals (Associated Broadcasting Development Company) failed to raise the money required and a merger was offered as an acceptable compromise. This went ahead and Associated TeleVision[8] was first awarded the London area at weekends (Associated Rediffusion got weekdays) and subsequently the weekday Midlands franchise. ITP subsequently became Incorporated Television Company Limited (ITC) and became a wholly owned subsidiary of ATV operating as its distribution arm.

Grade brought his experience in theatre, and specifically variety, to embrace light entertainment which was very popular in America. Amongst the traditional 1950s television fare, he filled

8. ATV was originally the Associated Broadcasting Company (ABC), but was forced to change its initials to avoid confusion with Associated British Cinemas that operated franchises in the North and the Midlands.

the airwaves with shows such as *Val Parnell's Sunday Night at the London Palladium*. However, such a striking contrast to the BBC's more staid output wasn't popular with everyone, and Bernard Levin famously referred to ATV's output as an 'incandescent cataract of drivel.' Nevertheless, ATV was immensely popular and financially an extremely successful venture, leading the way with the production of expensive television series shot on film.

Gerry Anderson recounts the first fateful meeting with Lew: "He (Connery Chappell) got me a meeting with Lew Grade and I went up there with a beautiful brochure that Reg Hill had drawn. Lew was sitting behind his desk with his enormous cigar. My voice was shaking from nerves and I said, 'We'd like to make this television series.' He just flicked through the pages and he said, 'How much is it going to cost?' I said, 'We've budgeted it out and it will cost £3,000 per episode.' And he exploded. '£3,000 an episode!? I can't afford to pay you *that*! This is for a *kid's* series!'

"He looked at me and could see that he'd shaken me. I was really quite frightened. He became very nice then – 'Uncle Lew' – and he said, 'Look Gerry, if you go back to your studio, it's five o'clock now, if you come and see me tomorrow morning at half-past seven and tell me that you've cut the budget in half, I'll give you an immediate contract for the twenty-six pictures.'

"Well, I drove back to the studio and all my partners said, 'You must be mad, Gerry. There's no way we can cut it in half.' I said, 'Well, it's either that or we go bust.' So they said, 'We'll have a go.' We sat up all night. We cut everything down to the bone. The thing I remember was that dawn was breaking and we *hadn't* cut it in half. I remember saying, 'Look, we've allowed for four cups of tea a day for the unit. What if we reduce that to two? It'll save the milk bill and electricity.' That's how desperate it was.

"I made my way to Lew's office and arrived at half-past seven in the morning. He said, 'Well, have you cut it in half?' I could feel my eyes welling with tears. I said, 'Mr Grade, we've been up all night and we've tried desperately.' I said, 'We've cut a third off the budget, but there's no way we could cut it in half.'"

Grade pondered for a moment, looking at Gerry, before rising from his desk. "Just a moment," he said, before opening a door into another room. Grade disappeared briefly and when he returned said, "OK, you've got yourself a series." Gerry says, "I was overwhelmed."

Alan Pattillo adds an amusing detail: "It transpired later that the room Lew Grade went into was not an accountant's office – it was in fact a cupboard!"

"When I was walking out, having thanked him," says Gerry, "I thought, 'If we're going to start production immediately, we've got to have money to go into pre-production.' So I turned back and said, 'Mr Grade, is it possible for you to let me have a letter of intent?' Then again he exploded. He said, 'A letter of intent!? My word is better than any contract or letter of agreement that you could ever get drawn up! Now, get out of here and make the series!'"

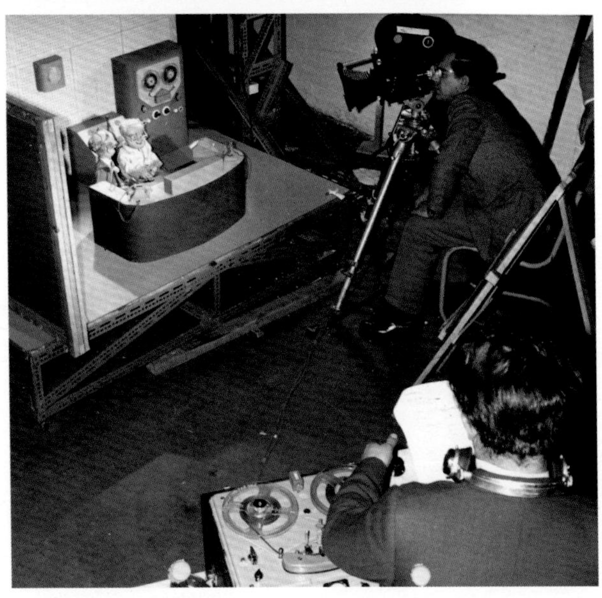

Grade's word was indeed as good as a contract, but he had one stipulation: the show must be on the air within six months. Pre-production swiftly began, in order to commence shooting in the middle of September.

Before anything could be filmed or recorded, the most important thing to get 'in the bag' was the opening set of scripts, which needed to be produced at alarming speed. Writer Martin Woodhouse starts the story: "My brother Hugh telephoned me and said that he had been given the job to write twenty-six scripts for an outfit which was doing something called Supermarionation. In other words, they were doing a television show – a drama show – which was done by puppets rather than human beings. He had been asked to do the scripts and he certainly couldn't do them on his own and would I come and help? So I said, 'Sure.'"

When his younger brother called him, Martin was fresh from his National Service in the Royal Air Force. Although a scientist (Martin built Lettuce, the first small computer capable of artificial intelligence in the '50s), he leapt at the chance to enter his brother's world of professional scriptwriting.

Martin Continues: "We knew from the word go that we were going to have a little file which contained, literally typed out onto half a sheet of paper, the next twenty-six stories. By and large, the stories themselves were only, oh, a paragraph.

"The great advantage about being a single scriptwriter, or in our case, two scriptwriters almost with the same mind, is that you don't have to have all these complex discussions. You're on the same wavelength already. Ok, so you have, 'Where will this be?' 'Oh, it will be in Panama?' So there were hardly any arguments, which was a very good thing because there was hardly any time for arguments!"

Martin continues: "A script would take us a fortnight; first to write the first draft and then to clean it up. What would happen is that one of us, whoever's turn it was, would write the first draft. If it was me that had written the first draft, I then fired it over to Hugh and he wrote the second draft. Meanwhile, he would be writing the first draft of the next one. I've got to say, I look back at this from my experience, as a scriptwriter, and it was an enormous pace to write adventure scripts at, even if they were only half-hour scripts. One a week? Shooting scripts, complete with all the angles and everything like that. Wow!"

Hugh adds his own recollections: "In the first thirteen episodes, I suppose he (Gerry Anderson) was tight up against it, or tight up against Lew Grade's pressures and there was *no* time for him and his team to do anything other than to shoot our shooting scripts."

On the stages, the pre-production process, now familiar to all, was instigated. As with *Four Feather Falls*, illustrations of

Opposite, above, L-R: Yvonne Cutler with Mike on *Island Incident* / Bill James with the medium-sized Supercar model / Preparing the puppets for a scene in the Black Rock kitchen. Below, L-R: Ray Soni films Beaker and Popkiss / John Blundall at work / Another view of the medium-sized Supercar model.

the main characters were provided by an ex-Disney animator[9], and Mary Turner and Christine Glanville set about producing the complete cast of main characters from these pictures, with Mary tackling Mike, Beaker, Masterspy and Mitch, and Christine doing Zarin, Jimmy and Popkiss. Meanwhile, Roger Woodburn and Jack Whitehead produced the bodies. With such a heavy workload, it became necessary to recruit extra help in the puppet department. Eddie Hunter and Yvonne Cutler[10] were hired as puppeteers, along with a much older husband and wife team, Cecil (Buster) and Madge Stavordale. The Stavordales were well-regarded puppeteers, known for their stage work, and had previously been recruited to assist for a brief period of time during *Torchy the Battery Boy*. For *Supercar*, Madge made the costumes[11] and dressed the puppets, while Buster helped out in the workshop. When needed, both would clamber up on to the Dexion bridge to manipulate the puppets. However, working on the series did not hold much appeal for them, as John Read recalls: "I don't think they enjoyed working on film. It wasn't real puppetry to them." Roger Woodburn concurs: "They weren't used to working on film. It took Gerry, or whoever was directing, quite a long time to try and explain to them that puppeteering had to be much more subtle on film than on the stage."

The task of designing Supercar itself fell to Reg Hill. "Supercar was Reg's baby," says Assistant Art Director Bob Bell. Director Desmond Saunders backs this up: "Certainly it was one of Reg Hill's proudest achievements; he really did love the fact that he was the designer of Supercar."

In the *Slough Observer* in 1961, Reg talked about his creation: "The modern audience, used in this science-minded age to seeing the real thing, can be especially critical of equipment and apparatus, even when it is used in a children's serial.

"Supercar itself took me six weeks to design, and I have to be able to explain most things about it to the fans."

Roger Woodburn recalls Reg's fascination with cars: "He was a bit of a boy-racer, even though he was a middle-aged man; I think he'd been a bit of a racer when he was a lad. He bought himself a Ford Anglia, but he had it 'souped up' with some amazing overhead this, that and the other. It went like a rocket. He parked in the same bay in the front of the studio every day. It was his little bay and he would 'vrooom' into it. When he left at night, 'vrooooom, vrroooom, vroom!' and he'd back out like *Starsky and Hutch*. Then one day, when we were at work, the council came along and put a lamppost in and they put it behind his car. He came out at night, jumped in the car and he backed out at about thirty miles an hour

9. The name of this animator is now lost in the mists of time. However, we do know that he was trained by David Hand, the Supervising Director of *Snow White and the Seven Dwarfs* (1937).

10. Eddie Hunter and Yvonne Cutler married a short time later.

11. According to *The Stage and Television Today* in 1961, Susan Fox made costumes too.

into this lamppost; the car just stopped dead. The lamppost was bent and the back of the car, which had a boot of traditional shape, had gone right in and I think cracked the rear window. He must have hit it at the most amazing speed. It was the biggest shock of his life, because it was like a routine for him. I remember laughing myself sick about it… He didn't think it was very funny!"

Three versions of Supercar were built in all; a miniature 12-inch version for flying shots, a larger one at 4 feet and, finally, a larger scale puppet-sized version, which caused Reg more headaches than his own car managed to.

The puppet-sized model was beautifully crafted from thin strips of balsa wood laid over a wooden frame in order to give it the sleek shape required. "We then had to have a canopy," says Gerry Anderson. "It was the early days of plastics. We went along to a plastics factory and said, 'Here is the plug.' In other words, it was the inside of the canopy made of wood, and they stretched the plastic over the top, heated it and then they sucked the air out from the bottom so that the plastic bent and wrapped itself around the plug, and when they lifted it off we had a canopy. The only thing was that we did this about six times, because each time as they heated it, it would explode. We got to the point that we'd spent so much money that we didn't know what to do. They said, 'Gerry, you can't go on. We've spent a fortune on this.' I said, 'One more try'… and it was all right."

The expense didn't end there though, as upon delivery to the studio floor for shooting, it turned out that the model was impractically fragile. "Supercar, if you dropped it, it broke," says clapper / loader Alan Perry. "If you didn't get hold of it in the right place, a piece could come off in your hand, because it was basically balsa wood. Also the Perspex would crack and cloud." Roger Woodburn concurs: "When you put it on the set, you were always terrified that someone would drop something from above. Even a pencil or a biro end-on down would have just punctured it. It used to get dented and you'd have to go to Reg.

"The wings used to come out on this electric motor – they had a screw thread – and it worked beautifully when it first arrived from the model-makers. Then after about a week, one of the rods that wound it up got bent. Reg had a fit because it all had to be taken to bits and this rod had to be straightened."

Supercar wasn't just problematic for the production crew, as writer Hugh Woodhouse states: "We liked writing certain stories, using certain characters, and to be perfectly honest we were quite pushed to bring Supercar into them. There was one which was called *A Little Art*, which was all to do with a Salvador Dali-like painting, in a desert with a cactus and a droopy folding watch, and this was a story entirely about finding treasure.[12] It was finally worked out that the cactus and the folding watch indicated that, at such a time, the shadow of the cactus would be long enough to point to exactly where the treasure was. Well, of course, there really wasn't any role

12. The treasure that Hugh refers to was in fact counterfeit money plates.

for Supercar in that at all, except just as a mode of transport. So, it's, 'Oh my gosh, we'd better get there before the others do!' Similarly, Scottish castle, phantom piper – typical ingredients – but where the hell does Supercar come in? But then, where the hell did Supercar ever come in, except simply as a mode of transport to get them to Scotland, or Ireland or Sumeria?"

Before *Supercar* could hit the main stage and embark on its own adventures, the APF crew had a couple of hair-raising missions themselves in order to capture footage needed for the series. Director, David Elliott says, "We would use a system called 'back projection', so that you had a screen, and a projector at the back of the screen, and you would project what was called a back-projection plate which could be a shot in the air, it could be a motorway, could be a scene at sea, and then in front of the screen you would have your actor, or, in our case, puppet."

Back projection[13] was used to create scenarios that, at the time, APF did not have the facilities or the technical knowledge to create convincingly in miniature. Therefore, various crews had to go off on excursions to capture the required footage.

"I remember spending a day on the motorway[14] with John Read, Alan Perry and a hired car which was a Jaguar," says David

13. Curiously, the feature run by *The Stage and Television Today* on *Supercar* in February 1960 states that all back-projection plates were filmed in colour. But then, this same article claims that Lew Grade invented the series, so this claim could be unreliable! However, it is stated in a couple of trade mags, so may well be true.

14. The sequences shot for *Grounded* were filmed between junctions 9 and 10 on the M1 near Dunstable.

Above: Who called Charlie Queen? Beaker and Popkiss find themselves manhandled by giant executives.

Elliott. "We were going up and down the motorway at speeds in excess of 100 miles an hour. We had special permission from the police, who always pounced on us when we stopped, to find out what we were doing."

"We also hired an Airspeed Oxford, which was a twin-engine aircraft," says Gerry Anderson, recalling the filming of the aerial shots to simulate Supercar flying. "We went to meet it at White Waltham and it landed. Because I'd been in the RAF, I looked at the windsock and I was horrified because it was landing down wind, instead of into wind. The pilot got out and said, 'Hi folks, sorry, I've got to go to the control tower for a bollocking' – to use his words! – 'because I came in down wind.' I thought, 'Yeah… and we're going to go up with you!' Anyway, we went up with him and he took us up to 12,000 feet, where you really need to have oxygen, but we had no oxygen masks. My other partner, dear old John Read (who was acting as camera operator), was very distressed; he was panting. I went over to him and said, 'What's the trouble?' and he said, 'Gerry, I've only got one lung.' I didn't know that until that point. So, I rushed down to the cockpit and I said, 'My partner has only got one lung and he can hardly breathe.' The pilot said, 'Well, I've got an engineer here who's got a cold and if I descend, I'm going to blow his ear-drums out.' So, we circled for half an hour to come down in order to save John and the engineer."

It was equally dramatic filming the sea shots for the first episode, as David Elliott recounts: "I took one of the cameramen, an Indian chap whose name was Ray (Soni)[15], down to Brighton to film some back-projection plates of rough sea. A fisherman took us out in his rowing boat and we went to the end of the pier. It was really, really rough. It was the first time I've ever seen a white Indian! He literally went white and was terribly sea-sick. It was so rough that the camera was getting soaked. I suddenly thought, 'Christ – is the camera insured!?' and threw myself around it. We got absolutely soaked. So of course, we didn't get our back-projection plates. I said to Ray, 'Well, we've got to get these shots.' So another week we went down and he was lowered on ropes from the end of the pier to film these scenes, which was just as bad because the electricity for the camera was 230 volts so we were lucky he didn't get electrocuted!"

Once captured, these 'plates' would be played on A.P. Films' back-projection system, which was installed during *Four Feather Falls*, and was a little more elaborate than the average set-up owing to the limited size of the studio. In order to get the required 'throw' (the distance the light has to travel – i.e. the further away the projector is, the larger the image area), a tunnel was constructed with a 90-degree corner in it, and a mirror was placed there at 45 degrees. When the image hit the mirror, it would reflect around the corner onto the back-projection screen, giving the correct 'throw.' It is interesting to note that in the surviving rushes featuring back projection, a recurring newspaper image shows a headline about Brenda Nash, a 12-year-

15. Known as Ray to the crew, his real name was Kumar Soni.

old girl who went missing in October 1960. It is poignant that her short life should have been memorialised in this way.

Roger Woodburn recalls the drama of using this Heath Robinson set-up. "The problem with back projection, which is a dead art now, is that you have to have a long tunnel, because if you use a wide-angle lens on the projector you get vignetting. You get a bright centre of the screen and dark around the edge. So the further back you put the projector the flatter and more even image you get. The communications between the unit – who were in front of the screen – and right down the other end of the corridor and around the corner, where there was somebody working the projector was a drama in itself. There was this telephone intercom thing. When the projector started up you couldn't hear what the guy at the other end was saying. The projector made an enormous noise. Clattering great monster.

"I had all these reels of film, clouds moving left, right etc. I also had these rehearsal rolls. Fifty times through the projector the film would get scratched so you had these rehearsal rolls. So once you'd done the rehearsal you'd then say 'Roll A21'. The film would come up and the clouds would be running the wrong way meaning Supercar was flying backwards. We'd say, 'No, not that one!' But he couldn't hear. So we'd have walk down the corridor, through the office, into the projector room which was (whirring noise) and say, "NOT THIS ONE!" We were constantly getting the wrong bit of film. When it worked though it looked great."

In the weeks before shooting began on the main stage, a new voice cast assembled in the make-shift recording studio in the rushes theatre, to record the dialogue. 22-year-old Canadian actor, Graydon Gould, was given the role of Mike Mercury, whilst *Crossroads to Crime* star, George Murcell, had something more desirable to work on this time, as he provided the vocal characterisations of Professor Popkiss and villain Masterspy. His *Crossroads to Crime* co-star, and *Four Feather Falls* actor, David Graham, also returned, this time to play Doctor Beaker, Zarin and rather unusually, Mitch the Monkey. "I practiced the Stanislavski acting method with Mitch," says David. "I spent a day at London Zoo at the Monkey House to get the correct interpretation!" Unlike Dusty and Rocky from *Four Feather Falls*, Mitch was unable to speak (dream sequences excluded!). "We did find it very challenging to write dialogue for him," says Hugh Woodhouse. "Mitch: 'Eek! Eek!'"

For the voice of archetypal 'nutty professor' Doctor Beaker, Graham found more conventional inspiration in the form of veteran actor Felix Aylmer, and his voice for the character is amusingly similar.

Another new addition to the voice ensemble was Sylvia Thamm, who not only directed the sessions, but persuaded Gerry to let her take the role of the young boy, Jimmy Gibson, in addition to all the female roles the series had to offer. However, she didn't manage to bag the role until the first recording session had already

Opposite: Gerry poses with the series two *Supercar* voice cast.

been done. Sound engineer, Jean Taylor, recalls the recasting: "At the start of the series, we had recorded the scripts but Gerry was not happy with the voice of Jimmy. He telephoned us to ask if we had studio time because Sylvia was going to record the voice. And so she came to Birmingham[16] to do the recording. It was the first time she'd ever done anything like that, so she was very nervous, but she did an excellent job of it."

Jean also recalls the set-up for recording dialogue: "Where the actors were was the actual theatre where they showed the rushes. We used the projection room as our control room. We did the rehearsal and the take. Lunch was usually sandwiches. Normally we would start around 9.30 and finish at 5.30. It was very efficient and usually a good day."

Graydon Gould also has fond memories of the recording sessions that took place once a month on a Sunday. "The challenge is to take a stack of 90 pages and plough through this, getting each scene done as well as you can. I'm still surprised at the standard that we came up with. If it's not obvious why we recorded on a Sunday, it's because we were on a trading estate in Slough and it was the only time it was quiet! Sylvia directed the sessions, and I was grateful to her because she would always point out when my Canadian accent was slipping through, as Mike was supposed to be American!"[17]

Finally, after weeks in pre-production, Mike Mercury and Supercar finally arrived in front of the Arriflex cameras to begin their brief television careers. Episodes were handled in rotation by David Elliott and Alan Pattillo, although Gerry Anderson helmed the first episode, *Rescue*. However, as a sign of how tight the cash-flow

16. The Taylor's recording studio was in Birmingham.

17. Sylvia had previously been married to an American.

was, Gerry was forced to be credited as 'David Elliott' in order to save on the cost of having an extra 'Directed By' caption produced![18]

In the first episode, *Rescue*, Jimmy Gibson and Mitch are flying with Jimmy's older brother Bill in a bi-plane. A fault occurs and Bill is forced to ditch the plane in the sea, where they board a life-raft and wait in the freezing cold, with Bill in a bad way. Thousands of miles away, in the middle of the Nevada desert at the Black Rock laboratory, the final touches are being put to five years' worth of work in the form of Supercar. Popkiss, Beaker and Mike overhear the radio announcement about the lost plane and, despite worries that Supercar is not ready for its first excursion, Mike boldly stages a dramatic rescue operation. Jimmy awakens and finds himself at Black Rock, whilst Mitch wastes no time in causing havoc. "It looks as though we've found a co-pilot!" says Mike.

The first episode does what any pilot should do in terms of setting the scene and establishing the premise: we are introduced to Supercar and all the characters. One thing it fails to do though, is explain why young Jimmy is able to stay at Black Rock ignoring practical matters such as schooling or, indeed, any family connections he might have. Jimmy's only relative appears to be Bill, who abandons him at the lab, returning a few times throughout the series, in each instance doing a different job and taking no more than a casual interest in Jimmy's welfare!

Filming continued smoothly, with each episode allocated a two-week slot on the stages. In late November 1960, during production of episode 10, *Island Incident*, various shots were filmed for the title sequence, including the first that involved the use of water.

Outside, in the back yard of the studio, a small round pool of water was erected and filled, with the aid of the helpful local fire brigade. On the evening of November 22nd, the rush-hour traffic that crossed the bridge behind the studio started to slow in order to peer at the preparations taking place. Finally, when everything was ready, filming began on two separate shots for the titles, of Supercar flying into and out of the water. It was then that the crew made a terrible discovery: Supercar was buoyant. Recently discovered rushes from the title sequence illustrate the agonies the crew went through in order to get the wretched miniature to behave properly, including one shot where it appears the model was simply hurled by someone across the screen! Eventually, the solution came in the less-than-satisfactory compromise of dropping Supercar unceremoniously into the water and then filming another shot where a stone is thrown in. During editing, the splash made by the stone was cut together with the shot of Supercar diving into the sea. Viewers were thus spared the sight of Supercar bobbing to the surface, like a plastic duck, a moment later.

Equally unconvincing was the shot of Supercar emerging from the water, which Gerry Anderson has particularly vivid

18. It is important to remember that in the 1960s (and indeed up until the 1990s!) captions on film were largely done by an expensive process called Optical Printing, involving a special film printer, lots of Letraset and much patience!

Opposite: Filming Supercar in the outdoor tank.

memories of, as it occurred on a special day for both him and Sylvia. "We had, in fact, been living together for quite some time and now and again she used to say, 'Aren't we going to get married?' and I would say, 'Yes, of course, but we can't do it right now, we're too busy.' Eventually we found the time and we went up to town and got married. I was driving back to the studio and it was quite late. At the back of the studio, I saw the round water tank which the fire service had filled with water. They had Supercar on a line, someone was holding it underwater, they would release it and pull it out... and it wasn't working. So I said to my, then, wife, 'Sorry, I'll be late.' So I spent the marriage night working outside, getting that particular shot. It's a very famous shot because everyone can see the line attached to Supercar to bring it out of the water!"[19]

Gerry and Sylvia's marriage marked the beginning of a winning creative partnership (albeit it a volatile one). "Very creative couple – absolutely beautiful together," says Keith Shackleton, who went on to oversee the merchandising division of A.P. Films. "The truth is we worked together," reveals Sylvia. "So I was able to provide the human side, and he was able to provide the technical side and work with our technical team."

Sylvia elaborates: "Characters were my thing. If you meet someone and see him with his family, then he goes into the office and he's shot dead – that's a shock. But it wouldn't matter, and you wouldn't care, unless you'd seen his character beforehand. And that was always my contention. The special effects we had were fantastic, but you had to have the human side for it to work."

Sylvia's interest in what she calls 'the human side' extended beyond the puppet characters to the crew. In many ways she became

---

19. Despite getting married fairly early on in the series, Sylvia would remain credited as 'Sylvia Thamm' for her Dialogue Direction role.

the mother of the company. “Sylvia was an absolute goddess,” says Special Effects Assistant Brian Johnson. “She was the one everybody went to if ever there was a problem.” “You do find that if you have a group of people that there are problems. There’s going to be,” says Sylvia. “I was naturally interested in their problems. You know, if they were having problems at home, or financial things – whatever it was they came into my office and we talked about it.”

As the years rolled by Sylvia’s role within the organisation steadily increased, culminating in her producing the two *Thunderbirds* feature films. She had an eye across all departments, with a particular eye towards character and story development as well as the fashions.

“Gerry was much more creative in different directions,” continues Sylvia. “He would be very good with ideas, all the adventures, all the hardware, everything.” “He was a workaholic, Gerry. He worked day and night. He didn’t have any other interests,” says former business partner, Arthur Provis. First wife Betty agrees: “Gerry was an extremely ambitious person. I mean, I don’t think he talked about anything else other than the film business. That was the main topic of conversation. Let’s get through the niceties and talk about the film business. There wasn’t much else in his life that interested him. Did he have a hobby? No. Not exactly. He loved gardening, growing vegetables and being out in the open air. The film business was really the love of his whole life. He didn’t really want to have much to do with puppets. It so happened that it took off. It was very popular. He didn’t expect it to be. It was a stepping stone to becoming a director. He was a good producer. He could phone people and get money out of them. I’ve known him sit for hours when we were going broke. When I say we, I mean the company, and us as well, because we were sort of involved in lots of ways. He’d sit for a couple of hours phoning all sorts of people to raise money to get the film made.”

“He was driven. A driven man without question,” says Editor David Lane. “He was an absolute visionary. He totally admired Walt Disney. He wanted to be the Walt Disney of England, no question about it. He was also an absolute perfectionist. Everything had to be right. Walt was like that. Steve Jobs was like that. They have this thing where everything has to be right. He wouldn’t let anything go. Nothing went out of the house without him looking at it. If it had to be re-shot, it had to be re-shot. If it didn’t work then he’d make sure it did work by the time it left. He was the guv’nor. The boss. No question about it.”

Lane speaks highly of his former employers. “One particular time I said to Gerry, ‘I’ve just got to take a break.’ I was shooting constantly for six weeks. And he and Sylvia were very kind. They said, ‘Well, take a holiday and go where you want to and we’ll pay for it.’ And they did. You had done your shift and they made sure you were recognised for doing that shift.”

The Andersons’ marriage had occurred without fanfare. The team were too busy working for any sort of party.

For scenes featuring Supercar underwater, an ingenious solution was needed, as David Elliott recalls: "To shoot underwater, we wondered how we could do this and Reg had this idea. I remember we were sitting down, Reg, Gerry and myself, and Reg said, 'Now there's a good thing!' We said, 'What's a good thing?' and Reg pointed to a calendar of fish. Reg said, 'I've got this idea. If we had an aquarium, put fish in and shone light through the top, it would look as if it was underwater.' So, we experimented and finally we had built a very, very large aquarium, which was probably about seven foot square and on wheels. Although it was seven foot square, it was only a few inches wide."

Camera Operator, Julien Lugrin, describes the set-up: "We put the camera on one side and the action on the other side, so you were shooting through this tank. We had to have people with a stick so that the fish would swim away to get into shot at the right time. We gave our fish some stick, I suppose you could say!"

Filming continued on the first thirteen episodes until the end of December 1960. Episode 12, *Ice Fall*, saw a new director added to the rota in the form of Desmond Saunders. Saunders had worked with Gerry as far back as the ill-fated *You've Never Seen This* and had visited A.P. Films occasionally over the previous few years. On *Supercar*, he was invited to edit one picture, before being asked to direct an episode. Des would go on to become one of the most important contributors to the company but, as he recalls, his first week shooting was far from smooth: "My strongest recollection of *Ice Fall* is the famous day when the time came to shoot in this ice cave. We were expecting this ice cave to come moving in and somebody said, 'What do you mean an ice cave? What ice cave?' So I said, 'The next thing I'm shooting is in the ice cave.' Everybody was looking at everybody else as if to say, 'Well I haven't got it! Where is it?' So one person disappears and another and another, but Reg Hill did not appear. The message came back, 'What's the set-up?' I said, 'What's the set-up!? How can I give you the set-up, until I've got the set?' So Reg comes out and says, 'What's the set-up, mate?' Anyway, there was a stupid discussion about what the set-up was, so I said, 'Look – just put the camera there, will you Julien?' It was facing the bridge and the platform on which the set was supposed to be and I said, '*That's* the set-up!' Reg then disappeared and there was a long, long wait and then a sack arrived full of blocks of ice! Under the red hot lamps, you can imagine how difficult it was to build an ice cave out of these blocks of ice! Anyway, another sack of ice was sent for, and another, and finally, we had to do it ever so quickly, but we got a shot." Julien Lugrin completes recollections of that day: "We always remember it by saying, 'What's the set-up?' He said, 'Put the camera where you want the set and we'll build it to it.' Which is completely backwards!"

Julien speaks highly of his association with Desmond: "I always liked working with Des, because he wanted the impossible. He wanted the shots that really you couldn't get, but we had to get them. It meant I was stretching my technical knowledge to the

ultimate extremes to get the depth of field that he wanted, which would be from the beginning point to the furthest point, all in sharp focus on the old-fashioned equipment we used. I had to pour on light and reduce the aperture and do tremendous things you shouldn't do. I remember on one occasion we had so much light generating heat that the zip fastener on the puppet melted. We had all these wonderful things happening, but it all made for a great experience and we really enjoyed it… afterwards!"

Desmond wasn't the only director with set issues. "I was shooting a scene with a helicopter, or a plane against the back projection screen and asked Reg Hill were my set was," remembers Alan Pattillo. "He said, 'Here it is' and held out a stick! I had to use it to look like I was shooting through a window."

Shooting broke for Christmas and in the first week of 1961, Alan Pattillo returned to the stages to direct *Phantom Piper*. Within a few weeks, on January 28th 1961, the first episode was unveiled to viewers in the London region, a mere four months after it had been filmed. The series immediately struck a chord with the audience and, once again, succeeded in being quite unlike anything else on television. Journalists from various magazines flocked to the studios over the coming months, writing a succession of articles. In February 1961, *The Stage and Television Today* ran a lengthy spread on the series, abiding by the old adage 'never let the truth get in the way of a good story':

> "*The project for* Supercar *was put to us last autumn," says Gerry Anderson, whose A.P. Films studio at Slough have already produced many commercials (the* Blue Cars

current series) as well as Granada's Four Feather Falls, Torchy *and others.*

In one of his typical crisp sessions, Lew Grade outlined his idea for an all-British series which would combine elements of the Superman *technique, plus action and drama to appeal to a wide age group.*

A series impossible to do with human characters.

Based on this outline from Lew Grade, A.P. Films went into an intensive session, scripting and creating characters.

In March 1961, A.P. Films became the subject of further newspaper attention when the first *Television Mail* Commercials Awards ceremony took place. Nicholas Parsons, whose adverts for Blue Cars were eligible for entry, explains: "The first *Television Mail* Commercial Awards came around and I said we should enter them and we put them in – not thinking we were going to get anything. A guy from *Television Mail* rang me up and said, 'Are you going to the banquet?' I said, 'No. I don't think we can actually afford it. It's quite expensive at the Hilton,' and he said, 'Well, I think you should go, you know.' I thought, 'This sounds like a message,' so I phoned up Gerry and said, 'Gerry, they're suggesting we should go to the banquet. I think we might have won something, probably only in our own category – there's not much competition in the Consumer province.'

"So we got together and we asked the client, Ken Box, and he brought his wife Eve along, and the six of us (Gerry, Nicholas, Sylvia, Denise Bryer, Ken Box and Eve Box) sat at a table and they showed all the winners. When we got two awards, the German and the Martian one in our category, it was very well received (1st and 3rd Award in the Consumer Services category).

Then we got to the Grand Prix and they said, 'We'll now show you the final commercials that won the Grand Prix. Now there were ten entrants; there were ten chosen. We had a panel of judges and they gave points for product image and impact and so forth.' I only discovered many, many years later why he (the compère) made that long speech: the judges had decided that ours had won... and they (*Television Mail*) didn't want us to win, because they had just formed a new magazine and thought, 'This won't go down well with the advertising boys!' So they said would the judges all look at the commercials again for the Grand Prix, hoping they would reconsider. They all came back and said, 'No, that's the winner.' We all sat there nervous as hell. Number 8... number 7. And I remember sitting there... 4, 3, 2... there's none left! And he said, 'And finally, this was the winner!' and up came the Martian commercial. I remember it vividly. Denise actually slipped onto the floor right under the table, Gerry was sitting there... and I sort of went 'aaaah!' and our client Ken Box and his wife Eve clapped hysterically. Gerry and I walked up to get our award in somewhat subdued silence. There were a few

Opposite, left: Buster Stavordale in the workshop.
Right: Madge Stavordale fits a costume. Note the puppet design for *Phantom Piper* in the background.

"Most satisfactory!" A selection of *Supercar* merchandising spin-offs.

claps and a cheer from Ken Fox. Denise was still under the table. She couldn't bear to be seen as she worked for all the advertising agencies on voiceovers! It wasn't well received.

"The result was that Gerry thought he might make some commercials. I thought *I* might make commercials. We both advertised in *Television Mail*... Not a bloody sausage! We had done what we shouldn't have done. We had gone, with sheer confidence and blind ignorance, into a world where people had spent their life in advertising, and on a shoe-string budget made a commercial that worked."

The April 1961 edition of *Television Mail* was almost like an extended brochure for A.P. Films, with various suppliers to the company clamouring to publicise their association. APF itself took out a double-page spread in the magazine stating: A.P. FILMS DON'T *USUALLY* MAKE COMMERCIALS. A.P. FILMS DO MAKE *UNUSUAL* COMMERCIALS.[20]

Television Mail also ran a small piece about the latest addition to the expanding A.P. Films set-up: *A.P. FILMS LTD. – who received the Television Mail Grand Prix Award for the best commercial in 1960 – have formed a new company to handle the exploitation of their new Children's TV series "Supercar." The new company will be known as A.P. Films (Merchandising) Ltd., and Keith Shackleton has been appointed as General Manager.*

The recruitment of Keith Shackleton, who had known Gerry from their National Service days, was to mark the beginning of what would soon explode into a rapidly developing merchandise empire of toys, comics and records, all generating the important revenue needed to fund further adventures with Mike Mercury.

Another addition to the A.P. Films set-up came later that year with Arrow Productions, formed by Gerry in the hope of creating a successful off-shoot from the parent company to produce commercials. In December 1961, *Television Mail* reported:

> *"A.P. Films of Slough have appointed Ken Davis to head a new associate company, Arrow Productions.*
>
> *It is the fourth in the AP Group[21] and will specialise in TV commercials and documentaries.*
>
> *Ken Davis, who began his career in the Kodak Laboratories, was formerly Producer / Director for Pearl and Dean Ltd., and has produced commercials for many well-known sponsors."*[22 23]

---

20. This advert lists A.P. Films as making films for H.M. Government. What these films were cannot be ascertained.

21. The A.P. Group companies were A.P. Films Ltd, A.P. Films (Merchandising) Ltd, Sound Effex Ltd and Evoca Sound Pictures Ltd. Arrow Productions Ltd made the total five.

22. Ken Davis had been introduced to A.P. Films through Nicholas Parsons. In February 1961, *The Stage and Television Today* announced that Davis would be involved in Parsons' company D.N. Productions Ltd.

23. Arrow Productions was based at 9 Orme Court which is where the Associated London Scripts agency was. It was this connection that subsequently got writer Dennis Spooner involved (see Chapter Four). It also lends support to Gerry Anderson's recollection that Terry Nation (a member of the same agency who went on to create the Daleks in *Doctor Who*) came up with the idea for Oxygen Pills in *Fireball XL5*.

Filming continued on *Supercar* until the beginning of April 1961, when Desmond Saunders shot the 26th episode, *Crash Landing*[24].

Roger Woodburn, who by this time was handling all special effects shots, has fond memories of shooting a dramatic sequence of Supercar: "We had a clapper / loader, which you always think of as being a sixteen-year-old boy who wants to get started in the business – 'Yes, guv, right guv!' – but we had a guy who was about seventy. He'd been in the film business all his life and he was *very* slow. He used to have a cigarette stuck on his bottom lip, which used to make me cringe!

"It had taken me an hour to hang up a model of Supercar and it was a spectacular shot because I'd managed to put a pivot in either end, so it was suspended in space, but it would pivot. The whole idea was that Supercar was supposed to be in some dramatic dive. I got it all rigged and it looked absolutely great, and I said, 'Let's do it! Can we put a slate on, please?' This old guy got up and chalked in 'SCENE 1, TAKE 1,' and he put it in (for the camera to film) and through all the wires! Then he brought it back and the Supercar model was hanging from the slateboard! He walked back, sat down, put the board down and went, 'Oh, what's this doing!?' I had to start all over again!"

During the second batch of episodes, numbers 14 to 26, Sylvia started to take a keener interest in the scripting of the series. Since the company's inception, scripts had always been provided

24. Although *Supercar: Take One* is usually credited as being episode 26 in production, it seems from extensive detective work that *Crash Landing* was the last in production. The jungle sets from the episode are still standing in the photographs of the press-launch day, and the episode contains edited-down footage from *The Magic Carpet* (which in current accepted Production Order was made after *Crash Landing*). Diary sources and surviving footage already contradict the accepted Production Order, so it is, currently, impossible to make anything other than a best guess.

Above: A motley crew of guest characters in the puppet dock.

by professional scriptwriters. However, Sylvia felt that she would like to put pen to paper. She had gained some writing experience with an annual for *Four Feather Falls* and now she persuaded Gerry that they should write scripts. Their first idea for an episode, *Flight of Fancy*, was put to the Woodhouse brothers, whose response was tepid, as Hugh Woodhouse recounts: "I remember the one that we never wrote which was a dream sequence which Gerry and Sylvia Anderson insisted be part of the repertoire. We said, 'Over our dead body!' and they said, 'Well, we're going to do it anyway,' and they persuaded us that they would write the script, but to save money they wouldn't re-shoot the credits so we were credited!"[25]

Gerry and Sylvia felt that their first foray into scriptwriting was a success, and it soon became apparent to the Woodhouse brothers that their usefulness was coming to an end. Hugh Woodhouse describes the events that led to their eventual demise: "Lew Grade financed the first thirteen, which we wrote for £80 per shooting script. Then there was a pause to see whether they would sell overseas. That pause went on for, I suppose, about six to eight weeks. Then the answer came back, obviously through Gerry Anderson, from the Grade office saying, 'Yes, you can go on for another thirteen.' We said, 'Well, obviously the thing is a success, we'd like to renegotiate.'

"We offered what we thought was very reasonable, either to up the £80 by 50% to £120 a script, or £100 plus a share of the residuals. To cut a long story short, they said, 'OK, you can have the £120.' And that's when the trouble started, because that was the first time they were able to pause and think, 'Can we get these people cheaper? Can we substitute our writing for theirs?' That's not mere conjecture, that is in fact what happened."

Martin Woodhouse remains bewildered: "We had a completely informal, conversational agreement. You must remember that we were beginning writers, so our price was bound to be cheap. We had an agreement which said, more or less, 'If you write the first twenty-six scripts and everything goes all right, we'll take you on for the proper rate for the job for the next twenty-six.' And that never happened. I have no idea why not. We must have done a competent job. It can't be that we did an incompetent job because we know that the series not only worked, but was popular. So it can't have been that."

Martin and Hugh wrote twenty out of the first series of twenty-six instalments.[26] However, they were not called on again to provide any further scripts for A.P. Films. Hugh Woodhouse concludes: "It was tacitly understood that we would be offered the opportunity to write the next series. In the end this did not happen.

25. Different prints of this episode carry different credits, some stating *Story By Martin and Hugh Woodhouse*, whilst others correctly say *Story By Gerry and Sylvia Anderson*

26. Martin and Hugh Woodhouse, according to the credits, wrote up to 23 episodes. However, we know that Gerry and Sylvia wrote *Flight of Fancy* and it is the author's opinion that, despite the credits, Martin and Hugh did not write either *The Magic Carpet* or *The Dragon of Ho Meng*. Neither episode features the characteristic trademarks of the brothers and in the case of *Ho Meng*, the only three regulars to appear are Mike Mercury, Jimmy and Mitch – characters which were unpopular with Martin and Hugh.

There was no falling out. They simply stopped talking to us! It's as simple as that."

• • •

It's the first British-made puppet series to crash the world in this way, reported *Kine Weekly.* Lew Grade was delighted that not only had his gamble paid off, but also he found himself with an unexpectedly big hit. Because of the ITV regional divisions, a large chunk of the country couldn't see the series until nine months after it began delighting audiences in the London region in January 1961. Even so, there was no doubt that *Supercar* was a success and, in the summer of 1961, the message came through to APF that the run of episodes was being extended to thirty-nine and that their immediate future was assured.

"I think ATV, or Lew Grade then started to say, 'Hang on a minute, there's something here, we're going to start pumping more money in'," says Clapper / Loader Alan Perry. In Director Alan Pattillo's opinion: "The second series of *Supercar* was rather more ambitious than the first one had been."

Over the summer of 1961, Gerry and Sylvia wrote all thirteen adventures themselves, ready for production in September. However, before shooting commenced, it was felt that improvements needed to be made to the production process. The biggest change was to the shooting schedule. Previously, one episode would be shot scene by scene across a two-week period, either making use of the large stage under the main bridge, or the small stage area against one wall with the back projection unit. From series 2, two units would operate at the same time (each unit supervised by Mary Turner and Christine Glanville respectively), with an episode now being allocated one week on the main bridge and a second week on the small stage. Meanwhile, the next episode would begin its shooting schedule on the main bridge. In order for this to happen, a new set of identical puppets was constructed of all the regular characters so that the two units could operate in tandem. Although the idea was fine in principle, both units were shooting in the same cramped studio space and it must sometimes have felt like trying to work in a crowded station during rush-hour.

Some puppets didn't just get a set of new sculpts, but also new voices, as actor George Murcell had left during the first series. A replacement was found in the form of Cyril Shaps, whom Gerry and Sylvia had seen in the West End play *The Tenth Man.*

The second series also marked the beginning of a full-time special effects unit. Throughout the first series, Roger Woodburn had become responsible for handling all the effects shots, and towards the end of filming, Gerry offered Roger the chance to become their Director of Special Effects. Roger declined, feeling that his joyful three years with the company had been enough, and that he wanted to take his now greatly increased experience and expertise into the mainstream industry. He departed in the spring of 1961.

In the dark and distant days of 1957, APF had approached special effects supremo Les Bowie, who at that time was best known for his work on the Hammer Horror films, and asked him if he would help them with their matte painting and any effects that they might need. Les pointed to his assistant, Derek Meddings, who later explained, "He didn't want to do it because I think he felt it was a little bit beneath him." Derek joined the company part-time as a matte painter, moonlighting in the evening alongside his day job at Anglo-Scottish pictures.

When Roger Woodburn left, Gerry, Reg Hill and John Read were keen to up the ante with the special effects, which until now had been little more than a few models flown in front of a back-projection screen with tolerable, rather than excellent results. Derek Meddings accepted the role of Special Effects Director and, in mid-1961, joined the company full-time, bringing with him a fellow scenic artist, Brian Johnson.[27]

In order to stand any chance of producing realistic special effects, it was essential that the newly formed unit had its own space to work in. Previously, all effects had been done either outside, or had been created on stages shared with the puppets. SoundEffex Ltd., Gerry Anderson's and David Elliott's company, formed during production of *Twizzle*, was by now doing extremely well. It left its small room in the Slough studio in 1961 and set up at the Gate Recording Studio at Elstree. Gate was responsible for dubbing all the marionette films supplied to them. As soon as SoundEffex left the premises, Derek took over the vacated miniscule area and arranged for a small stage to be constructed. Alan Perry remembers clearly the revolution that Derek brought with him: "Everything seemed to progress; we started to learn. The special effects weren't as hit-and-miss as they'd been in the early days, because we were pioneering."

Whilst by today's slick standards the effects on *Supercar* are far from realistic, the series is an interesting illustration of the company's rapid advances in the field. Derek's effects give the series a much larger feeling, thanks mainly to the development of landscape shots to set the scene of the world being portrayed. Bill Harris, who had previously edited several episodes of *Supercar*, and for the second series was elevated to a Director, remembers how Derek improved the sophistication of the shots. "I wanted to do a long shot with Jimmy walking into foreground and a small bi-plane landing in the desert in the distance (*The Sky's the Limit*). I said to Derek, 'Could we possibly do this in one shot?' He said, 'Yes, and also I'll get a small air-line and, as the plane lands in the desert, you'll see the dust going up,' which I thought was a very complicated shot which he handled beautifully."

This wasn't the only shot where special effects and puppets came together. Firstly, all the back-projection shots still needed to be filmed on the puppet stage and secondly, sometimes the puppeteers would require a little assistance. "The puppeteers used to hate us coming in," says Derek Meddings. Perhaps this isn't surprising as the safety of the puppets couldn't always be guaranteed when special

27. Brian Johnson was credited in the 1960s as Brian Johncock.

effects paid them a visit. Sculptor and puppeteer, John Blundall, who joined during *Supercar*, illustrates this: "Brian Johnson was involved early on and was very enthusiastic. There was one end of the studio that was reserved for insert shots and there was one shot through a window where Popkiss was making breakfast in his kitchen. He was side-tracked and was supposed to have burnt the bacon, or something.[28] I think Brian was rather enthusiastic and there was a damn great explosion, and when the dust cleared there was poor old Popkiss with an absolutely black face and singed hair!

"Another one was: there was a test shot of shooting a bullet into a wall. He was quite happy that it was going to work… It went round the set, round the studio, with everybody ducking!"

In order to increase the realism of water shots, John Read built a brick water-tank at the back of the studio, with a matte sky backing.

For the music, Barry Gray recorded a new arrangement of the *Supercar* theme tune, this time engaging the Mike Sammes Singers to perform the song and replace the previous version sung by Mike Sammes solo.

"There were a number of changes to the second series," says Director Alan Pattillo, "but most significant of all was this new famous caption saying, 'FILMED IN SUPERMARIONATION.' The term 'Supermarionation' was coined by Gerry Anderson, in an attempt to mimic the grandeur of the big technical movie processes hailed in huge letters at the cinema as *Technicolor, Panavision, Techniscope*... It is possible that Gerry was particularly inspired by Ray Harryhausen, the famous animator who used stop-motion animation to produce fantasy sequences for a number of epic movies such as *The 7th Voyage of Sinbad* (1958) and who coined the term 'Superdynamation' for his unique style. For his own portmanteau word, Gerry was supremely logical, combining 'super', 'marionette' and 'animation' to produce 'Supermarionation'[29].

Shooting progressed smoothly on this final batch of thirteen episodes and, by Christmas, filming had been completed and the last instalments were in the hands of editors. They would ensure that all was ready for transmission to begin in February 1962.

With such a runaway success on their hands, discussions naturally turned to the possibility of another twenty-six instalments, which Lew Grade agreed to. However, APF had the bit between their teeth and were keen to see where else they could apply their Supermarionation technique. It is no surprise, therefore, that in January 1962, Gerry presented Lew with a new brochure...

28. The shot that John is referring to is most likely the scene from *The Sky's the Limit* where Masterspy opens fire on the laboratory.

29. The term 'Supermarionation' first appeared in promotional material during the filming of Supercar's first series, although it didn't actually feature in the titles of the programme until the second season. In early literature, including adverts produced by the studio itself, the term is listed as being 'Super Marionation.'

FIREBALL XL5

•1962•

XL 5

A WONDERLAND OF STARDUST 4

Fireball XL5

Says Gerry Anderson: “I was thinking all the time that if I made really good puppet shows the broadcasters and the financiers would say, ‘Hey this guy makes great puppet films, let’s give him a live action film.’ So what happened? They said, ‘Hey this guy makes great puppet films, let’s give him some more!’”

Dear Gerry,

The success of a television show cannot be judged only by its sales and its ratings. You already know how well Supercar *is selling in the United States, and how high the ratings are. What I want to tell you is just how the car and its characters, headed by Mike Mercury and Professor Popkiss, have caught the imaginations of youngsters throughout the country. They have become part of family life.*

The kids are whistling and singing the Supercar *theme tune. They’re riding* Supercar *toys, wearing* Supercar *clothes, reading* Supercar *stories and strips in their magazines and books, operating their own* Supercar *puppets and playing with* Supercar *dolls.*

Mike Mercury and his friends have become very real to them and have won their love and affection.

I see this interest in Supercar *on all sides. Even recreation centres have made enquiries regarding the possibility of building* Supercar *rides.*

I am convinced that Fireball XL5 *is going to exceed everything* Supercar *has done. The space ship is going to capture the kids’ imaginations and young viewers are going to love Steve Zodiac, Venus, Professor Matic and the other fascinating characters you have created, like Robert the Robot and the loveable “Lazoon” pet from another planet.*

Sincerely,

MIKE NIDORF

President, I.T.C. New York [1]

With the rocket powered success of *Supercar*, A.P. Films did not have to worry where their next commission was coming from. By December 1961 *Supercar* had wrapped filming at their Ipswich Road studios and although the initial plan had been to produce a second batch of 26 episodes, it was decided to temporarily put the series on hold. It seems to have been a protracted decision whether

---

1 Letter reproduced from *The Stage and Television Today* (1962)

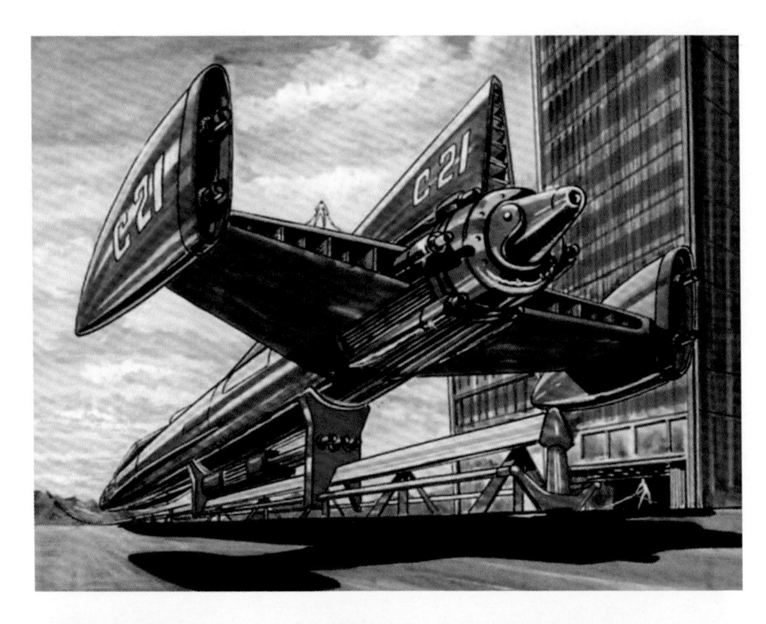

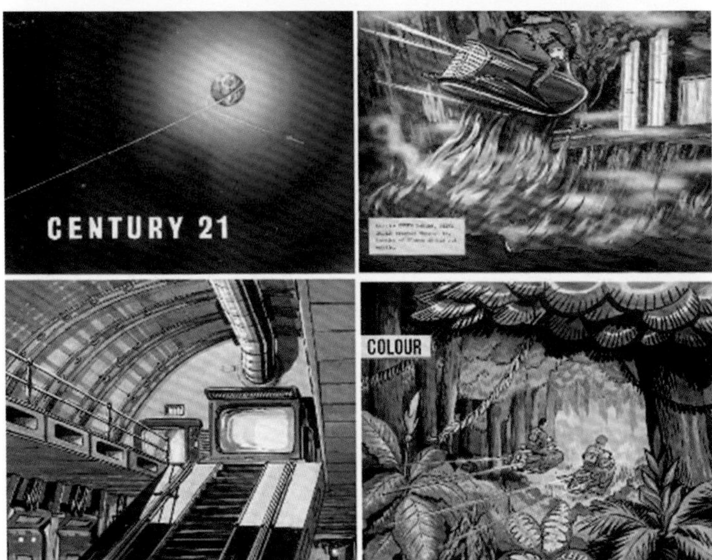

to continue with *Supercar*, or to produce an entirely new show. Plans for a new series had certainly been considered during early 1961, as there had been some preliminary discussions with the Woodhouse brothers about writing it. While the future of *Supercar* remained in the balance, Gerry attended one of his meetings with Lew Grade armed with not one new idea, but two.

A.P. Films Present

A new and exciting children's series

Prepared Especially for Associated Television Ltd

We present CENTURY 21 as our idea of a modernistic 'Evergreen' Space series. CENTURY 21 is the name of the spaceship and the century in which our action takes place.

The year – to be exact – is 2962 – a thousand years hence, when space travel is an everyday occurrence but still there are planets as yet unexplored. The nearer and more inhabitable planets are already 'humanized' and people from the overcrowded cities in Earth are emigrating as they did in the early days of America and Australia.

But not all planets are sympathetic to Earth Man's need to settle in the Universe. Many are hostile to the peculiar race of Man that Earth has produced, who think themselves superior to other planets. And in Man's attempts to find peace away from the crowded Earth - he only encounters Space Wars and evil races of creatures worse than Earth has ever produced.

No wonder then that the United States Space

Patrol has a fleet of interplanetary spaceships patrolling the Universe as our highways are patrolled today.

Let us take the adventures of one such patrol… our Hero Space Patrolman STEVE ZODIAC – the handsomest, most courageous 'all American' hero ever to enrol in Space Patrol. Make no mistake, he'll be every boy's idea of a real He-Man, but with a charm that will turn the head of every girl viewer… tall… powerful… all the stuff from which heroes are made… and his counterpart VENUS – our heroine – his beautiful, delightful female assistant, a Doctor of Space Medicine who shares in all his adventures, but of course, is never able to cope with a situation with the same cool nerve as STEVE ZODIAC – a perfect pair typifying Mr and Miss America of 2962!

But every space adventure must have a Professor and MATTHEW MATIC is ours. As his name suggests, he is the mathematical genius who navigates the Spaceship through the Universe. Quaint – kindly – a loveable character – his head full of figures (the dullest kind) and an expression that suggests he is constantly in the midst of solving a highly complicated mathematical problem.

In this age Robots are in constant use and ROBERT, our Robot, is the automatic Pilot – rather like 'George' is today. But because the year is 2962 we have allowed ourselves a little licence by injecting a small degree of temperament into our Robot. He can get literally 'steamed up' when things don't quite conform to his way of…well I almost said thinking! ... Well, let's say when we don't come in on his wavelength!

So much for our crew… And the spaceship itself – it is vast, streamlined, futuristic and is virtually the Space Headquarters for our crew. Over 300 feet in length, it contains Laboratories; Living Accommodation; Control Rooms; Masses of Equipment and apparatus to enable the crew to land on planets that have no atmosphere and vast stores of fuel and medical supplies, which include the crew's diet for a period of four months – in pill form, of course. In fact, the Spaceship is completely self-sufficient, a miniature town with everything necessary for journeys through the Universe that could perhaps take years.

The front part of the Spaceship – the nose cone – breaks away and becomes a completely independent unit when a landing is made on a planet, the remainder of the ship orbiting until the crew returns.

Jetmobiles – small space vehicles without wheels – are used for travel on planets. These are relatively small but deceptively powerful and enable the crew to manoeuvre their way easily on the strange uneven surfaces of the planets by use of an electro-magnetic force.

Our adventures are as limitless as the Universe itself… each holding a fresh danger and, above all, the excitement of the unknown. Our first story gets off to a rip-roaring start – within seconds of opening there is a savage air battle and we waste no time getting into our adventure

Opposite: Images from the *Century 21* promotional brochure.

and from then on we never look back. This is an action-packed undisguised Space Science Fiction Series but injected with all the ingenuity and technical achievement that made Supercar *a successful series. A.P.F. is already thinking Spacewise and raring to go!*

APF's pitch bears the indelible stamp of the era that it was written in; space travel was becoming a real possibility with Cosmonaut Yuri Gagarin, the first man to venture into this unexplored territory, making one orbit around the Earth in April 1961. The Americans followed swiftly with Alan Shepard making a suborbital flight on Freedom 7 as part of the Supercaresque-named 'Project Mercury'. Space was suddenly big news. "*Fireball XL5* came out at a time when the space race was hotting up," says Alan Pattillo. And of course it was the time of the Cold War between the West and the Soviet East. So there was a lot of paranoia in the air."

In May 1961, American President John F Kennedy stated: "I believe that this nation should commit itself to achieving the goal, before this decade is out, of landing a man on the Moon and returning him back safely to the Earth. No single space project in this period will be more impressive to mankind, or more important for the long-range exploration of space; and none will be so difficult or expensive to accomplish." Kennedy deemed space travel so important that in September 1962 he even went as far as to say, "No nation which expects to be the leader of other nations can expect to stay behind in this race for space." Therefore it is not surprising that, when it came to devising their new series, space was at the top of APF's list. On the flip side, it seems despite the introduction of the contraceptive pill in January 1961, the new prescription had yet to liberate women from rampant sexism, if the brochure's description of Venus is anything to go by. She lacks Zodiac's cool nerve "of course"! Sylvia Anderson responds to this saying, "At that time, in any of the big movies women didn't really take the lead at all. They were either waiting for the man coming home from the battles, or putting in their two cents worth of common sense, or 'feminine intuition' or whatever.

"We were leading towards women coming in as leads – or at least co-leads. And we were giving her something perhaps a bit more interesting to say than would be the norm. But it was still very early for her to actually take the lead too much. That wouldn't have been accepted really.

"I think I'd probably wince now at some of the scripts. But for the era in which they were written, I guess they were OK."

Alongside the colourful brochure illustrated by Reg Hill and Derek Meddings was another concept which would mix Supermarionation and live-action. The proposal revolved around live-action framing sequences featuring Joe, a young boy (American of course) who dreams of being a dashing, heroic space pilot named Joe 90. The fantasy sequences, intended to be filmed in Supermarionation, would follow Joe 90 and his crew: Debbie (his sister), Gary (brother-in-law), Cindy Lou (niece) and Professor

Matthew Matic (the only character to appear in both formats). Together they get into adventures aboard SPV 1 Zero or Space Patrol Vehicle 1 Zero. The outline for the first episode concerned the SPV1 Zero crew visiting a planet of giants where they become entangled in the web of a giant spider. Bernard Braden and his wife Barbara Kelly were listed as possibilities for playing Joe's parents in the live-action sections, while Kenneth Connor, Bernard Braden, Spike Milligan, David Graham and Sylvia Anderson were mooted as possible voice artistes on the show.

Of particular interest to fans now are the names suggested in these two brochures: Joe 90 would have to wait another 6 years before getting a series of his own, and even then in name only. It would be another five years before an SPV was pressed into service, albeit as a land vehicle, and Century 21 would go on to become a defining trademark of television and film in the 1960s… but not until 1965. Also of note in the brochure is the naivety and almost child-like innocence of the major mistake in the first proposal. Having hammered home that the ship is called Century 21 because that 'is the year the action takes place' we are then told the year is 2962, which is in fact the 30th century. Mistakes such as confusing a century with a millennium were not unique to A.P. Films, and at the time many film makers were liberally using terms they did not understand, with one of the most common sci-fi misconceptions being "light years" – described as a measurement of time rather than distance.

Despite unsubtle attempts to escape puppets by introducing a

Above: The rear view of the large Fireball model.

Below: Black Rock lab redressed as Space City control.

XL 5

WORLD
SPACE PATROL

live action element, Gerry Anderson found himself saddled exclusively with puppets once again, as Lew commissioned *Century 21*.

In early 1962, ITC found itself a target of an Equity strike which brought production on all filmed television shows (as opposed to those shot on videotape) in the UK to a halt. In an article in *Kine Weekly* in February 1962, Grade issued an ultimatum to the union that unless the strike was resolved by Easter, then ITC would close down production in the UK permanently, with consequent loss of jobs for its members. In this same article Grade talked about ITC's recent success and noted that "*Supercar* has got such terrific ratings in the States that ITC has been asked to produce another 26 episodes." He then went on to note a number of jobs that would be affected, for actors and technicians across numerous productions. He continued, "I am not including the colour pilot for *Espionage*, which was to have been the highest budgeted television film ever to be made in this country, or the 26 *Supercar* episodes to have been made under the title of *Nova X 100*." This statement is particularly interesting in that it implies that *Supercar* had been renewed, albeit it under a different title. It is possible, if not likely, that this is a mis-translation or confusion attributable to the reporting journalist. However, during the next two months this statement is repeated throughout the trade journals, who admittedly could have copied it from the original printed source, or mistook 'Supercar' for the term 'Supermarionation'. On March 15th 1962, *Kine Weekly* reported:

> *From Val Parnell I hear that the TV "Supercar" series which is produced by Gerry and Sylvia Anderson at Slough, has achieved a remarkable success overseas.*
>
> *So far the US sales have grossed 600,000 dollars and another regional sale has just been completed which will bring the series' earnings into the one million dollar bracket.*
>
> *[...]Thirty-nine episodes have already been made and a new series will soon be started.*

On April 5th 1962, *Kine Weekly* reported that the Equity strike had come to an end and stated: *ITC will also make 26 additional "Supercar" puppet films, produced by Gerry Anderson under the new title of "Fireball XL5".* This didn't stop them reporting later that month that Lew had commissioned a slew of new shows, including another run of *Supercar*.

Whilst it seemed very likely that *Supercar* would immediately take to the skies for another run of adventures, and indeed writers Alan Fennell and Dennis Spooner were commissioned to write new scripts, the show was temporarily abandoned in favour of the new

Opposite, above, L-R: Judith Shutt paints the wires out / Director John Kelly grapples with Zoony / Mary Turner poses with the XL5 stars and a visitor to the studio. Below: rare colour shots from *Space City Special*.

series, now christened *Fireball XL5*. "Where did I get the XL from?" asks Gerry. "It was a motor oil made at the time!" [2]

With the Equity strike resolved in April, filming could commence. However, when the first episode, *Planet 46*, went before the cameras the format had undergone a few more modifications: the year was revised from 2962 to the genuine 21st Century setting of 2062, and the United States Space Patrol became the World Space Patrol.

In the 2060s, the Earth is known to be one of many planets that support life. The stars are patrolled by the Fireball XL series of craft. Fireball XL5 is commanded by Steve Zodiac, the dashing pilot (blessed with better looks than his *Supercar* counterpart). Ably assisting him are the glamarous 'continental' doctor of space medicine, Venus, Professor Matthew Matic, the bespectacled scatty genius and, occasionally Zoony, Venus' pet Lazoon. Back on the earth, at Space City, from the massive revolving control tower, Commander Zero and his assistant Lieutenant 90 make strategic decisions and issue the orders to the entire space fleet.

As with *Supercar*, and perhaps more conspicuously so, the real star of *Fireball XL5* was not the square-jawed chisel-featured pilot, but the vehicle itself, beautifully brought to life from Reg Hill's concept drawings in the form of three models (of various scales). In official ITC publicity the craft was described thus:

> *[...] Fireball XL-5 is a spaceship, the biggest of its type and over 300 feet in length, rocket propelled. It can be away from its base, if necessary, for months at a time. Completely self-contained, it has living quarters for all its crew, with an ultra-modernistic lounge, observation window, a laboratory for research and an "astrascope" which, like the Clearvu in "Supercar", enable its crew to see in any conditions.*
>
> *It has a nose cone ("Fireball Junior") which detaches itself from the main part of the spaceship and can make a landing while the spaceship itself continues in orbit.*

Gerry says: "I had heard, and I don't know whether this is correct or not, that the Russians were experimenting with launching their rockets: instead of vertically they would go along and gain speed along a railway track and then, rather like an aircraft, lift its nose and fly." Inspired by this image, Gerry wrote this launch procedure into the title sequence, which he then handed over to his burgeoning Special Effects department.

Derek Meddings by now was settled in his new position of Special Effects Director and set about devising the effects sequences to be filmed in the tiny room allocated to him. In his book *21st Century Visions* [3] Derek says: "By now, we knew that part of the success of AP's programmes came from the impact their imaginative visuals made and we were always looking for new ways

---

2. Gerry is presumably referring to Castrol XL.

3. *21st Century Visions* by Derek Meddings and Sam Mitchell (1993)

to increase this impact. I was sure my unit could help by producing more spectacular miniatures, and *Fireball XL5*'s launch sequence is an early example of the approach we developed. Combining unusual camera angles with dramatic movement, either within a shot or by cutting quickly from one shot to another, is one of the most effective ways to produce visual impact. And as dramatic movement also distracts an audience from looking too closely at a miniature, it helped my shots if it was written into special effects sequences from the start.

"For a start, the stage we were working on was so small that it was impossible to build the length of track we needed to create a realistic launch and we had to rely on one of the advantages of shooting on film to create the results we were looking for.

"Our models were usually made from wood and card, partly because we couldn't afford other materials, but also because our model vehicles had to be light enough to be flown on the thinnest wire. Although we had a superbly detailed 7-ft model of Fireball built for close-up shots, we had to use a much smaller model for the launch itself. Unfortunately, it was so light that whenever we pulled it along the track any unevenness was magnified, and we had to spend hours carefully weighting it and smoothing the track to create the right movement. We had the same problems with the control tower. This was also built of wood and card, and was attached to an electric motor,

Left: Wood, card, and wobbly: Space City control tower.

but every time we turned on the motors, the tower wobbled, and it took hours of adjusting to make it revolve smoothly. Just when we'd succeeded, it would suddenly stop in the middle of a take because sand from the landscape set had found its way into the motor."

Derek's assistant Brian Johnson has equally vivid memories of the shoot. "The opening sequence for *Fireball XL5* where it gets fired up a ramp with all these rockets was a nightmare because Fireball had to be held on wires, and there I was hanging over the top of the set trying to match the speed of the vehicle being pulled up the thing and if you look at it it's terribly bumpy."

Gerry smiles wryly when he recalls the biggest question that his young viewers had about the title sequence: "The only thing, of course, was that it had to have wheels (in order to run along the runway) and the wheels would have been an impediment in terms of air flow. So, as soon as it took off, they would jettison the undercarriage. One of the things that a few kids would ask me was, 'What happens to all those undercarriages that they drop in that field at the end of the runway?'"

Fireball XL5 marked the time that special effects became as important as the puppets themselves, and Derek's small team had to use many ingenious methods to maximise both on-screen impact and use of their miniscule budget. One innovation was the use of an endless array of model kit parts to construct all manner of weird and wonderful craft. Kit parts, combined with ordinary household objects (such as toothpaste lids) dressed many a puppet and model set over the coming years.

Director Des Saunders speaks with great enthusiasm about Derek and his contribution. "Derek came along and made all these wonderful special effects shots for us. The industry outside seemed to learn from that that special effects were the thing to add real production value."

Puppeteer Roger Woodburn concurs, "There was certainly amazing, pioneering work done there. Although, it all seemed a bit Mickey Mouse at the time!"

Explosions were also becoming a part of every day life. Detonating charges proved to be a hit-and-miss affair, especially for any spacecraft that required rockets to fire. An electrical current would be fired down the ultra-fine tungsten wires that the craft was precariously tied to (often causing the wire to break, sending a model crashing to the floor) in the hope that the required Schermuly charges would detonate simultaneously. However, more often than not, charges would fail to ignite, or if they did fire, one rocket would be prone to extinguish before the others.

In addition to endless rocket motors, there was an increasing need to blow things up. Over the next few years, Derek and his team would hone their pyrotechnic skills to perfection, building from simple charges, to conflagrations enhanced with petrol jelly for a truly intense result. Sometimes the team got more than they bargained for. Alan Perry recounts: "There was a sequence where we were shooting against the back projection screen and Steve Zodiac was on his scooter, which had a gun built into it. We turned the camera over, and Steve was going through the foreground. We said, Fire!' and there was an almighty bang. The cloud of smoke cleared and there was Steve Zodiac on a pair of handlebars – the bike had disintegrated! Derek said, 'I think we put too much in there lads!'"

Steve's co-star was also the victim of the enthusiastic Special Effects department. Director David Elliott recalls this with glee: "This explosion went off and as the smoke cleared, there was the heroine (Venus) on fire. The body practically disintegrated. 'Let her burn!' I said. I don't think Gerry and Sylvia were very impressed!"

Detonating explosives was an imprecise science that would frustrate the special effects boys for many years to come. They would continue to experiment with whatever materials came their way in their quest for perfection. Brian Johnson recalls: "Derek and I once went out scouting around the Slough Trading Estate and found ourselves some bags of stuff, which we would use as rock formations. We would blow this stuff up and it looked terrific. What was this stuff? Blue asbestos!"

While Derek and his team worked in their confined space on the effects sequences, the puppeteers produced the new cast

Opposite above, L-R: Fly by wire – Derek Meddings with Fireball XL5 / Interior decorating at Space City / "Put out those flames, Lieutenant!" Ninety is made ready for some Firefighting.

members. For the first time, the entire cast was designed in-house by the puppeteers and sculptors. Mary Turner (Steve Zodiac and Lt 90), Christine Glanville (Venus and Zero) and John Blundall (Matt Matic, Robert the Robot and Zoony) undertook to design and construct the heads, and Eddie Hunter and John Brown helped John Blundall to build the bodies. At this time, the puppets were essentially the same as the *Supercar* marionettes, but slightly less caricatured and with minor refinements in the physical construction. Notably there was a new key difference between male and female characters (breasts aside…): for men, the head and neck would be moulded together, while for females the head and neck were moulded separately for a more delicate neckline. Previously, the heads and necks had always been separate, regardless of gender. [4]

Newcomer, writer Alan Fennell, met Gerry Anderson whilst working on the popular *TV Comic* for children. During his visit to the studios to discuss licensing opportunities, he was asked what he thought about the scripts for *Supercar.* After stating that he thought they were too sophisticated for children, Fennell was given the chance to prove himself by contributing heavily to *Fireball XL5*. For *Supercar*, Gerry and Sylvia had undertaken the task of writing the whole of the second series but, this time, they elected to write only the crucial opening episode, *Planet 46*, which, as usual, had the task of establishing the format and, later, *Space Monster.*

The remaining 37 episodes were distributed between Alan Fennell, Anthony Marriott (who despite writing eleven episodes would not contribute to the Supermarionation oeuvre any further) and new writer Dennis Spooner, who met the Andersons at a party hosted by writer Johnny Speight. [5] Over the next few years Spooner and Fennell would become APF's most prolific writers.

With the words written, the craft constructed and the stars born, the only thing left to do was to find them voices. Paul Maxwell, an American actor with a dramatic 'heroic' voice, was chosen to play Steve Zodiac, whilst David Graham was invited back to play XL5's resident scatty scientist, Matthew Matic and Lieutenant 90 as well as Venus' pet Lazoon, Zoony, with its catchphrase "Weell-cooooome Hoooooo-ome." Australian actor John Bluthal was given command of Space City as Commander Zero, and Sylvia Anderson cast herself as Venus. Robert the Robot, though, proved an interesting challenge. In this series, Gerry not only had a hand in the production, but a voice in it too. Feeling that the creation of the robot's voice was a technician's job rather than an actor's, Gerry set himself the task of finding a suitable buzzing monotone.

---

4. An interesting exception to this is Jock, the engineer. His head and neck are separate. In fact, Jock looks like Mike Mercury after plasticine surgery – they feature the same head shape, eye shape, mouth and neckline. Steve Zodiac would later find himself similarly demoted (though this time just re-wigged) when he appeared as Johnny Swoonara in the Stingray episode, *Stand By For Action.*

5. Speight and Spooner were represented by Associated London Scripts, which as previously noted, had its offices at 9 Orme Court where Arrow Productions was based. It seems likely that this is how the Andersons came to be invited to the Speight's party. In an interview featured in *Starburst* magazine, Spooner recalled his meeting with the Andersons and stated that he was initially commissioned to write scripts for *Supercar* which were unused.

"It had a robot," says Gerry Anderson, "And thinking of a name we came up with a very, very original name... Robert the Robot! The robot was built with new materials at that time, plastics and what-have-you. Basically, we would go out and buy lots of bits and pieces that were made in plastic, take them apart and reassemble them and make them look like a modern robot. Then we needed to have a robot voice. Today, with modern sound recording if you say to the engineer, 'We want a robot voice,' he'll go 'ding, ding, ding' and ask, 'Is that the sort of voice you want? No, you want a deeper one?' Whatever you want today they'll produce in two seconds. However, then it was difficult, if not impossible to produce the sort of robot voice that would have to be a monotone. So, we found that at Edinburgh University they were creating the human voice by actually painting the modulations on a clear piece of film and then running it under a light, and the light would vary as it went through and they produced a short sentence artificially. It sounded like one of our late kings who had an impediment in his speech. We went up there and we explained what we wanted, and they came up with the idea of giving us a vibrator, which of course everyone smiles at – not that kind of vibrator! – and it was a vibrator that people who'd had their larynx removed through cancer would be able to put under their chin, and it made a constant buzz. Then that sound was transmitted to the sound inside the mouth. I was then able to modulate that by mouthing the words. So, let's get

Right: Sylvia with Venus and below, comparing the original with Fairylite's Jetmobile toys.

this straight – it was not my voice. It was the sound of the vibrator that I modulated. That's why Robert always used to say, 'On our way 'ome,' because you can't sound an 'h' when you're modulating a tone in the mouth."

APF took the vibrator and adapted it for recording purposes. Gerry continues: "We designed a sound-proof box which at one end had an opening for me to push my mouth against. I had to push hard so that the sound didn't escape. At the other end there was a microphone. I'd hold the vibrator underneath my chin. The sound of the vibrator couldn't get into the box but it was coming out of my mouth, and by mouthing the words this formed the words which were then recorded by the microphone at the other end. Why did I do it? Because it was my idea, it was highly experimental and I knew what I wanted to achieve. I have nothing of the artiste in me and that was the only voice I did." [6]

Voice artist John Bluthal has fond memories of these recording sessions. "I was over the moon to be part of it! This was one show that was different from any show that I had ever done before – or since. Gerry was very serious minded. He would be nervous if an actor left the recording to go to the toilet for a few minutes. Notwithstanding that, he was brilliant at what he created. Sylvia was a joy to work with. She had a great sense of humour and she was disturbingly attractive. David Graham was renowned for his quips and general bonhomie. Paul Maxwell was a nice man. He lived close by in Putney and I would drive him to the studios. Although I was a joker, the recordings were highly professional." Bluthal admits though that there was one disappointment. "I would have liked to have gone on and done another series."

Once the individual elements (puppets, voices and special effects) had been filmed and recorded they were passed to the editors who had the difficult task of assembling them in the cutting room to produce yet another exciting episode. David Lane, who joined as an editor on *Supercar*, discusses the challenges of editing puppet shows. "The difficulty with editing is to get some expression out of the rhythm of the piece. When you see them at rushes the puppets are quite dead. But once you begin putting it together you start energising it a bit. Then you start your cross-cutting; pull scenes forward, push them back, change them around… When you're doing a TV show it's a sausage machine. So no one part is a hundred per cent finished. You never get a perfect script, you never get a perfect recording, you never get perfect shots. You just get the whole piece thrown at you at the end, and you just have to make it work. And with the puppets you need to make it feel natural, not stilted."

David, who was only in his very early 20s when he joined the company, has vivid memories of editing one particular picture. "It didn't work. To be honest, I thought it was OK, but Gerry was pissed off. I was editing it for John Kelly who was directing. After viewing the episode Gerry turned to me and he said, 'Well, you know it doesn't

6. Gerry also provided the other robot voices in *Fireball XL5*.

work.' And then he turned to John and said, '*and* you know it doesn't work.' He said, 'I'm going off for Easter and when I come back I expect it to work.' And that was it. It was a good lesson for me because I spent my Easter reading and re-reading the script and suddenly began to see the flaws in it. So I went back during Easter and re-edited the whole thing. I ripped the script apart and turned scenes around. So we went back into the theatre after Easter. I sat there trembling. Gerry watched it and said, 'Well, it works now!'"

David has enormous respect for Gerry and his talents. "Gerry was a terrific editor and had tremendous patience. So when we had a film that didn't work he would pull it to bits and try this here, try that there. He just had a very, very good eye for editing and sound. So whilst you were mechanically following his instructions you were also learning enormous amounts."

Art Assistant Keith Wilson who joined at the beginning of production on *Fireball XL5* concurs with David about the education on offer. "It was my passion to work in films. At that time it was extremely difficult to get into the industry because of the unions. You had to have a union ticket. And they would not supply you with a union ticket unless you had a job. It was one of those catch-22 situations. But there was an exception – Gerry Anderson's company. It was so specialised that there was nobody in the union that could actually do the jobs. So it was Gerry's idea to train people from the beginning. So people like myself who were passionate and enthusiastic about working in the film industry could actually be taught. And we were all young. We were all in our very early 20s and the atmosphere was extraordinary.

"I had no idea about the concept of actually making a film and how it was put together. But I learnt it very quickly. And that's what was so wonderful about working for Gerry and Sylvia at that time – it was like going back to school, but to learn all about film-making. It was a small complex. Everything was in one building. So when I wasn't actually working on a set I would go into the cutting rooms and actually see how films were assembled. It was a total education working there."

David and Keith were not alone in their admiration for Gerry.

In June 1962, in their lengthy spread about the new television series, *The Stage and Television Today* printed a letter from Lew Grade to Anderson:

> *Dear Gerry,*
>
> *We have just seen the first productions of* Fireball XL5 *and I want to tell you how delighted we are at the way they are turning out. Your enthusiasm when we discussed the project fired me with great expectations. The results match your enthusiasm.* Fireball *is going to be even more popular than* Supercar*, which is still the most successful children's programme we have ever handled.*

Opposite, above: Edmundo Ros and children in the booth on a studio visit / Puppet cast from the final production block of episodes.
Below: John Blundall and the Space Monster. Aquaphibian and Plant Man look on / Work in progress on *The Firefighters*.

FIRE

IT MIGHT BE HERE AGAIN!
IF YOU PUT IT BACK.

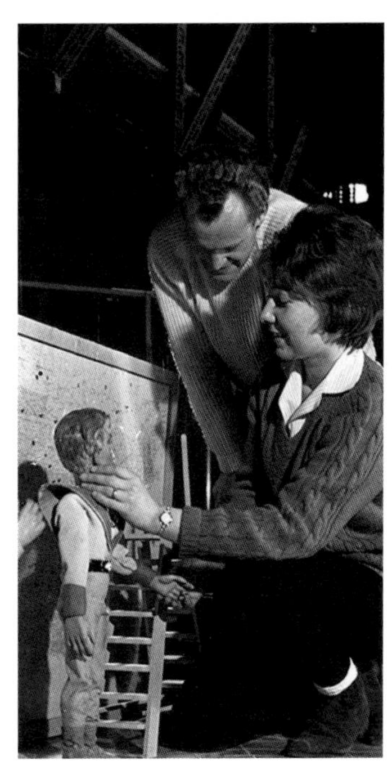

XL 5

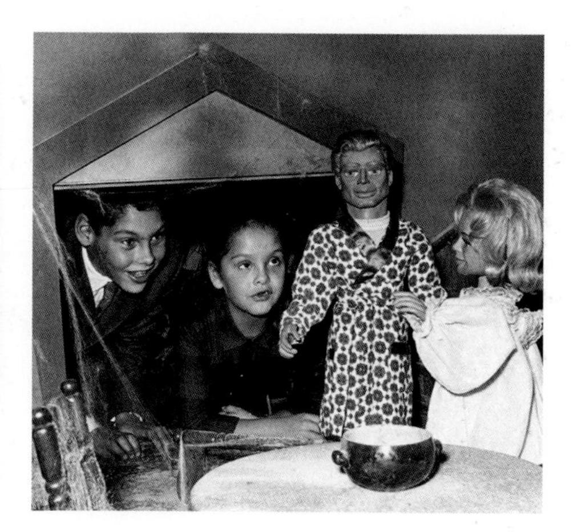

My primary interest in choosing any show is the reaction we can expect from the British viewing public. Sales to other countries are of secondary consideration, but are highly important for several reasons, one of which is to show that we can hold our own against all competition in all parts of the world.

Supercar *has met with gratifying success everywhere it has been seen, particularly in the United States. It is a valuable dollar-earner. More than this, it's winning plaudits for British technicians.*

I think Fireball XL5 *will do the same. It's vital that television should produce the right type of programmes for younger viewers, and this is the sort of series that will inspire a spirit of adventure and stretch young imaginations.*

I feel you will have every reason to be proud of your latest achievement, and I am happy to be associated with it.

Lew's feelings seem to have been mirrored by the public when the series was launched on British TV screens on October 28th 1962,[7] six months after the last new adventure starring Mike Mercury had taken to the skies. *The Stage and Television Today*'s review of one of the earliest episodes to be screened, *The Doomed Planet*, was extremely favourable:

The flying saucer formed the basis of this episode (November 4th 1962 ATV) with Steve Zodiac and his girl Venus in sparkling form. The stories in this new series are a sure-fire hit for the kiddies, and the amount of sound technical 'gen' imparted to the young viewers is quite considerable.

The ingenuity put into the series is remarkable considering the small scale on which the whole thing is worked.

---

7. October 28th 1962 was also the day that the Soviet Union agreed to remove all missiles from Cuba, in exchange for America removing its missiles from Turkey, thus bringing to a close the Cuban Missile Crisis. *Fireball* director Bill Harris recalls listening to news of the crisis on the radio whilst at the studio. "I remember thinking to myself; 'I wonder what Steve Zodiac would do…'"

Fireball seems to be much more exciting – both visually and in story line – than predeccessor Supercar.

Let's hope Lew Grade manages to succeed in selling this show to the States.

While the reviewer's assessment that a series with 'Oxygen Pills' and a variety of other suspect scientific devices contains 'sound technical gen' is rather dubious, reviews such as this must have been extremely reassuring to both A.P. Films and Lew Grade, who had ambitious plans for this wonderland of marionettes. Further welcome publicity was generated, when band leader Edmundo Ros visited the studio with his children during production of *Ghosts of Space* and *Trial By Robot*. It seems, however, that not everybody was enamoured of the show and its success. In 1963, *The Stage and Television Today* reported:

The BBC last week banned and then quickly raised its veto on the playing of a recording of the theme tune of 'Fireball XL5', ITV's popular puppet series.

The disc was banned as not being a "hit", although it is selling at the rate of 1,500 a day. "Fireball" was recorded by Don Spencer.

The puppet series is the work of A.P. Films, which also made the "Supercar" series (with puppets too). They had "thought about it again," stated the BBC, when announcing the abandonment of the veto.

The recording of the theme tune for *Fireball XL5* entered the popular music charts, climbing to number 32 and, as with *Supercar*, was part of developing a campaign to subsidise production costs with a range of merchandise. The song's success was also illustrative of how important Barry Gray's compositions were to each puppet series.

Fireball XL5 features heavy use of a new, unusual, instrument that Gray had acquired from France called the Ondes Martenot. Developed by Maurice Martenot in 1928, the Ondes Martenot was one of the world's earliest electronic instruments and produced suitably appropriate ethereal sounds for Barry to use in conjunction with his traditional ochestral compositions. Barry had first used the Martenot during *Supercar*. "I'd never seen anything like it!" says recording engineer, Keith Grant. "We spent a while working out how best to record it. It produced a great sound though."

Production on the series was winding down in the winter of 1962. The final episode was *The Firefighters*, written by Alan Fennell, and was left to the end of production as it required the total destruction of Venus' beach hut. Also left to near the end was *A Day in the Life of a Space General*, which entailed greater devastation with the destruction of both Space City and Fireball XL5.

"In America it was part of television history," says Gerry of the series. "At the time America wouldn't touch British product but in fact NBC took it for distribution in the States and it was a huge, huge success."

Opposite: Edmundo Ros's children visit the studio during production on *Ghosts of Space*.

XL5

As with *Supercar*, the success could be most visibly seen from the tie-in merchandising. By this point Keith Shackleton was increasingly focused on APF having control over the creative elements of the merchandise, rather than allowing licencees to have carte-blanche with what they produced. Shackleton recalls the genesis of what would eventually lead to the creation of their own record label: "I put together an album called *Journey to the Moon* in which a little boy goes to bed having watched an episode of *Fireball XL5* and he dreams about the moon and Fireball. To make it as authentic as possible I arranged to meet with Patrick Moore - the *Sky at Night* man who advised us on the science. Anyway, we put that out through a joint deal with had with Pye Records. Eventually, we went on to create our own label Century 21 Records. Which I think was right and proper. We were strong enough to have our own label."

In a very short space of time APF had gone from almost bankruptcy to being comparatively important players in the business. Lew Grade, rarely one to miss a good opportunity, wanted to increase his slice of the pie.

"I received a call at the studio from Lew one morning," says Gerry, "and he said, 'Gerry, can you come up and see me?' I said, 'Yes, sure. Tomorrow morning?' and he said, 'Can you come up now?' So, I said, 'Yeah fine'. I jumped in my car, drove up to ATV House, and I got into Lew's office and he sat me down in front of his desk, and he looked me straight in the eye and he said, 'Gerry, I've decided to buy your company.' Now, I have to tell you that I was deeply offended because we had our *own* company. And we had our own letterhead, with our names printed on it. And we had a telephone. And a filing cabinet. And here he was, wanting to buy our company and I thought to myself, 'What a bloody cheek this bloke's got.' I mean, he didn't say 'I'd *like* to buy your company.' No, 'I'm *going* to buy your company!' Not, 'Would you *like* to sell your company,' no, 'I've *decided* to buy your company.' I sat there thinking, 'What a damned cheek he's got!' And then he told me how much he was prepared to pay… and I remember thinking, 'What a *good* idea that he should buy my company!'"

STINGRAY

•1963•

STINGRAY
3

STAND BY FOR ACTION 5

Stingray

"I liked it so much, I bought the company," goes the now-famous slogan coined by Victor Kiam after he bought Remington shavers. Seventeen years earlier, in 1962, Lew Grade followed that philosophy with A.P. Films. As summer drew to a close, Grade was mightily impressed with the vast revenue and high profile publicity generated by one tiny warehouse in Slough. Even before *Fireball XL5* had premiered in the UK and had secured the much coveted award of a network transmission in the USA[1], Grade knew that the time had come to snap up APF and add it to the growing ATV empire. However, before Lew could get his wish, he needed to deal with a couple of matters…

THE MASTER SHOWMAN IS TO QUIT, announced *The Daily Mirror* in September 1962. *VAL PARNELL, the last of Britain's great showmen is giving up his £8,000-a-year job as managing director of Associated TeleVision Ltd.*

His place will be taken by his deputy Mr. Lew Grade. This was announced yesterday after a meeting of ATV's board.

Val Parnell's resignation paved the way for Lew to become, debatably, TV's most influential man. It was announced that Lew would step into Val's shoes as managing director on November 1st, and Grade duly notified Gerry Anderson that as soon as his feet were firmly under the desk, he would authorise the sale to go through. However, Lew had competition. Whilst the keys were changing hands and one dynasty was replaced by another at ATV, A.P. Films had been approached by advertising giant Pearl and Dean with a similar offer. How serious the Pearl and Dean proposition was, we cannot be certain. It seems likely that the offer may have come through A.P. Films' associate company Arrow Productions (A.P. Advertising) and

---

1. *Fireball XL5* began transmitting in the London area on the 28th October 1962, the Granada region on 26th December 1962 and in the Midlands on 25th March 1963. The show was sold to America in May 1963 and began screening there on 5th October 1963. It seems likely that Lew made the offer to buy APF in around August 1962. Curiously, the sale was extremely low key and no official announcement can be traced by the author. Indeed, in November 1962 *Television Mail* ran a short piece about the rise of independent producers, noting APF's success with *Four Feather Falls, Supercar* and *Fireball XL5.*

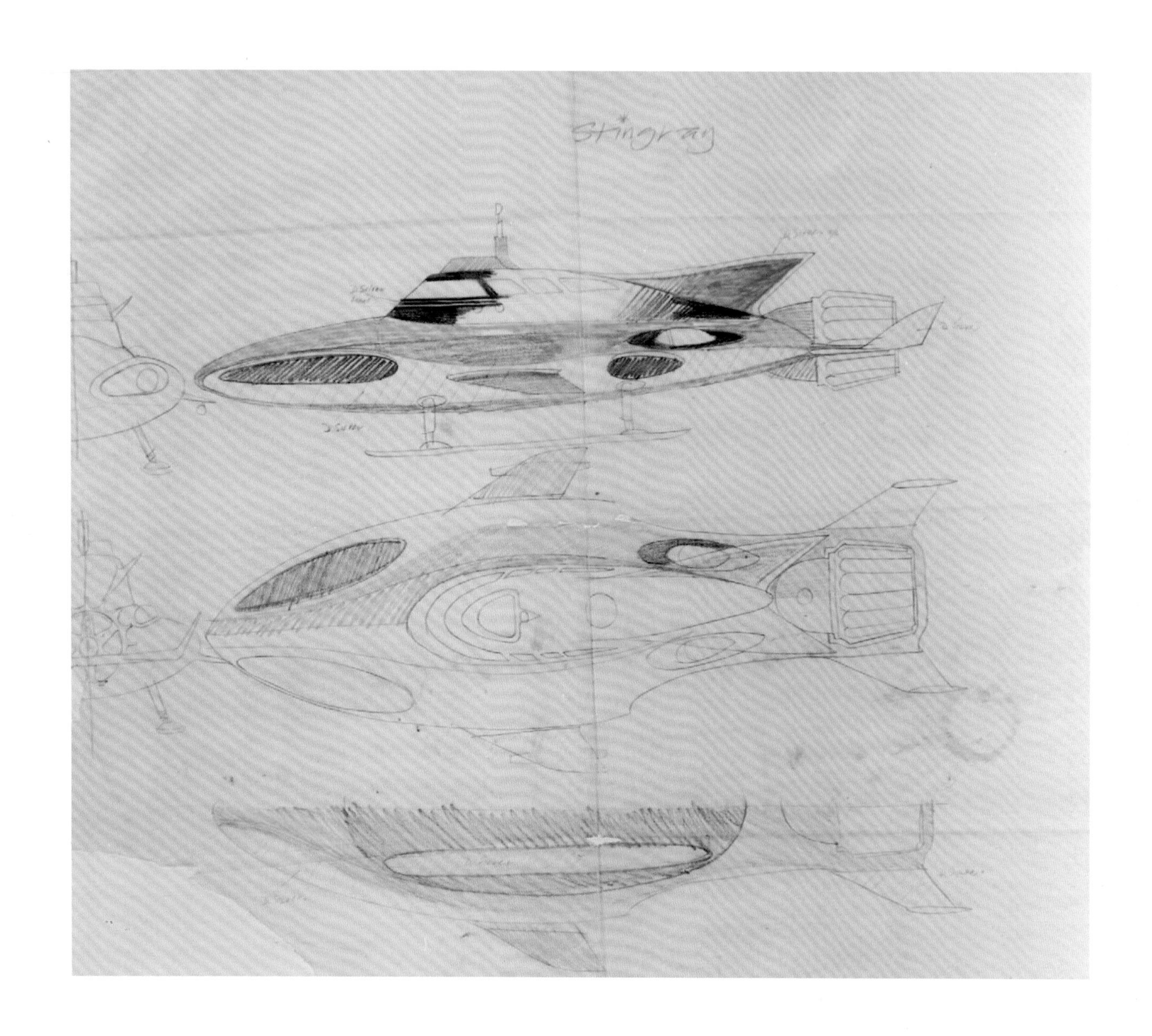

Elevation plans for Stingray.

Ken Davis, who had previously worked for Pearl and Dean. Sylvia supports this supposition to an extent: "Ernest Pearl had spotted us as a consequence of our highly successful Blue Cars commercial with Nicholas Parsons, for which we won top television awards. I am not convinced that Lew Grade believed us when we told him that we had another offer we could not refuse, and I think at that time he figured we had invented another mystery bidder. Of course, we were not at liberty to reveal the name of the other party, but, because it was the truth, we were able to bargain from strength."[2]

Lew was not a man to give up easily, however.

Sylvia comments on Lew's enthusiasm for the acquisition. "When Lew offered us the possibility of him buying our company we were absolutely thrilled. We thought, 'Wonderful! Wonderful!' Then we started thinking about the reality of it. 'This person won't be needed anymore. This person will be coming in. Will they do this or that?' Then we realised the reason Lew Grade wanted to buy our company - it was one big thing. It was the merchandising. The marketing."

Keith Shackleton concurs and adds a bit of backstory. "I first went to America in 1961. ITC assumed they had the merchandising rights for *Supercar* and they placed them with an American company called LCA (Licensing Corporation of America). So I went out and said, 'Excuse me these are not yours to place. So could you recall them please?' They did. And I met up with Stan Weston who had his own company, Weston Merchandising, and he was an absolutely fantastic guy who knew everybody in the industry. I showed him *Supercar* and he took it on. And I said, 'Well what have you got for me?' And I came back with the rights in *Doctor Kildare*. We had six books which had been published in America which were appalling! The story lines were absolutely appalling. But the covers of the books were beautiful and they sold very well. I bought them back and did a deal with Collins for the six titles and we sold a million and half copies of the six titles purely because of Richard Chamberlain. So that was our first foreign, not in-house property. We went onto handle *Man from Uncle*, *How the West Was Won*, *Bonanza* etc. I used to go back and forth to America quite regularly. It was a big contribution to the success of the group."

A.P. Films' cunning decision to retain merchandise rights made them a very attractive proposition indeed and ATV made them an offer they couldn't refuse. On the 20th December 1962, at the offices of APF's solicitors Messrs. Nicholas and Co. in Piccadilly, London, the deal was done. The contract makes for fascinating reading.

NOW IT IS HEREBY AGREED AND DECLARED by and between the parties hereto as follows:-

1. THE Vendors shall sell and the Purchaser shall purchase the shares in A.P. Films A.P. Merchandising A.P. Advertising and A.P. Accounting detailed in the schedule hereto (but

2. *My Fab Years* by Sylvia Anderson (2007)

excluding the said shares in A.P. Merchandising now owned by A.P. Films) and the vendors will procure the registration into the name of the Purchaser or whomsoever it shall nominate of the transfers of all such shares.

2. *THE aggregate price agreed to be paid for the shares as aforesaid is ONE HUNDRED AND TEN THOUSAND POUNDS which shall be paid to the Vendors on the completion date in the amounts set forth against their names respectively in the third fifth seventh and ninth columns of said schedule.*

The contract goes on to detail how much will be paid for each of the A.P. companies. For the subsidiaries the amounts are nominal; only £102 – or approximately £1,900 in 2014 - was paid for A.P. Merchandising, £100 of which went to Keith Shackleton, while the remaining 898 shares remained the property of A.P. Films which itself was acquired from the directors for a handsome price.

Reg Hill and John Read held 220 shares each in APF, for which ATV paid both men £24,170, or around £450,000 in 2014. Sylvia's 140 shares were sold for a more modest £15,382 (2014: £287,000 approx), while the big money was saved for the man at the top. Gerry Anderson's 420 shares were bought for £46,144 (roughly £860,000).

The contract also reveals that just prior to the sale of the company the four directors were on fairly generous salaries. Gerry was making around £430 a month; it doesn't sound like much now, but when measured against the 1962 average annual income of £799 *a year* it becomes apparent just how successful A.P. Films was. In modern money, 1962's £430 would be worth around £8000, which is an impressive remuneration package indeed. John Read and Reg Hill received around £300 per month. In a true reflection of the attitudes of the time, Sylvia, being what Lady Penelope would later term 'a mere woman', received a much smaller salary than the men: around £170 a month.

Although ATV was ostensibly buying the company and its assets, the real value lay in the creative team at the helm. The agreement goes on to stipulate:

> *THE present Directors of A.P. Films and A.P. Merchandising respectively shall continue in office.* [...] *On the Completion Date the Purchaser shall enter into and execute Service Contracts with Mr. Anderson Mrs Anderson Mr Hill Mr Read and Mr. Shackleton* [...]

Gerry, Sylvia, Reg, and John were given ten year contracts and enjoyed new upwardly-mobile lifestyles from the purchase of their shares. "I remember Gerry and myself going to Harrods and buying lots of things on the strength of this deal," says Sylvia. "I look at things I have now and think, 'Oh yes - I remember when we bought that clock!' We didn't have much before that time. It took us out of a small circle. From then on it was always Lew Grade as the godfather looking after us."

In his biography, Gerry rather sweetly recalls their reaction to their newly found wealth: "Bendix had introduced the first automatic washing machine, and at the time it was considered very expensive. I remember saying to Sylvia, 'Do you realise that we could buy a new Bendix washing machine every week for years?' It seems funny now, but that was my way of measuring our new found wealth."[3]

If it had been Arrow Productions that had sparked Pearl and Dean's interest in purchasing the outfit, then it is perhaps ironic that ATV's acquisition of the company resulted in Arrow being disposed of – possibly because it was not acceptable for a broadcaster to own a commercials production company.

With his new interest in the organisation, Gerry Anderson found it a much easier prospect to sell his new vivid ideas to Lew. "I went to see Lew Grade, which started a tradition," says Anderson. "Whenever I went to see him, he always wanted me there at half past seven in the morning. Always there was a silver tray, a couple of coffee cups, a silver coffee pot. He would pour two coffees and he would give me one of his cigars and we'd both light up and he'd fold his arms, sit back in his chair and say, 'Well, Gerry, what's the new idea?' The important thing is I had no script, no drawing, no budget, nothing. I would explain the idea to him and he would listen intently. Then he would ask a couple of questions. Then he would think for a moment and say, 'Ok, go ahead.' From then on, that's how every series was commissioned. I did sixteen years with him without a break. One production finished and I went straight on to another. A wonderful man."

One of the key features of Reg Hill's brochure presented at the pitch meeting to Lew for *Fireball XL5* (or *Century 21* as it was at the time) was vibrant and dramatic illustrations showing certain scenes as they might look in both black and white and colour. When the idea was mooted again, this time for their new proposed series, *Stingray*, Lew needed no further persuasion and sank an enormous amount of capital into the business in order that it could fully re-equip for colour. This new series was going to be the biggest thing television had ever seen…

"We were invited to ATV House to have a celebration lunch," says Gerry. "Champagne, wine, wonderful food… clink clink clink. 'Congratulations, you're joining a family.' It was quite wonderful. And then of course everything happened very quickly after that."

Before pre-production could commence, Lew authorised Gerry and his partners to go scouting for new and more spacious premises. Finding their base in Slough a convenient one (mainline station and all the major film studios are in spitting distance) the partners opted to relocate to new industrial premises, within the

3. *What Made Thunderbirds Go – The Authorised Gerry Anderson Biography* by Simon Archer and Marcus Hearn (2002)

trading estate, on Stirling Road. In his biography, Gerry recalls the vigorous procedure he had to go through in order to secure the new premises in late 1962[4]: "We needed bigger premises to shoot the new series, so I rather nervously asked Lew if this was OK. To my amazement he said, 'Yes, fine,' adding on that I should first contact Max Gumpel, who handled the property transactions for ATV. Max agreed to come down to Slough and inspect this newly built factory that afternoon. I waited for Max outside while somebody went to fetch the keys from the estate agent. Before long a chauffeur-driven Jaguar pulled up and Max got out of the back, swiftly followed by five poodles which he held on leashes. Max took one look at the factory, walked up to the door and peered through the letterbox. "Fine," he said to me. "Take it." Then he got back into the car and off he went."[5]

Keen to make sure his latest venture started generating income without delay, Lew ensured that the transformation of their new factory unit was a swift one, providing APF with previously undreamt-of resources. The old Ipswich Road studio was handed over to special effects guru Les Bowie, who found the converted warehouse ideal for his purposes. As usual, the majority of the crew were laid-off in between the shows and when they returned a few weeks later, in March 1963, they found themselves in what was described in ITC publicity as "*the largest, most modern studios of the kind in the world – a fairy-land Hollywood devoted to the making of "Supermarionation" films.*"

Even with this amazing regeneration of the company, Gerry found it hard to believe that the days of shoestring budgets and frugality were over. Now, if the company needed something, it would be provided for: "I remember that I phoned Lew some months after we'd been taken over and said, 'Lew, we really need to buy five Mitchell cameras.' In those days, Mitchell cameras were about £20,000. He said, 'Why are you calling me?' So I said, 'They're going to cost £20,000 each.' He said, 'So!?' 'Well, I want your permission.' 'Gerry! You don't have to ask my permission. Just buy them! And get on with it.' So we had everything we ever dreamt of in terms of equipment."

Lew's generosity extended beyond the running of the company, and provided his new executive with the ultimate status symbol, a brand new Silver Shadow Rolls Royce.

The new studio was described in detail in a *Stingray* publicity brochure in 1964:

> *The studios are completely self-contained. There are seven full-sized cutting rooms. There is a large property department. There is a scene dock, a carpenter's shop, a paint shop.*
>
> *The studio has its own dressmaking department in which hundreds of miniature costumes are hand-made. Nearby is the puppet workshop, where the puppet actors and actresses are created. Another part of the*

---

4. The January 4th 1963 edition of *Television Mail* includes a telephone directory which lists A.P. Films at their new premises, meaning that the building had already been leased by December 1962.

5. From *What Made Thunderbirds Go: The Authorised Gerry Anderson Biography* by Simon Archer and Marcus Hearn (2002)

building contains the executive offices and viewing theatre.

There are two production stages identical in every way, with mobile bridges for the ten puppeteers to operate from any position on the stages. The equipment includes full studio lighting and cameras, with television monitor sets so that directors and everyone else concerned can see exactly what will be shown on the screens.[6] *There is also a back-projection machine with automatic phasing and remote control.*

Next to these two main stages is an up-to-the-minute special effects studio, where much of the seemingly miraculous effects seen in productions are filmed. Here they create incredible scenes on and under water, violent explosions and mechanical wizardry. Much of the studio consists of a large water tank. It has its own complete crew of specialists to work on these important scenes.

The studio also has its own experimental section, vital for carrying out the work so necessary in the production of a form of film-making which progresses from day-to-day,

6. The booth, which had been so unpopular at Ipswich Road, was dispensed with. All the equipment was moved out onto the studio floor.

Above, left: APF's new home at Stirling Road in 1963. Right: "It's great being the richest man in the world..." Filming Troy's *Raptures of the Deep*.

A.P.F.
STINGRAY
CAM· J. READ
DIR: D.Saunders
SLATE C
COLOR
TEST
TAKE
1
DATE.

with new problems cropping up almost every hour. That's why "Stingray" contains so many scenes which would have been technically impossible only a short time ago.

Only two departments, normally found in a film studio, are absent. They are make-up and hairdressing. Puppet stars don't have to sit in the make-up chair: the painters provide their complexions for them. And chief puppeteers Mary Turner and Christine Glanville look after their hair.

Despite the enormous amount of money he'd ploughed into A.P. Films, Lew Grade was reluctant to interfere and left the running of the business entirely in the very capable hands of the original directors. As a result, his visits to the studio were few and far between. He did, however, organise a personal inspection of the new premises upon their completion. Company Director and Director of Photography, John Read recalls: "He walked into the building and went straight into one of the offices and picked up a phone and called his secretary. He said, 'Right, I've had a look around and everything seems in order, I'll be returning shortly.' He then put the phone down and said, 'The cow!'" Apparently his secretary had responded to his lightning visit by saying, 'What kept you?!'

"I can count on one hand the number of times Lew called me and asked me to specifically do something," says Sylvia remembering Grade's hands-off approach to the company. Mike Trim says, "We didn't often see him at the studio. I recall one occasion when he came in and tripped over the puppet-sized model of Supercar which was still in the workshop. 'Oh, Thunderbird 2!' he exclaimed!"

In 1964, extracts pertaining to their General Meeting in September that year from Associated Television's Chairman, Sir Robert Renwick, BT., K.B.E. were reproduced in *The Times*. It was noted:

Late in 1962 we acquired the share capital of the A.P. Films group of companies which includes a vigorous and expanding merchandising company. A.P. Films are the producers of the popular puppet film series "Supercar" and "Fireball XL5". Their latest and most advanced production in colour, "Stingray" is scheduled for showing in this country in the autumn and has already been offered a network showing in the U.S.A. I have never before predicted the success of any television series but, on this occasion, I do so without hesitation.

Stingray had been born at the end of 1962 as it became necessary to find a worthy successor to *Fireball XL5*. Initially, it had seemed that A.P. Films was going to get the opportunity to produce two television series simultaneously. *Television Mail* reported on March 8th 1963:

Associated Television is to spend about £1,000,000 on telefilm production this year, a drop on last year's investment on TV film, which amounted to more than £1,500,000.

Opposite, top left: Derek Meddings, Eric Backman and Brian Johnson build Marineville. Right: Atlanta is colour screen-tested.

Below, left: Lighting the Marineville miniature. Right: Gerry and Sylvia with the cast of *Stingray*.

> *The company [...] is preparing to go ahead with a new series called* Sentimental Agent, *another series of* The Saint, *a further 26 episodes of* Supercar, *probably another series of* Fireball XL5 *and a new project from AP Films involving an underwater world.*

A new series of *Supercar* had been on the cards since the original batch of 39 episodes had been completed in December 1961. In March 1963, Lew Grade gave the go-ahead to A.P. Films for a further set adventures with Mike Mercury. However, as they were gearing up for production to begin on their two forthcoming projects, the government proposed a bill which would ground *Supercar* permanently.

Clause 7 of the *Television Bill* introduced a heavy financial penalty for the Independent Television companies, by stating that there would be a levy on the gross profits of advertising, rather than the net. This had serious implications for ATV, who were forced to scale back expenditure in readiness for the new legislation. In May 1963, *Television Mail* reported: *Grade has already had to effect a small measure of economy – namely a second series of* Supercar (i.e. they had decided to cancel it).

Stingray went onto the stages alone in June 1963. The series, in essence, differs only slightly from its predecessor, *Fireball XL5*, mainly transposing the space setting to an underwater one.

It is the year 2065[7] and the World Aquanaut Security

---

7. 2065 is the year given in the episode *The Lighthouse Dwellers.*

Patrol maintains security in the seas. Their flagship craft is the sleek, streamlined and powerful submarine Stingray, piloted by Captain Troy Tempest, ably assisted by his Hydrophone Operator nicknamed "Phones". Operations are controlled from Marineville, a high-tech base situated somewhere on the West Coast of America, by Commander Sam Shore, a gruff hoverchair user, assisted by his daughter, Atlanta and Lieutenant Fisher. Marineville is no ordinary base; when under threat of attack "Battle Stations" is sounded and the entire complex of buildings is lowered on hydraulics to a bunker deep underground.

It is discovered in the first episode that there is intelligent life under the sea that fiercely protects its domains. The most vicious marine villain is the ruler of Titanica, Titan, who rules tyrannically over a multitude of enslaved underwater cities. He is kept informed of the happenings of the terraineans (land dwellers) by a series of Surface Agents (although we only ever see one), namely X-20, a bug-eyed, slimy, incompetent creature that inhabits a superficially ramshackle house on the Island of Lemoy in the Pacific. As with Marineville, his house is a façade for some extremely sophisticated gadgetry and, at the touch of a button, wall panels revolve, pictures slide away and his living room transforms to reveal the vast amount of technology at his disposal (although bizarrely, he still only has black and white television). He assists Titan in his quest to conquer the land masses and recapture his slave Marina, the beautiful merwoman who cannot speak, taken from him by Troy Tempest during his escape from Titanica in the first episode.

The oceans are populated with other sentient life, both good and evil (and often only seem to consist of two representatives) which Stingray and its crew encounter on the way. Troy Tempest may be our fearless hero, but there is one thing that scares him: the jealous rivalry between Atlanta and Marina competing for his affections!

The concept may not have been sophisticated, but the technology behind it was ground-breaking for a television series. The problem, though, with being the first to explore new technology, is that there is no text book to guide you out of trouble. While construction proceeded on the new series, there was a crash course in colour for the entire crew.

"While we were in America we saw colour for the first time. And it just knocked us out. We said, 'We've got to do our next series in colour," remembers Sylvia.

"(Previously) the only colour process was Technicolor," explains Gerry, boiling this extremely complex process down to a simple explanation: "This involved three, one thousand foot reels of film running simultaneously in a camera, and in front of the lens a prism split the colours into component colours and they were recorded separately. It was a very involved process and things like *Gone with the Wind* were filmed with it. Technicolor cameras were so heavy that they had to be put onto the camera dolly using a block and tackle. So it was a very slow, expensive, wonderful colour system. But then Kodak managed to produce a single strip of film which could be exposed like any other film and when it was printed it came out in colour (Eastmancolor). That meant suddenly it was possible for us, who were making television pictures, to make them in colour."

"We had to talk to Lew Grade again," says Sylvia. "We said Lew, 'You've got to do our next series in colour.' He agreed!"

The decision to film in colour was a landmark for television production in England: though colour had been tested on other productions, most notably ITC's classic series *The Adventures of Sir Lancelot* with William Russell, *Stingray* holds the distinction of being the very first show in the UK to be filmed *entirely* in colour.

A.P. Films' first official experience of shooting in colour came in early 1963, when they shot a *Fireball XL5* cinema commercial for Lyons Maid.[8] However, filming in colour for the cinema was vastly different from filming in colour for television, as Gerry Anderson explains: "It was quite a frightening experience. In black and white, if a man is wearing a white shirt and standing in front of a white background, the problem was he might sink into the background and we wouldn't be able to see him. So, we were constantly worried about separation, making sure that people wearing the same colour were brought out from the background with lighting. But with colour, that didn't matter. Nevertheless, being cautious, as I was, I sent Reg Hill to the American Networks where they had been shooting colour TV for some time. Whilst he was in America, we were busy in pre-production building all the (permanent) sets that were going to be used. Then Reg came back and said, 'Can't use that colour. Deep greens are out. Definitely can't use red – it bleeds!' So, we had to tear all the sets apart and rebuild them." Judith Shutt continues: "Everything had to be put back a month, because everything had to be painted and colours had to be changed because the spectrum for black and white television was different."

"It didn't take long to figure it out and we used it (colour) very successfully," says Gerry. Sylvia concurs: "As a result we got everybody coming along saying, 'What do you do about colour? What about the background? What about the blue? Can you use white? Can you use black?' It was quite a revolution. But it's nice to know that we started it in a way."

Gerry notes, "If you look at the first films we made in colour, they all have one thing in common: when you looked at the screen it said, 'We are shooting in colour!' Everything was colourful, which of course we wouldn't do today. It was very exciting. There was just one thing that used to really upset me: we would shoot in colour and get a colour print of the finished picture. They would make up to five prints in the lab, adjusting the colours to our satisfaction and then we would say, "Yes, that looks absolutely wonderful! Will you now make a black and white negative please?', because we had to make black and white prints for release."

---

8. According to a somewhat dubious *Television Mail* article from 1962, experiments filming in colour had already been done on *Fireball XL5*. Whether this is true or not is anybody's guess...

“We are shooting in colour!” Stingray’s vibrant palette.

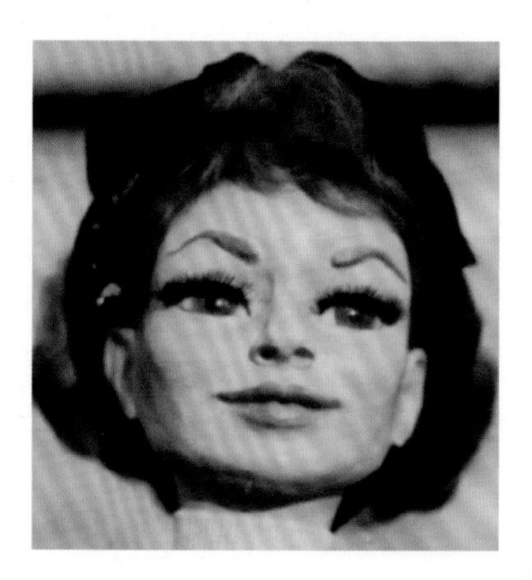

Stingray's vivacious colour palette remained hidden from UK audiences until the ITV Network began transmitting in colour in 1969, on one of *Stingray*'s many repeat runs. Gerry remembers with amusement: "I heard a funny story that I'll never forget, of a child who'd been watching *Stingray* week after week in black and white and then saw a repeat in colour. He called out, 'Mum! They've coloured it!'"

Although colour was the major innovation pressed into action on the series, existing technology in use at the studio was being upgraded.

The puppets underwent their most radical surgery since the Supermarionation process had been introduced with *Four Feather Falls*. In June 1963, *Kine Weekly* reported on a new innovation: *A former objection to puppets is that, no matter what they are saying, grave or gay, their expressions have remained unchanged; one might see Venus imparting the gravest news, still with her habitual smile. This is now being remedied.* For the first time, the puppets were now capable of expressions achieved by using four different heads: a 'smiler', a 'frowner', a 'blinker'[9] and a 'neutral' head. Whilst it wasn't possible for a face to change its expression, by cutting away from a character and then back again, it was possible to alter an expression within a scene. Another adaptation was to the eyes. Courtesy of a man impressively named William Shakespeare, the heads were fitted with glass eyes of the kind used for flesh-and-blood people who had lost theirs. New bodies were also introduced. Based on wooden formers produced by John Blundall, three types of body were cast in synthetic materials: a large male, small male, and female. The puppets were also furnished with bendable hands, constructed by an outside contractor that succeeded producing the hands in rubber, meaning that it was now possible to pose the hands as required.

---

9. 'Blinker' heads had first been used on *Fireball XL5*.

Despite the attempts to make the puppets seem more human than ever, APF could not resist giving their audience a tantalising glimpse of reality in the episode *Tom Thumb Tempest*, which features the marionette heroes acting in a human-sized set.[10]

As with *Fireball XL5*, the cast of characters was designed in-house, by Mary Turner (Troy Tempest, Marina and Lt. Fisher), Christine Glanville (Titan, X-20 and Atlanta), John Brown (Phones and Commander Shore), Carolyn Turner (the Aquaphibians) and John Blundall (Oink). This time the sculptors drew more heavily upon the facial features of real life actors. Troy Tempest was James Garner, Titan was based on Laurence Olivier ("Particularly his eyelids," said Christine Glanville), X-20 on Claude Rains and Atlanta bears more than a passing resemblance to her voice artist, actress Lois Maxwell.

The villainous Titan's most damaging encounter was not at the hands of Troy Tempest, but out of the hands of wardrobe mistress Elizabeth Coleman. Christine Glanville delivered Titan's newly finished head for dressing. "As I was leaving, I heard a crash and stood there as everyone went silent," says Christine. Swiftly turning back into the wardrobe department, Christine saw what she had expected: her evil creation lying cracked and damaged beyond

10. The 'Land of Giants' type of episode was also done in *Supercar* and *Fireball XL5*.

Opposite: Troy and Atlanta seen alongside their original plasticine sculpts.

Above: "Women – they're as fickle as the sea!" The three faces of Atlanta Shore. Below: Keith Wilson in the control room.

repair on the floor. Collecting the pieces, Christine returned to her bench and began the painstaking process again.

Emergency surgery was also carried out on the star of the series after Director Alan Pattillo casually noted that he particularly liked Troy's slight squint. Alarmed that their hero was anything but perfect, Troy was immediately rushed in for a spot of puppet ophthalmic surgery to have the disconcerting defect corrected. "He never looked as good after that," says Alan. "From certain angles, the squint showed more prominently and gave him great intensity of expression."

As the puppet crew worked on their innovations, the special effects department were hard at work in their new considerably bigger environment. Swapping alien rockets and spacecraft for ocean-beds and submarines, Derek Meddings was able to draw from and improve upon techniques used on *Fireball XL5* and *Supercar*.

As with *Supercar* there were two types of tank: surface water tanks and transparent aquarium tanks for shooting through for the simulation of convincing underwater shots. Derek discussed the water tank in his book *21st Century Visions*: "It was obvious that we couldn't use an exterior tank to shoot *Stingray*'s water surface shots as we had for the occasional water scene in *Supercar* and *Fireball XL5*, so new interior tanks were built that could be put up whenever we needed them. Reg designed a wedge shaped tank, which gave us a good horizon line at one end for static shots, and also saved space in the studio, but it couldn't be used for panning and tracking shots, so we also had a bigger rectangular tank built which was more adaptable. Both were fitted with an artificial horizon system, which continually pumped water over their edges into an overflow trough around their sides. This created a permanent ocean horizon all round the tank, and allowed us to position the camera as low as possible. The only problem with the tanks was that they both took hours to empty and fill; this meant that if we hadn't prepared another set ready to shoot on the other stage, we'd lose valuable time."[11]

Special effects technician Brian Johnson elaborates on this problem: "It used to take three hours to drain the tank. Whoever designed it had an engineering brain, not a practical brain. They put in a pump which used to get blocked. Someone would have to stand by it to stop the pump clogging every five minutes. So, I suggested we used a six-inch pipe at the bottom of the tank and let gravity do the rest. Reg Hill said it was too expensive – a six-inch wide piece of pipe! It's not as though the company was short of money, with the (company) directors turning up in increasingly flashier cars."

The decision was taken to construct two new aquaria for *Stingray*. "Reg Hill was a very cautious person," explains Gerry. "You need someone like that when you're detonating explosions five times a day in a building. He got the London Zoo to get their manufacturers to build the tank." However, the construction of the tanks was flawed. "This tank was manufactured on Slough Trading

---

11. *21st Century Visions* by Derek Meddings and Sam Mitchell (1993).

Estate," says Brian Johnson. "And it had really quite thick glass in it. We started shooting on it and when you put water in the tank you could see the putty bulging at the edges of the tank as the pressure pushed the glass further towards the metalwork. Unbeknown to anybody there was a welding spot of metal and the glass over a period of about three days got closer and closer to this point and the whole thing shattered."

"This tank exploded," continues Gerry. "The water and fish were all over the floor. Had it happened while filming there would have been some serious injuries."

Water was the source of considerable consternation for Reg, who had earned himself the rather unkind nickname, 'The Car Park Attendant', for his diligent adherence to health and safety rules. Director David Elliott recalls filming the episode *Set Sail for Adventure*: "I'd got a big full length galleon and it was crashing through the waves. Alan Perry and I got this tin bath which we filled up with water and threw everywhere. Anyway, Reg comes through and raises his eyebrows and goes onto the other stage where John Kelly was directing (*Tune of Danger*) and he'd got everything on fire. Reg came back and shouted, 'Knock a hole through the wall and then the water can put the fire out!'"

The effects team also discovered another problem, courtesy of the fish, that had not been an issue previously in black and white: algae forming in the tank altered the colour of the water. The advent of colour production greatly increased the work over on the effects

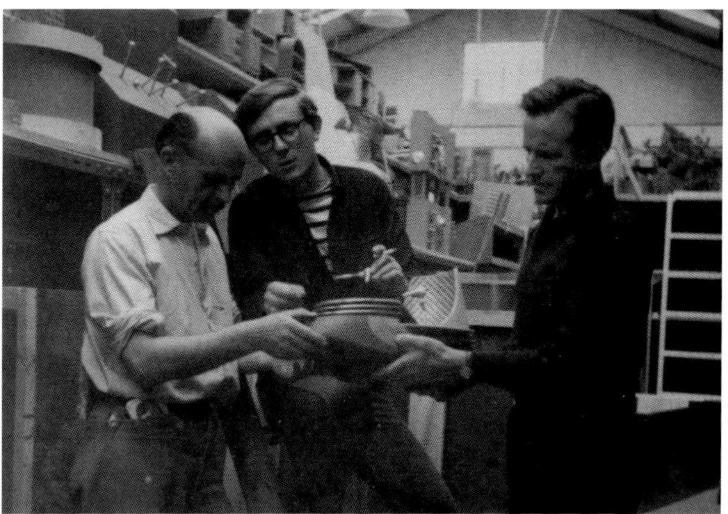

Above: Stingray alongside WASP Weather Station 4 (*The Invaders*)
Below: Making adjustments to Commander Shore's hovercheck.

stages for the crew desperately trying to produce world class visuals within tight time and budget constraints. Derek Meddings continues in his book: "Colour caused problems when we tried to create convincing water surface shots. Although it's easy to believe the sea is blue because it's usually seen under a blue sky, it is in fact only a transparent liquid that reflects light, and its colour depends entirely on the light reflected in it. As we couldn't use reflected light to create the kind of blue sea that would match the sky backings used, we had to dye the water."[12]

The special effects unit really pushed their 'underwater' photography to new limits with *Stingray*. Whereas previously, in *Supercar*, the team had been happy to use common-or-garden goldfish, *Stingray* introduced the use of tropical fish of varying sizes to give a sense of perspective. In order to propel the fish into action for a take, they would be fed moments before. An unfortunate side-effect of this was a very high mortality rate. As with *Supercar*, a carefully positioned airline would give a plume of bubbles when needed. The combination of these elements led to some of A.P. Films' most striking effects shots, including the iconic image of Stingray leaving the launch tunnel in which a matte painting on the glass of the tank, carefully lined up against the rock face miniature, hid a cunningly disguised air-line able to blow a jet of bubbles when the super-sub evacuated the tunnel.

Achieving spectacular shots was not always a headache though. For the second episode, *Plant of Doom*, a shot was required of Stingray leaping out of, and back into, the water, fast pursued by a Mechanical Fish. In a 1993 radio interview, Derek Meddings recalled: "It was one of those sequences that I was really panicking about because we had to get Stingray out of the water and the fish following it, all in one shot. Stingray was held on wires and so was the fish. We had Stingray under the water and we had a puppeteers' gantry above the tank and, on cue, somebody had to pull Stingray out of the water, do an arc with it, and go back to the water, and at the same time somebody had to pull the fish out. It happened in the first take and we were so surprised that I could hardly believe it!"

In order to give a lot of the special effects shots their impressive look, the unit frequently found themselves utilising high speed photography. In conventional cinematography, 24 frames are exposed every second. When projected on the cinema screen at the same speed, the action appears to happen in real time. As the name implies, high speed photography involves exposing *more* than 24 frames every second. In the case of miniature effects work, this process can be highly beneficial. For instance, traditionally, the most problematic elements to work with in special effects are water

---

12. *21st Century Visions* by Derek Meddings and Sam Mitchell (1993).

Opposite, top left: Behind the scenes on *Star of the East*. Right: "You take the bows, Phones..." filming *The Ghost Ship*.
Below, L-R: In the scene dock / Gerry, Sylvia, John Read and Reg Hill with the hero craft / Sylvia writes, with a little help from her friends.

and fire, as it is impossible to scale them down, and as such, very difficult to control their motion. However, when shooting at high speed (e.g., 72 frames per second), the camera captures the same amount of action, but across a higher number of frames. Therefore, when played back at the standard 24 frames per second, any motion is slowed down. So, with water, small ripples (generated with the aid of several fans placed around the tank) would become forceful waves. Also, with flying aircraft, any unsteadiness is smoothed out. In 1965, Derek Meddings said: "We shoot at around 72 frames, and sometimes as much as 120. There are very few shots we can do at 24 in special effects."

Always on the quest to try and refine their techniques, at one point the unit hired in a special camera that could shoot at 500 frames per second. Even on their comparatively generous budgets, this beast was too expensive for them as designer Mike Trim says. "It was a very, very high speed camera which was about the size of two cabinet fridges and ran at some stupid speed like about 500 frames per second. That really produced a wonderful result, but it chewed up film at an enormous rate. It was very expensive to hire and it just went through film like nobody's business. It probably got through a week's worth of film in a couple of seconds. It was incredibly expensive to have, so we went back to the 120."

High speed photography was also, occasionally, employed on the puppet stage, particularly for shots of Marina swimming underwater in order to make her hair flow beautifully.[13]

The star of the show, the powerful atomic submarine Stingray, was created in the traditional way. Reg Hill contributed his design for the craft, his final star creation for the APF fold, and several different-sized models were outsourced and created by Mastermodels in Feltham.

Another impressive visual element of the series, sure to set the pulse of any child of that era racing, was the "Battle Stations" procedure. A dramatic drumbeat reverberates across the complex, combined with Commander Shore's echoing voice, "Stand by for Battle Stations!... Five seconds! Four… Three…" before the buildings descend into the ground. In reality, the whole of Marineville was but a small model, built on two tiers. Through the implantation of a water hydraulic system, the miniature would rise and descend as required.

As filming commenced, the newly-cast team of voice artists assembled for the first batch of recordings. Canadian actor Don Mason played Troy Tempest, whilst versatile actor Ray Barrett took the parts of the gravel-voiced Commander Shore and cut-glass English-sounding villain Titan. Barrett, an Australian, had been living and working in the UK for some time and remained with the Andersons for the next few years. Lois Maxwell, well known for being Miss Moneypenny in the *James Bond* film franchise, played Atlanta, and American actor Robert Easton played Phones and X-20.

13. A side-effect of high-speed photography was that as each frame had less then optimal exposure time, the film grain increased greatly.

Easton remembers: "In 1961 I had done what I think was about my 35th film called *Voyage to the Bottom of the Sea* with the wonderful Peter Lorre. I was fascinated with voices and was listening to him all the time. One time they went to roll a take and Peter Lorre had gone to the men's room and the AD didn't notice, so we were doing the take without him. Walter Pidgeon did his line and everybody did their line, but when it came to his line he wasn't there. So I flipped it in (imitating Peter Lorre's voice), 'Well, you see the Van Allen belt that hangs up there in the troposphere at that altitude.' Peter Lorre came back and they said, 'Ok, Mr Lorre we won't need you for the rest of the day.' He said, 'No! I have a whole lot of important scenes to do today.' They said, 'No, no, no. Mr Easton will do your voice.' He said, 'You do my voice!?' I was kind of embarrassed but he said, 'Do that for me!' So I did it and he said, 'That's very good! A lot of people when they go to do my voice, they put the finger on the nose. I don't walk around with my finger on my nose!' So when I met the Andersons and talked to them about *Stingray*, we discussed the voice of X-20 and I did the Peter Lorre voice for them and they said, 'Ok, that's good.'

"And then for the other character, Phones, I used the voice that I had used for that same film. I had been the radio operator from the South called Sparks. So I just did a similar voice for Phones."

In a long production process, the last element to be added into this exciting mix was always the music. Once again, Barry Gray composed incidental music for a handful of the 39 episodes (which could then be recyled), as well as composing the opening and closing themes. As with *Fireball XL5*, a dramatic piece was used for the opening titles (although this time, Barry left the Ondes Martenot at home, relying on a dynamic orchestral sound), and, for the closing theme, a romantic song. Gary Miller recorded the, now-famous, *Aqua Marina*, in February 1964. The song was then set to a montage of Troy with Marina in various settings, whilst Atlanta looks on longingly at Troy's picture at home. The concept of a title sequence based around a puppet love triangle seems faintly ludicrous, yet the on-screen result is done with such conviction (albeit with a knowing twinkle) that somehow they get away with it.

"STAND BY FOR ACTION!" demands Commander Shore followed by an almighty explosion in the sea. We go to the APF logo in black and white which dissolves to another caption telling us we're watching 'Videcolor'.[14] Suddenly, we pull back to reveal Commander Shore and immediately we're in colour. "We are about to launch Stingray!" The opening titles for *Stingray* are a masterstroke in editing.[15] A viewer could search the airwaves at the time and not find a title sequence as striking or dynamic as this one. Using rapid cuts, exciting visuals, dramatic music and a series of what are now considered iconic catchphrases ("Anything can happen in the next half hour!") the viewer is delivered direct into the action and it is easy to see how the show secured APF's place in the hearts of children.

Puppeteer Judith Shutt recalls the difficult task of filming Commander Shore for the titles: "We did it on a Friday evening and had this special zoom lens which we had hired for one night only. We did take after take trying to get it right." Projectionist Tony Stacey has similar recollections about the evening. "Gerry said, 'In America, they've got a remote control with about 20 or 30 channels and if it doesn't catch their eye within the first 20 seconds, they change channels.' So that's the thing that was uppermost in Gerry's mind all the time; it had to be really punchy. I can remember doing the main titles for *Stingray*, being there gone 10-11 o'clock at night: I was doing a bit of back projection which features in the opening sequence. We couldn't get the timing right of the models moving, the puppets moving in conjunction with the background, so we kept going backwards and forwards over it. Gerry actually directed it himself. He said, 'It's so important, we've got to make this sell."

The series is a clear progression from, and a worthy successor to, its predecessors. Everything from the effects, the sets, to the photography is a clear step-up, and the storylines and characters are arguably more mature and better developed than in the comic-book *Fireball XL5*. "I don't think we ever said, 'Look guys, now is the time to make more of the characters," says Gerry Anderson. "I think what happened was that the people who were building the puppets were making them better and more attractive to look at. And we had some very good voice artists. So, it followed that if you had a good looking

14. No one remembers what 'Videcolor' was derived from. It was dispensed with after *Thunderbirds*.

15. The titles were revised during the final shooting block of 13 episodes, when the APF / Videcolor captions were altered from black and white to colour. Commander Shore saying "We are about to launch Stingray" was also reshot.

guy and a good looking girl, one of the writers would write a scene with jealousy in it. We always screened the finished pictures for our writers, and the other writers would think, 'That's a good idea, I'll build on that.'"

As with all their previous Supermarionation shows, the puppet cast mainly consisted of Americans. "One of the things Lew Grade had to suffer was criticism for our characters being American," says Sylvia Anderson. Gerry Anderson explains his reasoning for this decision: "At the time, if you put all the sales across the world together, America paid a much larger figure than the rest of the world combined. So the American market was very important to me, because our shows were very expensive. Also, it didn't make sense for us to try and make these shows set in England. Can you image a broadcaster saying, 'There's great excitement in this country at the moment, because the first rocket to go to the moon is being launched in Scunthorpe tonight!' So, we were able to use American characters to make the stories believable, but at the same time, it also suited our purpose."

Sylvia was interviewed in 1971 for the BBC's documentary series *The Tuesday Documentary* where she spoke at length about the use of American characters. "There are two reasons. The first one is financial, because our programmes sold to the American networks, which was quite unique at this time. In order to do this we had to have the characters Americanised if you like and speaking so that the American public would understand them. This was before the British accent was the in thing. People in the

Above: One of the *Disappearing Ships* awaiting detonation.

Below: "An ancient galleon?!" Filming *The Ghost Ship*.

COLONEL JOHN GLENN JR.
Revell

'sticks' and in America – they wouldn't understand at all. So our characters were geared for them.

"We needed that money – the American money - for our programmes. Although they were backed by ATV we needed the American sale in order to make the sophisticated programmes in the puppetry world that I believe we made, particularly in science fiction.

"The second reason is a creative one. In the early 60s, the British boffin was not a terribly glamorous character. Not the way he is today. You have the British lawyer, the British doctor – rather stuffy. I don't really think the stuff that TV puppet heroes are made of."

Puppeteer Judith Shutt remembers one rather irate woman who got upset about these all-American heroes being on display in England when the *Fireball* characters appeared at a stand promoting Pye cameras. "This American woman would not have it. 'Why aren't these characters in America?' They said, 'They're not American they're English. This is one of the puppeteers.' She would not believe it was made in England. 'No, no – it's American!'"

Following the initial commission for 26 episodes, Lew duly extended the run by thirteen to 39 instalments. An awkward situation arose among the voice cast around this time when Don Mason and Robert Easton discovered that despite assurances, the voice cast were not on parity with each other, with David Graham receiving a higher fee. A difficult exchange followed with both Gerry and Sylvia, where Gerry argued that it was unprofessional to have enquired what a fellow actor was earning, until it was pointed out that the source of the indiscretion was Graham himself. For a moment, it seemed that neither Mason nor Easton would return to their roles, but renegotiations led to them completing the final batch of 13 episodes.

Stingray proved to be as successful as the other Supermarionation shows when it was first screened in October 1964, and bolstered A.P. Films' profile considerably. Within a few months of *Stingray* arriving on the airwaves, at the beginning of 1965, a new comic from A.P. Films (Merchandising) arrived on the shelves of British newsagents, entitled *TV Century 21*. Based on the concept of a 21st century newspaper where the worlds of *Fireball* and *Stingray* existed together, the 'paper' was an exciting mix of dynamic comic strips and faux newspaper articles about the dramatic happenings of the 21st Century. Head of Merchandising Keith Shackleton explains the genesis of the comic. "I'd seen the Eagle which was created by retired clergyman Marcus Morris. And that was enjoying a circulation of about a million copies a week. But the standard of editorial and artwork and presentation was absolutely brilliant and that was our model for TV21.

"Alan Fennell and I spent hours putting this together and I was so excited about the thing I rushed off to Lew Grade and I said, 'Look, we've got this wonderful idea. I want £30,000 please to launch it.' He said, 'Go out and licence it.' I said, 'No. We want to control it.'

"Anyway, I went out and got one major taker. I met up with the joint General Manager of the *News of the World* and he loved the idea.

He said, 'Well how's it going to work?' I said, 'It's very simple. We'll put the thing together and produce it. And you will distribute it please.' We had the outline of a deal so I went back to Lew Grade and said, 'I've got a super deal here with the *News of the World*. He said, 'Have you heard of Hugh Cudlipp?' I said, 'Of course I've heard of Hugh Cudlipp!' Well, Hugh Cudlipp was *Daily Mirror* and *Daily Mirror* had shares in ATV. So I went to see Hugh and he sat me down with a guy called Tommy Atkins. We sat down and looked at the dummy and Hugh said, 'Oh yes. We'll match the *News of the World* deal!' I said, 'Well, you'll have to do a bit better than that.' I was a bit mercenary in those days! 'You'll have to do better than that if we're going to think about a switch.' Anyway, in the end we got into bed with the *News of the World*. And it was a brilliant success. We had creative control. They had distribution control.

"I remember going up to Liverpool to Eric Bemrose the printers, and I had the pleasure of pressing the green button to start the press to print our first issue which was 700,000 copies. We put this on the bookstalls on the Saturday. We were all out there, nothing happening... until the Tuesday when we had a complete sell-out! And it survived for two or three years and it would have survived longer if it had been more gently handled, I think.

"We had an office in Fleet Street. 167 Fleet Street and we had a staff of over 100 people, because it was weekly - if you start publication you're on the tiger's back. You've got to produce something every week on the button to meet the deadlines."

Despite its relatively short life, TV21 would go down in history as one of the most successful children's comics ever. Over the next couple of years, the demand for Supermarionation tie-in merchandise increased exponentially.

Curiously, *Stingray* seems to have fallen into a promotional limbo. For a series that was the first to be shot entirely in colour, being produced by the country's largest consumer of colour stock, it wouldn't seem unreasonable to suppose that the television trade magazines would have given the show a reasonable amount of coverage, as with *Supercar* and *Fireball*. However, the series remained relatively ignored. Why this was can only be surmised and may be due to any number of factors, including lack of PR from ATV, lack of interest generally in yet another puppet series, or possibly professional snobbery that a mere kid's show was attracting such financial success. Another factor is undoubtedly that by the time *Stingray* hit the airwaves, A.P. Films were already several months into filming their next series. *Stingray* was old news at the company before it had even been unveiled to the public.[16] With Robert Renwick's confident prediction of success for the series, ITC didn't even consider waiting to see the reaction to the series before moving on to a new show. "We had an audience who knew what Supermarionation was," says Keith Shackleton. "And they knew who Gerry was, so I think we were getting a bit complacent."

---

16. An example of this can be found in *The Daily Mirror* where they visit the studio to promote the series. The accompanying picture is of Stingray placed on wheels sitting in the desert set for the *Thunderbirds* episode *Pit of Peril*.

In *Kine Weekly* in 1964 the newspaper reported on a conference with Lew Grade:

> *Grade then shifted the emphasis of his conference to "Stingray" and the fact that two of the major networks were bidding furiously for it. Said Grade: "I am holding back until I get the time I want. We have sold this series at the prices we want and in the stations of the world we want. I have already commissioned Gerry Anderson to go ahead with another 39 puppet films in colour based on a marvellous idea."*

That marvellous idea was born ten months earlier in November 1963, as a result of a terrible tragedy …

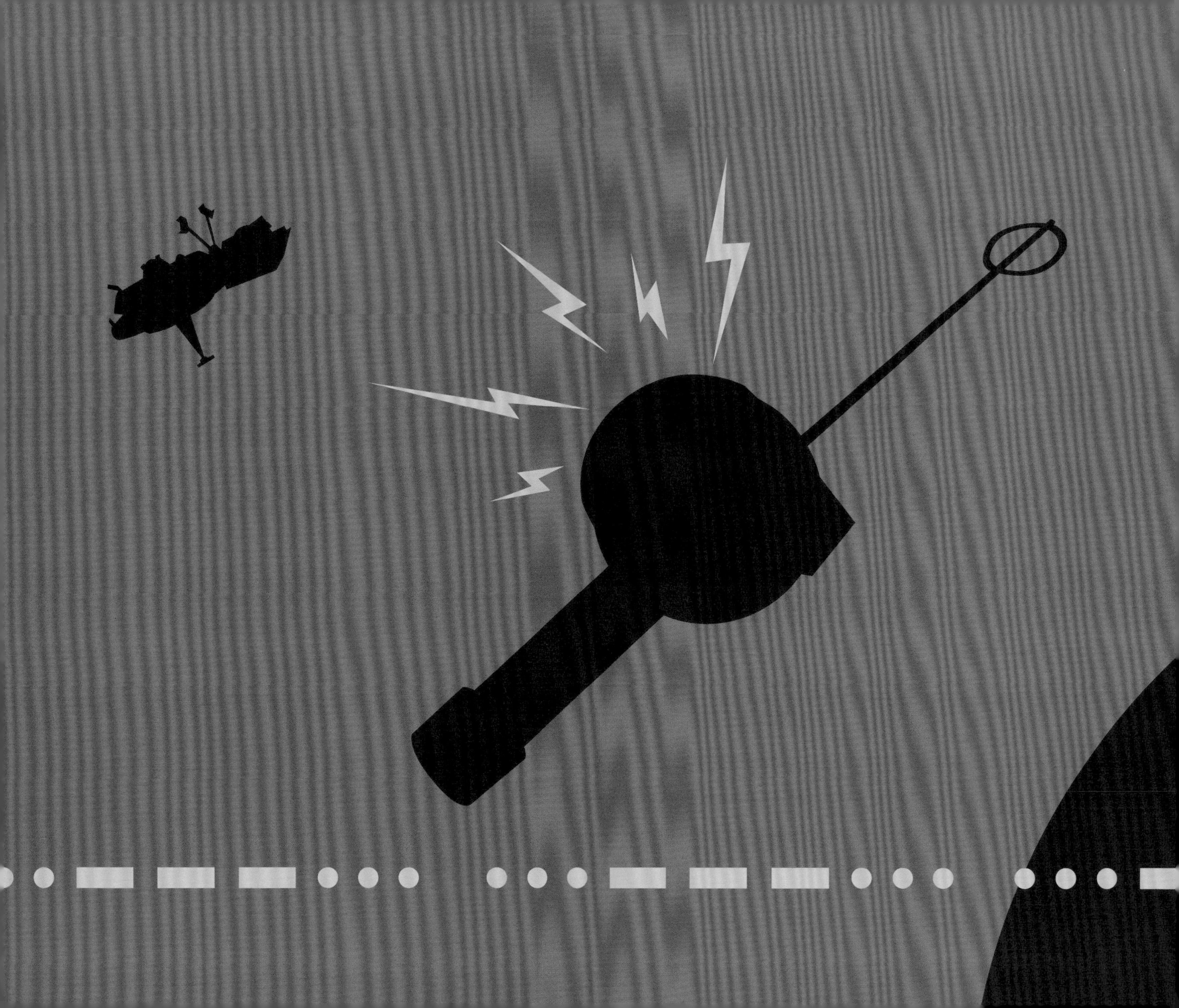

THUNDERBIRDS

•1964•

2
THUNDERBIRD 2

CALLING INTERNATIONAL RESCUE 6

Thunderbirds: Series One

Eight days and nights have passed since Lengede Mine flooded. For the three men trapped below the critical moments were drawing very near. This was the testing time for perhaps the most intricate rescue operation in mining history.

Pathe News – 1963

"I had the inevitable call from Lew asking me to come and see him for the next show," says Gerry Anderson. "But before that happened, there was a mine in Germany which comprised a central shaft along which miners were hewing iron. It's difficult to believe, but the mine was actually under a lake. One day, the bottom of the lake fell out and the mine was flooded. Miners were trapped underground – a long way underground. They worked out where some of the miners would be, in an air pocket, so they drilled a small hole down. They dropped a microphone down there but couldn't get them out. Then the rescue crews decided they needed to drill a large borehole, big enough to hoist a man up. The only drill available at that time was in Germany, but it was going to take eight hours to arrive, meanwhile this disaster was unfolding. Will the miners live or won't they? Then they drilled this hole, which took a long time. They also built a capsule so that a man could stand in it and be hoisted out. It was a very moving story and many of the men died. The thing that did it for me was, 'They've located the miners. They're trapped under there and the only way to get them out is to drill a big bore hole, but the only machine capable of it is eight hours away.' So I started thinking there ought to be rescue equipment dumped all over the place. So I went to see Lew and on the way up I was thinking about what I was going to say. I went into Lew. He offered me a cigar, sat down and said, 'What's the new series, Gerry?' I said, 'Look, Lew, I've got an idea, but I'm not sure you'd want to back this one.' He leapt out of his desk, strode around the desk, grabbed me by the scruff of the neck, hauled me to the centre of the office then said, 'Do you see that light bulb up there?' I said, 'Yes'. He said, 'Gerry, if you want to make a series about that light bulb, I'd back it.' So we sat down and I told him what it was going to be. It was going to be called *International Rescue* and he said, 'Sounds good,' and we embarked on the most difficult and most costly series I've ever made."

The new series was revealed to the studios in the dying days of *Stingray*. The first task was to hone Gerry's multitude of ideas down to a single, concise format. In conjunction with Sylvia, along with input from senior members of the team, the sea of ideas and scribbles on scraps of paper solidified into a basic premise. Sylvia describes the working process: "Gerry and I worked well together; we respected our individual ideas and talents, which rarely overlapped. Generally speaking, there was a division of labour, whereby I would create the characters and Gerry would devise the action sequences of the plot. The storyline was a blend of the two. On completion of the script, we would pursue our respective ideas of production: I followed through with the development of the characters – designing the clothes and casting the voices; Gerry would liaise with Reg Hill and Derek Meddings over the effects and the hardware content, such as the vehicles and craft."

The Andersons retreated in a creative ferment to their holiday home in Albufeira in Portugal to draft the first script and devise what would become the 'Bible' for the series – a document outlining the various characters, craft and scenarios.

Upon returning to the industrial and dreary Trading Estate in Slough, copies of the first script and format were circulated to the crew. *International Rescue*, as the show had been christened, dramatised the global exploits of a family-run organisation using the most advanced rescue equipment in the world. At the head of International Rescue is ex-astronaut and multi-millionaire Jeff Tracy who with the aid of his five sons, Scott, Virgil, Alan, Gordon and John, and a network of agents, has set up a base on a remote island housing equipment that pushes science to its limits, and has one aim only: the preservation of human life. Vital to this great humanitarian mission is a fleet of five 'Rescue' vehicles, which were detailed thus:

> *RESCUE ONE, the 15,000-m.p.h, rocket piloted by Scott Tracy, comes out of the swimming pool, palm trees swaying and smoke billowing from its tail.*
>
> *RESCUE TWO, transporter of heavy rescue equipment, is piloted by Virgil Tracy and housed in a hangar behind a cliff face. It is comparatively slow, travelling at a maximum speed of 2,000 m.p.h., and is the heavy duty arm of the International Rescue Fleet.*
>
> *RESCUE THREE, the spacecraft, awaits pilot Alan Tracy in the heart of Tracy Island. There is an eruption of sound as three giant engines kick into thunderous life. As they scream louder, the craft begins to shudder and then she is away, roaring through the Round House for the emptiness of space.*
>
> *RESCUE FOUR, the underwater scout, is carried aboard Rescue Two and piloted by Gordon, who is also Virgil's co-pilot.*
>
> *RESCUE FIVE, the super-satellite, appears. Its function is to orbit Earth and monitor global communications.*

Each of the five craft is allocated to a particular Tracy brother: Scott (Rescue One), Virgil (Rescue Two), Alan (Rescue Three),

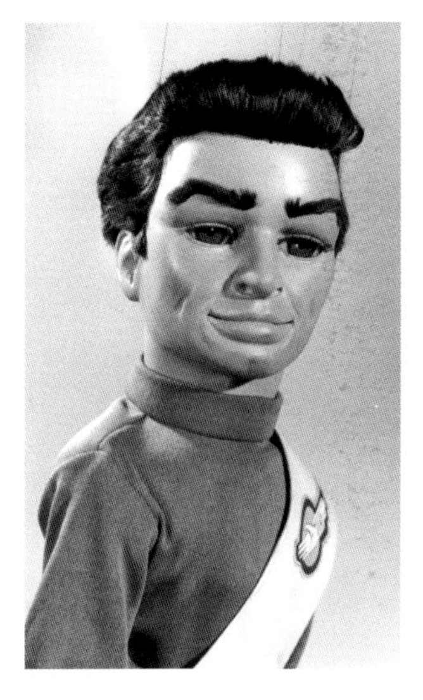

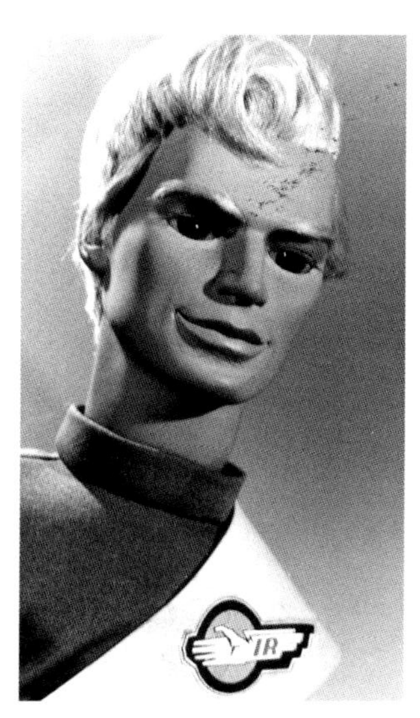

Gordon (Rescue Four) whilst the unfortunate John is lumbered with the lonely task of manning the remote satellite (Rescue Five). Though the series makes it clear that satellite duty is on a rota, in practice, more often than not, John is found relegated to the low-visibility role of scanning the Earth and informing Tracy Island of where the disasters are occurring. Indeed, it's a measure of how unpopular John was with the scriptwriters that in the one story where the space station plays a significant role (*Operation Crash-Dive*), Alan is manning the base whilst John looks on passively from the sofa in the living room. "The idea of the brothers and the father – that was a direct pinch from *Bonanza* as far as I was concerned," comments Sylvia.

Alongside the five good-looking brothers, there is a team of other characters, including three who would go on to eclipse the Tracy Family themselves.

"When we were preparing for the series," states David Elliott, "Gerry asked around for ideas for characters. I told him about a book I had just finished reading, which was about an imprisoned safe breaker who, just after the war started, was offered release if he would work for the government behind enemy lines. This he agreed to and was taken on commando raids to occupied France where he opened safes in various German headquarters – and Parker was born."

Parker, the loyal cockney butler and chauffeur, with his catchphrase, 'Yes, M'lady', and his aristocratic employer, International Rescue's London Agent, Lady Penelope Creighton-Ward, have attained immortality in popular culture. Gerry Anderson explains the reason for their inclusion and subsequent appeal: "Having had a whole bunch of American characters, I thought we ought to have at least two English characters and came up with the

idea of Penelope and Parker. Reason being, I felt, was that they could play a serious role, but would be heavily laced with comedy. I knew that we British have the capability of laughing at ourselves and the Americans love to laugh at us. So it worked very well."

Sylvia describes her thoughts on the conception of Penelope and Parker. "My favourite book of all time was *The Scarlet Pimpernel.* I loved the idea of someone by day being this person, and by night being something else. It just caught my imagination. I thought to myself, 'What can I create now that would appeal to the Americans?' And then I thought that at that time we (the English) were to them either the cockney character, or the posh lady with the twin-set and pearls. Well why not put them both together?"

What makes Penelope and Parker so memorable is undoubtedly two elements: their appearance and their voices.

Sculptor John Blundall describes the inspiration for Parker's look: "I was trying to think of the typical clichéd butlers in black and white English comedy films."

Gerry greatly admires John's craftsmanship: "I saw the clay sculpt and it was such a wonderful head I thought, 'God, we've got to have a marvellous voice for this.' Two or three of us used to go down to a pub in Cookham-on-Thames which had a nice little English restaurant there. They had a wine waiter called Arthur and he was a snob who dropped his aitches and then put them back, 'h-in' the wrong places. He was a wonderful character and had this lovely patter. So I sent David Graham, who played the voice of Parker, down to have lunch every day for a week and we picked up the tab, and after lunch he used to chat to Arthur and he picked up this patter. And that's how Parker got his voice. Parker was a smash hit overnight and we said, 'What are we going to do about Arthur? Are we going to tell him?' It was obvious that he was a man who was a cockney and had pulled himself up by his shoelaces… Would he be proud or would he be offended? We decided that he would be offended. We didn't tell him, and he went to his grave never knowing that the character was based on him."

Parker isn't just an icon in his own right, for wherever there is mention of him, 'er Ladyship' isn't far behind. Sylvia Anderson explains the creation of Lady Penelope: "We got Parker alright because Parker was caricature. But with Penelope it was more like a real person." "I modelled what I thought Lady Penelope should look like from what I had of the script. Sylvia was very interested in that character," comments sculptor Mary Turner.

Sylvia continues: "We couldn't get it right. I said, 'I don't know, it's just not working.' So she said, 'Look, shall I take it home for the weekend?' You get to a point where you don't know where you're going with it. So she took it home at the weekend and came back on Monday, she bought it into me – this is in plasticine, she'd painted it – as she walked in I said, 'Yeah! You've got it! Absolutely right!'"

"It seemed to get more and more like Sylvia herself!" says Mary. Sylvia denies any knowledge of the striking similarity: "When we first brought the reporters in, the first thing they asked me was, 'Who is she based on?' I said, 'Well, talk to Mary herself.' So I called Mary in, and she told this story which I'd never heard before. She said, 'Sylvia and I had been working on this' and she said she went home and said to her father who was an artist, 'I don't know what to do.' He said, 'Well, base it on Sylvia. Don't tell her.'"

Mary Turner verified this in an interview with the *Daily Mirror* in 1968 when she stated: "Lady Penelope, by the way, was modelled on Sylvia herself – we wanted a glamorous blonde and she was the obvious choice."

After initial consideration had gone to Fenella Fielding, Sylvia also bagged the speaking role of Lady Penelope, providing her with a now-famously distinct classy, breathy voice that was a

Opposite, right: "You rang, m'lady?" – Parker, and, left, Lady P in riding togs.

counterpoint to Parker's more plebeian tones. Despite Fielding missing out on the casting call, Sylvia later claimed that her interpretation of the role was a cross between Fielding and Joan Greenwood.

Penelope was originally a subsidiary character, there to back up the operations being fronted by the men. But, with Sylvia's persistence, Lady Penelope was raised from the sexist sub-plots devised by the all-male scriptwriting team to become a formidable star in her own right. For instance, *Vault of Death*, early on in the series, makes a lengthy sequence out of Lady Penelope's total inability to drive, whilst later on in *Brink of Disaster* she's shown to be extremely confident behind the wheel. Similarly, another early episode, *The Mighty Atom*, portrays Penelope as the timorous female who stays behind in Thunderbird 2 for safety and is scared of mice, compared to later adventures (*The Cham-Cham)* where she's leading the action and the Tracy Family are all but supporting characters.

Penelope even had her own strip in *TV Century 21*, which spun off into her own comic. Head of Merchandising Keith Shackleton discusses this: "Lady Penelope was cast as a key character in *Thunderbirds.* I think rightly so. It reflected the personal relationship that Gerry and Sylvia had at that time. Sylvia's voice was a natural for Lady Penelope. There was no problem in creating a strip for Lady Penelope; she had enough aura and background to tell her own story. And she survived very successfully in her own right as evidenced by the comic. It was never as successful as *TV21*, but the combined circulation of *TV21* and *Lady Penelope* did exceed 1.2 million for some time. She was very successful and the girls loved her. This was a nice way of building a girl interest into the show."

"The thing I noticed with Lady Penelope is that the fellas didn't understand it," remarks Sylvia. "I said, 'Look, we're going to need some more scripts featuring her. Now we're bringing out a publication we want to back it up with what's on the screen.' That was difficult. We had a team of writers by then. But they didn't understand how to write for someone like Lady Penelope. So I had a really hard job, and it made me realise for the first time that there was going to be quite a task to get her into the mix of what we already had. They said, 'What can we write for Lady Penelope?' and I'd say, 'I'll tell you what to write!'" "It was unusual in that particular type of action show for a lady like that to take the leading role, but she caught on," comments Director David Lane.

It is interesting to note in retrospect that Lady Penelope is in many ways a symbol of Sylvia's role in the company: originally considered a supporting female, her prominence and importance grew as time passed by until she was actually important in her own right. While Sylvia had been a controlling influence for some time, with *Thunderbirds* she came into her own, being responsible for 'character visualisation', script approval, costume approval, and

Opposite: Press launch for the *Lady Penelope* comic and below, right, Gerry and Sylvia peruse a copy.

Lady
PENELOPE
THUNDERBIRD
4

dialogue direction. Sylvia comments: "All the heroines in our previous series had been perfect foils to the action-man heroes, but now, with Lady Penelope, we had an action girl who was a personality in her own right. In a way, life was imitating art, as I began to find my own identity within the framework of our working life. However, I did not realise at the time that this would be the cause of much resentment later on. While I was perceived as merely the female contributor in the team and my female heroines walked several paces behind their action men, my role was acceptable to Gerry, and, indeed, he encouraged and supported it. Once that position changed, however, so did the fine balance of our relationship. It is important to understand that I was not a crusading women's libber or anything like that, but I was growing and learning and starting to have a voice, which did not always agree with everything that Gerry pronounced. More importantly, I was beginning to have a public face with the growing popularity of the series and my alter ego Lady Penelope." Despite Sylvia's support for Lady Penelope, the puppet heroine was still the subject of laddish humour on the set, where a 'three-shot' was the term occasionally used to describe a close-up featuring her head and breasts!

Sylvia confesses that there was a hidden perk in taking such a keen interest in Penelope. "When I was designing Penelope's stuff, I was often rather cheekily designing so that I could have an adult version!" In 1965, Sylvia was interviewed about the fashions of Lady Penelope. "As our series is based on the 21st century and is futuristic we try to, at least, make the costumes contemporary and at the best futuristic." When asked if she was trying to 'lead fashions by the costumes of Lady Penelope,' she replied: "Well, we are really, yes. There will be Lady Penelope dolls and fashions and I hope this will perpetuate the image that we create on the screen."

Lady Penelope wasn't the only female in this largely male-dominated environment. Tin-Tin Kyrano, an electronics expert and the daughter of Jeff Tracy's manservant Kyrano, was the romantic interest of the youngest Tracy brother, Alan. Like Penelope, she developed from being the submissive hired help to a more assertive, independent role, although to nothing like the extent that was granted to Penelope.

The third iconic character in the series was Brains, the designer of International Rescue's magnificent machinery, remembered for his big blue-rimmed glasses and stuttering American accent. David Graham discusses Brains' voice: "Sometimes, with very intelligent people, they think so quickly that their mouth can't keep up with their brain, so they stutter." Ironically, while the stutter is one feature that helped Brains to enter popular culture, it was eventually phased out in the series, possibly because it slowed the action.

Completing the ensemble in later episodes was Jeff Tracy's elderly mother, Grandma Tracy.

The first script, *Trapped in the Sky*, was circulated in the

Opposite: "There will be Lady Penelope dolls and fashions..." 'er Ladyship and two of her outfits.

spring of 1964 and pre-production got underway immediately with preliminary photography (stock shots, etc) scheduled for the summer, and shooting of the series proper to begin, with luck, in September. The scale of *International Rescue* was epic compared to what had gone before. Even though, like *Stingray*, *Fireball XL5* and *Supercar*, each episode needed to be told in a 25-minute adventure, the number of regular sets, craft and characters was significantly higher than in previous shows. With thirteen regular characters – almost double the number of characters in *Stingray* (all needing to be made with various expressions, plus a set of duplicate heads) – and six star vehicles (five craft and one car, all required in various scales and possessing different functions) – *International Rescue* was given a much longer pre-production time than its predecessors.

As scripts were delivered and designs were drawn up, Gerry looked back, as he so often did, to his childhood.

Growing up, Gerry lived in the shadow of his dashing, heroic brother Lionel. Gerry was quiet and shy; his brother was outgoing and popular. Gerry's introversion was made worse by his parents' internecine war. First wife Betty remembers Gerry's parents, Deborah and Joe. "His mother liked to go for a walk and we would go for walks down to the park. Most of the time we went for a walk she moaned about her husband. The minute we got out of the gate

I have already written to tell you about the film we have been making here. It has helped me to meet a few celebrities, Jack Holt, Gene Tierney and Preston Foster, Ralph Bellamy, Gracie Fields, Brian Aherne and Joan Fontaine have also been here. We have practically finished the film which will be called "Thunderbird". It is in technicolour and will be showing in a couple of months. I don't know how long it will take to reach England, but when it does, be sure to see it.

You ask me if I prefer the heat of Arizona to the cold of Moncton. Well, I definitely prefer the heat, as sunshine is much more pleasant. Up to a week or so ago, it was winter here and the temperature was about 60°-70°. It is spring here now and the temperature has shot up to 85°.

Extract from Lionel Anderson's letter to his family.

it would be, '…and that bastard.' That was her favourite expression. 'And he doesn't do this … And he doesn't do that …' He was a little man. Gerry was really tall. I loved Joe, he was always kind to me. He was obviously putting on his best show when I was there. He didn't look like he was the sort of man who could behave in the way she was saying. It wasn't a love match. It was an arranged marriage and she hadn't wanted to marry him. She never came to terms with anything. It was quite difficult in those days in terms of people's attitude if you hated each other. And she hated him. She never stopped moaning about him. I felt sorry for him."

At the outbreak of the Second World War Lionel joined the RAF and was fortunate enough to find himself initially stationed in America, away from the hostilities. He kept in touch with the family through a series of letters, regaling them with tales of his adventures. On Monday, 30th March 1942 he wrote to his family from Falcon Field, Arizona, updating them on all the latest news. One exciting piece of news was that he had recently made a cameo appearance in a film:

> *"I have already written to tell you about the film we have been making here. It has helped me to meet a few celebrities. Jack Holt, Gene Tierney and Preston Foster, Ralph Bellamy, Gracie Fields, Brian Ahern and Joan Fontaine have also been here. We have practically finished the film which will be called 'Thunderbirds'. It is in technicolour and will be showing in a couple of months. I don't know how long it will take to reach England, but when it does, be sure to see it."*

These letters sparked Gerry's imagination, whose own life was mundane. Although the seven-year age gap between him and his brother prevented them from being very close, Lionel was a hero to Gerry.

In 1944, the Andersons received the news all families dreaded: Flight Sergeant Lionel Anderson had been killed in action. He was aged 22.

"Poor old Gerry," says Betty. "His older brother Lionel got killed in the war - he was a pilot. It turned Debbie's brain quite a bit. She never came to terms with his death. She was a nice looking woman, but very neurotic." For many years Deborah, traumatised by the loss of her eldest son, kept a large picture of Lionel above the fireplace. "It should have been you that died," she would mutter to her remaining son.

Gerry was a man who, like so many creatives, wrote from what he knew. Many of his shows were based around heroic military men, which can very clearly be traced back to his admiration for Lionel. However, there are, perhaps, more subtle manifestations of his influences too. The large wall portrait of a heroic pilot, for instance...

In 1964 Gerry recollected details from the letters his brother had written two decades earlier and a memo was quickly circulated noting that the name of the series was being changed to *Thunderbirds* and that the five main 'Rescue' craft would be re-christened Thunderbird 1, 2, 3, 4 and 5. "I remember saying, 'Oh fine'," says Alan Pattillo on this new announcement, "and thinking, 'It'll never catch on.'"

Previously, the design of the hero vehicles had fallen to Reg Hill, but this time he was fully ensconced in his managerial position as Associate Producer, and so the task of designing the star craft fell to Derek Meddings. Derek explains: "The first vehicle, Thunderbird 1, was International Rescue's high speed reconnaissance craft. As it was to be launched vertically, like a rocket, but also had to fly in the atmosphere and land at the danger zone, it needed wings for stability and manoeuvrability, so I came up with the swing-wing rocket design. I thought this would result in a more dynamic machine than a simple fixed-wing or rocket-shaped vehicle. But although it was intended to be the 'star' of the show and appeared in practically every episode, it was upstaged by its less glamorous sister ship."

The less glamorous, but more popular sister ship was Thunderbird 2, the green transporter craft. Derek continues: "After a great deal of thought, I eventually developed an aircraft with a pod integral to is fuselage, horizontal and vertical rocket motors to either side, and telescopic legs to raise the main body of the craft to allow loading and unloading. As finishing touches, there would be a tailplane connecting the two rear thrusters, and stub wings. I was very pleased with the overall result, apart from one detail. The stub wings just didn't look right. Experiments showed that larger wings looked wrong, as did no wings at all. In the end, I came up with a solution that became one of the main talking points of the vehicle. I turned the wings around so that they pointed forward." [1]

---

1. *21st Century Visions* by Derek Meddings and Sam Mitchell (1993).

For Thunderbird 3, International Rescue's space ship, Derek looked to a Russian Soyuz rocket for inspiration, whilst Thunderbird 4, the small, yellow underwater craft of the fleet, was visualised with relative ease. The original description of the satellite station, Thunderbird 5, however, failed to inspire Derek. A glimmer of an idea was provided by the newly-constructed model of the Round House – a secondary house on the main island (which incidentally, never appears to be used in the series) beneath which Thunderbird 3's rocket silo is situated and through the centre of which the giant red spacecraft passes on its way to the stars. Derek liked the shape of the house and echoed its outlines when he created the final Thunderbird machine.

However, the work was not quite over for Derek, as there was one more vehicle to go: Lady Penelope's bright pink Rolls Royce, FAB 1. Meddings' design bore no resemblance to any Rolls

Derek Meddings' pre-production drawings of FAB1 and Thunderbird 3.

Royce on the road beyond the grill and the famous 'flying lady' motif – The Spirit of Ecstasy. Approval was sought from Rolls Royce, who not only allowed the car to be used, but also provided a full sized radiator grill for close-up shots. FAB 1 proved to be rather more popular than had been anticipated and in the early days of filming the model unfortunately disappeared. *The Slough Observer* carried this article:

WHO'S PINCHED THEIR 21st CENTURY ROLLS?

Production of a new science fiction series by the Trading Estate firm A.P. Films – creators of "Supercar" and "Fireball X-L 5" – may be held up by the theft of two models from their Stirling Road premises.

The models are a "futuristic" 21st Century Rolls Royce and an underwater craft. The car model, 15 ins long, has four front wheels, a central driving position, and six headlamps among its special features. It is valued at £173.

The underwater craft, eight inches long, is worth £65.

Mr Gerry Anderson, the managing director, said the models were the only ones in existence.

"It will take at least two weeks to make two more," he said. "Meanwhile, we are filming parts which do not include the car and craft.

"But if they take much longer than a fortnight to make, the series may be held up."

Mr Anderson said he did not know who could have stolen the models. "There was no evidence of a break-in. We have children looking around the studios all day and we cannot keep our eye on all of them."

The missing models were never recovered.

Whilst the main craft were being attended to, the special effects department had to construct the models of Tracy Island and Lady Penelope's mansion house. Such was the volume of work that the model shop needed more assistance. An advertisement was placed in a newspaper and in response to their cry for help, three young model-makers answered. James Channing built Creighton-Ward Manor (based very closely on Stourhead House in Wiltshire) and a few other features of the series, before leaving APF a short time later. Consequently, his two colleagues who had also answered the advert found themselves with plentiful employment. Roger Dicken and Mike Trim were skilled model makers, and the latter rose very quickly through the ranks, thanks to his amazing design work. Mike Trim remembers his arrival: "On my first day at the company I was greeted by Derek Meddings who immediately said to me, 'You can draw plans, can't you?' And I said, 'Yes, I can.' And he said, 'Right, come with me.' So I was sidelined off into his office and worked with him for, I think, about two or three weeks, drawing up the visuals that he created of all the major craft on *Thunderbirds* and turning them into plans and elevations that would then be sent to an outside model making company." Mike set to producing his own designs for the Round House (which, as previously mentioned, gave Derek the inspiration for Thunderbird 5) and the cliff-house over Thunderbird 2's hangar entrance. Once these designs had been created to his satisfaction, Mike took up the position in the workshop he'd originally been hired for, helping to add details to models and carrying out the 'dirtying down' process, as explained by Derek Meddings: "We would draw panel lines on to the model, apply graphics, paint mud splashes around wheel arches and smear oil spills at the jet intakes. One of the simplest and most effective techniques we developed was to smudge soft pencil lead from a piece of paper held against the model to create the effect of weathered panelling. The same technique was applied to buildings. We would simulate rain streaks and plaster cracks, and add grime to windows to make a house look weather-beaten."[2]

It was important that the exterior models of craft and locations designed by the special effects department should complement the puppet interiors being designed and constructed by the art department, led by Bob Bell and assisted by Keith Wilson and Grenville Nott. For the futuristic sets, everything from egg-timers to toothpaste lids would be used to dress the sets, and Bob would occasionally take trips into Soho to raid old electrical shops. David Elliott recalls one of these trips: "Bob told me he'd been up to Soho to see a guy. He was walking down the street and a 'Lady of the Night' approached him and said, 'Are you looking for a woman?' Bob replied, 'No, I'm looking for a man,' and she said, 'Quick! Scatter girls – he's one of us!'"

Although innocuous domestic items scavenged from a variety of household goods worked well for the designs of consoles and aircraft, greater sophistication was required for some of the more conventional sets, such as the Frank Lloyd Wright-inspired main lounge on Tracy Island and particularly for the interior of Lady Penelope's mansion, which required meticulous attention to detail, down to fake miniature Tudor paintings made by four miniature prop construction specialists, Tony Dunsterville, Arthur Cripps, Stuart Osborn and Eddie Hunter (who also designed the International Rescue logo, featuring the motif of a hand reaching across the world).

David Elliott recalls Bob Bell's zealous pursuit of detailed accuracy: "I needed an exterior set of the Bank of England for *Vault of Death* and asked Bob if he could do this. Next thing I know, he tells me he's been to London and actually measured the real thing up! You'd get shot if you did that these days!"

Elsewhere in the studio, the team of sculptors, puppeteers and costume designers worked to prepare the miniature stars of the show. Thirteen main characters were the work of five people; Mary Turner (Lady Penelope, Brains, Gordon Tracy and John Tracy), John Blundall (Parker and Kyrano), Christine Glanville (Scott Tracy, Alan Tracy and Tin-Tin), John Brown (Jeff Tracy, Virgil Tracy and The Hood) and Carolyn Turner (Grandma). By this time, the team of sculptors was drawing heavily on real life (as opposed to the early days when characters were designed by an animator), following the successful use of this approach

2. *21st Century Visions* by Derek Meddings and Sam Mitchell (1993)

on *Stingray*. The actors' casting directory, *Spotlight*, provided more than a few faces from which to draw inspiration, with Scott being based around Sean Connery, Jeff Tracy having a slight resemblance to Lorne Greene from *Bonanza*, Brains has a hint of Anthony Perkins, and Alan Tracy to Robert Reed – characteristics which were in turn passed on to his brother Virgil by virtue of the fact that sculptor John Brown, struggling for a starting point, turned to Christine Glanville's sculpt of Alan. This very *slight* resemblance is curiously the only facial characteristic shared by any of the five brothers!

Nearly six years on since the first Supermarionation marionettes were designed, modifications were still being made. Associate Producer Reg Hill explained in 1965 to *Television Mail*: "For this *Thunderbirds* series, the size of the puppet heads has been slightly reduced to give added realism and the human figures are now perhaps more 'human,' less a caricature."

Above, left: TB2 in the model workshop and, right, the large TB3 model mounted in readiness for filming.

As had been the case since *Stingray*, heads would first be sculpted in plasticine[3], from which a cast would then be taken to produce the final head. *Television Mail*, which in 1965 devoted an entire special 'supplement' issue to *Thunderbirds* and discussed the materials used in the construction of the skulls reported:

> *"Mrs P. Smith, wife of the creator of one of the techniques used, says: "For the creation of* Thunderbirds *characters we supply AP Films with special glass fibre cloth and a polyester resin, similar to that used in the automobile industry for glass-fibre car bodies. However, a "mat" is used for coachwork, whereas the glass-fibre cloth is smooth and suitable for modelling. A plaster mould is made, as described by Mr Anderson, and then the constructor of the figure starts to laminate, putting on various layers of cloth, each of which is soaked in resin. It becomes touch dry in 30 minutes, completely dry in an hour. The final colour is a natural beige: the resin itself is merely translucent.*
>
> *[...] Thunderbirds figures also involve use of a material known as Bondapaste, a putty-like compound which is used to fill cracks and contours, although it is not intended to be a moulding medium.*

Whilst the various departments toiled day and night, Gerry and Sylvia turned their attention to an area of production that they liked to keep a close eye on: the voices. The call was put out to casting agents, who by now were familiar with the Andersons' requirements: 1) artists capable of coping convincingly with American accents (essential); 2) a good range of other accents (highly desirable); 3) able to adopt strange, idiosyncratic voices (if possible).

Aside from guest characters, Sylvia decided to focus on Lady Penelope and allowed the two other female regulars, Tin-Tin and Grandma to be allocated to Christine Finn, who at that time was probably most familiar to viewers as Barbara Judd in the highly successful 1959 six-part BBC television serial *Quatermass and the Pit*, starring André Morrell.

David Graham, as well as scoring the roles of Parker and Brains, was also given the comparatively minor roles of Gordon Tracy and Kyrano.

Ray Barrett was the only other member of the *Stingray* cast, aside from Graham, to be invited back for *Thunderbirds*. This is, of course, excluding Sylvia Anderson who made one guest contribution as Marina in her sole speaking scene from a dream sequence in *Raptures of the Deep* – a voice which incidentally sounds similar to Lady Penelope's. Barrett was given the role of John Tracy and also the arch villain of the series The Hood. Whilst both of Barrett's regular characters played minor roles in the series (The Hood only appearing in six of the television episodes, and John generally relegated to notifying the base of the latest disaster), he got more than his fair share of the vocal acrobatics through a long list of guest characters. Most memorably for the cast was when Barrett undertook the role of

3. Previously, the heads had initially been sculpted in clay, before being moulded in fibreglass.

The Duchess of Royston in *The Duchess Assignment*. Both Sylvia Anderson and Christine Finn suggested voices for the Duchess (who was referred to on set as 'The Old Boiler'), before Barrett dropped in his impersonation of theatrical legend Dame Edith Evans. His routine had the cast in stitches and, along with the marvellous face for the character, certainly lends the episode an enjoyable quirky charm making it one of the most unusual episodes in the *Thunderbirds* canon.

Although the Andersons generally found Australians like Barrett to be the best at affecting convincing American and English accents, English-born Peter Dyneley had no problem with either and was another highly versatile member of the voice cast, and the person most frequently called upon to play any older upper-class gent. Described by Sylvia Anderson as "A real Hemmingway look-alike, larger than life and great fun," Dyneley was cast as the patriarch of International Rescue, Jeff Tracy. His deep, distinctive, gravel voice launched each episode with the now famous countdown: "5! 4! 3! 2! 1! Thunderbirds Are GO!"

Another memorable voice amongst the cast was that of Canadian-born Shane Rimmer, who was doing variety in Leeds when a call was put in from Sylvia. "I didn't really want to do it," says Rimmer, who was reluctant to travel the distance from Leeds to Slough. However, as most actors are cautious about turning work down in a notoriously precarious business, Rimmer took the

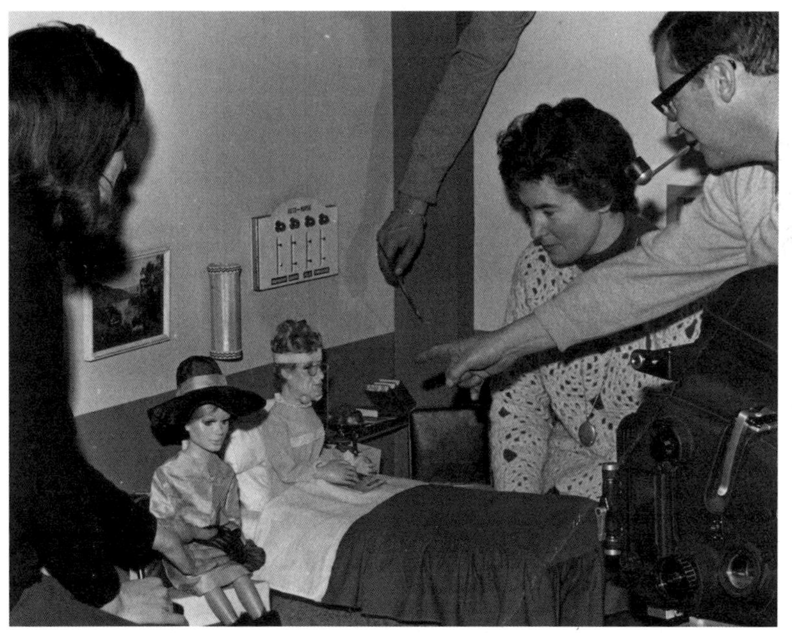

Right, above: Puppeteers at work al fresco.

Below: "Penelope, dear!" Attending to 'The Old Boiler'.

Above, L-R: Reference shot of Parker / Derek Meddings' original designs / The Hood flies his stolen aircraft in *Martian Invasion*.

Below, right: Rock crusher from *Martian Invasion* and, left, revamped into the Restraining outfit in *The Duchess Assignment*.

Above, Left and centre: Scenes from *Trapped in the Sky*. Note the studio floor beneath the control tower. Right: Tenders prepare to tackle the *City of Fire*. Below, L-R: Sunprobe meets the Mole / An unused version of the Round House / Alan in TB2 seat from the opening titles.

opportunity to record a voice track, and not long after found himself in the role of Scott Tracy.

For a series dominated by Americans, it is remarkable that David Holliday, cast as Thunderbird 2 pilot Virgil Tracy by Sylvia Anderson after seeing him in a play, was the only bona-fide American actor amongst the cast.

Rounding off the cast of regulars was another Canadian, Matt Zimmerman, who came to the party quite late, after the first recording session had been completed. "I was appearing at the Savoy Theatre and my friend David Holliday had already been cast as Virgil," says Matt. "Sylvia Anderson mentioned that they were having difficulty casting Alan Tracy and he recommended me. I went along to Sylvia and when I walked in she said, 'Don't speak!' The Alan puppet was on her desk and she remarked how much it looked like me, except he was blonde, and about the identical cleft in our chins. She then told me to speak, which I did, and she said, 'That's Alan's voice!' and I was hired."

The only other vocal contributor to the first 26 episodes was occasional participant John Tate, an Australian-born actor, who was on hand to voice some of the 'starring' guest characters.

Matt Zimmerman has fond memories of those days: "The recording sessions were always very enjoyable. They were done on a Sunday at the studios in Slough and we did two scripts at a time, once a month. Lunch was always provided and we all worked hard and laughed a lot."

Sylvia, who oversaw the recordings, describes the sessions in more detail: "We had a lot of fun doing them. In those days, actors didn't work at weekends. So we would get the actors to come in on a Saturday or a Sunday when there was extra money for them. It was a bit like having a class in school. You'd say, 'What have you been doing over the week?' So I let them all talk about what this nasty director did etc. And then, finally, we'd say, 'Let's have a look at the script.' I would say, 'Have you got any comments?' Which, I shouldn't have done really because everyone's got a comment. So I would then say, 'OK, you've made this suggestion, but if we do it that way we're going to have to alter page 58 because we've already referred to it. So we'll have to go back and you won't get to go home soon.' So, I treated them like adults but they behaved like children!"

"Part of my projection room was divided up so that the sound recording people – a company up in Birmingham who Gerry knew – used to come down every couple of months and record half a dozen episodes and the artists then all used to march into my little preview theatre and record all the dialogue," says projectionist Tony Stacey. "While we were recording in there, practically everyone was tip-toeing around the building because even though it was insulated, it wasn't like a sound booth. So eventually Gerry, against Sylvia's best wishes, because she didn't want to change it, insisted they moved to a proper recording studio.

"They used to come every couple of months. I had a great

big glass partition between the two projectors in the projection room. We used to take that out and you could see straight through to where the actors were. I used to sit and listen to it sometimes and some of the banter was absolutely hilarious when they were codding things up – but it was very professional and they got on with it."[4]

As usual, once the tapes had been recorded, they would be edited and transferred onto ¼ inch tape for playback in the studio. In one alarming moment, an entire dialogue track for an episode went missing and had to be re-recorded urgently. However, the tape materialised again a few days later.

It was not until September that the lengthy pre-production process was complete, with all the models, sets and characters built for the first episode. During the summer, a catalogue of stock-shots had been built up (such as the launch sequences), but once these were in the can *Thunderbirds* was indeed ready to go.

The first episode to hit the stages was Gerry and Sylvia's 'pilot' script *Trapped in the Sky*, which was helmed by veteran director Alan Pattillo, and as with the name chosen for the series, drew upon Gerry's personal experiences. "In the pilot film of *Thunderbirds* we had a futuristic aircraft which couldn't land," says Gerry. "One day I was on my bicycle, cycling around Manston (where Gerry was stationed for National Service) and I saw a Spitfire coming in to land and its undercarriage wasn't down, which obviously meant it was going to crash. The runway controller fired a red light and the Spitfire immediately accelerated and went around again. Down came its undercarriage and it made a successful landing. These little incidents stick in the mind and that's one of the things that helped me to write that sequence."

The Spitfire evolved into the Fireflash – a giant supersonic aircraft capable of flying at six times the speed of sound, and the story was developed into a plot, by The Hood, to lure International Rescue out on their first mission, simply so that he can obtain photographs of their super-secret technology. He plants a bomb in the undercarriage of the Fireflash, notifies London Airport's authorities and awaits the arrival of the Thunderbird machines.

The first script provided major headaches for Derek Meddings, most significantly the climactic sequences featuring the Fireflash trying to land on International Rescue's elevator cars, which are attempting to act as a makeshift undercarriage. For the shots to be convincing, exciting and spectacular, it was necessary to be able to track along the runway with the stricken aircraft. To 'fly' the model above a long runway was not possible for many reasons, not least space constraints, and there was no way of flying the model convincingly whilst the operator was moving. Another solution had to be found. During *Stingray*, Derek had introduced 'roller' sky backings: stretches of canvas that would be placed on rollers. When the model was suspended in front of the backing and the motors were switched on, the moving sky would give the illusion that it was, in fact, the model

4. Interview by Richard Farrell for *Andersonic* magazine (2013)

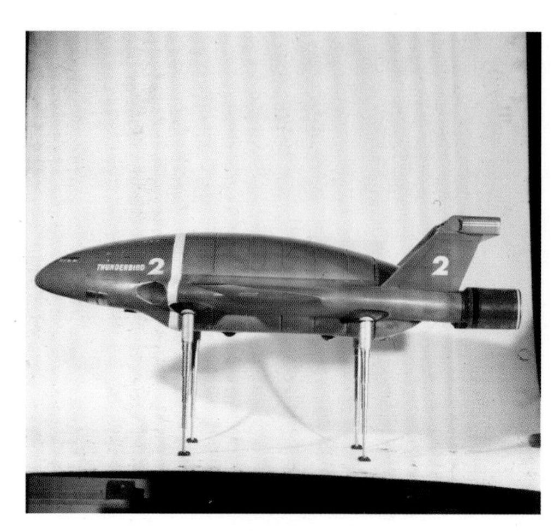

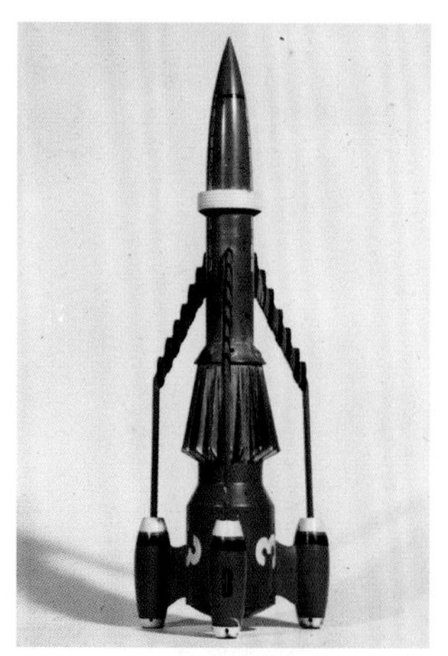

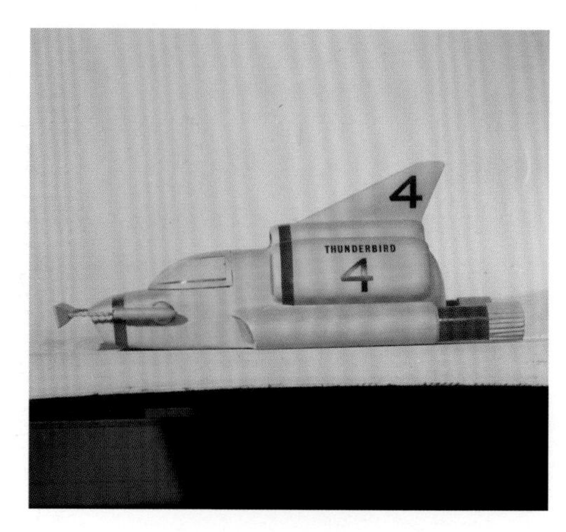

that was flying. Derek toyed with the idea that this system could be developed into a more sophisticated version that could include land elements. The solution he struck upon was ingenious and involved using a number of 'loops', for instance: a foreground element (e.g. a picket fence), a middle element (the runway), a background element (grass) and distance element (the roller sky). Derek realised that he could exploit the way in which the human eye perceives perspective. He worked out that by running each roller at a different speed (the foreground element fastest, the furthest element, the sky, slowest), the viewer is tricked into believing that it is the model that is flying, or the car that is moving, rather than everything around it. The effect worked so well that in one instance, when one of the elevator cars went astray careering off the runway, it was so convincing and dramatic, that a new sequence was written in to show the vehicle crashing into an unoccupied aircraft. It is undoubtedly Derek's genius creating this sequence along with his skilled technicians, and the inspiration of Gerry's experiences translated onto the page, that secured *Thunderbirds* its place in television history.

The creation of any filmed series in the '60s was a lengthy business. Even with each episode being turned around on the shooting stages every two weeks, the post-production processes of editing, dubbing, scoring, grading and then finally printing the completed show were complicated. Reg Hill explained in 1965: "We must do three or four times the amount of cutting as (they do) in live-action. This is made necessary, for instance, by the fact that you cannot hold the interest of a scene for more than a few seconds since a puppet's facial expression cannot be altered... except by cutting, of course, to a different strip, shot when the puppet is fitted

Above and opposite: Studio reference shots of the *Thunderbirds* vehicles. Note the different style numeral on TB4.

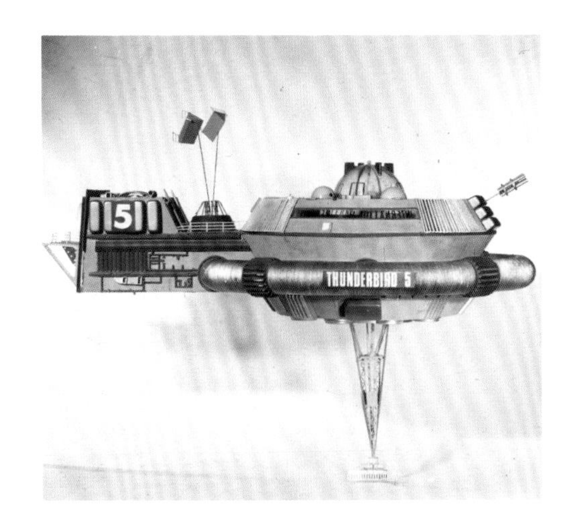

with a different head."[5] With such a long, meticulous post-production process, it was not until approximately nine episodes had completed filming, around Christmas 1964, that Gerry went to see Lew with the finished opening instalment, for which the incidental music had not been recorded until December 8th.

Gerry recalls the agonising wait for Lew's reaction: "We went upstairs to his private preview theatre and we sat side by side. He remained silent. Then the lights went up... He was silent for a moment... My heart was thumping because I'd spent a fortune on this thing. He walked all the way down the theatre to the screen and then he turned around to face me and he said:

"'Gerry. This is not a television series.'

"I thought the ground had opened and I was going to be swallowed up. I was absolutely distraught. Then he walked all the way back up and he wagged his finger right in front of my face.

"'Gerry! I'm telling you, this is not a television series!'

"He then said...

"'Gerry... this is a feature film! You *have* to make them an hour!' I said, 'But we've already made nine pictures as 25 minutes.' He said, 'I don't care. You'll have to make them one hour.' So we had to turn everything into an hour."

Christmas 1964 was both exciting and daunting for the Andersons and their team. Alan Pattillo, who later assumed the role of script editor for the series, was in Scotland with his parents when the call came through telling him that he needed to get his thinking cap on and work out how to expand the existing stories.

When the crew returned in January 1965, after the Christmas break, a decision had to be taken on whether to keep the cameras engaged in filming new work (half hour scripts waiting to shoot), or to

5. Reg Hill speaking to *Television Mail* (December 1965 edition)

Derek Meddings and assistants attend to the monorail miniature in *Brink of Disaster*.

halt production in order to do the summersaults required to produce the hour-long shows that Lew Grade demanded. Ultimately, it was decided that the production line couldn't afford to be delayed, so rather than waiting for the first rewrites to be finished, the next few half-hour stories went ahead, while the rest were expanded to fill 50 minutes, and more scripts were commissioned at the new length. Lew accordingly increased the budget, offering up to a reported £40,000 per instalment, making *Thunderbirds* one of the most expensive television series in the entire world.[6] Sylvia is sceptical about this figure though: "It was never *that* expensive. Lew Grade was a true salesman. He would always tell the press it cost more than it actually did. Every interview we did they would quote Lew Grade and we'd have to say, 'Oh yes… It was expensive.' Even though the series had cost half that."

Once the crew had recovered from the initial shock of the gruelling routine that lay ahead, they settled down and rose to the challenge. There was an excitement that pervaded the studios; Lew's ecstatic response to the series generated a warm atmosphere of enjoyment that resulted in possibly the happiest studio environment since *Four Feather Falls*. Most of the crew felt that they were making something special, and more than ever the pioneering spirit bubbled irrepressibly through those otherwise bleak warehouses. They worked day and night, sometimes resorting to grabbing a snooze on the stages which smelt of paint and fibreglass.[7] Rod Allen, writing in *Television Mail* in 1965 said:

> *It's worth noting that APF is one of the happiest film studios I have ever come across from the staff point of view, that staff-turnover is relatively low, and that there is a great deal of promotion from within on the studio floor; first names are the rule all the way up and down the shop, and in an operation that depends to such an extent on team work, the team seems to be really united.*

"It was very, very busy. A wonderful, wonderful atmosphere," says Assistant Art Director Keith Wilson. "It was the beginning of the Swinging Sixties. And we were an integral part of it." "Anyone who was involved in it was very proud. Especially us newcomers," says Art Assistant Ken Turner. "We worked hard and we partied hard," remembers Sylvia. "People often say to me, 'I always remember you in those days Sylvia.' I say, 'Why's that?' and they say, 'Well, you always gave good parties!' Humour was the thing that kept us going. When we were dead tired, no money and everything was going wrong – we'd either have a party or we'd just collapse with laughter."

One poolside party at the Anderson's home was particularly memorable for many of the crew. "There was talk of going swimming and somebody said, 'Well nobody has got any costumes," says David Lane. "And Des (Saunders) said, 'Well I've

6. For perspective, the average half-hour episode of *Doctor Who* cost £2500 to make!

7. The crew weren't the only ones to occasionally sleep on the stages. Sometimes, certain puppets would be found lying in compromising positions...

had enough of this!' He shot into the little chalet bungalow they had there by the side of the pool, strides out stark naked and just jumps into the pool!"

Des picks the story up: "Everybody screamed and laughed. And then a little voice spoke up, a little lady's voice, and she said, 'Well, what's all the fuss about? I didn't think that was very much did you!?'"

Des relates another amusing anecdote: "We were always looking for ways to make the puppets more life like. I felt sorry for them. There they were worked to death during the day, hung there all the night. They seemed to have no fun or anything. So one morning I went in early, I went along and chose all the men and I put little willies on them! When the girls got in in the morning there was the most terrible uproar. I said, 'Well, you've got to bring 'em to life somehow, haven't you!?'"

In between the frivolities the crew worked extremely hard. This did not go unnoticed. During those early, quaint days of *Twizzle*, the crew had worked with similar selfless energy, but now such success had brought A.P. Films to the attention of the unions, namely the A.C.T.T (Association of Cinema and Television Technicians) who questioned, unsuccessfully, the filming schedule. "I seem to recall that they suggested we should go on strike," says sculptor Ernest 'Plugg' Shutt, brother of puppeteer Judith Shutt, "But, we refused to." The unions had attempted to exert some control over the studio before, and in the early days they forced the company into nominating a Shop Steward. Curiously, this role fell to John Read leaving him with the uncomfortable compromise of being a company director and having to work against the company with the unions, if required. "John Read was a director of the company. And he was also the shop steward so it was a crazy situation. It was like A.P. Films wasn't in touch with the reality of Britain," says Roger Woodburn. "In the '60s and '70s the unions were all-powerful, so they had to go through having the token of a shop steward. I couldn't get over it. It was usually 'them and us'. But John was both. So if you turned up late in the morning his great joke was to say, 'Now listen here. You're five, ten minutes late. We're on set, everything is ready to go and you live upstairs and you've only just arrived. If that happens again we're going to have to seriously look at your salary.' And then he'd turn around in a circle twice and go, 'Don't let the management speak to you like that sonny!' Being rather green I initially used to take it all seriously and then I realised that everyone else was sniggering away."

Alan Shubrook, who joined the company towards the end of *Thunderbirds*, explains the power of the unions in the 1960s: "We had finished filming at around six o'clock that evening after numerous miniature trees had been destroyed in one of the studio's regular 'fire and destruction scenes'. As I had no plans that evening and loved my new work, I decided to stay late and create some new trees to replace the damaged ones. I was quietly working for a few hours when, at around two o'clock, the workshop door burst open and a very disgruntled gentleman came bounding towards me. "I didn't realise any overtime had been authorised tonight!" he said, approaching my bench. "It hasn't," I happily replied. "I'm just working because I enjoy it." It was only then that I realised that the man standing before me was the head union representative at the studio (by this time cameraman Nick Procopides). I could almost see the steam rocketing from his ears. "Nobody works for nothing!" he shouted and he stormed from the room, slamming the door behind him. The following morning I had to appear before a union committee to be reprimanded for what I had done and had to assure those present that I would never work purely 'for the love of it' again."[8]

Unions fulfil a useful role in ensuring that their members aren't exploited or abused in the workplace, but during the '60s when the unions were at the height of their power, they controlled many industries in a vice-like grip and the film industry was no exception. During this period, if any overtime was required, it would need to be noted some two hours before the 6pm wrap time, and the amount of money involved was phenomenal, with high overtime rates that increased even more if exceptionally long hours were worked. Whilst a degree of protection was appreciated, many felt that the unions were too heavy handed and it can be argued that in a highly skilled artistic environment like this, with so much depending on individual impulse and bursts of creativity, the unions were being counter-productive, enforcing the rules with destructive precision.

Alan Shubrook continues: "It had taken much longer to prepare (the shot) than anticipated and the clock was fast approaching 6pm, the official finishing time at the studio. The shot in question was finally ready. It was fairly complex and, due to the nature of many similar special effect shots, would only allow us the opportunity for one take. Bill Camp was the unit director and with great relief he finally shouted, 'Action!' The scene unfolded and was running perfectly but, halfway through the shot, the studio clock struck six. Before it turned one second past, the entire stage was plunged into total darkness and a look of horror fell upon the crew. After a few seconds, one of the sparks (lighting assistants) strolled calmly from behind the backdrop. He looked at his watch and simply commented, "It's six o'clock. No overtime – no lights!" and he walked off the set. Only official electricians were allowed to turn the power back on and you simply didn't cross that line."

The actor's union Equity also tried its luck. Noticing that the live-action inserts of hands picking things up etc., were being performed by non-union members, they attempted to coerce the studio into using professional hand-artistes (a different artiste for each character, no less!). They were less successful than the ACTT in getting the studio to conform to their wishes.

However, Mary Turner recalls that the unions weren't always keen on enforcing their rules: "The puppets had to have two electrical plugs put into each puppet that needed to 'talk' in a scene in order for the lips to move. An electrician suddenly realised this

8. Alan Shubrook quotes on the unions from his book 21st Century FX (2007)

and started making a fuss about Judith Shutt and myself putting the plugs in as, 'It was the job of an electrician.' When we told him how many times we had to plug and unplug – which meant him climbing up and down the puppet bridge every time – he thought better of it, not being an 'overly energetic' person! It would have slowed down the proceedings considerably."

A.P. Films was in overdrive in 1965: pairs of half-hour episodes and then, later, hour-long episodes were being filmed simultaneously. Meanwhile, filler material was being generated and shot to bring the existing 25-minute instalments up to the required 50. Alan Pattillo, in his role of script editor, was largely responsible for seeing that suitable additional material was being written for the half-hour shows. The task was a gargantuan one, especially in addition to his other roles as a script-writer and director, and so newcomer Tony Barwick was brought in to write supplementary material, albeit uncredited. It wouldn't be long before Tony became one of the company's most important contributors.

It was not always an easy task to try and shoe-horn an extra 25 minutes' worth of material into an existing story, and generally it is straightforward to be able to identify episodes which were originally half-hour through the appearance of scenes that fail to move the story along. The writers attempted to make their new material fit in seamlessly, using the opportunity to expand on character development, or add a new exciting dimension into the plot (the oil rig fire at the start of *Terror in New York City*). However, sometimes the end result merely came in the form of a failed rescue attempt, carried out before putting in the call to International Rescue (*Trapped in the Sky* and *Pit of Peril*).

Shooting schedules were revised and eventually each hour-long episode was allocated four weeks' production, with a pair of episodes going before the cameras simultaneously. The four directors, stalwarts David Elliott, Alan Pattillo and Desmond Saunders, alongside newly promoted editor, David Lane (replacing John Kelly who departed after *Stingray*), were supposed to operate on a one-month-on, one-month-off schedule, meaning while two directors were shooting, the other two were planning their next episode. However, in practice this did not work out as there was such a vast amount of material to shoot.

The special effects stages were in similar chaos. In order to ease the burden on the overworked Derek Meddings, Brian Johnson was offered the chance to become head of the newly-formed Second Special Effects unit. Brian, who enthusiastically accepted, says, "I was keen to show that our stuff on the Second Unit was as good as the stuff Derek was shooting on the main unit." Eventually, as the

Opposite, top left: Where's the Firefly when you need it? Flames roar on the effects stage. Right: Betty Coleman dressing a puppet. Below, left: Judith Shutt gives Brains a coat of paint. Right: Lip-synch playback in the foreground during filming on *Security Hazard*.

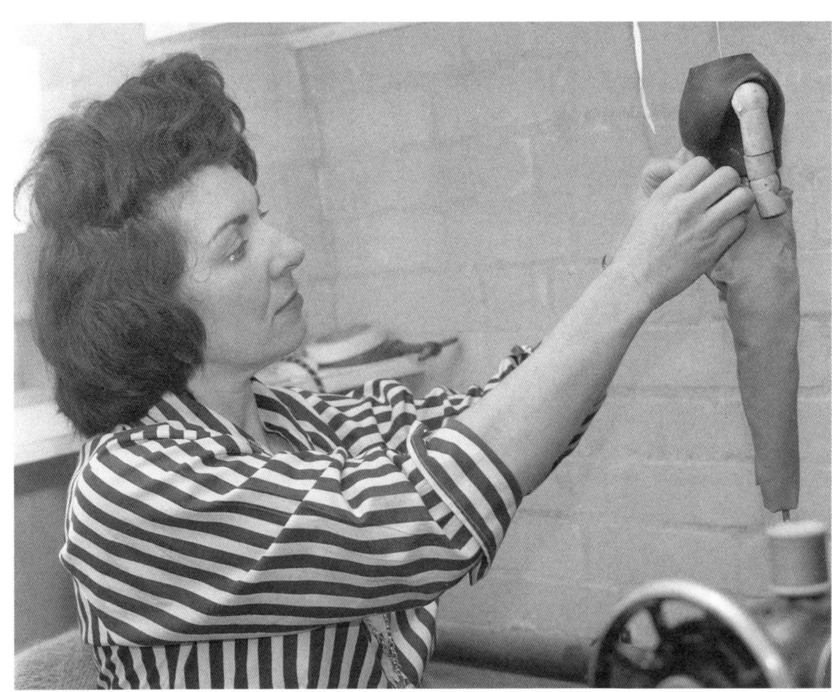

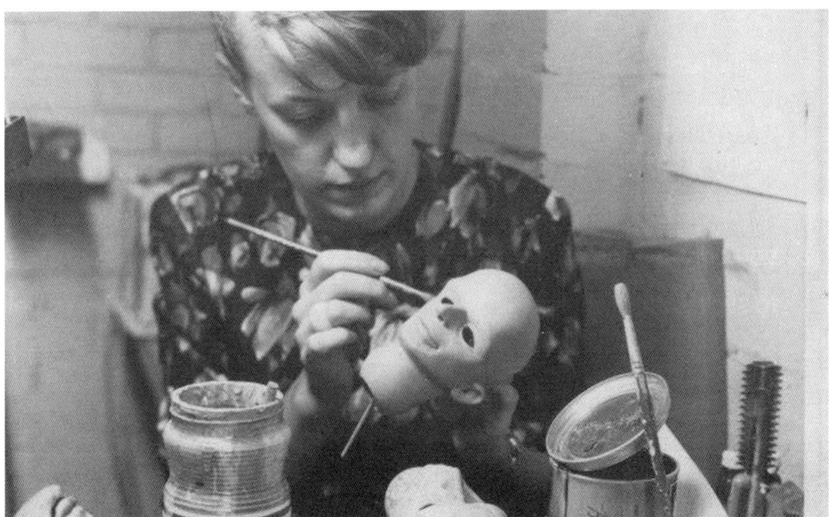

workload increased further at the studio, a third unit was formed to deal exclusively with flying shots, under the control of Peter Wragg, who, as an ex-dancer, was known for being exceptionally adept at 'flying' the models. Unlike the puppeteers, who had a securely constructed bridge to work from, the model-operators balanced precariously on the edge of planks (to allow the models increased manoeuvrability) often blinded by the smoke from rockets jets. Health and Safety was clearly not a priority in the 1960s!

Second unit effects Director Ian Scoones remembers: "None of us liked getting up under the lights, the Brutes, because the temperature rose to more than 120 degrees. So hot, but we needed those lights for the high-speed photography. We had this plank, like a scaffold plank, with a rope around it, and you would hang off this rope, holding the model which was bloody heavy, made of fibreglass – Thunderbird 2 being 3' 6" – with rockets in it which were detonated by current running down the metal puppet wires, all on a cruciform which you held right over the set, balancing with one leg in the air. None of us likes to do it because nobody gets the credit for all of it as you only see the model on the set, not the guy holding it. So we used to stick Wraggy up there. 'Oily Wragg' as we used to call him. He'd get so hot that the sweat would be coming off him. 'Stop sweating, Peter!' we'd say, as these little drops would be coming down into the sand."[9]

---

9. Interview by Rob Hammond for *Auton* magazine (1995)

The production line was a slow one, as David Elliott told *The Windsor, Slough and Eton Express* in 1965 when he said that he was happy if he got two minutes in the can each day.[10] Both the effects and the puppet units suffered from the same time-consuming problem: the wires. Alan Perry recalls: "Everyone was saying 'We've got to get rid of them. I seemed to be quite good at toning them down with anti-flare, and puffing powder paint on them, to make them blend in with the background." However, despite valiant efforts, many wires still managed to escape into the final films. Christine Glanville says: "The girls used to spend over half an hour on each shot getting rid of these wires, looking through the camera, puffing a bit more (paint) here, anti-flare there, and I mean it's very depressing when somebody will say to us, 'Of course the wires showed.'" Desmond Saunders describes the daily nightmare: "The time one spent getting everybody and everything ready for the moment when the camera was going to be switched on to make a take. There would be three or four puppeteers all holding this weight, waiting for the moment when you were going to turn over (the camera). There are strings that have to be dusted and got rid of because they would glisten in front of the camera. There might be somebody that has to do something at a particular moment. Everybody's got to be ready. After all this time when we've been waiting, rehearsing, lighting, getting the right lens and doing all these things, everything is ready and so you say, 'OK, turn over. Action!', and a string breaks! Or the puppet's gone wrong, or the eyes have gone up in the air, or the arm has come off. Every day was like that and when you've got to make a certain number of shots in that day, it just makes everything very tense."

Over on the special effects stages, the atmosphere could be equally stressful. In 1965, Special Effects Director, Derek Meddings, concurred with the puppeteers when asked what his biggest problems were: "Anything that flies, because we always have to lose the wires against clouds and blue skies."

A snapped wire in the effects department could have dire consequences, resulting in many models crash diving to the floor and sustaining serious damage. Increasingly elaborate sequences involving explosives, which now included the use of bags of petrol, and magnesium strips, also added to the chaos. Mike Trim remembers how busy the repair shop was during this period, and recalls one particularly serious incident: "One of the problems that we had when we were flying models was that quite often we were doing landing shots – like with Thunderbird 2 say for argument's sake. And in the bottom of TB2 there were four tubes set into the balsa wood body, and these were to take what was known as the Schermuly charge, which was just like a little rocket charge which would provide all the smoke as the craft came in to land. The only problem with these was,

10. Interview conducted during filming of *The Duchess Assignment*.

Opposite, left: "I'll take the strain" – Shaun Whittacker-Cook and technicans filming *End of the Road*. Right: John Blundall creates a character.

while the craft was in the air, the charge could actually pour the smoke downwards towards the set. But the closer you got to the set the smoke and the flame would have a tendency to start going upwards as it bounced off the set and all the models in those days were sprayed with cellulose paint, which is highly flammable. So it was not unknown for some of the flame to just touch the cellulose and for the cellulose to ignite. And then you would have a problem. If the shot was over then people would rush in with fire extinguishers and try to douse it before it got too bad. I do remember one occasion where one of the assistants walked into the model shop just before lunch with TB2 cradled in his arms and said with great understatement, 'We've had a bit of an accident.' And when he turned it around, the side that was towards him had completely burned. It was charred to a crisp. And so my friend and I spent the entire lunch hour taking green plasticine, which was fortunately not too different from the Thunderbird 2 green, and remolding the side. Then I very crudely painted 'TB2' on the side of the plasticine. It weighed an absolute ton when it went out of the workshop and when they redid the shot, we didn't see any of the side that we created so we really could have just left it charred. But that's the film business for you, isn't it really?"

Despite the daily dramas, David Elliott has fond memories of shooting some of those episodes: "There was a castle in one episode (*30 Minutes After Noon*) and the set had three sides, all with torches mounted. I told Alan Perry that I wanted a track around all three sides of this tiny puppet set. 'You're bloody joking!' he said. I was, but didn't let on. So, he rehearsed the moves. Then I said, 'Light the torches'. I'll never forget Alan, on the dolly, operating, with his backside in the air wobbling about every time it got burnt by a torch!"

Practical jokes were not uncommon in those days, and one of these is a testament to the lighting genius of John Read. David recalls: "Whatever the set was, John Read always managed to light it. So I said to Alan, 'Right, put the camera down the barrel of that cannon.' John came along and we told him what we wanted him to do, and blow me he actually did it!

"We were busy, but always found time for a practical joke. When we were shooting the London Underground set for the bank episode (*Vault of Death*), the Camera Operator, John Foley, said, 'What we need is a dead ticket inspector!' We spent an hour searching for this bloody puppet skeleton that had been made for another film (*The Uninvited)*, but couldn't find it anywhere. Eventually we gave up, which was a pity, as I'd loved to have seen Gerry's face at the next morning's rushes!"

However, sometimes, the boot was on the other foot, as Elliott recalls, laughing. "I had a Jaguar at the time, and frequently I'd come out and find a bloody great pretend scratch that the effects boys had put on there. One time I came out, and there were these fake bullet holes right across the windscreen! So, you can imagine what I thought the time that Una Scott (Gerry Anderson's secretary) came in and told

Opposite: Lady P poses with a *Zoom* lolly. (Her Ladyship would later switch allegiance to *Fab*, 'the ice lolly especially for girls'.)

ZOOM
Lyons Maid
CREAM
Lyons Maid
6d

me that a lorry load of ingots had been dropped on my car. 'Yeah, yeah,' I thought, as I went out there. Except, it was true! There was a bloke in reception who drove the lorry who was ever so apologetic!"

One film assigned to Elliott was *30 Minutes After Noon*. However, Elliott found himself lacking inspiration: "I'd started this film and didn't know what to do with it. It was a Friday when we started shooting and I went to the pictures that night and saw a film with Michael Caine in, *The Ipcress File*. The director used all the old fashioned shots – looking through a lampshade, etc. On Monday morning, Paddy (Seale – lighting cameraman) came in and said, 'I saw a film this weekend,' and I said, 'So did I!' 'Was it *The Ipcress File*?' 'Yep. Right, that's what I want to do.'" The result was certainly interesting. However, the impact of the quirky visuals is heavily diluted by the fact that the entire opening of the episode is filmed as normal.

Thunderbirds featured a lot of striking ideas and imagery, and its array of catastrophes was mirrored in the 1970s by a string of 'disaster movies' such as *The Towering Inferno*. The world of the future is a dangerous one; a place where even man's greatest achievements can still go horrifically wrong. With hindsight, we see that the world envisaged is not too far from the one we live in today, where supersonic airliners fall out of the sky, nuclear power stations explode, and New York skyscrapers collapse into dust. Alan Fennell's aptly named *Terror in New York City* was inspired by news of a Japanese department store which was being relocated to a new site, but the operation was deliberately carried out at a snail's pace to enable its customers to continue shopping uninterrupted. Fennell swapped a department store for the Empire State Building and, in his version, poor construction work leads to the eventual collapse of the famous skyscraper.

The award for the most unusual episode should without doubt go to Alan Pattillo's story *Attack of the Alligators!*, based on H.G. Wells' *Food of the Gods and How it Came to Earth*. The plot concerns a phial of Theramine, a chemical capable of enlarging the size of animals, carelessly washed down a sink and out into the Ambro River in South America, where it comes into contact with three alligators which then grow into leviathans.

The filming of the story was easily the most complex and ambitious shoot the A.P. Films' crew had ever undertaken. Early on, it was decided that the giant alligators would be played in the film by dwarf crocodiles, which were specially brought into the studio by a handler. With the marionettes being so diminutive in stature, even these small crocodiles (which could still grow to the fearsome size of five feet!) would give the appearance of being gigantic.

"We worked closely with Derek Meddings on that film," says puppet-unit camera operator Alan Perry. "He came on to the puppet stage and we had a tank for the 'alligators'." Derek discussed the episode during a radio interview in 1993: "It was the one episode that gave us so much trouble. We had to work night and day and we were using real crocodiles which they put on to miniature sets. We had a lot of fun, but it was a lot of heartache trying to get these things to do what you wanted them to do."

Whilst it was unlikely that the crew thought that task would be a 'walk in the park', it seems that none of them had anticipated how difficult the process would be, and that the unpredictable creatures would take no direction at all. "We warmed the tank up, because if you put them in cold water they just go to sleep," says Alan Perry. However, even if they weren't asleep, the recalcitrant reptiles managed to give a convincing impression of having nodded off by remaining totally motionless. In the end, it was decided to give the creatures minor electric shocks to motivate them; a decision that greatly divided the studio both then and now. "There was no ill-treatment whatsoever. They were taken back at the end of the shoot. There was no harm done to those animals at all," says Alan Perry, adamantly. Desmond Saunders disagrees: "It was terrible. So many of them died from pneumonia. I think at the beginning that they were being looked after, but they were left in the water overnight… In the end it took much longer than it was ever intended to keep them there and some of them died. It was scandalous. It was one of the great episodes. Nevertheless there was a price to be paid for it." Director David Elliott had completed shooting on his final episode for the first series when *Attack of the Alligators!* went before the cameras, and so has no definite opinion on the way the creatures were treated, but remembers the following incident: "There was one crocodile in particular that was massive, it was about five feet long. Anyway,

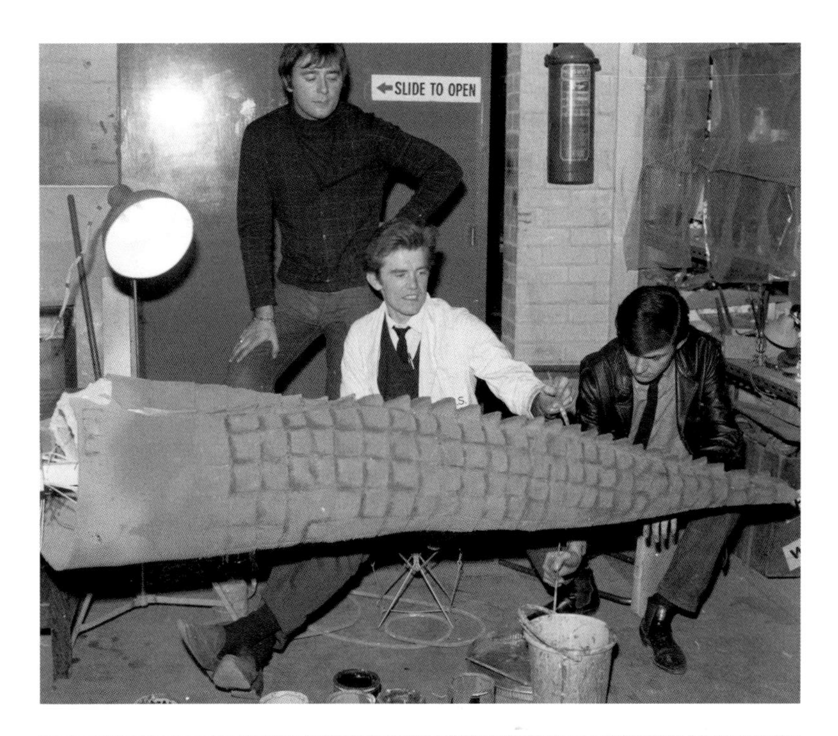

Right: "Relax? With three giant alligators knocking the house down?" Work in progress on *Thunderbirds*' most unusual episode.

they gave this thing an electric shock and it jolted so suddenly that it dislocated one of its legs."

The whole issue was highly contentious, and certain members of the crew refused to be involved. This disharmony led to the RSPCA being notified. Gerry Anderson tells the story: "We were shooting and I was in my office and I got a call from the receptionist to say that the RSPCA are here and they want to see you. They said we were ill-treating the 'alligators'. I could see my name in the *News of the World* immediately, so I said, 'Bring him straight through,' because I didn't want him to think that we were preparing anything. So he came in and he was polite enough. I said, 'Look, let me take you straight onto the stage. I've had no time to warn them that you're coming and you see for yourself what we're doing.' So, we went onto the stage and the RSPCA inspector said to Derek Meddings, 'What are you doing with the alligators?' Derek said, 'We're having a great deal of difficulty because we put them down on the side of the water and they're just frozen. They don't blink. They don't move. It's almost like they're cast in brass or stone.' So he (RSPCA inspector) said, 'How do you make them move?' Derek said 'Well… we give them an electric shock.' So he said, 'Well, now. That's interesting… Oh! Is that Parker over there!?' Derek said, 'Yes.' He said, 'And that's Lady Penelope.' I said, 'That's right.' 'Do you make *Thunderbirds* here!?' 'Yes.' 'Oh,' he said, 'that's my favourite programme![11] What's the chance of looking around the studios?' We said, 'Fine!' and took him around the studio. When he came back he was absolutely full of it and he said to Derek, 'So you've giving them an electric shock. What voltage are you using?' Derek said, 'Well, we're being very careful. We're only giving them 12 volts.' He said, '12 volts!? 12 volts!? These animals have got very, very thick skin. Try turning it up to 60!' So, we were all friends and when he left he said, 'I've got two weeks holiday coming up. Could I come and work here and take care of the alligators?' I said, 'Yes' and that was that."

Electric shocks weren't the only things used to keep the crocodiles in line, as Derek Meddings recalled on radio in 1993: "We used to sometimes put a little noose around them and pull them through the water because, like all animals, when you wanted them to do something they wouldn't do it. We did have one large alligator which was something like five foot. I remember having it in the tank and I had to pull it towards the camera. […] We had it through a loop so that all you saw was the alligator coming towards you and the rope was concealed under the water. I stopped to regain my breath from tugging this thing through the water. And then I said to the crew, 'OK, let's go for another take,' and I pulled the rope and there was nothing on the end. This thing had come free in the water. I'm sure it's exaggerated but the crew reckon I leapt out leaving my boots in the water!"

Despite the reptiles' extremely vicious appearance, only one member of the crew got seriously hurt. Lady Penelope

---

11. *Attack of the Alligators!* was shot in around October / November 1965. So, the series would have been fairly new to the public when the inspector visited, having only begun on TV on September 30th (and later, in October, in certain regions).

Lady P shortly before her amputation.

was brought onto the set for a photo-shoot with the 'alligators' (even though she doesn't actually appear in the episode) when one of them took a fancy to her and bit her leg off, leaving crew members frantically trying to remove the disconnected limb from the creature! The children were left unaware of the heroine's major surgery, but any fears they may have had about the enormous creatures would have been dispelled at the end of the episode, when Tin-Tin presents Alan with "a special kind of pygmy alligator." The final shot shows one of the miniature reptiles running around in a full (not puppet) sized bath, thus giving the game away!

Attack of the Alligators! was directed by David Lane, much to the annoyance of Alan Pattillo who, as the writer, had wanted to direct. The episode overran its allocated month's filming. David Lane recalls: "They had a closing date for the studio and I was shooting the alligator episode. That was the last episode to be shot (in 1965). Gerry said to me, "I don't care what you've shot, we are closing the studio on Friday. So wherever you are, that's it. End of story. We did a forty-eight hour shoot. You had two editors. One would go home and the other one would come in. We were constantly editing and I'm going back to Derek on the stage and saying, 'I really need a shot here.' I think Derek went three days, non-stop, just shooting."

Because of their prevalence throughout the story, both in the effects shots and the puppet shots, there was an unusually high amount of collaboration between the two units, who usually kept themselves relatively separate. The puppeteers tended to be rather 'arty', whereas the equally talented special effects unit inclined more towards laddish antics. "There was *huge* rivalry between the special effects and puppet units!" says Brian Johnson. Model maker Alan Shubrook affectionately remembers the two units: "The lads in the special effects team used to do puppet walks when passing the puppet stages on the way to the rushes!"

"I think probably the people that worked on special effects would have to admit they were probably louder, dirtier and noisier in all sorts of ways, whereas the puppet people always seemed quite quiet. They always sat there at their desks and they whittled and they carved and they moulded and they seemed a slightly sort of saner, quieter bunch," says Mike Trim. "We were called into a meeting once and told not to be rude about the puppeteers!" says Effects Director Shaun Whittacker-Cook.

Despite different approaches, the atmosphere between the two units was extremely friendly, although news that special effects would be visiting the puppet stage remained unwelcome. Derek Meddings explains about loading guns with explosives: "Nine times out of ten the gun would explode because it was too small. You'd pack a few grains of black powder into it with an igniter. The puppet couldn't really hold the gun perfectly still. So when the gun went off, usually the gun went up in the air or shot backwards and sometimes a little bit of damage was done to the puppet." However, David Elliott recalls the perils of not calling in the team from special effects: "It was a Friday and I wanted to blow a lock off some gates and I asked special effects to do it. The message came back that they were too busy. Grenville Nott, who was a real crash-bang-wallop merchant, was the set dresser. He used to pick up a six foot flat (sheet of board from a set) swoosh it around and knock all the puppets off their strings. Gren said, 'When I was in the Army I did some demolition. I can blow that up.' Alan Perry went, 'Oh my god!' So, Alan starts putting barricades around the camera. It was getting late on Friday and was almost time to finish. 'Right, turn over... Fire!' Nothing happens. Gren goes over and tinkers. Again, 'Turn over... Fire!' Nothing happened. This kept going until eventually six o'clock arrived and we went home. So Monday morning comes and Alan Perry is on top of the barricade, chatting away. 'Turn over.' Alan very casually just switches the camera on. There was this enormous explosion with bits of metal flying everywhere! The lock disintegrated and Alan Perry fell off the camera. Marvellous!"

The crew were not the only people in danger from explosives. In a now infamous story, Lew Grade brought a number of high-level executives to view his miniature empire. A demonstration of a scene using explosives was staged, and at the appropriate moment, Derek Meddings cried out, "Action!" As the landscape detonated, the shock-waves disturbed a sheet of plaster board lodged in the rafters and as the smoke cleared, Lew,

Miniature set of the monorail from *Brink of Disaster*.

NEWS OF THE WORLD
EXCLUSIVE
IAN SMITH in a remarkable interview ...
SHE WILL ALWAYS BE OUR QUEEN
Doddy's Here!
THE BOBBY SMITH STORY
Make a luxury housecoat
Pools firm sued for a million
Pirates fight for radio fort
L.B.J. is on his feet
AND NOW—LORD EXPORT
AGENTS
WARWICK

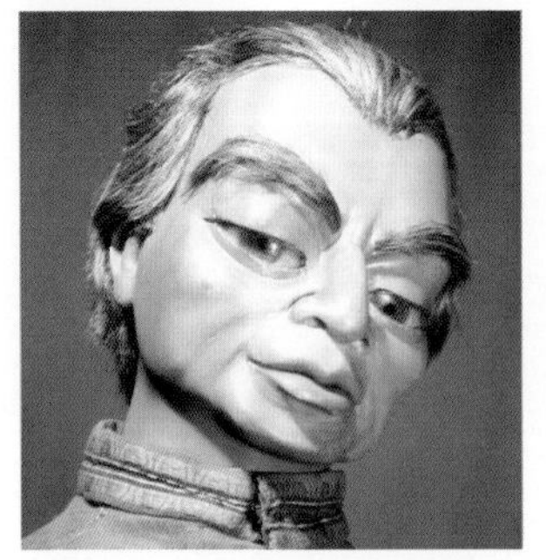

puffing on his cigar, and the other executives with their immaculate suits, were covered head-to-toe in white dust. Fortunately, the matter was met with much laughter. Whether the incident was an accident or an elaborate practical joke remains unresolved to this day.

Attack of the Alligators! exemplifies the vision and daring of Alan Pattillo. Due to his three-way role in the series as script editor, script writer and director, not to mention the input he would have had as an accomplished film editor, it would be fair to say that a lot of the on-screen result was heavily influenced by Pattillo. Alan in particular favoured Lady Penelope and gave the character her first major storyline in *The Perils of Penelope*, an episode based on Pearl White's movie series *The Perils of Pauline*. "I always tried to get the puppets to do something a bit different. For instance in an episode called *The Cham-Cham* I had Lady Penelope do a slow foxtrot." "Alan Pattillo was the rare animal who understood Lady Penelope," says Sylvia. "He wrote some of the best episodes for me. *The Cham-Cham* when I got to sing in my Marlene Dietrich voice – lovely. What I call 'Pearl White' adventures. He was very, very good for Penelope's stuff."

In *The Cham-Cham*, Lady Penelope poses as a singer, Wanda Lamour, at a hotel in the Alps, to uncover the truth behind The Cass Carnaby Five, a band that seem to be involved in the destruction of military aircraft. *The Cham-Cham* is a glorious example of *Thunderbirds* at its best, combining all the elements that made the show so popular: the characters, the adventure, the rescues and, of course, the humour which, as always in *Thunderbirds*, was carefully pitched for two audiences: firstly the adults ("I think I might take Cook out for a punt," says Parker gleefully) and secondly the children (Parker doing a 'Mary Poppins' floating down to earth with only an umbrella). "They were family shows," says Gerry Anderson. "We had scenes or lines of dialogue that were a little risqué at that time, so that they could be enjoyed by an adult watching but go over the head of the little ones watching."

By the time *The Cham-Cham* was made, in the final few weeks of shooting on *Thunderbirds*' first series, walking a puppet in full shot had been virtually abandoned. Walking the puppets convincingly had always been a problem and it was decided that in order to obtain any sort of walking shot, nothing below the waist should be shown. An out-of-shot floor puppeteer would then move the marionette from below the waist to give the impression of movement. Even this type of shot was a compromise as the resulting 'bobbing' motion wasn't terribly convincing either. However, *The Cham-Cham* flies in the face of what puppets can and can't do, and features some terrific protracted sequences of characters dancing and skiing.

The price to pay for such a strenuous production period was the need to produce one 'budget' episode. Before embarking

Opposite, above: Two rare images of Lady Penelope. Below: Some of the series' well-loved characters. And the Hood.

on filming *The Cham-Cham*, the epic season finale, the team resorted to an old favourite: the flashback episode in which tales of previous adventures could be told. Alan Pattillo undertook scripting duties once again and produced *Security Hazard,*[12] a charming tale of a little boy named Chip, who stows away in Thunderbird 2. Once discovered back at the island, crisis talks ensue, whilst one by one each of the brothers tells Chip about their daring adventures. In a cunning act of compression, four stories that began life as half-hour adventures were boiled down to around ten minutes each, leaving the crew with minimal new material to shoot.

During work on these final adventures, the earliest episodes were completing the post-production process and being made ready for their unveiling to the public. In late 1964, musical maestro, Barry Gray, produced his most striking title theme yet: the *Thunderbirds March* was a hit with the crew and would go on to become one of the most instantly recognisable television theme tunes. Barry did not find the task of producing a closing theme so easy. As with *Fireball XL5* and *Stingray*, Gray aimed to write a tuneful, romantic song for the end credits. In August 1965 he recorded *Flying High* with Gary Miller, which he wasn't entirely happy with and re-recorded again twice during September. Upon hearing the theme tune, Gerry Anderson decided that the song was a mismatch for the series and instructed that an instrumental version of the main 'march' be used instead. A mere two weeks before first episode was broadcast, the closing song was replaced with the instrumental tune that had been used to accompany Thunderbird 1's launch in *Trapped in the Sky*, before being subsequently replaced by a specially composed arrangement which was used from *Pit of Peril* onwards. Another alteration to the titles from week two was the addition of The Mole to the closing sequence of images. The only major special effects shot for either sequence was at the end of the opening titles, when a refinery of some kind is obliterated by a series of explosions and a conflagration results. David Elliott remembers with amusement the colourful language heard from the special effects unit on the day of filming: "I was shooting one of my episodes one day, while the boys from special effects were shooting the titles. Suddenly there was a cry of, 'Christ! The roof's on fire!' after a lump of petrol jelly had ignited and shot into the roof! This was followed by Derek shouting, 'If any of you turn that fucking camera off I'll fucking kill you!'"

In the weeks running up to the premiere the series was well-promoted. Stills photographer Doug Luke was charged with capturing the all-important publicity pictures. He remembers his job with great fondness: "I had access to all the puppet and model effects stages. I also had my own little studio too, about 30-40 feet

---

12. Although episode listings place *Security Hazard* as being the last episode in production of the first series of 26 episodes, an old black and white newsreel from the time shows that this clearly isn't the case. In the film we see a number of sequences being shot for various episodes, including *Security Hazard*, *Cry Wolf*, *The Man From MI.5* and *City of Fire*. We can hear the dialogue tracks being played in the studio for *Security Hazard* and in the puppet workshop we see that Olsen from *The Cham-Cham* is being sculpted. Therefore, *Security Hazard* cannot have been the last episode of the first series produced. It is also worth nothing that the special effects unit were considerably behind the puppet unit, shooting effects for episodes that had long-since completed on the puppet stages.

square. I could do portraits and whatever was needed. I also had a lighting electrician and a puppeteer to assist me. I'd tell the puppeteer to move the head or arm as I looked through the camera. It was easier to have an assistant, as it saved me going back and forth to change position of the puppets. They could do it for me as I directed them. We would pinch a puppet and cut the strings off for photos. I remember I used to annoy the puppeteers, as I'd put gaffer tape around the arms to keep them posed and cut off the head strings for a photo. They then went potty having to re-string them up again. It took them ages to do because the strings had to go through the wig, to the eyes and solenoid for the mouth. I did that a few times and they would always groan, 'Arrghh, he's done it again!'

"Eventually, Gerry said I could have my own Penelope and Parker puppets to myself. So I had a couple of puppets made just for me, for use on stills only. Penelope had different heads, one normal, one smiling, one serious and so on. So I had to have the right head for the right photograph. I used a gauze filter for the female puppets, made out of a pair of black nylons (chuckles). Like a person, every puppet had a good or bad side, and I had to choose a good angle for them when doing portraits."

"5! 4! 3! 2! 1! Thunderbirds Are GO!" came the rallying cry to viewers on Thursday September 30th 1965 at 7pm.[13]; a thunderclap,

Above: Work hard, party hard. An APF fancy dress party in Cookham. Sylvia (left) and Gerry (far right).
Below: Reg Hill poses beside his Mercedes-Benz.

---

13. The World premiere of the series was on ATV Midlands. As with *Supercar*, *Fireball XL5* and *Stingray*, different franchise areas would screen the show at different times. In certain cases, the films were split into two (or in one case three!) segments for screening as separate episodes.

then crash into a montage of fast cutting images showing us what's in store for this episode, before a series of photographs introducing us to the vehicles and craft. Following the destruction of the refinery and the cinematic captions 'FILMED IN VIDECOLOR AND SUPERMARIONATION', the first episode got underway.

CAPE KENNEDY WAS NEVER LIKE THIS, cried *The Daily Mirror*. *SLOUGH'S THUNDERBIRDS HAVE ROCKETED TO THE TOP*, reported *The Windsor, Slough and Eton Express* when they visited APF in November 1965 during the filming of *The Duchess Assignment*. The article continues abrasively:

> *Who killed Noddy, first of the TV puppets? The children. And what did you expect? They had had enough of green grass, red-roofed houses, philanthropic Big Ears and jolly corpulent policeman like Plod. Give us action, they cried, attacking the breakfast table array of sauce bottles and salt and pepper pots with spaceships from the cornflakes box. So along came A.P. Studios on the Slough Trading Estate, and dosed them up with all the imaginable terrors and wonders of science fiction.*

The children also wrote in by the sackload:

> *September 30 (8.5 pm)*
>
> *Dear Gerry and Sylvia,*
>
> *After watching Thunderbirds for the very first time just over five minutes ago, I just can't wait to express my feelings. The most up-to-date, fantastic, supernatural (Supermarionation), suspense, unbelievable…*
>
> *No more words to explain it. Well, I would just like to say (on behalf of all my friends) thanks, thanks a million for all the hard but worth while work you (and the APF team) have put into this weekly one-hour-26-series-programme! […]*
>
> *Yours faithfully,*
>
> *Michael Stott*

Lew Grade's intuition about the success of the series was spot on and before it had even hit television screens he decided to put *Thunderbirds* where he felt it belonged: on the *BIG* screen ...

THUNDERBIRDS ARE GO

•1966•

NOW, ON THE BIG SCREEN! 7

Thunderbirds Are Go and Thunderbirds: Series Two

Such was the confidence in *Thunderbirds* that news of a feature film was released to the press before a single television episode had been screened. A budget reported to have been between £250,000 and £300,000, according to various media pundits, was set and in the last quarter of 1965, Gerry and Sylvia Anderson retired to Portugal to write the film.

With the real-life Space Race to get to the moon at its peak, the Andersons decided to reflect this in their screenplay, *Thunderbirds Are Go*. In their 21st century setting, man has long since reached the moon (indeed, Jeff Tracy himself was one of the first men to go there). Narrowly avoiding incineration, man has even made it to the Sun. The next stepping-stone into the universe is Mars. Aboard the giant spacecraft Zero X, a crew of five men become the first humans to venture into this unexplored territory. As always though, the technology of the future is prone to sabotage or malfunction, and when the call goes out for help, Thunderbirds Are Go!

In anticipation of the vast scale of the operation required to complete both a movie and a second run of television episodes, A.P. Films acquired two neighbouring factory units. Both units were expensively decked out to fulfil the new requirements, and by the end of January 1966, the transformation was complete.[1]

Despite being no more than the equivalent of two and a bit episodes, in terms of length, the preparation and filming time needed to bring *Thunderbirds* to the big screen was a long one, and approximately six months was scheduled to complete the film.

"*Thunderbirds Are Go* was just an enormous amount more problems," says Director David Lane. "Everything had to be that much better." "We were going on the big screen," says cameraman Alan Perry. "We're blowing up here. The sets had to be immaculate, the props had to be that little bit better. These are puppets but they're going to be 30-foot tall by the time they get into a cinema. Attention to detail quadrupled really."

Before beginning pre-production, some test footage of the

---

1. Child visitor to the studios, Peter Thornley, sadly remembers that the expansion meant that children were no longer as welcome at the studio as they had been in the past, thanks mainly to the appointment of ultra-officious security guards.

puppets and models was shot and taken to be screened at a local cinema in Slough. Whilst the results were far from disappointing, it was realised that a lot more effort and care would have to be put into a feature film as any faults that would normally be hidden on a small TV screen would be glaringly apparent when magnified at the cinema. Special effects designer Mike Trim recalls: "When we shot *Thunderbirds Are Go* we did a test of a model of Thunderbird 1 and we took it down to the local cinema and projected it on a 40ft screen. We sat there and there was the original model of Thunderbird 1 which had the wings that opened. The top half of the fuselage could be lifted up to get at the mechanism to wind it up. Suddenly there we were with this Thunderbird 1 that was now about 20-30ft long on the screen and we could see straight through the gap between the two halves of model. And Derek said, 'We're gonna have to go bigger.' And we did, we went bigger."

Copies of the feature script *Thunderbirds Are Go* were circulated to the studio at around the same time that further scripts for a second television series of *Thunderbirds* were distributed. Although the studio effectively divided into two units to handle the separate projects, the reality was that most of the crew had some involvement with both shoots and needed to shuttle between the stages.

Before either unit could commence filming, a vast construction operation was instigated: the regular puppets, models and sets were rebuilt or refurbished, in addition to a new set of sculpts required for the guest characters in the movie, which were moulded in fibreglass, rather than plasticine (with the exception of very minor puppets which were built in the traditional way). The art department had an easier time than the puppeteers and the model makers, as their new versions of the sets did not try to slavishly match the originals. Unfortunately for the puppeteers and model makers, they had no choice but to attempt to recreate what had gone before, as viewers could make the credible assumption that interiors of buildings and aircraft have been refitted, but it's less plausible that the cast have all opted for cosmetic surgery and altered their faces!

The puppet makers achieved a relatively high degree of success in matching the original characters, although it is possible to tell the new ones from the old (especially Scott and Virgil). In 1966, however, it is highly unlikely that anyone noticed and a comment such as this could only be raised in the modern world of DVDs and videos, where instant replay and comparison is possible. However, one problem clearly visible on screen (for those watching in colour) was that a new delivery of flexible hands to the studio had been crafted in the wrong colour. Unable to get a new order of hands delivered soon enough, the television stage marionettes were forced to carry on with hands much darker than their faces.

For the model makers, the task of creating new models based on the original ones was familiar and not very popular. Thunderbird Two proved to be particularly problematic. In *21st Century Visions*, Derek explains: "The design did have its drawbacks.

Above, left: David Lane and Alan on the set of the refitted Thunderbird 3.

Right: "There's something wrong with your face..." Studio reference shot of Dr. Grant... or is it the Hood?

Without its pod in place, Thunderbird 2's main body was very weak. [...] As a result, we were constantly sending the model back to the workshop for repairs, and eventually the damage was so great that it had to be replaced. Unfortunately, its replacement was not only the wrong colour, it was a completely different shape. Although we had several more built in different scales, I never felt our model-makers managed to recapture the look of the original." If one major criticism could be levelled at the special effects department, then it would be their apparent indifference to getting the various scale models of certain craft to match, which often resulted in appalling lack of continuity between shots. For instance, Thunderbird 1 would often be seen descending with landing wheels and 'Thunderbird 1' markings on its underside, only for it to land on skids a second later, with markings on its topside! Scale itself also seemed to be a matter of little concern, as can be seen prominently in *Operation Crash-Dive*, where Thunderbird 2 is shown to be roughly the same size as the Fireflash, only for it to inexplicably shrink to the size of one of the Fireflash's wings once in flight. It is curious that a team which dedicated itself to producing top-end special effects should have had such a cavalier attitude towards an important part of the trade: namely maintaining continuity, which is rightly seen as an essential part of the film-making process. Fortunately, *Thunderbirds Are Go* largely eliminated these problems.

Gerry Anderson asked Alan Pattillo to direct the feature. Alan declined. He felt that he had worked with the puppets long enough and, like some of the other long-serving crew, felt that the company lacked the family atmosphere it once had. He relinquished his role at A.P. Films, although he contributed two further scripts to the series. The role of Director was then given to 24-year-old David Lane, who had directed several of the TV episodes. "It came out of the blue," says David. "I remember having meetings with Gerry and Sylvia and then Gerry called me in one day and he said, 'Well, you're going to direct the feature film.'" David's promotion is the best example of how the Andersons were happy to promote from within the company. To this day, many crew remember gratefully how they were given opportunities that few, if any, other film studios offered at that time.

Among David's first tasks was to decide, with the help and input of his colleagues, what format the film would be shot on. Panavision was considered the glamorous format as it was widely used for Hollywood movies, but its anamorphic lenses proved unsuitable for the A.P. Films crew as David Lane explains: "There was a complication with the actual shooting from the point of view that it had to be in Scope. Panavision was no good at all because the Panavision lenses – and Panavision period – wasn´t good enough to shoot the high-speed photography that Derek required. So, we had to use prime lenses. Also, with Panavision the lenses just weren´t fast enough and they didn´t have enough variety. They didn´t do 80mm lenses and that sort of thing that Derek used all the time to make all the sets look big and wide. So it was decided we would shoot it in Techniscope, and Techniscope is 16mm equivalent because it´s half of the 35mm frame one way, and the 35mm frame the other way."

A.P. Films invested a lot of money in overhauling the equipment during pre-production. The trusty Arriflex cameras that, with repairs and updated models, served the company's puppet requirements since the beginning, were taken out of service and replaced with Mitchells, which had been used on the effects stages for some time.[2] The reason for this changeover was to pave the way for an overhaul of one of the company's greatest inventions.

Despite tweaks over the previous seven years, the electronic viewfinder system, that allowed people all over the studio to see what the cameras were shooting, was a fairly rudimentary system that still involved a Pye video camera looking through the film camera viewfinder. After several discussions with Prowest Electronics, in nearby Maidenhead, John Read worked with the company to develop a new, superior system. The technicians at Prowest went to Germany in 1965 to look at a video-assist unit in use over there, and upon their return, set to developing a system of their own. That system was Add-A-Vision, developed especially for A.P. Films.

What made Add-A-Vision such a great leap forward was that the electronics boffins at Prowest had managed to develop

Director David Lane behind one of the huge Mitchell cameras.

2. Arriflex cameras were occasionally used later on, as can be seen in certain behind the scenes shots. However, they were incompatible with Add-A-Vision.

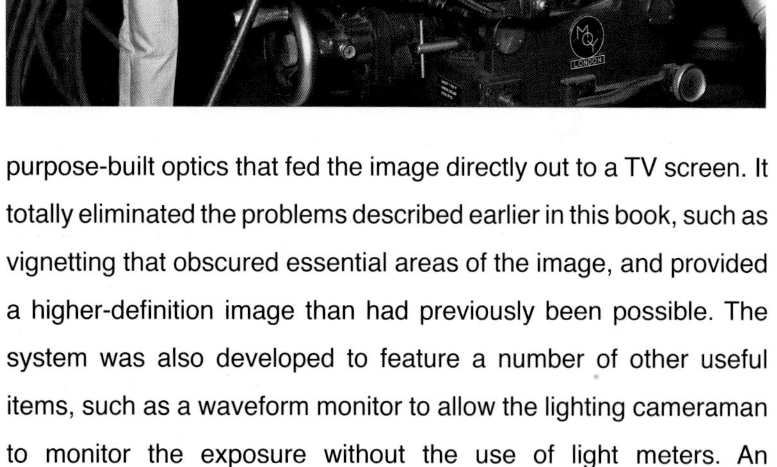

purpose-built optics that fed the image directly out to a TV screen. It totally eliminated the problems described earlier in this book, such as vignetting that obscured essential areas of the image, and provided a higher-definition image than had previously been possible. The system was also developed to feature a number of other useful items, such as a waveform monitor to allow the lighting cameraman to monitor the exposure without the use of light meters. An extremely crude form of video playback was also possible, allowing the Director instantaneous playback of rushes. *The Daily Cinema* ran a short piece about the system in late 1966: *Gerry Anderson, whose A.P. Films has been filming the first "Thunderbirds" feature for Christmas release, says he found the new Livingstone Add-A-Vision system an enormous help in "creating my space age image. We viewed rushes 30 seconds after completion of the shots and it*

Above, left: Brains makes some adjustments to the Add-a-Vision system. Right: Alan Perry and Ian Spurrier with the system in action.

speeded up our working time enormously."

In 1968 the BBC's *Tomorrow's World* paid a visit to the sets of *Joe 90* and *Doppelgänger* to investigate this new innovative system. Add-A-Vision was described thus:

> *The system works like this: a prism fitted behind the zoom lens of a standard film camera reflects the image through a right-angle into a television camera attached to the side. The television image is then fed into a control room and then onto as many television screens as necessary. [...] The television picture can also be recorded on videotape. This means if the director or cameraman want to check something that's already been filmed they can play it back immediately. Before, if there was any doubt in their minds, they'd automatically have shot the scene again just to be sure.*

Having been unpopular with the crew that worked on the early shows, the booth (a prominent feature of the Ipswich Road studios) was not in use at the Stirling Road studios by the time shooting commenced on *Stingray* in 1963. The equipment it had housed, such as the lip-sync unit and director's monitor, had been relocated to the studio floor. For the second series of *Thunderbirds* it was decided to reinstate the booth in order to give the new, very expensive viewfinder installation a home. It was mounted about four feet off the floor for a clear view across the stage and, unlike its predecessor, was constructed almost entirely of glass. Within it there was room for two people to move about without becoming hopelessly entangled, and here the director and lip-sync editor could work in reasonable comfort. By this time, however, the drawbacks of directing from such an isolated platform had been realised, and directors spent relatively little time in there. A large monitor dominated the room with various other bits of equipment connected to the Add-A-Vision viewfinder, as well as a microphone to communicate with the floor personnel, and a tape-deck for the lip-sync unit.

A source of consternation for the Directors of Photography was that the new system only worked with zoom lenses. Indeed, just weeks before the new system was introduced, John Read discussed the problem of depth-of-focus and the use of zoom lenses: "Our biggest sets are no more than 10ft deep, and with standard lenses, this brings depth-of-focus troubles, so the only solution is to stop down and illuminate at a higher level. At the present state of the art, zoom lenses are no material help, although we are continually experimenting with zooms."[3]

David Lane elaborates on the problems with Add-A-Vision: "It was fine for the crystal clear (video) picture, but it wasn't so clever for the film. The zoom lens wasn't right for all the shooting. You couldn't get in close enough. It was a big lump. A huge thing. Whereas if you use an Arriflex, or something like that, with a 40mm lens on, you could get the camera right into the set. But Gerry

---

3. John Read speaking in *Television Mail* (December 1965)

insisted on using it and he had it looped through to his office so he could watch the filming. It was really good for him and it looked good in his office.

"Alan Perry was the camera operator and I said to him, 'We can't get the shots with this, Alan. What are we doing?' So what we did is we used an Arriflex with the correct lens on it and then we'd use the zoom lens system for the benefit of Gerry. We'd line up a shot as close as we could get to the one we were actually shooting. Then if he came on the stage we'd quickly put the camera down and shoot with the other one. I think he knew..."

Despite the inherent issues, the system was revolutionary. "It was brilliant," says Lane. "Brilliant idea, but it was more suited to live-action I think than to puppet work." Add-A-Vision was later successfully sold to Elstree Studios, where it went on to be used in productions such as *The Avengers*. Its roots, though, were firmly grounded in the pioneering work of APF.

As David Lane set about preparing and storyboarding the epic adventure ahead of him, Sylvia Anderson was settling into her role as Producer. David's task was to get the whole thing in the can, while Sylvia focused on the style of the film, overseeing all elements of construction from costumes to sets, a job she carried out with aplomb, visualising some stunning items for Lane's team to capture on celluloid. However, she had great difficulty in getting the crew to follow her ideas to the letter, as she recounts of the Conference Centre set which appears near the beginning of the film: "For *Thunderbirds Are Go* we had more money and a bigger budget so I knew I could go to town a bit on the sets. So I described the Martian Exploration Committee in this big committee room and it was a very important scene. I thought, I want to do something different here. I specified it should be just two colours – tangerine and black. And the only colour relief would be the uniforms of this Martian Exploration committee in a pale blue. I was convinced it was going to work. So I explained it to Bob Bell and to Keith (Wilson). I think Keith got it and Bob said, 'Yes, I see.' It was a beautiful set. The only thing was every time I walked on set someone had put another colour on. And I would say, 'No! I just want it two colours!' In the end I got my way and it really was a stunning scene." With so many people working in concert on the multifarious elements of the film, attribution is impossible, and no one can state definitively who created what. The whole process must be regarded as very much a team effort. It does seem very clear, however, that one thing Sylvia had in spades was style, and she lavished it on the productions wherever she could, either through her own ideas or through her supervision of others, whether it be Lady Penelope's wardrobe, or the striking Swinging Star set, where all the background elements, including the puppets (which were photographic blow-ups), are in black and white and all the foreground characters are in vivid colour.

Everything about *Thunderbirds Are Go* is visibly a technological progression from the TV programmes; the whole production looks more polished. The visual effects became more

Shaun Whittacker-Cook prepares to launch Thunderbird 2.

2
1

2
1

impressive. When the new special effects warehouse was taken over, the increased floor space allowed for bigger landscape scenes, and Derek Meddings arranged for pits to be built into the floor, to allow the camera lens to get down to floor level for access to a greater number of dynamic angles. The puppetry also developed. It suddenly became markedly more restrained. Whereas previously, exaggerated hand movements were used to emphasise that a character was speaking, now movement was more subtle and realistic, less puppet-like. Full-length walking shots had also seen their finale. Meticulous attention was paid to the strings in order to eliminate them. "The biggest problem of all was, 'Well, we don't want to see any strings,'" says David Lane. "I said, 'But you're going to be putting this on a 70ft sheet, how can we avoid the strings?' He (Gerry) said, 'Well I don't want to see any.' The extra attention paid dividends and but a handful of visible wires escape into the final production. "That's why some of the compositions are a bit tight on the head," continues David. "We could paint a certain number out and puff them out, but you couldn't lose them completely. We tried all sorts of things. The problem is, if you get over-technical you can lose sight of what you're really doing and the fact it's supposed to be entertainment."

The set design had also matured. It was no longer acceptable just to stick a few toothpaste lids on a panel and hope it would look like futuristic instrumentation; all sets were now comparable with the slickest designs in live action. The presentation in all aspects was amazing, but the last vestiges of the cottage industry that had begun in a spooky mansion in Maidenhead were now gone: APF was in the major league with the big players now.

The star of *Thunderbirds Are Go* was, surprisingly, not the Tracy brothers or their amazing machines, but Zero X, the dark blue space vehicle, which in the film is destined to be the first manned vehicle to land on Mars. The craft is another great piece of design from Derek Meddings, though cynics would suggest that the various detachable segments (wings and nosecone) had less to do with the storyline and more to do with potential toy manufacturing!

The interior of the craft had its origins firmly in reality, as David Lane explains: "When we were trying to design the interior of Zero X, Bob Bell was coming up with different ideas, and Gerry suggested we went down to Filton airport to actually see the building of Concorde. We went down and flew the simulator of Concorde and saw the flight deck, and the interior of Zero X was based on Concorde and the type of look at that particular time."

After a lengthy period of pre-production that had run through early 1966, the shoot was eventually ready to begin. The special effects building worked to produce shots for both the television and movie sides of the operation, whilst the puppet stage based in the original building, was entirely devoted to the film. A weekend was scheduled in Portugal for filming back projection plates to be used throughout the movie, for the climax in which Zero X is minutes

Opposite: "This is Assembly Control..." Technicians get to grips with Zero X.

Above, L-R: "There will be a great disaster!" Effects shot for *Lord Parker's 'Oliday* / Manhandling TB3 / Cliff Jnr. gets a leg-up.

Below, left: Salvaging the burnt-out Zero X. Right: Technicians prepare to catch TB2 on take-off.

Above, left: "I don't want to see any strings." Losing the wires on Thunderbird 3. Right: Derek Meddings' design for the Crablogger.

Below, left: Building the launching ramp for Thunderbird 2. Right: Lighting the TB2 hangar and runway.

away from crashing, and for an earlier sequence which required an aerial shot spinning towards Tracy Island.

The shoot turned out to be largely fruitless. The 'spinning' shot was done by contra-rotating a helicopter and descending rapidly whilst under-cranking the camera. This resulted in nothing more than a very shaky shot with the water behaving in an extremely odd manner. The bulk of the aerial shots suffered the same fate with far too much judder to be of use. Less than a handful of these made it into the final film. The discarded shots were replaced with special effects created with the usual ingenuity, and less heartache.

More successful, in the realms of outdoor filming, were the shots done by the special effects unit. It was decided that a greater degree of realism could be brought to some effects by filming selected shots outside, against the real sky, in natural lighting. A gantry at nearby Slough power station was requisitioned and used as a lofty launching point from which to fly Zero X. The idea certainly paid off and resulted in some of the most realistic shots APF ever produced.

It was decided that no material from the television series would be reused (TV material was in full screen, not the required widescreen) and so all shots, including the oft-repeated sequences of the Thunderbird craft launching, were re-filmed.

As well as the staple ingredients of the successful APF recipe, such as explosions and amazing futuristic aircraft that are featured heavily, *Thunderbirds Are Go* also boasts what is perhaps the most bizarre sequence ever produced by APF in its entire history (which is quite a feat considering they used to produce films about toys that lived in fruit...). This was a dream sequence involving Cliff Richard and the Shadows. Sylvia explains: "We got to know Cliff and the Shadows when we had a holiday place in Portugal and we approached them and asked, 'Would you agree to write the music for our first feature film? And we'd like puppet duplicates of you.' It worked beautifully."

In the sequence, Alan returns to base in time to hear that Scott and Virgil are off for a night out with Penelope at a nightclub called The Swinging Star. Unable to go out with Tin-Tin in case an emergency strikes, a disgruntled Alan heads off to bed…

A plume of pink clouds (well, dry ice) fills the screen and, standing on a platform in space, we see Alan dressed in a colourful top-hat and tail-coat, awaiting his chariot in the form of a flying FAB 1. Parker at the wheel takes Alan and Penelope to the Swinging Star nightclub in space. There they watch Cliff Richard Jnr (they couldn't always accurately predict the future!) and The Shadows perform *Shooting Star*. This in turn leads to an even more surreal sequence involving Cliff stationed at the wheel of FAB 1 and an oversized guitar being launched from a rocket gantry. "I think it's in the best tradition of all the Hollywood movies," says Sylvia Anderson. "We kind of recreated a Busby Berkeley sequence." More importantly though, as Sylvia notes, "Of course it created a lot of publicity for the film."

Opposite: Hank Marvin meets his alter ego while, right, the puppet Cliff is prepared for lift-off.

These unusual sequences illustrated the versatility of the studios in all departments, and it was a new challenge to the puppeteers to have to re-create exact likenesses, rather than casually finding starting points in elements of other people's facial characteristics. Photographs of the five stars were taken for the sculptors to work to: John Brown created Cliff, whilst Terry Curtis crafted Hank Marvin, Christine Glanville produced Brian Bennett, Mary Turner was responsible for John Rostill, and newcomer Tim Cooksey modelled Bruce Welch. Cliff and The Shadows visited the Slough studios and posed on set with their diminutive look-alikes. "I was never really sure whether I looked like my puppet or it looked like me!" says Cliff Richard. "I thought Hank Marvin's puppet was really good, but then he always looked like a puppet anyway!"[4]

With such a large guest cast, the repertory of regular voices was expanded. Captain Paul Travers, commander of the Zero X, was played by Paul Maxwell, former voice of Steve Zodiac in *Fireball XL5*. The remaining characters were played by newcomers Alexander Davion (Space Captain Greg Martin), Charles Tingwell (Dr Tony Grant), Neil McCallum (Dr Ray Pierce) and Bob Monkhouse (Space Navigator Brad Newman). In 1998, Bob Monkhouse recalled his casting: "I had gone to the studios to seek Gerry's permission to

4. *Sci-Fi on Strings* broadcast on BBC Radio 5 (1999)

CRABLOGGER

have Stingray jump out of Des O'Connor's bathwater between his knees in a sketch I had written, and, after he had agreed in a rather preoccupied way, he explained that the actor he had hired to play one or two roles in the film, the late Alfred Marks, had pulled out due to a disagreement about the fee. Then he looked at me shrewdly and said, 'How much would you charge for the job?' I said, 'Gerry, I'd do it for nothing.' And that was the first time I ever heard the phrase, 'The price is right.'"[5]

Alfred Marks wasn't the only problem the Andersons had amongst the voice cast: David Holliday, the voice of Virgil Tracy, had returned to his native America following the completion of the first set of 26 episodes. Consequently, the search was on to find a suitably similar replacement. That person was Canadian actor, Jeremy Wilkin.

The studios had never been so busy. As one side of the studio ventured into the new territory of a Supermarionation feature film, the other side continued to feed the vast monster that was the television side of the operation, with two episodes constantly in simultaneous production. The first episodes up were *Atlantic Inferno*, directed by Desmond Saunders, and *Path of Destruction* directed by David Elliott.

Atlantic Inferno is an excellent start to the show's second series, showcasing some particularly fine special effects work in the form of giant fire-jets in the middle of the Atlantic. The finale to the episode featured the total destruction of the Seascape drilling rig. In the tradition of the "Ready when you are, Mr De Mille" gag, a technician misheard his cue when the shooting of this sequence was about to commence. Unfortunately, owing to a technical hitch, the cue he actually heard was the director shouting "Cut" as one of the cameras had malfunctioned; the entire model disintegrated in front of them without a single frame having been exposed.

The special effects unit had become world-class by this time; an assessment of its merit endorsed by a call to the studios from movie director Stanley Kubrick in 1965. Both Gerry and Sylvia relate identical stories of how Kubrick called one (or more likely both of them) and asked to see them for lunch. He was told that would be lovely, but if he wanted the team to produce effects for him (for his upcoming film *2001: A Space Odyssey*), then that would be out of the question. Apparently he immediately lost interest, said he didn't want lunch and put the phone down.

However, Kubrick wasn't to be put off so easily and approached several members of the effects team with a view to them leaving A.P. Films to work for him. He succeeded with second-unit special effects supervisor Brian Johnson, who had wanted to make the transition into movies for some time, and had become increasingly disillusioned with APF. Although Brian enjoyed the

5. *Sci-Fi on Strings* broadcast on BBC Radio 5 (1999)

Opposite: Work in progress on the final six episodes of *Thunderbirds*.

work, he was not entirely comfortable with the management, as he explains: "Reg Hill told me that he didn't have any faith in my abilities and that I had only got the job because I was friends with Derek." Brian was given his own effects unit, which created visuals indistinguishable from Derek's team, but despite his promotion failed to secure a pay rise to £40 per week. Brian says: "I was still being paid the same amount of money for directing as I had been as an assistant. I was directing, I was doing all the flying of the models, holding on for grim death, perched precariously on a plank above the set. It was about 140 degrees up there with all the lights. I thought I should have been paid extra, but I was told that there wasn't enough money." So when Brian was offered his break with Kubrick, he had no hesitation in accepting.

The news was not greeted with smiles by the board. "We were working until 9, 10 or 11pm. So I said that I was going to hand in my notice and Derek said, 'I'm not going to stop you.' I gave a month's notice and nothing was said at first. Then, one day, someone came down and said could I go and speak to Gerry Anderson." Brian was summoned to a meeting with Gerry, Sylvia, Reg Hill, John Read, Norman Foster and Ken Holt and was offered £100 a week by Gerry, a staggering increase over the £10 extra he'd been looking for. Brian ultimately declined. "Gerry said, 'We've spoken to Lew Grade and he's said we can pay you more.' I didn't understand it, as they'd hardly need to go to Lew Grade for the sort of money I was asking for. I said that I was leaving and Gerry said, 'Is that your final decision?' I said, 'Yes,' and he said, 'Well f**k you!' and slammed his cigar into an ashtray with sparks flying." Brian worked out his notice, and left A.P. Films before the first series of *Thunderbirds* had been completed, to join Stanley Kubrick's team. "I was in Kubrick's office at the time that Gerry called him and said that I wasn't any good," says Brian. Despite the call, Johnson remained on *2001*, and went on to a highly successful career as one of Britain's leading effects men; so good in fact, less than ten years later Gerry and Sylvia asked him to work as the Special Effects Supervisor on the live-action series *Space: 1999*. In his biography, Gerry reflects on the matter saying: "He (Brian) had every right to do what he was going to do, but I was absolutely furious because I knew he would take with him many of the secret processes that we were using."[6]

Brian was not the only casualty at this time. In 1966, after nearly a decade at APF, David Elliott had also grown disillusioned. Halfway through filming *Path of Destruction*, Elliott finally decided to leave the company. He dutifully completed shooting his episode before going to see Reg Hill to hand in his resignation. For an hour Reg tried to persuade David to stay, but to no avail. "I'd become disenchanted with the way that Gerry Anderson was treating me," says David. "We'd been extremely close in the 50s; I remember

---

6. *What Made Thunderbirds Go* by Simon Archer and Marcus Hearn (2002)

Opposite: "Mind the gap, Alan..."

Lighting the Shadows for the Swinging Star sequence.

helping Gerry decorate his house when he was with Betty. We were great friends and in the early days we all pulled together. Gerry had some great ideas and could be really nice. I remember after *Twizzle* that he bought me a car, a Ford Popular, which then cost about £350, and I was really pleased with it.

"We worked long hours in those days when there was no money. Gerry always said that when the money came in and the company became successful we'd be looked after. But, after he got successful, when Lew bought the company, he changed. He lost interest in our sound effects company and our friendship fell apart. During *Thunderbirds* I received a cheque for the nearly ten years of overtime via John Read: £400. Gerry always got someone else to do his dirty work. I was on £70 a week and had just had my kitchen done for £600, so it was a pittance for a decade of overtime.

"It wasn't any one event; it was just Anderson's attitude towards me. We were no longer friends and eventually I got fed up and decided to leave. I finished my film, went to see Reg, worked out my week's notice and left."

A phone call from John Read asking David to return also proved fruitless. It was time to get out. Elliott returned to film-editing, beginning a long association with the BBC. Despite leaving under pressure, David looks back with great affection on his time at APF: "They were great days," he says, "Great days." With his departure, the studios lost one of their greatest collaborators, who had been there with them from the beginning.

In any close-knit environment people are going to have arguments and disagreements. That's a fundamental part of human nature. However, many of Anderson's former colleagues draw attention to the fact that if you fell out with him the rift was unlikely to be healed. Gerry's youngest son, Jamie, talks about his father non-judgementally. "He would sometimes get very offended if someone was seen to be defecting to another side. He fell out with a few people along the way because they would go and work for another studio or might suggest something contrary to what he was thinking about, whether that be something creative, or a design, or a story, or anything like that. So sometimes he would fall out with people unnecessarily and burn bridges, which was a shame because that never really helps." Gerry's first wife, Betty, comments: "He felt if you had an argument that you ended the marriage. He couldn't see that if you had an argument, you had an argument. You might resolve it or you might agree that you'll do something. He was so frightened that he wasn't going to be happy, because he hadn't had any experience of his parents being happy." Jamie continues: "He was a product of his upbringing and had some really tough times. Those things not only caused these 'ructions' I guess you'd call them, later in life, but those are also the things that made him so successful."

Another of the stalwarts from the early days, Alan Pattillo, still had a presence on the series. Despite relinquishing his full time employment with APF, he was the scriptwriter of two of the second series episodes: *Alias Mr. Hackenbacker* and the Christmas special *Give or Take a Million*.

Alias Mr. Hackenbacker revolves around Brains designing a new aircraft, and has the dubious distinction of introducing the myth that Brains' real name is Hiram K Hackenbacker. It's not, as can clearly be seen from the fact that even Brains doesn't respond to it! It was merely an alias (as the title clearly suggests). As usual with a Pattillo-penned show, the episode is a showcase for the improved characterisation and the talents of the costume department, who get to show off their 1960s couture credentials in a story that involves a *lot* of fashion.

Although key contributors departed, their shoes were quickly filled. In the case of Pattillo, his successor was Tony Barwick, who previously worked, uncredited, on much of the filler material for the early half-hour episodes. With that mammoth task put to bed, Barwick devised his own scripts, *Lord Parker's 'Oliday* and *Ricochet*, the latter featuring a pirate radio space station inspired by the famous pirate radio ship, Radio Caroline.

At the beginning of 1966, A.P. Films was flying high. Merchandise sales were at a record high, leading the company to acquire its own toy firm.[7] A movie was in preparation for a Christmas release, and a second television series was about to go into production, for launch in the autumn to an eager audience that was still devouring the first.

7. J Rosenthal (Toys) Ltd was acquired by A.P. Films in 1965.

One day Lew called and asked Gerry to go and see him. "I went to see Lew and I thought he was going to say, 'Let's go on with *Thunderbirds*,'" says Gerry. "But he said, 'I want a new show.'"

The news was a bombshell for Gerry and sent shockwaves through A.P. Films. At the height of their success with their biggest property ever, Lew brought the axe down on *Thunderbirds*, one of the most expensive television series in the world. Despite a promising opening to proceedings, Lew failed to secure a sale in America for the show.[8] Head of Merchandising Keith Shackleton reflects on this: "*Fireball* was unique and special and the first of our shows to have a Network show in America. It shouldn't have been the last. Lew Grade in fact turned down a seven million dollar deal for NBC to screen *Thunderbirds*. We couldn't believe this when we heard it on the wire. He said, 'I want ten million dollars.' He should have taken the seven."

Without that crucial sale, *Thunderbirds* was dead. Millions of pounds worth of toys, a forthcoming movie and a recent major expansion of the studios was not enough to withstand the lack of American support. Gerry says, "I appealed and he said, 'Gerry, it's easier for me to sell a new show.'" Salt was rubbed into the wound, when in May, *Thunderbirds* was awarded a silver medal, for

8. Lew admitted to *The Daily Telegraph* in February 1966 that he had, at that time, failed to secure a sale, citing difficulties agreeing a suitable timeslot for the show. The precise details are lost to history. An article in *The Times*, also in February, reported that ATV had ordered another six episodes of *Thunderbirds*, indicating that the final six episodes were made knowing that they were to be the last. In his cue sheets, Barry Gray refers to 'Thunderbirds – Series of Six'.

Outstanding Artistic Achievement, by the Royal Television Society, further illustrating its success.[9]

Even as filming wrapped on the final six episodes, there was still the excitement of a glittering premiere ahead for *Thunderbirds Are Go* on Monday 12 December 1966. Once shooting was complete, Len Walter began editing the picture, which was then scored by Barry Gray. In a 1979 interview, Gray recalled discussing the music with Gerry: "In the case of the film *Thunderbirds Are Go*, he said he wanted to get a real symphony orchestra sound. He said, 'What's the least amount of musicians you can have to get a really symphonic sound?' I said, 'Well you couldn't do it much under 70.' So he said, '70 you have then.'"[10] The score was recorded in six sessions over three days on October 9th, 10th and 11th at Anvil Studios.

Aside from overseeing the incidentals, Barry also took time to attend the filming of the closing titles, which featured the band of the Royal Marines, marching in formation, playing the *Thunderbirds March*. The whole thing was shot in a morning at the Royal Marines School of Music in Deal, and was conducted by Lt Col. Vivian Dunn. Director David Lane recalls: "The gentleman who was conducting would insist on being on the back of the cherry picker (crane on which the camera is mounted), but every time he started conducting, we started rocking with the camera, and the

9. Gerry was made an Honorary Fellow of the British Kinematograph Sound and Television Society later that year.

10. Barry Gray speaking to Ralph Titterton for *Viking Radio* (1979)

Bigger than Bond? The London premiere.

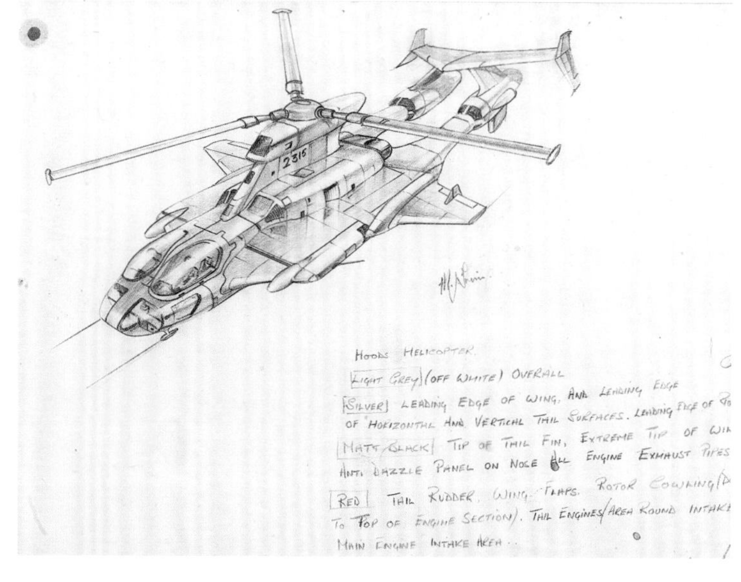
2316
HOODS HELICOPTER
LIGHT GREY (OFF WHITE) OVERALL
SILVER LEADING EDGE OF WING, AND LEADING EDGE
OF HORIZONTAL AND VERTICAL TAIL SURFACES. LEADING EDGE OF
MATT BLACK TIP OF TAIL FIN, EXTREME TIP OF
ANTI DAZZLE PANEL ON NOSE ALL ENGINE EXHAUST PIPES
RED TAIL RUDDER, WING FLAPS. ROTOR COWLING
TO TOP OF ENGINE SECTION). TAIL ENGINES/AREA ROUND INTAKE
MAIN ENGINE INTAKE AREA..

camera was beginning to rock more and more as he got more and more excited with the *Thunderbirds* music, until we thought we were going to come off the crane! I had to ask him if he would be good enough to do the conducting from the ground, rather than the crane."

Following all the optical work by the labs, and the addition of animation elements created by Studio Film Laboratories and Li Pearce of Pearce Studios (who had created some of the animations as far back as January 1966, well ahead of the main shoot), the film was then handed over to the skilled team of Dubbing Editors who, when furnished with the moving images of silent models and marionettes, created an entire soundtrack for the film, laying down every sound effect, piece of music and dialogue, to create a vibrant soundscape that brings the pictures to life. The film was then submitted to the British Board of Film Classification and received its 'U' certification (suitable for all audiences) meaning that it was ready for cinema release.

Shortly before the premiere, in early December 1966, it was finally decided to discard the old A.P. Films name. The title hadn't meant anything since Arthur Provis had departed nearly seven years previously, and judging by the official BBFC record for the film, it seems that the name 'Animated motion Pictures' had been shoehorned into the ill-fitting label. At the suggestion of Merchandising Executive Keith Shackleton the name was changed. "We were living in the future and Century 21 was a wonderful umbrella under which to set the future," he says. Thus, *Thunderbirds Are Go* was the first picture to feature the words: *A Gerry Anderson Century 21 Production*. From this point, all *Century 21 Productions* would begin with a distinctive animation of the logo travelling through a tunnel of concentric circles before being pierced with a dart, all accompanied by a distinctive, piercing cascade of violins before a cymbal crash.

This was the logo that opened the film on the night of December 12th 1966 at the London Pavillion in Piccadilly. Outside, in giant letters the words *THUNDERBIRDS ARE GO* twinkled, and the façade of the building was dominated by cut-outs of the Thunderbird craft. In the lobby, guests – both human and puppet – assembled amongst glittering showcases of the models used in the film. The Royal Marines played the *Thunderbirds March*, whilst Gerry and Sylvia met and mingled with the attendees, which included Cliff Richard and The Shadows, Lew Grade, Barry Gray and many other members of the cast and crew.

As the new Century 21 logo faded from the screen, a booming voice intoned commandingly, "THUNDERBIRDS ARE GO!" It cannot have failed to be an impressive sight as, on the big screen, the white lettering on a bold red background declared, "FILMED IN SUPERMARIONATION" before launching into the finest showcase of Century 21's talents.

"It was absolutely magic," says Sylvia Anderson. "It was a really exciting time," says David Lane. "You have to remember that we'd all

Opposite, top left: Flying the Zero X model. Right: Mike Trim sketch for the Hood's helicopter.

Below: Picking through the debris of Craigsville / Shooting the end credits for *Thunderbirds Are Go* at the Royal Marines School of Music.

come up from *Supercar*, and our own private showing down at Ipswich Road. But now we were at Leicester Square. We'd hit the big time boys! It was a glamorous time for such a small company."

Following the screening, Lew held out his keys to Gerry and said, "My villa in Portugal is yours any time you want it." Gerry Anderson recalls the enthusiastic reception the show got: "I thought it was a great picture and so did everybody else. I was sitting in the Hilton Hotel, where they'd made all the Thunderbird craft in ice, and I was with an executive from the American company that had co-produced it with Lew. He was swirling his scotch around in a glass and thinking, and he said, 'You know, Gerry, I can't make up my mind whether this is going to take as much money as *Bond*, or more.'" This comment echoed the response from the cinema manager a few hours previously: "As we left the cinema, we said to the manager, 'Good night, sleep well.' And he said, 'You're joking, I'll be up all night. They'll be queuing up at 5 o'clock in the morning to see this.'"

Kine Weekly agreed, stating in their review: *This colourful extension of Gerry Anderson's very popular television series is remarkably well done and cannot fail to have a wide success, especially in the holiday season.* ***Certain money maker.***

The following day, Gerry and Sylvia began their tour to promote the film. What began with euphoria, turned to gloom and perplexity, seemingly in the blink of an eye. The blockbuster success that had been predicted, indeed, taken for granted, didn't materialise. As Gerry says: "They didn't queue up. In fact the theatres were empty. The only thing we could think was that at that time the audience was not used to seeing a feature film version of a television show. So people would see *Thunderbirds* and think, 'We've seen it on television.'"[11]

Another problem for the film was competition in the form of numerous family films including *Batman* and *Born Free*, as well as a number of re-releases in certain theatres, including Disney's *Lady and the Tramp*.

The film received mixed reviews: The *Slough Observer* stated:

> *A heartening counter to America's* Batman, *this £300,000 production, shot in Slough and on location in Portugal in six months, is basically a Technicolor large-screen extension of this popular television series.*

The Times was rather more tepid:

> *It was a mistake when the animated science fiction dramas made by Gerry Anderson and his associates for television expanded from half an hour to an hour. The elementary plots and even more elementary characterisation possible with marionettes used realistically could just about fill 30 minutes, but beyond that the makers had to use more and more padding in the way of sheer process: launching and putting away rockets and other weapons, getting characters from one place to another.*

---

11. Although Gerry makes a valid point about a possible reason for why the film failed, it should be noted that *Thunderbirds* was not the first television show to transfer to the cinema. Indeed, Doctor Who had its *second* big screen film released in 1966, although, unlike *Thunderbirds*, it did not feature the same cast and was very different to the television series.

This is even more true of a 94-minute feature film: even very young children are likely to get very tired indeed of Lady Penelope and the Tracys long before they finally thwart all the attempts of evil humans and unpredictable nature to destroy the Mars-rocket Zero X and its wooden headed occupants.

Whilst *The Times*' criticisms are harsh, there is an element of truth in them. Despite no doubt being an impressive experience when released from the confines of a television set, the film misses the mark on a number of counts. A *lot* of time is devoted to set-pieces (such as the Zero X assembling) and the Tracy family and the Thunderbird craft appear very little in the film (it's 20 minutes until they turn up!). This must have been disappointing to the children that did persuade their parents to let them see it.

"The movies, well I don't know if I should say it. But they never worked as well as they did on the small screen. I think it got slightly lost," says actor David Graham. "At the time we thought we were doing a good job and we thought it was great. But, on reflection, I think it's difficult to move that type of show onto the big screen," says David Lane. "The fact was no one knew what something from television would take in the cinema," says Sylvia. "It wasn't the thing that really worked. We had Lew pushing up to United Artists how much it was going to take – and of course it didn't."

The idyllic land, painted by the press as Britain's answer to Disney, was crumbling. "It was just a terrible time because our marriage was breaking up," says Gerry. As 1966 drew to a close, the husband and wife team were feeling the pressure, and *Thunderbirds'* reign was over before it had really begun…

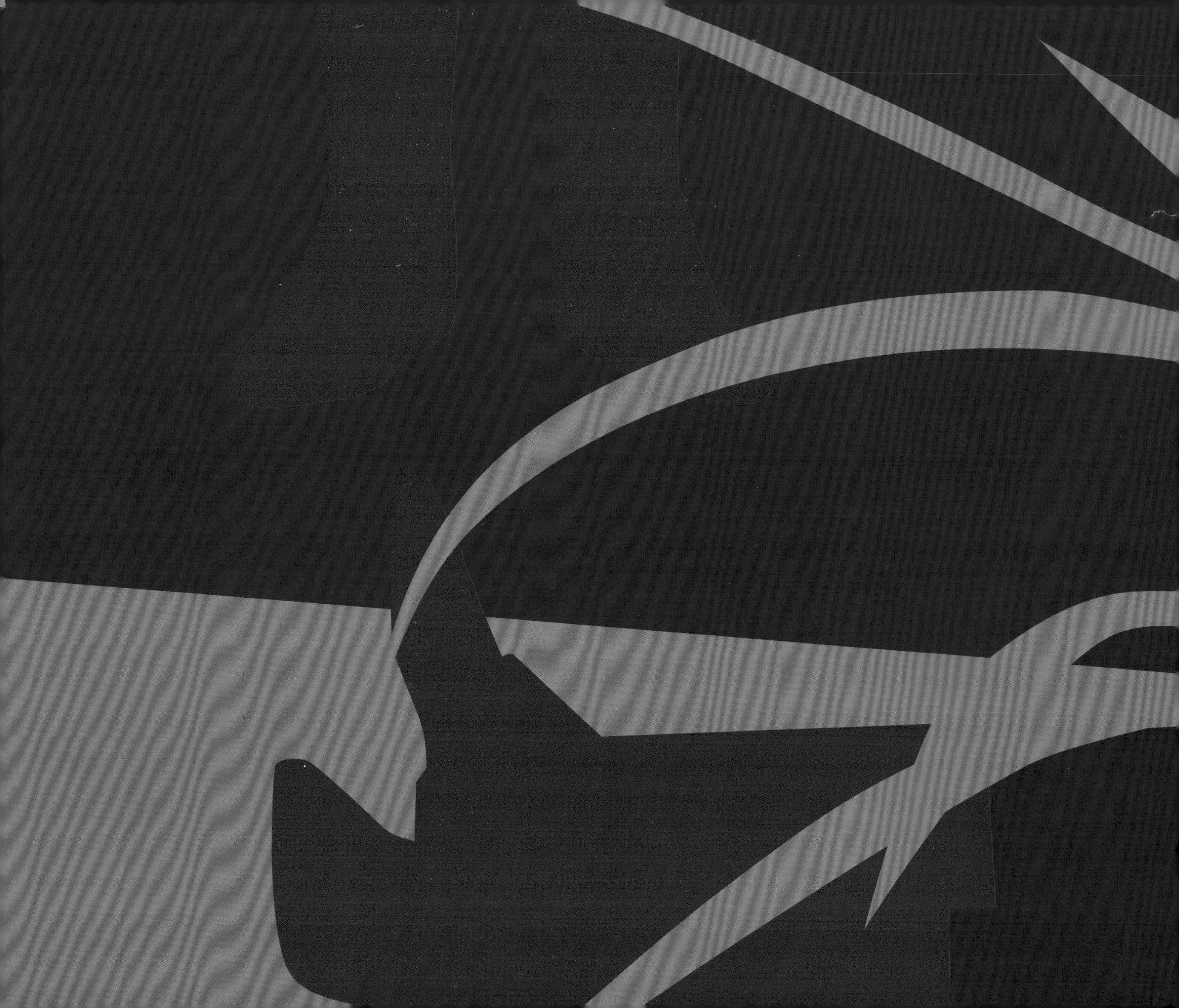

CAPTAIN SCARLET

AND THE

MYSTERONS

•1967•

SPECTRUM IS GREEN 8

Captain Scarlet and the Mysterons

Though Thunderbirds *is continuing beyond the original 26 episodes, there will be another, new, TV series. 'I can't tell you anything about it yet,' says Gerry Anderson; 'but I can say this: it will be bigger and better than anything we have ever done before.'* Those were the optimistic words of Gerry Anderson in 1965 when *Television Mail* asked what would be next. In retrospect, despite working in a place where explosions were happening daily, nothing could have prepared him for the bombshell that was to be detonated in 1966 with the termination of *Thunderbirds*. However, in late 1965, when it seemed that nothing could go wrong, Anderson was confident that the studios would go from strength to strength, and that if they could handle a movie and a TV series at the same time then there was no reason why they couldn't produce two different television shows simultaneously. As usual, Gerry went off to see Lew to outline his new idea:

"Let's get a big star in a long running series of, say, 52 episodes. We build and build the ratings, and every week the audience is on the edge of the seat, despite the fact they know the hero is never going to get killed. Then, about half way through the series… the hero dies! Then you bring in a new big star, which gives the series a new boost and lots of publicity and you prove that the star really can die."

"Are you mad?" replied Lew. "Kill off the lead? You need your head examining!"

Gerry took away his idea despondently, and developed a new idea – one where the leading character gets killed off in the *first* episode.

In August 1966, whilst post-production on *Thunderbirds Are Go* and the cancelled *Thunderbirds* television series continued, Gerry and Sylvia set pen to paper once again and, with a little input from Tony Barwick, devised the first script for their new TV series: *The Mysterons*. The show's title was subsequently expanded to become *Captain Scarlet and the Mysterons*, although the Mysterons themselves would struggle to maintain their headline billing, as people became inclined to truncate the title to simply *Captain Scarlet*.

It is the year 2068: we find the Martian Exploration Vehicle

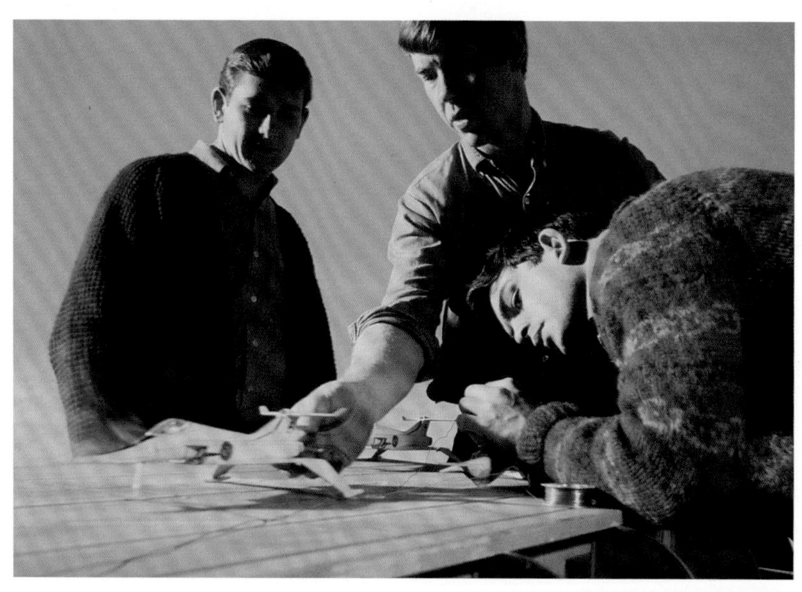

(MEV) from the Zero X spaceship trailing across the surface of Mars. "Those signals we monitored at Spectrum," says Captain Black, "they must have come from somewhere. Let's just take a look over that ridge and then we'll return to Earth." Beyond the ridge, the astonished four-man space crew find a giant, glowing city. Inside, the city pulsates. *"The first of the Earth space travellers have arrived,"* booms the raspy, deep voice. *"We must welcome them. Let us take a closer look."* A strange optical device rotates. Startled by the sudden attention, Captain Black orders his crew to open fire: the Martian city is obliterated. Before they have a chance to take samples, a blue, misty light falls upon the wreckage and the city is resurrected before them. The disembodied voice resonates: *"Earthmen. We are peaceful beings and you have tried to destroy us, but you cannot succeed. You and your people will pay for this act of aggression. This is the voice of the Mysterons. We know that you can hear us, Earthmen. Our retaliation will be slow, but nonetheless effective. It will mean the ultimate destruction of life on Earth. It will be useless for you to resist, for we have discovered the secret of reversing matter, as you have just witnessed. One of you will be under our control. You will be instrumental in avenging The Mysterons."*

Back on Earth, Captain Black cannot be located by Spectrum, the military organisation that operates from 40,000 feet above the Earth on a floating aircraft carrier, Cloudbase. Captains Brown and Scarlet are assigned by Colonel White, Commander-in-Chief of Spectrum, to look after the World President. Unexpectedly, their car swerves off the road and both men are killed instantly. Their dead bodies lie amongst the smouldering wreckage, before being dragged off into the foliage by... exact likenesses of themselves. Clearly the Mysterons' extraordinary powers are at work. While The Mysteron reconstruction of Captain Brown is eventually destroyed, the Captain Scarlet construct is released from the control of the unseen Martians when he falls 800ft from the futuristic car park, the London Car-Vu, after having kidnapped the World President. It is soon discovered that he has retained the powers of 'retrometabolism', which, as Doctor Fawn explains to him in *Winged Assassin*, means that a bullet will cause him to bleed, feel pain, "but after a few hours, even a fatal wound will heal completely." It is this Captain Scarlet, now virtually indestructible, that rejoins Spectrum in the epic fight against The Mysterons.

If *Thunderbirds* had been about saving lives, then *Captain Scarlet and the Mysterons* is the complete antithesis.

"*Captain Scarlet* really is a war film; a war between Earthmen and the Mysterons," says Gerry Anderson. "I didn't want to make the Earthmen aggressors," he continues, "Although, of course, I'm

Opposite, above: "Captain Brown – are you all right?" Before and after shots on the set of *The Mysterons*.

Below, left: Wiring up the flight deck of Cloudbase in preparation for an Angel launch.

Below right: Derek Meddings puts the finishing touches to Cloudbase.

afraid we are an aggressive people, and so the story was arranged so that the Mysterons were friendly aliens – they wanted to welcome the Earthmen and they trained their telescope onto the SPECTRUM craft. The people on board thought they were going to be attacked and opened fire – and so the war was triggered, really by accident, if you will."[1]

One element that was never dwelt upon, or indeed even mentioned again after the first episode, is that the protagonist we follow for the entire series is in fact, nothing more than a duplicate, a doppelgänger; the hero initially introduced to us is killed within two minutes of our first encounter with him. The exact nature of how Captain Scarlet, or indeed any other Mysteron reconstruction, is created is never revealed in the series. The original concept had been to make the duplicate Scarlet a mechanical man, in essence a sophisticated robot, as mentioned in the pilot script: The description for the opening titles reads:

MT1. *C.U. CAPTAIN SCARLET*

We are looking at him through a glass panel, on which is etched a printed circuit in silver and gold. The set-up symbolizes a mechanical man.

The notes for the closing titles confirm this conception of Scarlet: "*These will comprise still shots of Captain Scarlet in association with computers, printed circuits and electrodes, thus conveying the premise that Captain Scarlet is a mechanical man.*" By the time the first episode entered production, this idea had been abandoned, and it is later established that Mysteron reconstructions are identical to humans, except for being impervious to x-rays (they merely leave a silhouette), and can only be killed by high voltage electricity (although on occasion anything is lethal, as long as it's convenient for the script!).

Captain Scarlet and the Mysterons is an alarming departure from the traditional playgrounds of APF. "Captain Scarlet was a much colder, darker series," states Gerry Anderson. "With *Captain Scarlet* we were moving away from more of the family thing," admits Sylvia Anderson. The inaugural television episode, bearing the legend: *A Gerry Anderson Century 21 Television Production*, features: Captains Brown and Scarlet being killed in a car crash; a dead bleeding body being dragged into nearby foliage; Captain Brown physically exploding; and Captain Scarlet being shot and subsequently falling 800ft to the ground. Violent stuff!

For these darker, more realistic portrayals (no more gravity-defying descents using an umbrella, as in *Thunderbirds*) *Captain Scarlet* introduced a revolution in the Supermarionation process. For as long as he had been making puppet films, the one thing that tormented Gerry was that if he was unable to get live-action commissions, then he wanted to ensure that the puppets were as realistic as possible. However, there was always something wrong,

---

1. From the documentary *Captain Scarlet S.I.G.* (2001).

whether it was the way they walked, the way they talked, or that glistening wire that no amount of anti-flare would cure. Over time various ingenious devices were used to minimise these irritations. The one intractable problem though, was that no amount of ingenuity could by-pass the disproportionate scale of the heads. The size of the 'Super-marionettes' had been determined long ago, in the dim and distant days of *The Adventures of Twizzle*, based on the dimensions of Joy Laurey's own puppet creation, *Mr Turnip*. Once these dimensions had been decided, the stages, bridges and associated equipment were all manufactured to the appropriate relative size. When the lip-sync unit was introduced in 1958, the placement of the solenoid in the head dictated a minimum size for the puppet cranium. Because of the height of the bridge etc., it was not considered practical to scale the bodies up to compensate and so the puppets remained macrocephalic. Realising this deep-rooted concern, the puppet workshop finally managed to make Gerry's flight of fantasy come true: they produced the first correctly proportioned Supermarionation puppet.

"The change of the puppets was the biggest shock I ever had in my life," says David Lane. "Gerry asked me to go into his office and he said, 'Let's see what you think of this.' He had a miniature box. It was like the sort of wooden box you get port in. It was a very nice presentation case and I thought there was a bottle of drink in there. He lifted the lid up and there was this body lying in there. All perfect. Perfect size. Everything in proportion. It looked like a miniature dead body. He said, 'This is what we're going to do. We're going to make the next show with these scaled puppets. No more big heads.' I thought, 'Blimey!' I couldn't see any character in it at all."

In the early days, there had been much debate about the form the marionettes should take, and the style of performance to be expected from them. Some members of the studio (usually the puppet makers) felt quite strongly that puppets should look like puppets, and should specialise in what they do best: being and doing things that humans can't. In the beginning, despite the innovations that made these marionettes unique, they remained 'puppet like'. With *Fireball XL5* came a very subtle shift towards realism, and by the time *Thunderbirds* entered production, the main characters were definitely sculpted to echo real faces, and a miniature repertory of recognisable Hollywood stars was created. In 1965, during shooting of some of *Thunderbirds*' later episodes, Sylvia Anderson discussed the process of creating the faces in a filmed interview: "What we do is we take a composite face, in other words we take the eyes of someone, the nose of someone else, so that we can then produce the perfect face for the character that we've invented. We don't have to rely on the casting agency to provide us with an actor with the perfect voice, perfect face and acting abilities." The ability to create stars with "perfect faces" was frequently cited as an advantage by the husband and wife team (sometimes as if they felt the need to justify their continued association with puppets, rather than working in the more legitimate medium of live action) and Gerry made the same point, rather wistfully, in the same programme: "I would very much to like make films with live actors, but of course the problem is with live actors that you have to accept their faces as they are. I don't think it would be quite as possible to get the strong characters that we succeed in getting in our films and of course there would be many difficulties in creating the sort of situations we do at the moment with a live artist." Remarkably, it is something that a lot of personnel held opinions on, as *Supercar* writer Hugh Woodhouse comments: "Anderson's view was that *Supercar* should be so life-like that people would think they were live actors, which totally missed the point. Early Disney was always great – *Snow White* and so on. However, although they were fine with caricatures and with the animals, when it came to Prince Charming – no. You cannot caricature Prince Charming, whereas the Wicked Witch, etc., are all splendid."

"The weird characters were always popular with the public and the technicians," says *Supercar* puppeteer Roger Woodburn. "The heroes never had the sympathy." Sculptor John Blundall, who had created Parker, the last real caricature produced by the studio, was trenchant in his opposition to anything other than traditional puppetry approaches: "Gerry and Sylvia had this ridiculous idea that puppets should be like humans. Whereas, really, puppetry is about doing things that you cannot do with humans. The idea that you could copy faces out of *Spotlight* was stupid." Blundall felt so strongly about the direction the studio was taking, that he left A.P. Films during production of *Thunderbirds.*

Desmond Saunders also has a perspective on the appearance of the marionettes: "Gerry's idea was that we should be making these as normal as possible. He was constantly frustrated by the idea that these couldn't look like human people. We would all try different devices, like making them smoke, finding ways to put glasses on. Anything to get them to look like ordinary human beings. But they are not ordinary human beings! I was more in favour of keeping the big heads and making them more like puppets like on *Four Feather Falls*. There seemed to be a problem about enjoying puppetry. We were trying all the time to make these puppets like real people. I often wonder if it would have been better to make them *more* like puppets, not less like puppets." "Gerry didn't take kindly to my quips about, 'Have you ever tried actors?'" remembers Roger Woodburn with a mischievous grin. "His eyes would narrow and I'd think to myself, 'Shut up Rog. Before you end up back on the dole!'"

Much of this resistance to humanising the characters was counterbalanced by the appeal of pushing the technology to its limits. During *Thunderbirds Are Go,* attempts were made by 'Plugg' Shutt, along with the other sculptors, to produce heads that had a completely articulated mouth, capable of opening and closing fully, instead of just a moveable lip. Plugg explains: "We were trying to get a more flexible face movement; something more animatronic. We spent a lot of time on it. We were trying to get the jaw to move and we were using latex mounted on a fixed skull." So enthusiastic

were Gerry and Sylvia about the chance to upgrade the puppets that they announced the new development prematurely. In 1966 it was reported about *Thunderbirds Are Go*:

> *Guest stars will be Cliff Richard and The Shadows in puppet form but with a difference. Instead of a fibreglass head there will only be a skeletal frame of fibreglass over which will be stretched rubber to give the flexibility of skin. "Basically, this is closer to the human form," maintain the Andersons. "Instead of the mouth having two positions, open and shut, it will be more sensitive, opening and closing more realistically."*

However, despite numerous experiments, the fully articulated face never worked. "The technology wasn't advanced enough," says Mary Turner.

With the rigid fibreglass faces safe from the revolution, consideration was still given to conquering the problems of scale. In 1966, during production of the later episodes of *Thunderbirds,* John Brown in conjunction with Terry Curtis, presented the first perfectly proportioned Supermarionation character. The nameless character was promptly photographed with Lady Penelope and the result was distributed to the studio and, predictably, some loved it and some hated it. The answer to the technology issues was to relocate the solenoid inside the body of the puppet and run a cable from the solenoid to the mouth. However, Brown and Curtis weren't the only ones working on solutions for size. Plugg Shutt worked on producing a lip-sync system that required smaller components: "I found magnets small enough to fit inside the head, but powerful enough to operate the lips." However, the studio decided to go with Brown's design. Plugg continues: "By the time I'd developed it, they felt they were too far down the line with the new ones."

The eye mechanisms remained situated in the heads. However, it was no longer practical to use glass eyes, and so photographic reductions of fake human eyes were stuck on to plastic hemispheres.

Another innovation, originally used on *Thunderbirds Are Go*, was pressed into regular service with *Captain Scarlet and the Mysterons.* This was the use of under-control mechanisms. Ignoring momentarily the old problem of glistening wires, which reveal, even to the most myopic viewer, that these characters are not members of the human race, the wires did actually present some serious restrictions to filming. One of the problems was: how do you film a puppet sitting in the cockpit of an aircraft? Ever since the days of *Supercar*, when the top of the plastic dome had a hole to allow strings to pass through, canopies had been a problem. Mary Turner, determined to do away with this restriction, presented to John Read (who in turn showed it to Gerry) the ingenious idea of controlling the marionettes from below. Ultimately, whilst the method was used frequently, the traditional overhead crosspiece remained the preferred method of operating for most shots. However, the process was refined over time by Plugg Shutt.

Despite the lack of strings, the "under-controlled" characters somehow managed to seem even less human, being very static and moving with even more rigidity than was perhaps desirable, even for a team trying to stamp out puppet-like swaying and bobbing. Sylvia Anderson says: "The more realistic our puppets became, the more problems we had with them performing the mundane human actions of walking, standing up and sitting down in shot; of picking up objects; all of the simple movements which the human body performs with such ease. It was just possible to get away with the awkward moments in *Thunderbirds* because the proportions of the characters were still caricature. It was later when we had developed a more realistic approach – as with *Captain Scarlet* in 1967 – that the still imperfect walk was the more obvious." Forty years on, the debate still rages. Was it right to change the puppets? Gerry Anderson answers: "It's a matter which has been discussed repeatedly and the answer is… I don't know." Sculptor Terry Curtis says: "The *Thunderbirds* characters from the feature film were probably my favourite, but the involvement and attention to detail from *Captain Scarlet* on was far greater. However, as far as I was concerned, they somehow lost their charm."

Needless to say, at the time, Gerry loved the fact that at last his stars could be presented in perfect 1/3 scale, and with *Captain Scarlet and the Mysterons* he had the chance to develop a format that played to the dramatic potential of the more human characters.

When pre-production began in the latter third of 1966, the

'Under-controlled' Captain Scarlet puppet.

new marionettes replaced the old as a new cast of characters was born. *Captain Scarlet* featured a company comparable in size to *Thunderbirds*. However, the episodes were back to the 25-minute format and so, with 14 regular performers, any serious development of character was unlikely to happen for more than a handful of them. In the end, none of the cast received any kind of in-depth fleshing out. This is ironic, considering that the series was the first since *Torchy the Battery Boy* to be named after the central protagonist, and the first since *Four Feather Falls* not to be named after a star vehicle. Indeed, *Captain Scarlet* is devoid of any single stand-out craft, although it does feature a range of machinery which some would argue don't capture the imagination in the way that the earlier vehicles had. The emphasis had definitely shifted, and the characters themselves became the focus of the dramatic action.

The eponymous lead was sculpted by Mary Turner (who also made Symphony Angel), despite Gerry's initial exclamation upon seeing John Brown's original properly-proportioned prototype: "That could be Captain Scarlet!" Terry Curtis sculpted a veritable rainbow of characters: Scarlet's friend and close colleague, Captain Blue as well as Captains Grey, Ochre, Magenta, and the leader of The Angels, the all-female fighter pilots, Destiny. Curtis discusses Captain Blue's creation: "I based him loosely on myself, but I made him about ten years older, as I was only about 20 at the time and I felt that that would be too young. The eyes, the lips, the chin – all my features – but the nose was made a little smaller, because I always felt mine was too large! But, if you were to measure him, virtually all the dimensions are a third the size of mine: length, eye distance, head diameter. It was easier to work with a mirror and copy what I could see. It was only later, after screen testing (he had brown hair to begin with) that I wigged him with blond hair. In fact, I had spent so long looking at myself in the mirror that I made his parting to the right instead of the left!"

Tim Cooksey created Spectrum's Commander-in-Chief, Colonel White, and Lieutenant Green, who has the distinction of being the first black character in any of the Supermarionation shows. "I think it was Gerry Anderson's idea to have a black character on a popular show," says voice artist Cy Grant who played Green. "He was far ahead of his time in doing so." It was not the first time that Gerry had attempted to introduce black characters into his shows. Gerry recalls an incident that occurred during *Supercar*: "Right at the very beginning of working with Lew, I made an episode of, I think it was *Supercar*, where Supercar landed in a jungle and they were surrounded by black people. Lew had an American adviser unfortunately (Abe Mandell), and the American adviser said, 'Gerry, I want to run that show with you. I want some alterations made.' 'Oh yeah?' So he ran the show and he said, 'I want every coloured person taken out.' I said, 'What's wrong with it!? They're landing in a jungle, it's like a tribe.' 'I want every coloured person taken out, because on the Bible Belt, they will never accept that. No, you either take them out or we cancel the series.' So, I had to take them out."

Creating a truly realistic black character required a little more attention to detail than usual, as sculptor Tim Cooksey wanted to create authentic African hair, with texture and curl very unlike that required for the previously all-white casts. To achieve the look he wanted, he found a special mohair which could be curled on heated tongs. Lieutenant Green wasn't the only black character in the series: Melody Angel, who was from the Deep South, was also dark in colour, although her features betrayed the fact that she was ostensibly a white puppet painted black. Melody was sculpted by Christine Glanville, who also modelled the remaining Angels (Rhapsody and Harmony), and had the interesting task of creating the walking cadaver that was the villain Captain Black.

In addition to the regulars, nearly fifty 'revamp' characters were produced. Whereas previously, guest-stars were merely plasticine faces moulded on top of a blank shell, for *Captain Scarlet* it was decided that such a method would be impractical, as the heads had now been greatly reduced. It was time to build a permanent repertory company of fibreglass actors, bearing in mind that these could be modified and adjusted as needed. Director Ken Turner remembers that the new method of casting guest parts brought new issues: "One of the problems was that we had two episodes being filmed at the same time. I might take myself over to the puppet store and think to myself that I'll grab a certain one for a scene only to find that Alan Perry had already got him for the episode that he was doing that week. Another time, I might have said to Christine, 'I like that blond-haired good looking one we used the other day. Is it available?' and I would be told, 'Yes, but he's got black hair, a flat nose and glasses now.'"[2]

One 'character' from the series required no attention from the sculptors, as Gerry Anderson explains: "At the time *Captain Scarlet* was being prepared for shooting, there was a great deal of discussion about the possibility of life on Mars. I remember that people had observed lines on the planet's surface and there was the theory that these were canals made by an alien race. But we really weren't sure if there was life on Mars in any shape or form and I didn't want to be caught out, so I decided that I would make the Martians invisible."

The Martian race, known as Mysterons in the series, whilst supposedly invisible, did have one, now very famous, visual representation. In his biography, Gerry explains: "Film stock was getting faster and faster and it was now possible to project a picture on to someone's face, with sufficient light for the image to be photographed. I'd seen a television commercial for wool and I'd been impressed by the way the Woolmark logo had been projected over the contours of a girl's chest. I mentioned this to Reg (Hill) and John (Read), and when we actually came to shoot the programme, I suggested that we should illustrate the presence of the Mysterons by projecting two green rings over the people or objects that were due to be 'Mysteronised'."[3]

---

2. From an interview conducted by Martin Gainsford for *FAB* magazine, issue 40.

3. *What Made Thunderbirds Go – The Authorised Gerry Anderson Biography* by Simon Archer and Marcus Hearn. (2002)

The idea, which had originally been suggested in the pilot script as a way of projecting the series' then title, *The Mysterons*, was achieved by the very simple method of projecting a 35mm transparency of two green rings across the set. The result was undeniably very effective and is one of the most remembered elements of the series.

Whereas the sculptors had a relatively free hand to visualise their creations, the opening script dictated with vivid precision what the various sets looked like, as with this description of the main Cloudbase control room:

> *The control room comprises the usual array of instrumentation with one notable difference – there are no consoles as we know them. Instead, we find the Controller, Lieutenant Green, a man in his early twenties, and assistant to the Commander-in-Chief of the Spectrum Organisation, sitting behind an entirely new type of console. It is a long sheet of glass approximately 2'6" in height and approximately 15' in length. It stands on its edge and runs parallel to the ground supported at intervals by stainless-steel legs. The whole area of the glass is etched in silver and gold and is, in fact, a printed circuit. Along the bottom of the glass are the normal controls, switches, flashing lights and so on.*
>
> *All these components are slender and futuristic in design. Lieutenant Green's chair is mechanically propelled, and slides up and down the length of the console, thus enabling him to reach any of the many controls. The control room is divided in two – in the second half the floor is raised, thus giving it a split level. On the higher level and seated with his back to Lieutenant Green we see Colonel White, Commander-in Chief of Spectrum. He faces into a semicircular modern desk and when in this position is facing a giant illuminated chart which occupies the whole of the wall.*

Designers Keith Wilson and John Lageu divided the sets between them, with Lageu specialising in the technical design, such as the computers, whilst Wilson tended to the aesthetics. Grenville Nott was then charged with turning Wilson and Lageu's designs into blueprints and subsequently into physical sets.

Meanwhile, on the special effects unit, business continued as normal with Derek Meddings handling the major vehicle

Opposite, top left: Reference photographs of the SPV, MSV and Spectrum Helicopter.
Top right: Mike Trim design for the Spectrum Maximum Security Building.
Below left: Derek Meddings' concept sketch for the Angel aircraft, and right, as seen on screen.

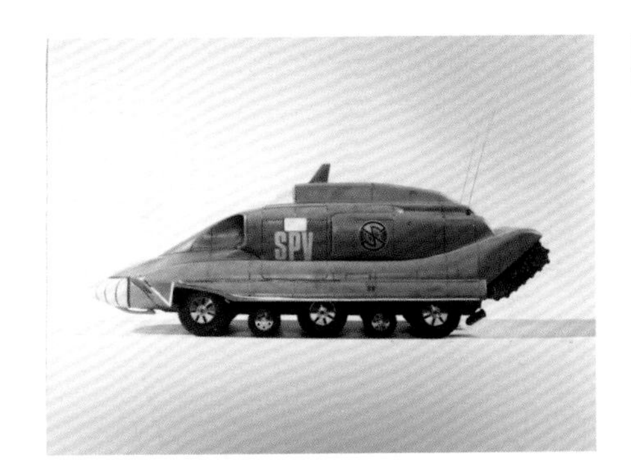
SPV

SPV

M.J.TRIM.
THE MAXIMUM SECURITY BUILDING. 1/25 Scale.

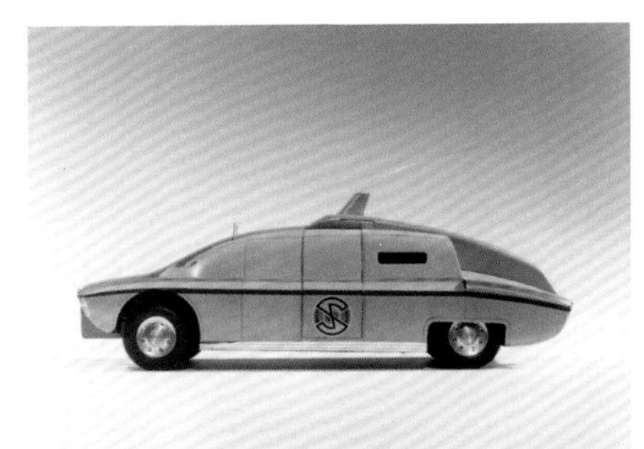

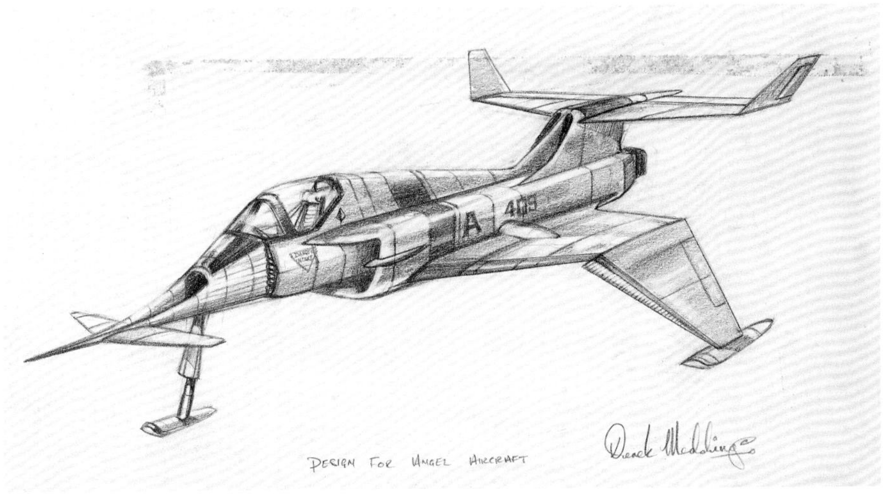
A 409
DESIGN FOR ANGEL AIRCRAFT
Derek Meddings

A
757

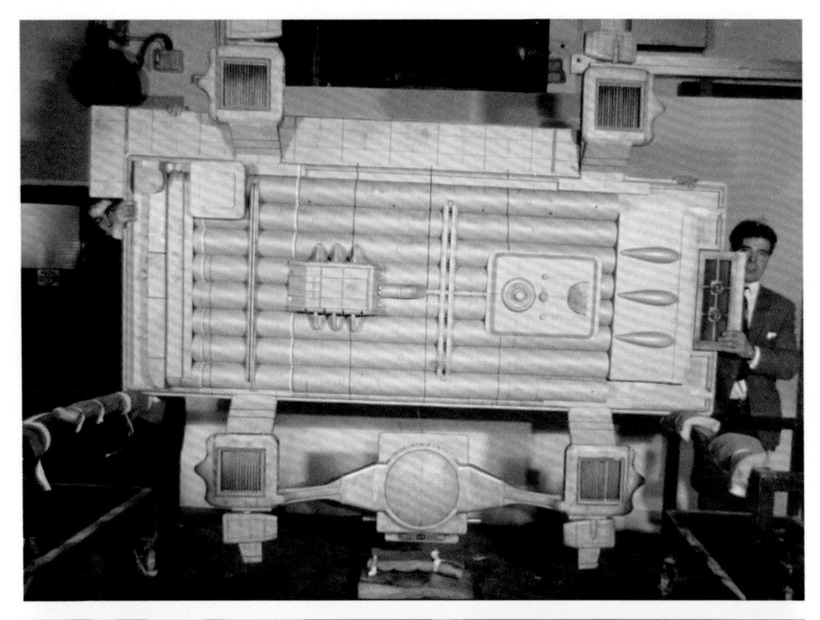

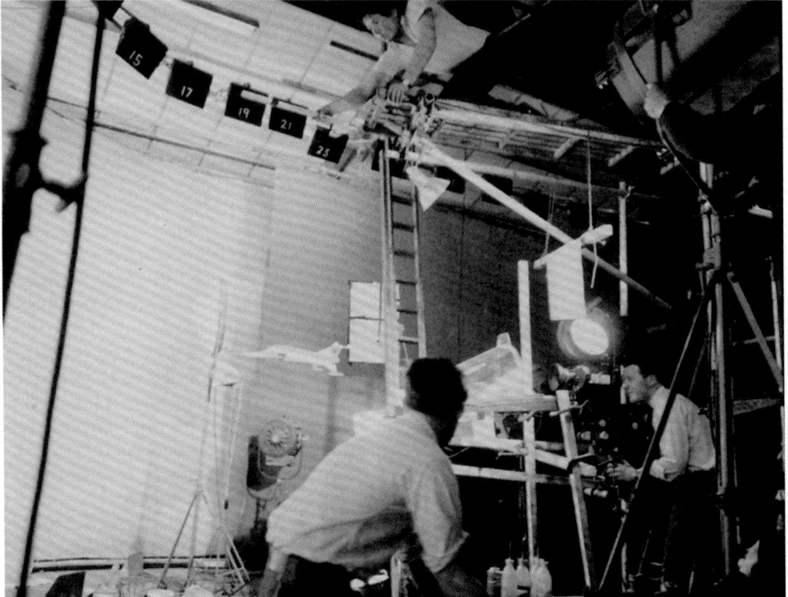

designs. Firstly, there were the Angel aircraft, built to a much more conservative design than previously used. Unlike Thunderbird 2, which required a bold leap of imagination to take to the air, the Angels looked as if they *could* fly, featuring a more conventional delta-wing design.

Derek also contributed the design of the SPV (Spectrum Pursuit Vehicle), a blue armoured tank-like vehicle, fitted with rear-facing seats, requiring the driver to watch the road by TV monitor (overlooking how useful wing-mirrors are). Gerry Anderson explained on a documentary in 2001 why he now feels this was a faux-pas: “The SPV represented one of my big, big mistakes. At the time, when we were planning *Captain Scarlet*, there was a big move afoot to have rear facing seats in airlines, because in the event of a crash-landing, people would be forced into their seats as the plane decelerated, as opposed to being thrown forward and, perhaps, rupturing their spleen on the safety belt. So this was all the talk and I thought, ‘I’ll be very smart here and on this futuristic SPV we’ll have the seats facing backwards. How do they steer? Well, very simple,’ I thought, ‘we’ll have a television camera on the front and that front view will be on a monitor that they’re looking at, and we’ll flip this picture over so that they’re steering the right way.’ And I was very pleased with myself.”

He continues: “As we started to script the series we began

Left, above: Never seen on screen - the bottom of Cloudbase.
Below: An Angel miniature is flown in front of a cyclorama.

to realise that the audience was going to say, 'Why are these people facing backwards?' So we started to write in explanations. We would stop at a petrol pump and the attendant would say, 'Why don't you guys sit facing the front of the vehicle,' and they'd say, 'Ah, you see…' and they'd give this explanation. But, then of course I realised that not everyone would see that episode, so how many times would we put it in? Would we put in, say, five times? It would become boring. If we only put it in once, other people wouldn't know. It was something I totally regretted."[4]

Derek Meddings' other major contribution to the series was Spectrum's headquarters, Cloudbase, a giant aircraft carrier suspended high in the sky. Gerry explains his reasoning: "I thought that if UFOs were coming in fast, it would be better to launch fighter planes from 10 or 12,000 feet." Ironically, these quick launches meant that one of the key elements that had made *Thunderbirds* so appealing, the protracted launch sequences, was removed entirely.

Responsibility for designing other craft of various shapes and sizes, including the Spectrum Saloon Car, the Maximum Security Vehicle and the Spectrum Passenger Jet, fell to Mike Trim, who also found himself charged with visualising all manner of buildings and structures – historical, futuristic or downright bizarre as with the London Car-Vu, a giant spindly car park several hundred feet in the air.

The models which were then produced to these designs often featured an array of household items discreetly, or in some cases blatantly, used as pieces of detailing. Although model kits provided copious pieces that could be cannibalised for models and sets, sometimes ordinary everyday objects could be utilised just as effectively. This goes someway to explaining why the Tracy family television set comes with a cooker temperature control! Mike Trim recalls the art of using what he calls 'gubbins': "The business of using household objects was a quick way to arrive at something that, if you decided to try and make it from scratch using raw materials, would take you forever. A classic example of that would be when you read the words 'Atomic Power Station' in a script; trying to build an atomic power station or an oil refinery, with all its pipework and things like that, from bits of rod and detail would take you forever. Whereas you could go down to Woolworths, which was where we usually ended up, or a hardware store. You'd come out with a lot of plastic boxes, beach balls, salt and pepper sets – anything really that we thought might be useful. And you would use these as the basis of your model and then you would detail on top of those shapes and try and disguise them so that people wouldn't look at them and say, 'Oh yes there's a beach ball.' If they were doing that you'd failed miserably, but normally we got away with it. And we carried that process right the way through. Wherever you could, you'd find some ready-made thing that you could perhaps adapt, hack about, add other things to, and then detail over the top of, which would give you something that looked believable. It was far easier than getting out a block of wood

4. From *Captain Scarlet S.I.G.* (2001)

One of Ron Embleton's iconic paintings from the end titles.

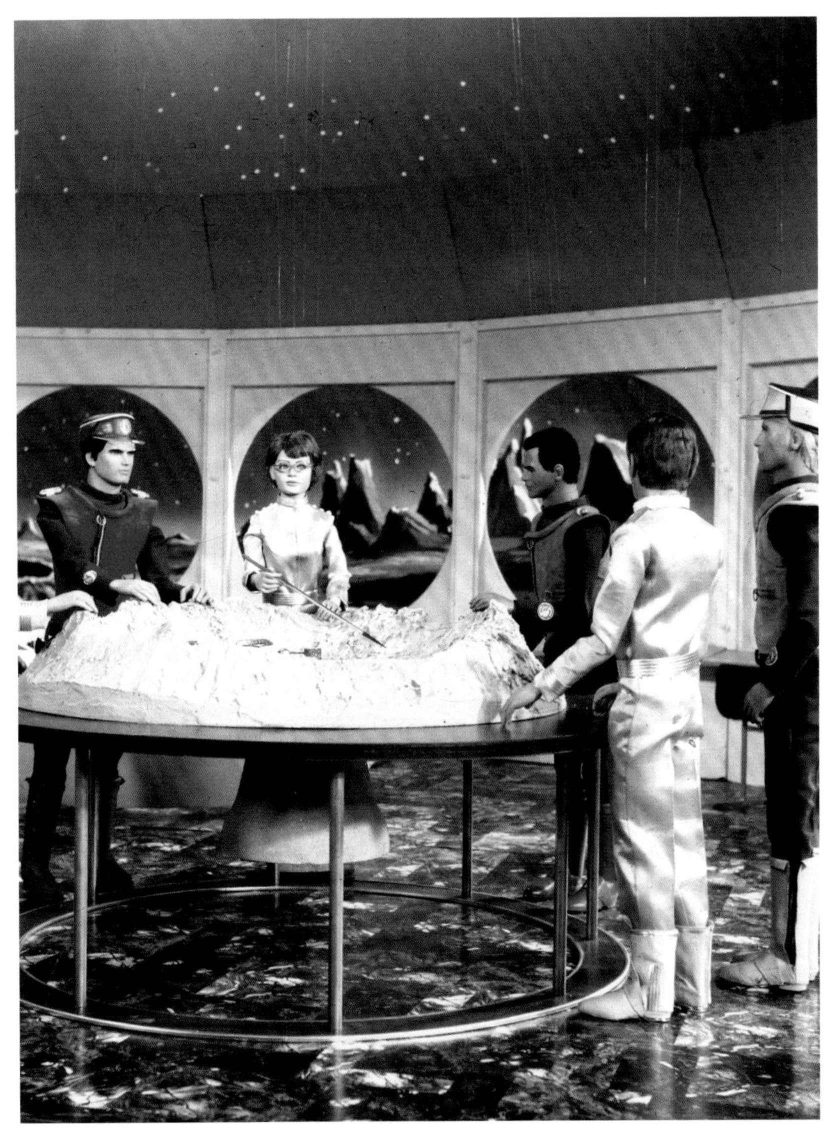

Above, left: "His name... Captain Scarlet." Right: Preparing for the assault on *Crater 101*. Note the star backdrop visible through the roof. Below: Members of The Spectrum clown around with members of Spectrum in the Cloudbase control room.

or sheets of Perspex and trying to create it from the word go." Years later, Mike feels that sometimes they should have worked harder to disguise certain objects. "Sometimes we got it wrong and we used things that we shouldn't have and there is one thing that haunts me and that is a lemon squeezer, which was stuck on the wall at the back of Thunderbird 1's silo. Every time I see that I shudder and think that we really should have disguised that or done something else with it. But we didn't and you win some, you lose some."

In these fantasy lands where everything had to be manufactured from skill and ingenuity, it was easy to let the imagination blast off in directions that might not be possible when dealing with a more conventional series. Although the sky was the limit for designs, the effects department was restricted by a far more mundane problem: the art department manufacturing the puppet sets. Mike Trim explains: "In an ideal world, we (the effects department) would have always found ourselves several weeks ahead of them (the art department) and therefore their large scale sections and sets would have had to follow our designs for the completed craft or vehicles. In reality, they were often ahead of us, and when I started to design a model, I would often find myself trying to work around an existing puppet set.

"Although liaison between the two departments was usually good, this situation could create horrendous problems. For the most part, these were caused by the fact that the art department sets were mainly created from flat sheet material – thin marine plywood, hardboard and clear plastic sheeting, etc., all of which could only be bent in one direction. Therefore, their ability to create smooth flowing designs, with their compound curves, was almost impossible. It was not unknown for us to end up with a fairly sleek and futuristic looking model that suddenly, and sometimes violently, changed character in order to match their set."

However, sometimes the boot was on the other foot and the effects team would get their designs off the drawing board first. Mike continues: "I always tried to be aware of just how easy it was for me to produce some streamlined design, compared to the struggle the art department would have trying to match it – but to have tried to avoid using such shapes, given the futuristic world we were trying to create, would have resulted in some extremely dull looking craft. And so, as you can probably imagine, despite this apparent understanding of each other's problems, the air was often fairly blue on both sides of the artistic divide."

As the master craftsmen toiled away combating the problems that had become familiar to them in the decade that had passed since the far-removed days of *Twizzle*, the Andersons began their search for a new cast of voices, but this time they set out with a slightly different brief.

By the time that *Captain Scarlet and the Mysterons* entered production, ATV's distribution arm, ITC, had become a major player in the international markets, selling many of their expensive filmed television series abroad, such as *The Saint* and *The Baron*. 1967 would see ATV become the recipient of the prestigious Queen's Award for Industry. Therefore, with characters like Simon Templar (*The Saint*) and John Steed and Emma Peel from ABC's hit series *The Avengers* surfing the U.S. Networks, it was now altogether more acceptable to have English lead characters. As a consequence, the Andersons relaxed their casting brief and gave the star role to 39 year old actor Francis Matthews. "Gerry Anderson had heard me do a spoof imitation of Cary Grant on the Pete Murray radio show *Open House*," remembers Matthews. Liking his uncanny impersonation of the Hollywood star, the Andersons decided that he would be perfect for *Captain Scarlet*. Giving the lead role to an Englishman was certainly an act of faith, and perhaps the Andersons felt that the voice would be more acceptable in the States if it already sounded familiar.

Also breaking the American casting taboos was, as noted earlier, the casting of Cy Grant to play the first black Supermarionation character. Grant at that time was well-known for his regular appearances on the *Tonight* show singing topical calypsos. It was Grant's casting that in turn led to another of the Super-marionettes finding its voice, as American actor Ed Bishop explains: "I was with an agent who represented Cy Grant, the black folk singer who was the UK's answer to Harry Belafonte. The Andersons called the agent as they wanted Cy to be in *Captain Scarlet*. The person at the agency told the Andersons that they had just taken on a new American actor and would they be interested in meeting me? They were. We met. They auditioned me. I got the job!" Bishop duly became the voice of Captain Blue.

Actor Donald Gray was given the chance to be both hero and villain when he was awarded the part of Spectrum's Commander-in-Chief, the severe Colonel White, as well as Captain Black and, for good measure, the evil Mysterons, for which his voice was slowed down in order to produce a deep, resonant, unsettling timbre. Gray's acting career after World War II had been a precarious one as he had lost an arm when his ship was hit by a German anti-tank shell. In the 1950s he was a newsreader for BBC television, before he took the lead role in the Danzigers' ITV series *Mark Saber*, a part which he always felt he had got purely because the producers liked the originality of a one-armed detective.

Actress Elizabeth Morgan played three of the Angels, namely French girl Destiny, English-born Rhapsody and Japanese Harmony. An experienced member of the BBC Radio Repertory Company, the job was an ideal one for Liz. She recalls the audition: "It was quite rigorous getting into it, because they were seeing lots of people. Gerry and Sylvia Anderson had this beautiful house in Gerrards Cross and I remember my agent taking me there. In those days, a very long time ago, your agent used to take you to the people you were hoping would employ you. Anyway, it was done in their house and I had to be Destiny and I had to do Rhapsody and they tried me as Harmony, who I did sometimes, as well as the other two." Liz also recalls that the puppets' limitations were just as frustrating to the actors as they were to the technicians: "I remember once, Destiny Angel was getting in a real tizz because

Captain Scarlet was heading straight for the Mysterons, or something. Destiny, who we (the actors) worked out was having an affair with Captain Scarlet, was saying, 'No, no, no, no! Please, Captain Scarlet! Please, please!' I remember the button going down and Reg (Hill) who was in charge that day said, 'Er, excuse me Liz. Got a problem there. Puppets can't cry, luv.'"

Of the two remaining Angels, Canadian actress Janna Hill played Symphony, while Sylvia Anderson herself took the role of southern-belle Melody. Sylvia was, as usual, occasionally responsible for dialogue direction, though increasingly it was a job done by others.

Other parts were given to a team of repertory actors, who would step in to provide the voices of guest characters and semi-regulars. The most notable of these was Paul Maxwell, the voice of *Fireball XL5*'s Steve Zodiac and *Thunderbirds Are Go*'s Captain Paul Travers, making his final contribution to the Supermarionation oeuvre as semi-regular Captain Grey.[5] The final, and most curious piece of casting, was the late addition of Asian actress Lian-Shin, who was cast a third of the way into the series to take over the role of Harmony Angel from Liz Morgan who had already played the character in five episodes. The reason for this re-casting is lost to history, although it seems likely that the producers felt that Lian's ethnic origins may have lent Harmony more authenticity. However, despite being credited on twenty episodes of the series, Shin only provided Harmony's voice in a single episode, *The Launching*.

The actors remember this period with enthusiastic nostalgia. Liz Morgan says: "We had a lot of fun doing it. It was once, every fortnight, at Denham. Sometimes people who weren't in all of them all the time would come and do their bit and then go. It was a day when everybody was in and out."

Ed Bishop recollects warmly: "(It was) an outstanding, pleasurable experience in over a 40-year career. We all got along very well. There was a lot of humour, friendliness, etc. We worked two days a month and did two scripts a day, so it was a long job and it enabled me to do very badly-paid theatre work and still pay my rent and buy nappies and Heinz baby foods for my kids. The first thing all the actors did was to read the back of the script to see if their puppet got killed off! If you were killed off you were out of a job. The only one who didn't have to worry was the wonderful Francis Matthews – his puppet was indestructible! Everyone was on the same money, so there was no tension on that score." With equal remuneration and friendly interaction, few can recall any friction, but Ed recalls one difficult moment between actors: "The only tension point I can recall was during the Rhodesia crisis. Donald Gray turned up one day with a 'Hands off Rhodesia' sticker on his car. Cy Grant took exception to this and there were a few terse words exchanged and it came to nothing." Cy remembers nothing of this, but comments: "It sounds very much like how I would have

5. It appears that Captain Grey was originally intended to be as prominent, if not more so, than Captain Blue. However, after Paul Maxwell left early on, Grey was reduced to a few silent appearances.

reacted to stickers like 'Support Rhodesia'! I have objected to white privilege and colonialism all of my life." Cy vigorously applauds the Andersons' decision to push the boundaries and introduce a black leading character and repudiates the accusations of racism levelled at the series in the 1990s for featuring a villain called Captain Black. Speaking not simply as an actor but as a black actor, he explains his perspective with great clarity: "There was nothing racist in the scripts. Lieutenant Green was someone in authority and trust, chosen as a team member for his expertise in electronics. He was embraced by, rather than excluded from, the group. Perhaps it is our language and the still common usage of the word 'black' to denote evil and unworthiness that confuses the 'politically correct lobby.' In any case, the 'darkness' of the Mysterons is most easily seen as the psychological rift – the struggle of 'good' and 'evil' – of the Western world as personified by Colonel White and his team. Dark and light are but aspects of each other. Incidentally, Green is the colour of nature that can heal that rift."

Cy's reference to the struggle between good and evil raises an interesting point that has been alluded to by commentators today: *Captain Scarlet* is in some perverse way an unlikely Christian allegory; Captain Scarlet being the man who falls to Earth, is killed and then resurrected. He lives among Angels in the sky and his adversary comes in the form of Captain Black, the fallen angel. It seems likely though that such overtones were accidental rather than intentional.

Just as the sculptors were getting to grips with changing working practices to produce the new generation of marionettes, the production crew on the floor were also finding their feet as they too had to adapt. Many of the first generation team had left, so *Captain Scarlet* marked the coming-of-age for some of the younger members. Of the five directors that had worked on *Thunderbirds*, David Elliott and Alan Pattillo had departed and David Lane found himself being assigned to the surprise project of a second *Thunderbirds* feature film, meaning that he would contribute no more than one episode to the new series. Brian Burgess remained, but he had previously directed only two episodes, *Lord Parker's 'Oliday* and *Ricochet*, meaning that Desmond Saunders was the only seasoned director left. Saunders was allocated the tricky task of directing the first episode. Following that, he was promoted to the position of Supervising Director to oversee the new team of youthful enthusiasts.

Having been at the studios since he was 18, first as clapper/loader on *Supercar*, then as focus puller and finally as camera operator, Alan Perry received the ultimate promotion and was given the chance to direct. The other elevation from within the company was that of Ken Turner, who had graduated from the art department to become the Assistant Director on *Thunderbirds Are Go* – this led to him being asked to become one of the regular pool of four directors on the *Captain Scarlet* series. The next addition was newcomer Robert Lynn who, despite being the outsider in this miniature fantasyland, was by far the most experienced film-maker in the company. He had recently directed shows such as *The Saint* and had worked extensively in the film business in various capacities since the 1940s. This included being First Assistant Director on Powell and Pressburger's celebrated film *Black Narcissus*.

In the quest for greater precision, the lip-sync unit was further refined for the new series. The optimistic goal was that it would automatically distinguish between long and short speech sounds. For long sounds such as 'Ah' and 'Oh', the lip would open fully, but for short sounds in words like 'it' or 'at', it would open halfway. Judging by the final episodes, it seems to have been a hit-and-miss process, requiring the lip-sync operator to do a fair amount of manual keying (which couldn't differentiate). Also, the ¼ inch tape that had been used right from the beginning was phased out, and all dialogue tracks were now played back into the studio on 35mm magnetic tape.

With these changes and with the prominent position that Century 21 had carved for itself in the British film industry, the company finally shed the last vestiges of its cottage industry approach, and the transformation into a well-oiled machine, churning out product, was complete. Supervising Director Desmond Saunders recalls the ad hoc organisation as the situation slowly evolved: "By the time we got to *Thunderbirds*, after *Stingray*, we had got ourselves slightly better organised in terms of pre-production and co-ordination between the various departments that all contributed to making this series. You have to remember that we had the puppeteers, the wardrobe department, the special effects department and another several people that all needed to be consulted as a team in order to get things ready on time, so that when you wanted it, it would be there. Up to a point we got that right, *without* the assistance of production managers and people to co-ordinate these things."

As *Thunderbirds* had progressed, elements were slowly introduced to aid the efficiency of production, from small touches such as issuing various personnel with electronic bleepers, through to a major organisational change with the appointment of dedicated Production Managers, Norman Foster and Ken Holt. For *Captain Scarlet* it was finally decided to bring Century 21 in line with the major studios. "What they wanted to do with *Captain Scarlet* was make it more like a professional film studio's production in keeping with the way other television series were done," says Leo Eaton, who was brought in as an assistant director on the series. "I was a Second Assistant Director on *The Saint,* and Frank Hollands was my First Assistant. Gerry Anderson asked him to come over to be Production Manager on *Captain Scarlet* and then he called me and asked did I want to be a First Assistant which would be a jump up for me. If I did well, and everybody liked me, I would get a chance to direct, which is what happened."

Eaton was the Assistant Director on the first episode of the series, *The Mysterons*. Like other new crew members, used to the traditional labours of working with actors, Eaton found himself undergoing a brief adjustment period, getting to grips with a variety of factors, including the fact that all the sound was artificially produced

and dubbed later, meaning that studio noise was unimportant. He explains: "Part of a First's job is to keep the crew quiet and call, 'Silence everyone!' I remember that the first time I called for quiet on the stage, one of the puppeteers said, 'Why!?'"

Eaton continues: "The thing that I remember is how noisy those stages were. I mean, if it rained hard, you really couldn't hear yourself think. There were tin or corrugated iron roofs and the rain would just beat off them. You were literally yelling on the floor to get things done."

Some of the 'old hands' whose work consisted entirely of Century 21 films were hit by a culture shock, when organisation resembling a factory line was implemented. Eaton laughs this off: "Remember, I had come from a real factory. When you're doing an episodic series like *The Saint* where you're shooting one episode every seven days and you have a huge crew – *that* is absolutely a well-organised machine. I think the people on *Scarlet* that were saying that it was a bit more factory-like, were saying so because of innovations that people like Frank brought in. To me, coming from a *proper* factory environment, *Captain Scarlet* was playing!"

Although Leo feels that Century 21 was still a more relaxed environment than other studios at that time, the attempts to make the company 'more professional' left a sour taste for many of the personnel. David Lane feels that the attempts to bring in 'old pros'

Left, above: Smoke is applied on the set of *Seek and Destroy*.
Below: The Magnacopter from *The Trap*.

to the company at such a late stage didn't work. "I remember us trying quite a few times to bring in old hands who had done feature films. Stage managers who'd done features, cameramen who'd done features and bigger television shows. But somehow they never really worked. There was a team spirit about this group of people who had grown up with this whole thing, and to come in at the back end of it wasn't good because you didn't have the history. Also, I knew what kind of wages everybody was on. I knew what I was being paid. These guys were off the Richter scale as far as we were concerned in our little beehive. We couldn't really afford them."

Shaun Whittacker-Cook, who joined the special effects team at the beginning of *Thunderbirds*, has strong feelings about the sudden change in culture. "The studio started to be destroyed by what I call rotten management. As the studio expanded, and people took credit for ideas that they hadn't invented, a certain sort of, 'Oh sod the place. I'll stay here until I get the sack,' crept in. And that I think was a shame because there was skill, inventiveness and artistic endeavour that was just thrown aside." Shaun illustrates with an example of what he felt was mismanagement. "The studio didn't go in for museum notices at first. But we were suddenly told, when we saw electricians working all over the building, that time clocks were going to be put in. It was that sort of management that was steadily eroding the atmosphere." Understandably, after many years of supporting the studio, many members of the team that had enjoyed the casual environment and had often done unpaid overtime because they loved what they were doing were hurt at the sudden lack of trust shown by the management. Model maker Alan Shubrook, who joined A.P. Films not long after the clocks had been introduced at the tail end of *Thunderbirds*, witnessed the resistance to the machines on his very first day. "I was taken into the main office and given my clocking in cards. I went over to my studio stage to ask where the clocking-in clock was and the cards were taken out of my hands, torn up and thrown into the bin in front of me." Eventually, it was realised that the crew had no intention of obeying the new rules and the policy was abandoned. The machines languished unloved and unused in dark corners of the studio. "It took a while for the atmosphere in the studio to recover after that," says Mike Trim.

Whereas once the crew had been united, slowly a feeling of 'us and them' crept in between the management and the crew on the studio floor. Shaun Whittacker-Cook recalls, "Norman Foster (Production Manager) came in on one occasion and said, "I'm sorry lads. I know this lavatory is closest to where you are working, but I've had a lock put on the door because if I'm wearing a £250 suit I don't want to brush against dirty walls where you lads have been."

The division even threatened to manifest itself on the on-screen credits. "They decided that the effects would be credited as 'Team One Special Effects' and 'Team Two Special Effects,'" says Shaun. "Somebody, I think it was Harry Oakes, the Lighting Cameraman, said, 'Where will you be Derek?' 'Oh, well I'll be on screen as Supervisor.' That nearly provoked a strike until the union got involved and everybody got the credit that they're entitled to."

It wasn't just the incoming managers that certain members of the team objected to. The old crew found themselves the target of sharp comments too. "Harry Oakes said, 'Why don't they give Reg Hill £10,000 a year providing he stays ten miles away from the studio?" remembers Whittacker-Cook.

Roger Woodburn, who left during production of *Supercar* and speaks warmly of the family atmosphere at the company in those early days, recalls going to the studio many years later. "I was working in Soho making TV commercials and I had to make a commercial which required some *Thunderbirds* puppets in it. It meant liaising with Century 21. I was going to shoot all the product stuff, and the special effects because the special effects unit couldn't help me. But for the puppets themselves I was going to liaise with the girls, Christine and Mary. I had to go for a meeting at Stirling Road and I arrived and I went in. There was nobody in reception. So I waited and waited and waited and in the end I went into the corridor. There was a long corridor with doors and I could hear things going on. I thought, 'Well I've got to see somebody,' so I chose a doorway and opened it and there was a meeting going on in there of crew, all looking very fed-up. They all looked like they'd been caught in the act. You could feel the atmosphere of dissatisfaction. It was a wake-up call for me and I thought, 'It's not the same.' The old days of Islet Park and Ipswich Road were great. Everybody was there. Everybody was mucking in. The vibes I got from doing this commercial was that Gerry hadn't been seen in a week and a half and that the gold Rolls Royce would occasionally turn up. He was probably doing a deal somewhere. But what he was unaware of was that things were festering. And he should have been onto that. But I could see it had become them and us. Whereas it was only 'us' when I worked there."

After years of successfully operating with minimum interference, the unions finally clamped down on the studio. Overtime was now only worked if it was properly paid for, and failure to arrange overtime at least a couple of hours before 6pm would result in the electricians pulling the plug, regardless of whether it would ruin a shot. The unions flexed their muscles wherever they could. Ken Turner recalls a frightening example of this later on during *The Secret Service*. "The union suddenly decided that we wouldn't do overtime and we would work-to-rule." Working-to-rule is a form of industrial action where members do no more than the minimum required by their contract in order to cause disruption. "I decided to do my own ballot of the crew," Ken recalls. He diligently went around to the crew asking what their view was on the situation and found that, contrary to what the union had suggested, they were perfectly happy to continue working as before. He presented his ballot to the union who responded angrily. "I was summoned to Gerry Anderson's office where members of the union were sat in a circle. I was told to step into the circle and set fire to my ballot." Ken did as he was told and the union got their way.

Alan Shubrook notes that the most enthusiastic union

Above, left: Filming live action inserts. Right: Lip-synch operator at work, showing the feed from the video assist. Below, left: More live action work. Right: Applying anti-flare to the wires supporting Cloudbase.

Landscape set as seen in *Seek and Destroy*.

members tended to be the electricians, and that the rest of the crew, whatever their occasional grumbles about management, were often totally dedicated to their work. "Unions affected the day to day running of each of the stages. The electricians who were, as far as they were concerned, the only people that could switch things on and off, move lights around etc. were just doing a job. For them, they were doing a job they could be doing anywhere. Whereas us on the creative team had far more responsibility for what we were doing."

Although the success of the studio had definitely begun to erode the family atmosphere, many of the crew still speak warmly of this time at the studio. It remained a largely friendly environment and a much better place to work than many of the alternatives. Team members who joined the studio in the latter years have fewer complaints, having missed out on what some of the long-serving crew felt were the 'golden days.' Nothing stays the same though.

Filming officially commenced on January 2nd 1967 and problems with the new marionettes soon became evident. "The heads were *so* much smaller that they would always jerk," says Eaton. "The heads would never turn properly." Operating the puppets from a protracted distance had always been a problem. However, after this radical reduction in head size, what control there had been was greatly diminished. One must bear in mind that the puppets were supported from the heads, rather than the shoulders, as is traditional. Ironically, Century 21 had vastly exacerbated the problems that they were trying to remove. Although they had created perfectly proportioned figures, the upshot of this was that the characters were so realistic that any 'puppet-like' movements were more unacceptable than ever, and as the figures lacked the former scale and proper weight distribution, they were more difficult to operate smoothly than their predecessors.

Orders were orders, however, and the team strove to overcome such problems. "We had a directive from Gerry Anderson not to make them look too puppet-like; to avoid puppet-like movement. We were discouraged from showing them walking – we were told to do it in cuts, rather than in one shot," says Eaton. Walking, oddly, became one of the smaller concerns on a day-to-day basis, as simply standing properly was a serious challenge for these puppets. In order to stop them drifting, and to help keep them rigid to avoid any sign that might give away the trade secret that they weren't human, the characters would frequently be secured with a G-clamp and gaffer tape. "When you had them standing, they always looked very artificial," says Eaton, whose complaints extend to the technology: "Everyone was so proud that you fed the pre-recorded dialogue down the strings and they flapped their mouths automatically. I bet if you talked to any of the lip-sync operators, they'll tell you that it worked smoothly 5% of the time."

Another problem, as evidenced by the completed episodes, is the old depth-of-field issue. The heads were so small that tight close-ups were impractical, if not impossible. With these difficulties in mind, it is a testament to the Century 21 crews that some of the most visually stunning work the company ever produced was contained in these episodes, and the viewer would never suspect the agonies endured to produce each week's exciting instalment.

Night time. A dark, deserted alleyway. Imposing buildings. Footsteps. Gone are the bang-crash titles brought to us by *Stingray* and *Thunderbirds*, and the dynamics of Fireball XL5 launching and Supercar gliding through the air; the titles for *Captain Scarlet* are much more sinister. Any distant memories of anthropomorphic toys singing lullabies are quickly crushed as a cat screeches, flood lamps activate, and a hail of bullets fired by an unseen assailant fail to harm their target, who calmly returns a single shot. His name: Captain Scarlet.

The shift in tone is remarkable, especially considering that even International Rescue, who were charged with dealing with the most dramatic situations, found time to laugh. With only a couple of exceptions, *Captain Scarlet* is devoid of humour and, far from saving lives, features an antagonist that has to destroy in order to resurrect. There are graphic electrocutions, car smashes, train wrecks, plane crashes, even a character crushed by a hydraulic lift in a garage – all displayed in vivid detail: the corpse lying there, blood soaked, before a pan up to reveal its duplicate, perfect in every detail. Because the show was being enacted by puppets, no matter how lifelike, it seemed that such gruesome depiction of tortured deaths was acceptable on TV screens at 5 o'clock on a Friday afternoon. Had the show been live-action and yet still aimed at the family audience, it is most unlikely that it would have survived the censor's knife. In a last minute twinge of conscience, certain ITV regions played a warning from Colonel White over the opening titles: "Captain Scarlet is indestructible. You are not. Remember this. Do not try to imitate him."

Production on the series took up most of 1967 and continued into the autumn before all 32 episodes were safely 'in the can'. As previously, certain episodes were selected to have incidental music specially written, which could then be put into a library for use on the remaining episodes. Barry Gray began recording in February 1967, and got to grips with the first version of the end title music which was used on the first 14 episodes. The arrangement, which features a chorus singing the words "Captain Scarlet," followed by an echoing 'electro-voice', was recorded at Barry's house in Esher, where he provided the electronic voice himself. The music was rearranged, however, when Gerry Anderson's chauffeur drew Anderson's attention to a band he had heard on the radio called The Spectrum, a group manufactured to compete with singing sensation The Monkees. Realising the publicity potential, Anderson immediately signed the group up to perform a new arrangement of the end title music, this time with lyrics, enabling it to be used as a promotional tool. The new version was recorded on July 29th 1967 and featured in episodes 15 to 32.

Perhaps the most famous contribution Barry made to *Captain Scarlet*, though, was the seven beat staccato drum motif played at various scene transitions. Despite an initially highly unimpressed Gerry Anderson, who had hoped more for a dramatic fanfare, the drumbeat has become iconic in its own right.

The Mysterons officially arrived on Earth on Friday September 29th 1967 when the aptly titled first episode, *The Mysterons*, was transmitted, although it is reported that they had managed to sneak onto the airwaves during a test transmission on April 29th. Very few viewers would have noticed this fleeting appearance, however. A special press launch was held for the series on the first day of transmission and, fortunately, an environmental disaster was averted when Gerry Anderson wisely decided to ignore Bill Johnson, of Century 21 Merchandising, who suggested using vast quantities of dye to turn the River Thames scarlet!

Voice artist Gary Files recalls seeing an episode for the first time: "I can remember watching the first episode of *Captain Scarlet* at a wide-screen 'film like' preview set up for management by Gerry at the Colombia Theatre in Shaftesbury Avenue. I looked at it with total and utter amazement. Some of us 'voices' had been shown around the Century 21 studios in Slough not long before this, and had watched the tower that is blown up in that episode being demolished in model form and in controlled conditions using a high speed camera. It was a supreme disappointment. Just a quick 'Paff!!' and the thing shattered before our eyes. Very wimpy and very unsatisfactory. Boy, you should have seen it on the big screen! They had laid in an incredible sound track to go with it. We all tottered out into the night, convinced that we were onto a winner." Francis Matthews' children, however, didn't get as far as

the finale: “I had two very tiny children, a five year old and a four year old, both boys. Reg Hill, who was the producer of the series put on a special showing for them – they were the first children, as far as I know, to see it – because he wanted to find out what children’s reactions to it would be. They settled down and it was put on the screen at Gerry’s studio. The film started and ‘This is the voice of the Mysterons’ – my eldest son screamed and ran terrified from the studio! Reg said, ‘Oh my god, what have we done!? We’ve made a series that no children are going to watch!’”

The series left the crew with mixed feelings. “I thought it was a very cold show,” says David Lane. “I found the puppets difficult to work with. They looked good. The shows looked good. Everything worked. But it was cold to me. A bit characterless.” Sylvia Anderson agrees. “It was one of the best things we did. But you don’t really care about Captain Scarlet do you? He’s indestructible. It’s not like Parker is in trouble.”

“I remember seeing the first episode in the rushes theatre and Mike Trim came out and said, ‘What do you think?’” remembers Alan Shubrook. “I was a young, green 19-year-old kid and I thought, after *Thunderbirds* it was so different was it really going to be as big? I think we all knew deep down, even though we all loved what we were doing, nothing would ever emulate the magic that *Thunderbirds* had.”

In spite of the crew’s concerns, the child audience responded enthusiastically to *Captain Scarlet and the Mysterons*, which was another success story for Century 21. However, as Alan Shubrook suggests, its lustre was dimmed by the long shadow of the phenomenally popular *Thunderbirds*, which still had one thrilling outing left to go…

THUNDERBIRD 6

•1967•

TIGER IN THE TANK 9

Thunderbird 6

Thunderbirds undoubtedly had the magic formula that catapulted A.P. Films into the big time. It was loved by the crew and was clearly adored by the public. When 1966 brought the catastrophic double-whammy of no-sale to the USA, followed by the failure of *Thunderbirds Are Go* at the box-office, no-one could quite understand why. The cancellation cast a pall of gloom across the studio and even the prospect of continued employment, in the form of *Captain Scarlet and the Mysterons*, struggled to lift the mood. Leo Eaton, who joined Century 21 at the beginning of *Captain Scarlet,* recalls: "I remember being told very clearly that you should have been here *then*. We were all aware that we were never going to be as good as *Thunderbirds* partly because we were half-hours and they were hours, partly because, even then, *Thunderbirds* was cult. When *Captain Scarlet* came out reviewers said, 'It's no *Thunderbirds*.' One was very much aware that… not that things had passed their best, but that things had changed and that *Thunderbirds* was the series that was going to survive."

Lew had inititally been so confident in the success of the *Thunderbirds* franchise that he had done a three-picture deal with United Artists back in 1965 before the series had even aired. In spite of the disheartening returns for *Thunderbirds Are Go* he still believed the show had the potential to spin-off into a successful cinema series. This was a sentiment echoed by hard-nosed businessmen and it was decided that *Thunderbirds* needed another chance. Therefore, against the background of disappointing receipts from *Thunderbirds Are Go* (which had aroused expectations of "bigger than *Bond*") United Artists entered into another deal with ITC, and £300,000 was budgeted for International Rescue's next foray onto the big screen.

Getting *Captain Scarlet* (billed as using 'the most advanced techniques ever in a production of this kind') off the ground was a long task, but Century 21, with its usual efficiency, soon had the production under control, meaning that selected members of the crew could be split off to turn their attentions elsewhere. As with the previous cinema outing, Sylvia Anderson took the role of Producer and David Lane was assigned to directorial duties. Sylvia confesses though that her heart wasn't in it. "I wouldn't have gone on to do anything else. We've done the film from the successful TV series. Let's leave it at that. Go

Above: Thunderbird 6 to the rescue.
Below: Derek prepares Skyship One.
Opposite: Virgil's lighting is checked.

on to something else. The second film didn't have it for me at all."

The characters were already well-established, so there was no question of reducing their heads to match the new generation of marionettes. The International Rescue team, after a few months on holiday, were brought out of storage, either in the form of the brushed-up originals or re-makes, and prepared for their next trip onto the silver screen. New characters were constructed where needed (such as the main villain Captain Foster), but largely the guest characters were resurrected from the repertory company of previous guest stars. As usual, once they were physically prepared, they were passed to the costume department, now headed by ex-studio-tea lady Iris Richens. This interesting promotion followed the departure of Elizabeth Coleman during 1966.

Over in the effects department, the task was equally demanding. A number of the main vehicles were remade or repaired, and once again some of the stock shots were re-filmed. The nature of the story provided a large number of unusual challenges for the personnel in visual effects.

In December 1966, *The Daily Mail* reported on a potential second *Thunderbirds* feature film concerning a "Russo-American space project." If there was any truth in this report, it seems that this original concept was abandoned in favour of an idea influenced by Director Desmond Saunders. "He had a great interest in airships and was always telling me how his ambition was to be involved with a picture about them," recalls Gerry Anderson. "Desmond fired my imagination and I read a number of books on the subject, particularly ones about the R100, R101 and the Graf Zepplin." Once again, the Anderson retreated, and wrote their third and final contribution to the *Thunderbirds* saga.

In the film, the New World Aircraft Corporation (previously credited on the end titles of *Thunderbirds Are Go* as the designers of Zero X) has invited Brains, in strictest secrecy, to pitch to them a bold idea for a new, revolutionary type of vehicle. "And now, gentlemen, the time has come. What is it to be?" ponders the chairman. "An aircraft that flies ten times the speed of sound? A space vehicle that travels at the speed of light?" There is a tense moment of awkward silence before Brains replies: "An airship." The room erupts with derisive laughter as the executives wipe the tears from their eyes, in what is, unintentionally, a contender for the most horrific scene ever produced by Century 21. Every character has been specially sculpted for a series of quick-cutting shots, so that their mouths gape rigidly wide open, and the camera swings in, showing in extreme close-up the menacing teeth of faces that appear insane.

Back on Tracy Island, Jeff Tracy feels that it is time for International Rescue's fleet of craft to be expanded. "We now need a Thunderbird 6," he says. "Sure Mr. Tracy. Can you give me some sort of a steer?" enquires Brains, "I like to work to a specification." "Specification?" Jeff gruffly retorts. "You didn't need a specification when you designed that airship for the New World Aircraft Corporation." "That's right. I didn't. And what happened? They laughed," winces the

bespectacled scientist, before Jeff reminds him: "Yeah, that's right. They laughed - and then they built it."

From here the film splits in two: the around-the-world maiden voyage of Skyship One (soon to be the subject of a hi-jack), involves Alan, Tin-Tin, Penelope and Parker; while back at base the focus is on Brains' frustrated attempts to produce a new design.

The two 'guest star' vehicles couldn't be further apart in concept. Derek Meddings undertook to produce the design of the futuristic airship, Skyship One, which, like many good Supermarionation guest vehicles, was destined to meet its end in a series of spectacular explosions. The other craft required no imagination at all, as it was already an existing design...

In the film, Alan and Tin-Tin travel to England from Tracy Island in a World War Two Tiger Moth plane, first in a small number of sequences showing their journey to, and arrival in, England, and then later when the antiquated craft becomes an unlikely rescue vehicle, with the stricken Skyship One precariously balanced on top of a mast, perched above a missile base (of course!) near Dover.

For the various sequences involving the quaint old relic, it was decided to hire a genuine Tiger Moth and, for the first time, mount a major location shoot, across Buckinghamshire. In most of these sequences (barring the air acrobatics featured early on in the film) ace-pilot Joan Hughes was at the controls. "Joan Hughes was a wonderful pilot," says David Lane. "But you wouldn't think she could ride a bike let alone fly Lancasters during the war!"

In the plot, the crew and passengers have been lifted to safety from the doomed airship by clambering onto the Tiger Moth - Penelope in the pilot seat, with Brains, Alan, Tin-Tin and Carter on the wings, Captain Foster in the rear seat, and the unfortunate Parker clinging on for dear life to the undercarriage! To perform this task as a piece of live-action, using a real plane, required dummies to be strapped to the relevant positions on the wings, with Joan taking on Lady Penelope's role of pilot. "They called Joan in," remembers David, "and she didn't bat an eyelid when I said to her, 'Joan, we want to put some bodies on the wings and one on the undercarriage.' She said, 'Well, I'll just have to do a few test flights to make sure it doesn't alter the characteristics of the plane.'" A test flight was duly organised and Hughes was satisfied that she could still control the plane sufficiently with the dummies attached. "And then Gerry got this bright idea saying, 'Why don't we fly it under a motorway bridge?'," recalls David Lane, smiling.

Lane continues: "The M40 was being built at that time and one section was finished and it was due to open in about three weeks. We got permission to use the motorway before it opened for tracking shots and back projection plates. And then we had to fly the plane under the bridge. Well, actually, we didn't have to fly under the bridge because we weren't allowed to! They said, 'You can't fly under the bridge, but you can land and taxi under the bridge and then take off again.' I said to Joan, 'Alright. Well if we must we must.' And she said, 'Oh well, if we must we must.' I said, 'Well, anyway Joan. Whatever you do I'll get it. I've got three cameras on it.' So she takes off and she comes in and does a run, but flies over the bridge just to get the whole thing sorted in her mind. And then she comes down, she goes lower and lower..." "She shot underneath there," continues Sylvia Anderson. "The official nearly fainted, everybody applauded... and then we were served with a court order."

However, as David explains, Hughes had more than just the visual impressiveness of the shot on her mind at that moment: "She *couldn't* land. She got caught in a crosswind and the wind would have pushed her the wrong way. It was safer to fly under the bridge than taxi under it."

In 1968 Hughes commented on being in flight a matter of mere feet from the bridge: "It was the only time that I have ever been scared."

Prosecutions were mounted against both Hughes and Production Manager Norman Foster. "As producer, and the person ultimately responsible," says Gerry Anderson, "I tried to persuade the police to charge me instead, but they wouldn't."

In March 1968, the case was finally heard. Sylvia continues: "Joan's defence was – and it was perfectly true – that it was more dangerous to do it the way they wanted with taxiing under the motorway bridge than if she got some speed up to get under the bridge."

David Lane says: "It was a foolish thing to bring before the court, because even the aviation authorities said that the pilot is in charge. If the pilot decides it's dangerous to land, then the pilot will continue to fly." The seven charges of dangerous flying against Hughes, and the three charges against Foster for aiding and abetting,

Filming the flying sequences with the Tiger Moth.

were dismissed after more than two days' deliberation by the jury, who had seen footage and even a model of the motorway built by Century 21. Following his acquittal Norman Foster told the *The Daily Express* that the verdict was, "A breakthrough for the film industry," and that, "Our Lady Penelope has opened the way for much greater realism in film-making."

In a story that David Lane admits might well be apocryphal, it's suggested that perhaps the judge was persuaded to direct the jury to acquit. David explains: "Before we went to court, Norman Foster said to Derek, 'Can you make me a model of Thunderbird 2? You know, a nice model. The sort of thing you can't get in the shops.' So Derek said, 'I think we can do that Norman.' So we went to court and Norman says, 'Hello Judge, have you got any grandchildren?' He said, 'Yes, I have. Three boys.' Norman said, 'Do you think they would like this?' and he gave him this lovely model of Thunderbird 2. He said, 'Just a little gift from the crew really,' and the judge said, 'Oh that's wonderful!' Anyway… case dismissed!"

It seems unlikely that such a blatant act could occur in a court, but another story David Lane relates shows that the company was not above bribery when it suited their needs. "We needed to get shots of the Tiger Moth flying low into the trees. So Joan does it brilliantly. She just clips the top of the trees with the wheel. And then we get a complaint from the farm nearby. The farmer's wife complained because the plane

Above right: David Lane disposes of a corpse.
Below right: The motorway miniature takes shape.

came too low over the house. But that was the only place where the trees were. Anyway, she sent a stinking letter to Booker Airfield (where the production was partly based) and they went mad at us. So, Norman Foster got the biggest bunch of flowers you've ever seen, knocked on their door and said, 'We've come to profusely apologise. We didn't know she was going to do it like that…' We never heard another word from them again throughout the whole film!"

It wasn't just the full sized Tiger Moth that caused the company headaches. In the months before acquittal, the Ministry of Transport had withdrawn permission to film on the M40. With the footage incomplete, Century 21 had to revert to tried and tested methods: the problem was handed over to Derek Meddings' special effects team. A large scale miniature of the motorway was erected at Booker Airfield which was situated near the motorway allowing for authentic natural scenery. Also, as the master footage had also been shot outside, it was essential to film the model work in natural light to avoid any discrepancies between the real and 'staged' footage. While the use of models was an old technique, a new technique was implemented for actually flying the craft. Because of the plane's conventional design, it was possible to use a system of radio control on the miniature. This model was used for various sequences in the film, including the motorway scenes. Despite proving to be inherently unreliable and crashing frequently, the team persevered and, free of the wires, managed to produce some of the best effects work Century 21 would ever create. It is a testament to their skill and ingenuity that, in the motorway sequence, the model shots are indistinguishable from the live-action footage.

Visually, *Thunderbird 6* is gorgeous, with a vast array of beautiful set-pieces designed by both the art and special effects departments. The effects unit had to replicate a number of locations and structures across the world in model form, including the Great Sphinx of Giza, the Pyramids and the Grand Canyon, all impressive in their own right and needing to look equally amazing when the small replicas appeared on the big screen.

Bob Bell's art department also found themselves going to town, producing a number of outlandish sets for Skyship One's interiors. However, one set, nearly led to a fatal accident. The Bottle Room, which was quite literally fashioned from an array of bottles, featured a transparent floor mounted on numerous ping-pong balls. David Lane explains: "Keith had this idea to light through ping pong balls on the floor. The girls were up on the gantries and we were working all day, which meant the lights were on all day. Suddenly the whole lot went up in smoke. Just like a bomb. There was no warning. The girls screamed. There were about three or four of them up there all on this gantry scrambling to get off. It was the most goddamn awful smell. You couldn't inhale it or you'd die."

The fire was extinguished, fortunately with no casualties, and the set was painstakingly repaired. "I don't think Keith ever decided to put ping-pong balls under the floor again. Good lesson," says David.

Attention to detail on *Thunderbird* 6 was perhaps even higher than it had been on *Thunderbirds Are Go.* Even though

Above, left: David Lane preparing for a scene with the Tiger Moth. Right: Paul Travers turns villain!
Below, left: Our heroes lashed to the Skyship's gravity compensators. Right: Lady P's drawing room.

Above: BANG! The missile base is destroyed.
Below: Filming at Penelope's mansion.

Sylvia claims that she was less interested in the second feature film, puppeteer Wanda Webb disputes this. "There were things we did on the earlier *Thunderbirds* episodes that we wouldn't have got away with on the later productions such as this. Like the odd hair out of place, a string showing, or even certain hair styles that simply weren't good enough. Sylvia wouldn't stand for it." Recalling a scene where Lady Penelope is sleeping Wanda says, "I had placed the plasticine sleeping eyelids on her and made the eye shadow a little too blue. We had to re-shoot the whole sequence."

Thunderbird 6 is a complete departure from what the audience had come to expect from the series and David Lane confesses that following *Thunderbirds Are Go* the team purposefully set out to make something very different. "I think what we tried to do is to lighten it up. It had more action and more fun. *Thunderbirds Are Go* was very serious, whereas *Thunderbird Six* had much lighter moments in it. Out came this script with a Tiger Moth in it, which was as far removed from the hardware that was in *Thunderbirds* as anything I can think of." So far removed, in fact, that it is possible that children watching the film may have felt let down by the lack of adventure (indeed the whole film feels like an extended puppet version of holiday magazine programme *Wish You Were Here*).

Also, the gag that results in the ancient Tiger Moth being named *Thunderbird 6* was probably more appealing to adults than children. It is certainly a joke lodged in the era, based on the advertisements for Esso at the time, which featured the catchphrase "Put a Tiger in Your

Tank". Virgil even borrows a version of the line to introduce the new member of the International Rescue fleet. The younger generation had likely spent the entire 90 minutes eagerly waiting for the most fantastic piece of hardware to arrive. They got an old plane.

Thunderbird 6 is great for fans of the series, as any chance to spend time relishing the characters and revelling in special effects is a must-see. As a film in its own right though, *Thunderbird 6* misses the target, lacking a number of elements that made the series so iconic. The stirring *Thunderbirds March* is heard only briefly and, beyond the briefest of shots, the launch sequences, so popular with the audience, are absent. The film has an unfamiliar air about it, almost trying to distance itself a little from what has gone before. The characters seem more mature, especially Lady Penelope who Sylvia Anderson plays with a new confidence. Voice artist Ray Barrett's absence (he had returned to Australia) also adds to the different atmosphere of the film, and his regular roles of John Tracy and The Hood are re-allocated to actors Keith Alexander and Gary Files respectively.

A metaphor for *Thunderbirds*' decline may be found in the fact that in the very first episode, we see a supersonic, atomic aircraft hurtling along a runway, and in the final outing for International Rescue, we watch a bi-plane chugging along a motorway.

The film is redeemed by an impressive and somewhat gratuitously long series of explosions at the climax of the film when Skyship One finally crashes into the missile base. Sound editor Tony Roper recalls this vividly. "The explosions were so big that they even had the fire service there on standby. Tony Stacey (projectionist) and I crept in the side of the stage to watch: all was well until Derek said, 'Action!' The plane crashed onto the airfield with such explosive power that Tony and I were blown about 15 feet back through the swing fire doors!"[1]

The final sequence is an astonishing spectacle of what could be achieved at that time on a miniature scale and in hindsight it seems incredible that less than a decade earlier Torchy's rocket had been launched using common-or-garden sparklers. Sylvia is equally appreciative stating, "If you ask me if I would name one person who was genius in the true sense of the word – it was Derek Meddings. We owe so much to Derek. We really do. I regret one thing with Derek. Derek came in to ask Gerry if he could be part of the company - literally part of the company and not just employed by us. And Gerry said 'no'. To me it made great sense and I think that's when Derek lost heart. I felt it was a terrible mistake because I felt no one could have done what Derek did and I felt we owed that to him."

Thunderbird 6 was completed at the end of 1967 and classified in January 1968. In the run-up to the film's release, Century 21 commissioned a full-sized version of the Rolls Royce, FAB 1,[2] [3] for

---

1. Interview by Richard Farrell for *Andersonic* magazine.

2. The irony is that FAB 1 is destroyed in the film, although this is not explicitly stated. It was on-board Skyship One when it crashed to the ground. An oversight on the part of the scriptwriters?

3. The car wasn't a real Rolls Royce. It was a specially constructed shell mount given an engine. Rumour has it that, in later years, Rolls Royce wanted the car destroyed.

publicity purposes with model Penny Snow playing Lady Penelope. In a rare bit of promotion for 'the other side' the BBC's flagship children's magazine show *Blue Peter* featured the car with presenters Valerie Singleton, Peter Purves and John Noakes showing off all the car's gimmicks which included a gun in the radiator grille (not real, of course) and a revolving number plate.

The film was released in July 1968, when it premiered at the Odeon Cinema in Leicester Square on the afternoon of the Monday 29th. Gerry and Sylvia were chauffeur-driven in FAB 1, but it unceremoniously broke down on the way, forcing them to jump into a taxi.

Gerry remembers that the screening was well received by an unlikely group of youngsters. "They had enjoyed the movie, but they specifically wanted to congratulate me on the puppets' teeth. It turned out they were dentistry students and they thought the fillings were wonderful!"

Unfortunately, the appreciative audience was small. *Monthly Film Bulletin* carried this rather po-faced review:

> "*Puppet films are clearly the answer to parental worries about the sex and violence content of children's pictures; and these particular homogeneous, plastic people achieve a refined degree of asexuality (it's significant that Lady Penelope's impeccable English manners rub off on ever her moustachioed captor), while bloodless corpses and gun battles on an obviously pea-shooter scale are unlikely to overstimulate anyone's aggressive or sadistic instincts.*
>
> *But though overlong, the Andersons' second feature film (modelled like its predecessor on their popular TV series) also holds some charm for adults, or at least for those who enjoy playing with miniature trains. The mechanical models in this Dinky toy* Space Odyssey *are beautifully constructed, as are the glossy sets, many of which appear to be made from boiled sweets; there's even a splendid* Lady from Shanghai *shooting match set amid the revolving metal spirals of the skyship's gravity compensation room. But unfortunately, the puppets themselves, with their eerily monotonous voices and unvarying facial expressions, prove inadequate vehicles for so prolonged exercise in suspense.*

The decision to premiere the film in the afternoon was indicative of United Artists' loss of faith. Lew's disastrous decision to cancel the series back in 1966 sealed its fate and the future of Supermarionation as a whole. By the time the film was released, it had been a year and a half since the last new episode, and the public had lost interest. Sylvia states though that, in reality, the films weren't unsuccessful, but that they were the victims of unrealistic expectations. "It was only really greed. Everyone wanted so much out of it. It couldn't possibly have been as big as *Bond*."

Thunderbird 6 was the end of the line for International Rescue, and no further adventures would ever be produced. At the time it seemed obvious that *Thunderbirds'* life had come to its conclusion. In retrospect, however, it appears that this was only the beginning…

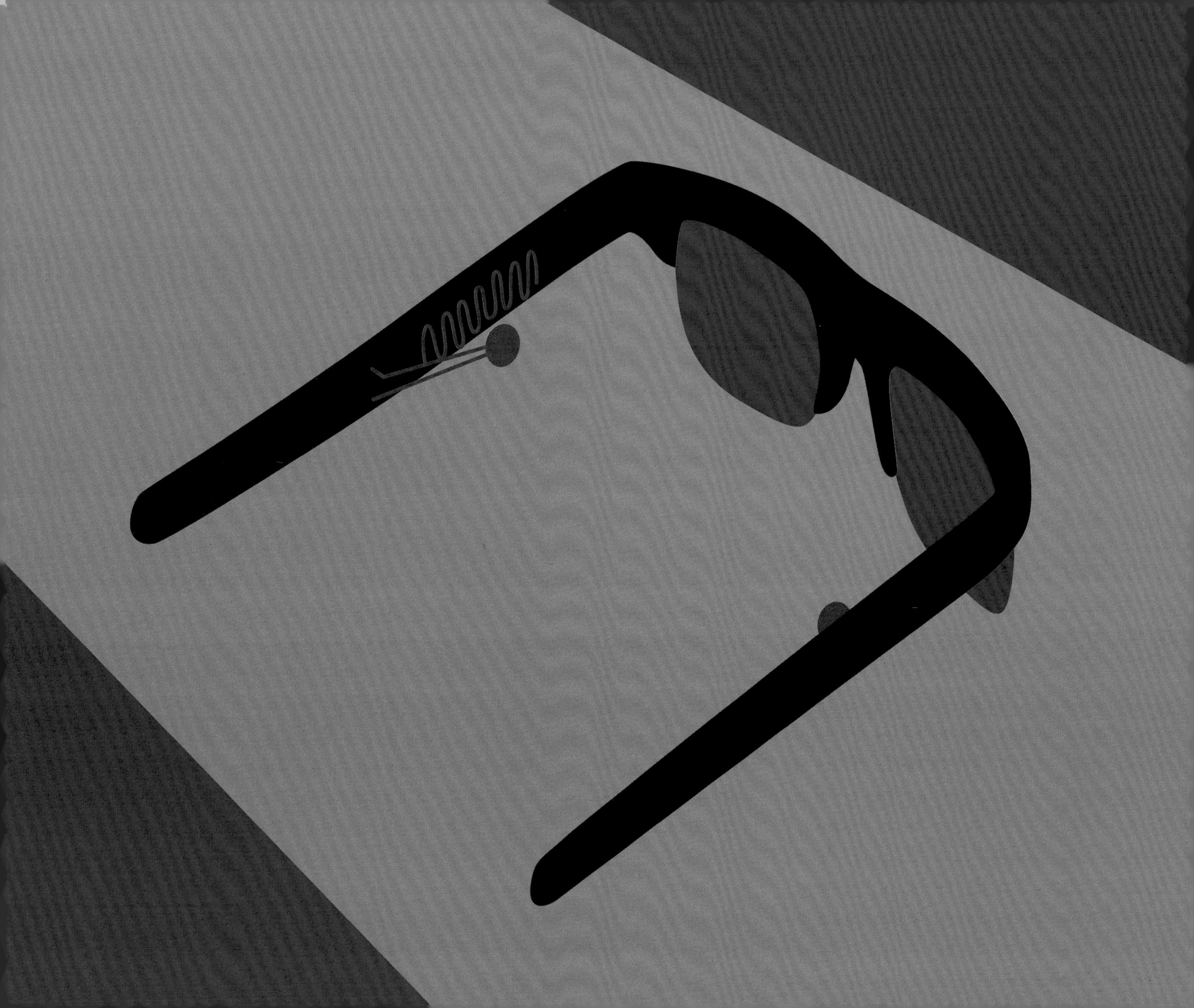

JOE 90

•1967•

MOST SPECIAL AGENT 10

Joe 90

1967 was another busy year for the Andersons, who had their attentions split in four directions: *Captain Scarlet* was in production on two of the small puppet stages; *Thunderbird 6* was progressing on the large puppet stage; Lew Grade had requested that Gerry outline his idea for a new series to take over from *Captain Scarlet* and, most difficult of all, they had to contend with the arrival of their first child in the midst of their disintegrating relationship. Sylvia recounts her memories of this busy but troubled time: "As the promotional tour for *Thunderbirds Are Go* progressed, Lady Penelope attracted more and more attention. This reflected well on me as the press latched on to the angle of a woman producer, who was also the creator and voice of the puppet star. For the first time the spotlight was then turned away from Gerry. He was used to being the centre of attention, although I had been coming gradually to the fore. Despite the fact that on every production Gerry insisted on his name above the title, we were known as a husband-and-wife team, yet now with *Thunderbirds Are Go*, I was considered newsworthy in my own right. This pleased the publicity department greatly, but Gerry less so.

"He found it difficult to deal with this new turn of events, although, for my part, I did not think of myself as competing with him and only of it being our success. In retrospect, I understand better his bruised ego, but at the time it came as a shock to me that he should resent me so bitterly. Unfortunately, there were angry scenes in the privacy of our hotel room and some public sulks at receptions.

"The situation was becoming impossible and I made plans to return home before the end of the tour. I got as far as booking a flight for the next plane back to London. This alarmed Gerry and he realised that he had gone too far. He begged me to carry on with the tour. He must also have realised that our problems would be made public if he was forced to continue alone. As much as he wanted to be solo centre stage, he was not prepared to face the final round of public appearances without me in my role as Lady Penelope, and was astute enough to know that this would harm our image on tour.

"I agreed to carry on, but the enthusiasm left me. We were on an exhausting schedule and I was beginning to feel the effects of the rigorous work programme that had become the pattern over the

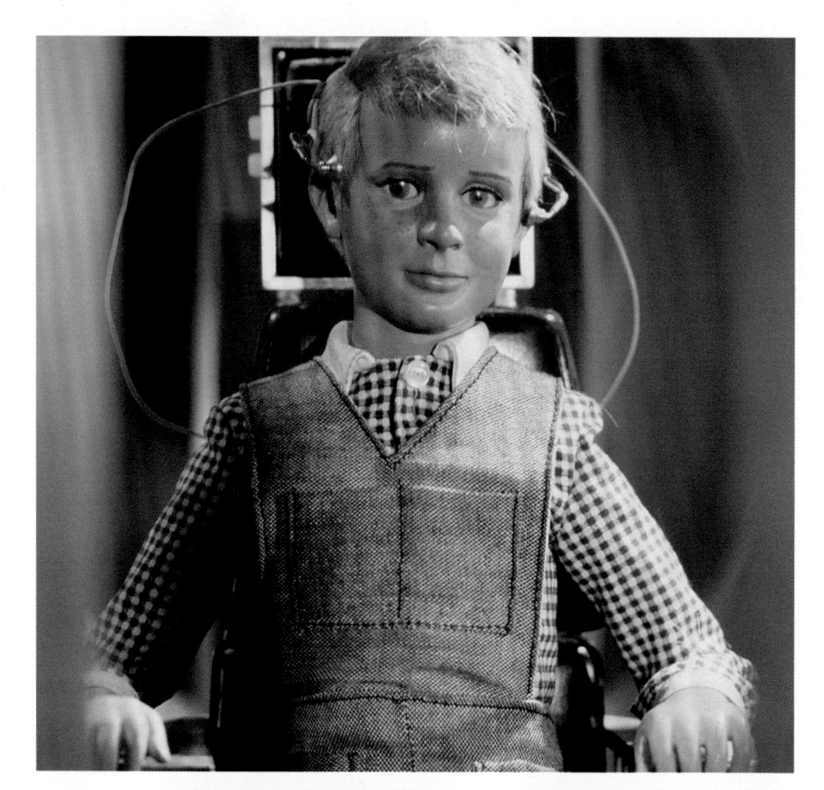

past ten years, and my health was beginning to suffer. In addition, the cinema returns were now coming in and proved disappointing, much to the amazement of all concerned. The distributors were beginning to eat their words. Obviously, we had failed to put across the message that *Thunderbirds Are Go* was a specially made film for the cinema and not a television compilation. Although we still had our loyal television fans, they remained just that – firmly seated in front of their television screens and not in the cinema. So, from the elation of the premiere, just a short while before, we were now firmly down to earth.

"Christmas 1966 came and went, and on Boxing Day there was another domestic crisis. Gerry was still nursing his resentments about my public role and the change in balance of our professional relationship. The change was inevitable: there was no way I could work series after series with Gerry – so heavily involved in the creative production – without getting some media attention. Of course, this was not a new problem between showbusiness partners. Eventually one or the other will start counting their lines, resulting in bitter resentment and a sense of injustice. It was now happening to us.

"I threatened to walk out again and this time I did. Packing a few things, I went to stay with my parents. I had decided that things had gone far enough and I needed time to think and have a little peace. I was still feeling unwell and had had no opportunity to go for a check-up. In any case, I knew I had to get away from the stress and strain of our relationship.

"Once again, Gerry grew full of remorse and wooed me all over again, to which I relented. He took me off to Paris, for a romantic New Year's Eve and lavished me with gifts. We became reconciled without ever really solving the underlying problem. In my heart, I knew that it was only a matter of time before the old resentments would resurface and I did not really have much hope for our future. I offered to give up my role in the company but that only made things worse as it was felt that would be making our problems public. I seemed to be in a no-win situation. Fate, however, decided to play a part in the next sequence of events: when finally I got around to having that medical check-up, I discovered that I was pregnant. It now made complete sense to me that my fatigue and illness during the tour were a major contribution to our problems. Thus I consoled myself. I wanted to believe it and looked forward to the arrival of the new baby. For the time being, this would heal the rift. But it was not to last."[1]

When asked about Sylvia, Gerry merely replies: "I have to say that it was one of the greatest mistakes of my life to get married on that particular occasion and to that particular person and I'm sure that she would say the same about me." The Andersons went through an acrimonious divorce in the '70s and, by Gerry's own admission, this colours his feelings towards his former wife. "I find it too painful to talk about, so I leave others to talk about her contribution." He is a little more revealing in his biography, where he tells broadly the same

1. From *My Fab Years*, by Sylvia Anderson (2007)

story, but obviously with his own take on events: "The more successful we became the more it seemed that Sylvia moved to the forefront. She was aided and abetted by the press, who made it very easy for her," he comments. "I noticed something about Sylvia while we were on the plane approaching each city. As the plane began to lose height, she would disappear into the loo and come back all dolled up, wearing the wig she'd brought with her. As soon as the plane stopped she was on her feet and down at the door. I was always behind her because I liked sitting next to the window. She would come down the steps onto the tarmac while I filed out with all the other passengers. She would stride towards the local mayor, or whoever was there to greet us, while I struggled behind her on the steps. After a while I took her to one side and asked her, 'When we get to an airport can you please wait for me so we can get off the plane together?' She responded by telling me I was jealous of the attention she received from the press. Of course my blood boiled and we started a row that went on for the rest of the tour."[2]

Sylvia counters this by suggesting that in the early days it was her outgoing personality and ability to talk to anybody that had helped their partnership, both in the personal and professional sense. "In the early days Gerry wasn't very social. He didn't enjoy meeting people or going to any event – he had a problem with that. Probably to do with his upbringing. But I never have. I just enjoy people. So, in the beginning that was very useful for him. I was supplying the sort of things he didn't have. We were complementary to each other. And then as time went on, I got stronger in the things I liked to do. He carried on obviously, but I didn't see any difference except that I was getting to know things a bit better. I didn't see it as a competition. Unfortunately, he did."

Gerry and Sylvia's relationship and subsequent divorce was to become one of the most high-profile feuds in the entertainment business. However, at the time, they managed to withhold their problems from the studio. David Elliott comments on how surprised he was, when he found out there was something wrong following his departure: "I spoke to Sylvia on the phone and she apologised about how I'd been treated, but said she simply couldn't speak to Gerry about it because of the problems. I was stunned, because until then I had no idea." In any feud it is difficult, if not impossible, to identify the reality, and so the precise history and context of Gerry and Sylvia's relationship will never be known. Sylvia is, however, rather more magnanimous towards her ex-husband: "When Gerry and I split up, the creative force was half as effective. Despite statements to the contrary, we *did* work well as a team. I've described our partnership as being a balanced act. As the creator of the characters and the director of the dialogue, I gave the 'heart' to the show; Gerry gave the action and adventure element. The success of the partnership is evident in our past work. Had we stayed together, I believe that there was nothing we couldn't have achieved. As it was, our parting broke up a winning combination.

2. From *What Made Thunderbirds Go* by Simon Archer and Marcus Hearn (2002)

After all, neither of us has equalled or bettered our past successes since our 'solo' careers." It was not always an unhappy relationship though, as Desmond Saunders recounts: "It was a very happy time and I'll always remember the image of Gerry and Sylvia walking around arm in arm, just enjoying it. I can always remember that, which makes up for all the unpleasantness later on."

The Anderson's son, Gerry Jnr ('A Gerry Anderson Production, Produced by Sylvia Anderson', according to the announcement cards), was born in July 1967 as *Captain Scarlet* was in its final weeks of production. "I had a very difficult time with the pregnancy," says Sylvia. "The first person that wrote to me to say, 'I don't want to hear of you going into the office,' was Lew Grade. He and his wife couldn't have children. He wrote to me and said, 'Nothing is more important than having your baby.' So I had everyone come to me at home! Then when I had the baby they all came into the hospital. I was in hospital in Windsor and I was okaying all the drawings etc."

As the barrage of flowers swamped the hospital, Sylvia sat up in bed approving various elements for the Anderson's other new child: *Joe 90*.

"Back to my days in the cutting room, along came magnetic recording," says Gerry Anderson. "You hold a strip of film and you can't see anything on it. But, if you ran it through a sensing head, it produced dialogue or whatever it was we were recording on it. I just stared in wonderment because there was a

Announcing the birth of Gerry Junior, in Century 21 style.

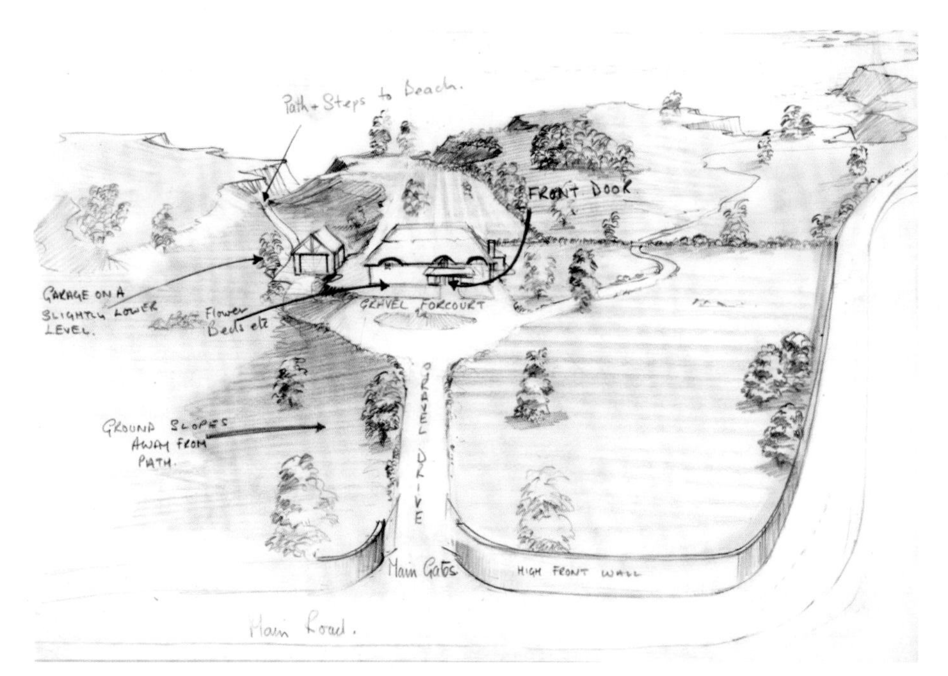
Path + Steps to Beach.
FRONT DOOR
GARAGE ON A SLIGHTLY LOWER LEVEL.
Flower Beds etc
GRAVEL FORCOURT
GRAVEL DRIVE
GROUND SLOPES AWAY FROM PATH.
Main Gates
HIGH FRONT WALL
Main Road.

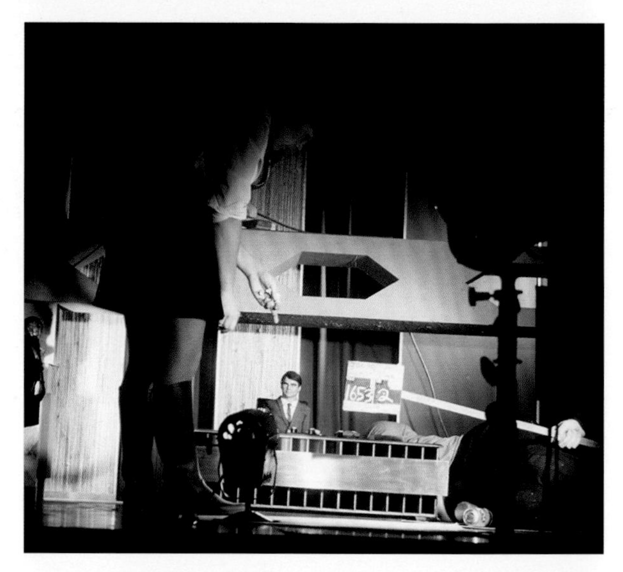

recording on it that I *couldn't see*, but it was apparently possible to wipe that recording and then record something else on the same piece of film. Of course, this was very, very exciting. That was what led me to think, 'Well, our brains work on electrical impulses, so theoretically, it should be possible to record somebody's brain impulses and then transfer them to another person's brain,' so enabling Joe 90 to become anything from a fighter pilot to a surgeon, or whatever, which allowed him to spy on behalf of our country. Always good against evil, don't forget!"

The premise that drives *Joe 90* taps into the fantasy indulged by most boys that they, even at nine years old, can be James Bond. Young Joe is the adopted son of Professor McClaine (Mac) and together they live by the sea in a thatched cottage, on a cliff-top in Dorset. As you would expect from any self-respecting Century 21 production, this prosaic exterior is but a façade, hiding something more exciting lurking in the basement: the BIG RAT (Brain Impulse Galvanascope Record And Transfer), a machine designed by the Professor.

ITC's publicity brochure introduces Joe, explains how the ingenious machine works, and outlines the stirring concept that this new series will embrace:

> *"He's only nine years old – but he is the world's most audacious special agent! There has never before been a special agent like JOE 90 – and television has never before presented such an original, imaginative and intriguing series. For nine-year-old Joe can do anything, thanks to a fabulous electronic device which can transfer the brain patterns of those who are the greatest experts in their field. When he receives these brain patterns, Joe, with the aid of a special pair of glasses which have built-in electrodes, becomes a man in thought and deed... he can become the greatest of all astronauts, a dare-devil pilot, an ace motorist, a brilliant brain surgeon or whatever else may be necessary for him as the most daring of all agents attached to the World Intelligence Network... yet he still looks what he really is – a normal, healthy schoolboy. Every assignment brings new excitement, new hazards and unexpected situations – for JOE 90 and viewers alike!"*

In the first episode, Mac's remarkable device is demonstrated to family friend Sam Loover, with Joe receiving Mac's brain patterns. Mac is curious to know how much such a device is worth, but all mercenary thoughts are swept aside as Loover invites Mac to the headquarters of W.I.N. (World Intelligence Network) in London to meet the boss, Shane Weston. Excited by the machine's possibilities, Weston outlines the sort of scenario that little Joe could find himself in, if he joins the organisation as a secret agent. Mac and Joe listen intently while Weston summarises a potential mission, in which Joe hi-jacks a fighter plane from the Russians and flies it

Opposite, above left: Mike Trim's design for Mac's cottage and surrounding landscape. Right: Preparing for a shot from *Big Fish*. Below, L-R: Puppeteer on set with Joe / Ken Turner sets up a shot / Preparing to shoot Shane Weston.

back to England. "But Joe is so young!" protests Mac in the ensuing argument about sending a mere child into such dangerous situations. It is only a matter of minutes until his scruples are overcome and Joe is awarded his W.I.N. badge. "Don't come crying to me if you get hurt," says Professor McClaine (who suddenly seems prepared to abnegate all parental responsibility) and his son becomes W.I.N.'s Most Special Agent and is assigned the codename Joe 90.[3] [4]

Amusingly, having outlined to the audience a story where the Russians are the villains, Shane Weston makes it quite clear at the end of his little tale that England is not at war with Russia. "I'd always tried very hard not to put my ten cents in to create World War Three," says Gerry Anderson.

Joe 90 rolled onto the stages immediately after *Captain Scarlet and the Mysterons*, with pre-production having taken place during shooting of *Scarlet*'s latter episodes. "We finished *Scarlet* and had to start on *Joe 90*," says Producer David Lane. "We finished one on the Friday and started the other one on the Monday. So it was very tough."

---

3. According to the series, Joe is assigned the codename 90 because the BIG RAT is W.I.N.'s File 90. However, publicity literature says that he is simply W.I.N.'s 90th agent.

4. The name 'Joe 90' originally featured in the discarded proposal for *Century 21* submitted along with the outline for what became *Fireball XL5* in 1962.

In contrast to the previous two series that had gone before the cameras, (*Thunderbirds* and *Captain Scarlet*) *Joe 90* was a much more intimate series with only five regular characters. The reduced cast meant that there was not such a burdensome workload to put through the puppet workshop as there had been in the past. Two of the regulars, Shane Weston and Sam Loover, were selected from the repertory of revamp characters built for *Captain Scarlet*. Casts were taken of the 'expressionless' faces to create one duplicate of each. This allowed the same character to appear on two separate stages simultaneously. For Sam, additional heads were made with 'expressions' – 'smiler', 'frowner' and 'blinker' – as well as another head mounted on a unit controlled from below.

Professor McClaine was specially sculpted by Mary Turner, and he was given the four heads that had become the norm for major characters (with the exception of Shane Weston, who remains curiously expressionless). Unusually, an outside contractor that was working on Century 21's comic series *Candy and Andy* got the task of building the star himself, Joe 90.

Previously, the only difference between adults and child characters, of whom a small number had popped up in various Supermarionation episodes, was the body height and facial features. No change in the head size had been thought necessary. For Joe, however, there was pressure to create the perfect child marionette in

Opposite, above: Captain Black, reborn as General Valdes in *Viva Cordova*.
Below: Mrs. Harris? Before and after.

keeping with the new realistic portrayals. Before visualising the face, an accurate set of body and head dimensions which could then scale down by one-third were required. "We used Norman Foster's kids for dimensions," says Plugg Shutt. "We took pictures, just for general shapes, sizes and characteristics." Joe's tiny size exacerbated the problems already facing the puppeteers with regard to movement, as he was a diminished version of puppets already reduced to the point where there was little scope for positioning the control wires effectively. The finished character is a testament to the skill of the sculptor though. Joe was furnished with three regular heads (one for each of the puppet stages and one controlled from below), plus 'smiler', 'frowner' and 'blinker' heads. He also had the luxury of a deliriously happy head sporting a huge grin, but this seems to have been used exclusively for publicity purposes.

The only other regular character was the much underused (and rather boring) housekeeper, Ada Harris. Curiously, Mrs Harris seems to have begun life as a man, as her head and neck are made in one (female puppets had a separate head and neck); without her wig she looks extremely masculine.[5] Ultimately, she was seen in only four of the thirty episodes, so any cross-dressing did not come under scrutiny!

The remaining guest characters were mostly drawn from the permanent catalogue of revamp characters (with a few new

---

5. Mrs Harris isn't the first Supermarionation puppet to be a man disguised as a woman. In the *Thunderbirds* episode *The Duchess Assignment*, a man in a wig and a dress is clearly visible in the art gallery!

Above, L-R: Cave set from *Child of the Sun God*. Note one of the Shadows' Vox amplifiers mounted on the wall! / Cornered in Coletti's hideout / Joe's WIN identification. Below, L-R: Filming Coletti's hideout in *Hi-Jacked* / The President's train from *Breakout* / Mac's cottage.

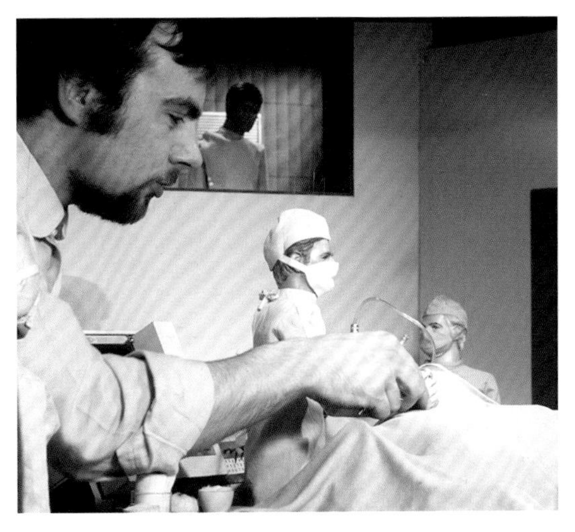

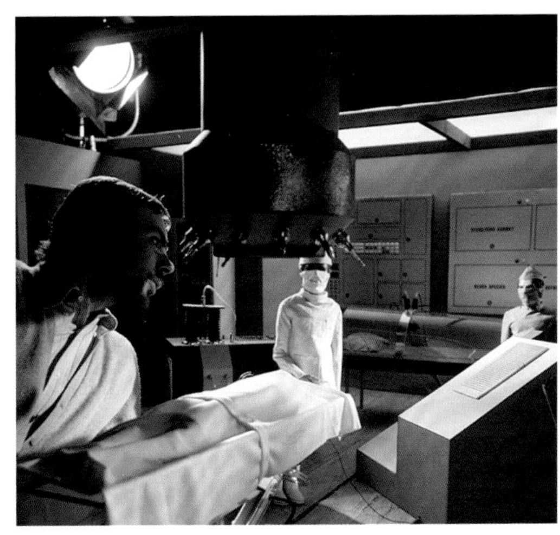

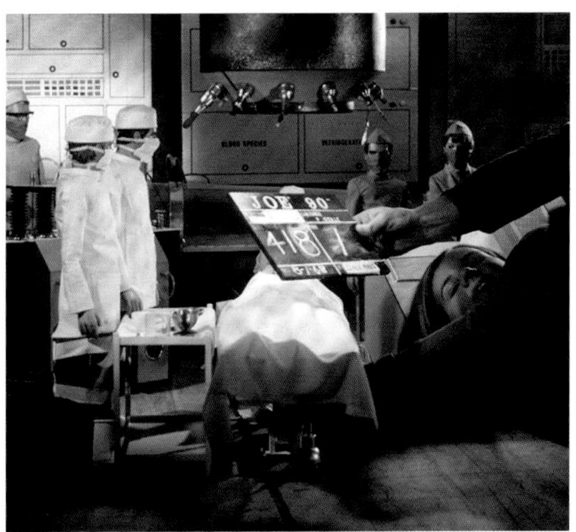

Above: Mac's lab. Below, L-R: On the set of *Operation McClaine*.

additions), which now included the *Captain Scarlet* regular cast. Eagle-eyed viewers can spot a number of well-known Scarlet cast members turning up in new roles, including Colonel White as Sam Loover's father in *Relative Danger* and Captain Black as the villainous General Valdes in *Viva Cordova* (he must just have that sort of face…).

As the Andersons knew well by now, a good face is worthless without a great voice. Having abandoned their requirement for an American cast, Gerry and Sylvia looked instead for voices that pleased them. The most celebrated actor to join the cast was Rupert Davies as Professor McClaine. At the time, he was best known for playing the French detective Maigret on television. Fellow voice artist Gary Files, who featured as a number of guest characters in the series, recalls Rupert with great affection: "I was tickled pink to be working with Rupert Davies. We became quite friendly and on one memorable day, we had to drop by his house on the way to somewhere, and he showed me some of his collection of vintage cars. Amazing! He also used to take some of us to the BBC Club for the occasional lunch or for a drink after work when we were recording in town. I hated the way that so many so-called producers wouldn't meet his eye. He was Maigret forever, you see, in their eyes. He was a terrific warm human being and a very talented *classical* actor, as well as anything else. Why do those who should really know better still assume that you can *only* play the last character you did? It's an insult to the profession."

Australian Keith Alexander, who had been brought in on *Thunderbird 6* to help fill the shoes of Ray Barrett, was given the role of Sam Loover, and David Healy, who guested in *Captain Scarlet*, was cast as the wise-cracking Commander of W.I.N., Shane Weston.

For the role of Joe, Gerry felt strongly that the widespread expedient of casting an actress to play a young boy was no longer acceptable, and so for total realism the Andersons cast child actor Len Jones. Sylvia has particularly vivid memories of her first encounter with their would-be child star. "He thought he would shock me, I think, when I was auditioning him. He started swearing at me. I said, 'Hey, hey, wait a minute – why are you swearing? Why are you doing this? Do you think it's clever saying the 'f' word to me?' Obviously someone had said something to him, 'Oh be shocking,' or something like that. Anyway, we cast him – but he didn't do the swear words!"

Sylvia's attention was no longer focussed on the puppet characters and her commitments lay elsewhere in the studio with *Thunderbird 6* and *Doppelgänger* (their first major live-action commission). Also, by her own admission the pressures of work and home were starting to take their toll and so she relaxed her grip on

Opposite, above: The puppeteers in a tight spot to operate an under-control Joe 90 / Explosives Tractors on an impressive landscape set. Below: Bill Camp loses the wires on a redressed Angel Interceptor / Fixing the tiny heads was a delicate operation.

the day to day running of things. Perhaps that is why *Joe 90* features no significant female characters. Indeed, out of thirty episodes, only ten contain female characters. *Joe 90* is very much a boy's own adventure. Sylvia's attendance at voiceover sessions was more infrequent than previously, leaving others to direct the gatherings. She contributed voices for some minor female characters, but her largest role was Mrs. Harris.

Surprisingly, considering how well-known Century 21 was for special effects, *Joe 90* is a character-driven series. While it does feature a variety of craft, its setting in the near future (certainly nearer than any series since *Supercar*)[6] means that the designs aren't as visionary as before, and there is only one 'star' vehicle, Professor McClaine's jet car. The car, in essence an updated version of Supercar (though with fewer features – it can only drive and fly), is unique in Derek Meddings' Supermarionation portfolio in that it has little, if any, aesthetic charm (indeed Gerry Anderson goes on

---

6. Some sources place the series as being set in 2013, while the Writer's Guide says 1998. *Thunderbirds* is either set in 2026 or 2065 (depending on whether you believe the huge calendar seen on screen *in Give or Take a Million*, or the date given in the comic strips) and *Stingray* was set in 2065 (c.f *The Lighthouse Dwellers*). *Supercar* was set in 1961/2.

Left, above: Ken Turner during location recce for *The Unorthodox Shepherd*. Below: Mike Trim's design for Mac's cottage.
Opposite, left: "Who made those mountains?" work in progress on the effects stage.
Opposite, right: Mike Trim's train on the set of *Lone Handed 90*.

record in his biography as saying he disliked the craft). The concept, basically a jet-engine with wheels and a cockpit, fails to capture the screen in the way Derek's previous designs did and falls short of the beautiful, sleek design of its predecessor, Supercar. Mac's car was Derek's only major design contribution to the series, produced while he was acting as Supervising Director of the effects unit. With his focus first on *Thunderbird 6* and then on the new live-action film, *Doppelgänger*, it was simply not possible for Derek to control everything within his remit. However, he always turned up to rushes every morning at 10am to oversee the work being carried out by the various units. Once seated in the rushes theatre, the crew would watch the models and landscapes creep silently across the screen. "Derek never screamed or shouted if he didn't like something," says Alan Shubrook. "He'd perhaps say something like, 'Who made those mountains?' and when you responded, 'Me,' he'd give you a look and you'd know, 'Ah. He didn't like it. Must do better next time.'"

Although the series was undeniably more character-based and lacked the perfect balance of effects and models that had made *Thunderbirds* so popular, the effects team still had to be as ingenious as ever. Often, making a familiar object convincing is more difficult than when dealing with an unfamiliar object, such as a space rocket. Mike Trim recalls *Lone Handed 90*, an episode written by Production Controller Desmond Saunders and set designer Keith Wilson, in which Joe falls asleep and dreams of being back in the days of the Wild West with steam trains crossing the prairies. After reading the script, Mike considered how he might achieve an effective on-screen result: "Knowing that I had an avid train lover, or 'chuffer-nutter,' named Charlie Bryant on the model making team, I was certain we could do a good job. Having talked it over with him, I decided to build the model at 'O' gauge in order to take advantage of commercially available wheels of the right type. And so I went ahead and did a piece of full-colour, side view artwork to that scale.

ATLANTIC RAIL COMPANY 4-4-0 LOCOMOTIVE 1865

"While I was doing this, I began to turn my thoughts to the vexed problem of getting realistic smoke puffing, rather than just pouring from the smokestack. I should have known better. I should have simply said to myself, 'We've got a tight schedule, a lot to do, so just forget it. It would be nice, but it is only a children's puppet film after all, and there's a limit as to how realistic we can be.' But I didn't. As I painted, a cunning plan began to reveal itself. If we put a small electric fan in the boiler that would blow air up in the chimney and placed a simple sliding valve, which was attached to the wheels, to interrupt that airflow, the result would be puffs of air directly related to the speed of the train. With something in the top of the chimney to produce smoke, the results could be very effective. Slow speed, long puffs of smoke. High speed, short puffs – perfect!

"As expected, Charlie did a superb job on the model and soon the time came to test it. Through various experiments, we had determined that a smouldering oil-soaked rag produced good smoke and that this could easily be concealed in the large conical chimney. We set up a test in the workshop, and to our delight, after a few minor teething problems, the system performed flawlessly. However, our celebration was sadly short-lived. No sooner had the locomotive been delivered to the stage for its triumphant debut than aggrieved special effects assistants appeared, cradling the said masterpiece. 'It's doesn't work,' they said, with more than a hint of annoyance. 'What do you mean it doesn't work?' 'Just that. It doesn't puff smoke.' 'Well, it worked fine when we tried it,' we replied, secretly wondering what they hell they had done to break it. 'That's as may be,' they went on – their tone now somewhat defensive, 'but it isn't working now.' And thus saying, they departed.

"After much head-scratching, Charlie examined the mechanics, made a few adjustments, proclaimed it to be in good working order, and returned it to the stage. And then it went quiet. We waited apprehensively for their reappearance but all seemed well. He and I exchanged a cautious but, we felt, well deserved, smile.

"Other duties conspired to keep me away from the model shop and stage for the rest of the day and so it wasn't until later that I finally headed across to see how things had gone. 'So the train worked okay then?' I casually, but not too smugly, remarked to one of the assistants. 'Eventually, yes.' 'What do you mean eventually?' He gave me an old-fashioned look. 'Well, it was fine once we'd disconnected all that smoke-puffing business and just rammed a black smoke pot down the chimney each time. Once she was on the move, it looked fine.' My inventive genius was crushed, my creative flair violated. But watching rushes the following morning, I had to admit it did look fine – damn it! All that work, all that time, all that genius wasted!"

Set design was undertaken by Keith Wilson and Gren Nott, as Bob Bell too was engaged on *Doppelgänger*. By this time, the two talented designers were producing some of their best work, with the interior of Mac's rustic cottage proving to be a highlight on their Century 21 CV. To assist the art department, a new company was incorporated called Century 21 Props, which was run by Don Fagan. The new organisation's first job was to produce the BIG RAT prop, which is not only prominent throughout the series, but features in the colourful psychedelic display that is the opening title sequence.

Opposite: Mike Trim's painting of the locomotive from *Lone Handed 90*. Above: Mike Trim's design for the explosives truck in *Colonel McClaine* and, below, as seen in the televised episode.

JOE 90
DIRECTOR
LEO EATON
EPISODE 28

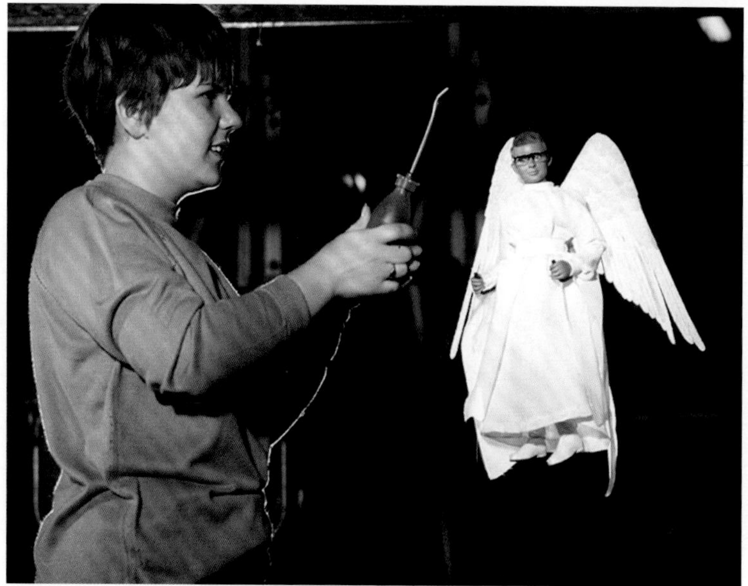

Shooting commenced on the two small puppet stages on Monday November 13th 1967, with Desmond Saunders taking charge of the first episode *The Most Special Agent*. Alan Perry and Ken Turner continued directing, along with Peter Anderson who had been promoted from his role as Assistant Director to fill the hole left by the departures of Brian Burgess and Robert Lynn. Leo Eaton, who had been promoted to director on *Captain Scarlet* when he submitted his own script, was also assigned to the director's roster.

Eaton explains his rise through the ranks: "When I joined *Captain Scarlet*, I asked Tony (Barwick) if I could write a script and he said, 'Do me an outline and if I like it, yes.'" Eaton duly submitted his outline for a story involving a Mysteron agent stealing a deadly virus to contaminate Los Angeles. "*Place of Angels* was sort of based on a sci-fi short story that I'd been writing for some time and it seemed like a good *Captain Scarlet* script. So I did the outline, Tony agreed to commission it, I wrote it and then Gerry asked if I'd like to direct it. So it was both my first professionally produced script and my first directing gig." Although *Place of Angels* was Eaton's first foray into directing for television, he had already gained some limited experience filming ice-lolly commercials featuring the stars of Supermarionation, past and present. "Gerry got me directing the ice lolly ads – I remember directing one of the FAB adverts, in fact, with Lady Penelope. It was then that I decided that commercials weren't what I really wanted to do because I remember sitting with a whole bunch of advertising people, talking about the exact angle that a puppet should hold the lolly, thinking, 'No! This is not me!"

The established pattern of two episodes filming simultaneously across two weeks continued, as had been the tradition for some time. However, despite the routine, every now and again there would be a scene that posed unique difficulties. Those who remembered dealing with the dangerous crocodiles for a month when filming the *Thunderbirds* episode *Attack of the Alligators!*, must have assumed that having a rattlesnake in the studio for a brief scene would be a piece of cake in comparison. However, as the adage goes, never work with children and animals. So when Joe 90 encountered a snake in the jungle in the episode *The Fortress*, things were not destined to go smoothly. Eaton explains: "There's a scene in it where Joe is escaping in this hovercraft, down this river. We had built a section of the jungle at full puppet size. When he's sleeping, a rattle snake comes up and almost bites him. We had the rattle snake brought in by a handler. But you know what these puppet stages were like – they were up on those rostrums and... it kind of got away under the rostrum with everybody trying to find it. I think it was de-fanged, but they were still freaking out. A rattle snake lost on the set is not an ideal scenario."

Opposite, above: Ken Turner on the set of *Operation McClaine* / Mac the tealady in *See You Down There* / Joe is clamped down for a close-up. Below: "Angel One skyborne..." Joe gets some anti-flare spray during *The Unorthodox Shepherd* and an adustment with a pair of scissors.

Leo has happy memories of those days when he was working with a high-spirited, youthful crew, many of them trained under the previous generation at the studio: "It was such a game. On *Scarlet* and *Joe 90* we really had fun. Most of us were young – it was a young crew. We used to play. I suspect that Gerry and the others used to do the same when they were young when they started with *Four Feather Falls*, but by the time they got to *Captain Scarlet* it was, 'this is serious.'

"I always found," continues Eaton, "that *Joe 90*, which I think was a fascinating series, always got short shrift. *Joe 90*, I think is my favourite of them all." Fellow director Alan Perry concurs in praising the series: "I quite liked *Joe 90* as a series. It was different and it was imaginative; the kids could put themselves in the position of Joe 90."

While the 'kids play Bond' theme seemed a winner, some of the crew had reservations about the reality of the plots in which a nine-year-old would, week after week, risk his life and frequently end up killing people (for instance in *Hi-Jacked* where Joe ruthlessly kills an enemy with a grenade). Desmond Saunders explains his views: "With *Joe 90*, some people – and I think I agreed with them – were very mystified by this boy being so sophisticated and doing quite unpleasant things. There was an unpleasant side to it which I never really understood. There was something about it that was very strange and sinister." Leo Eaton endorses this view somewhat, commenting: "By today's standards it's a bit, 'Oh!'" Director Ken Turner laughs this off saying, "It never occurred to us that we were brainwashing a young kid because it was for the good of mankind!"

This uneasiness about Joe's antics led to the recording of a special warning, which was played in some regions: "These are Joe 90's special glasses. Without them, he's a boy. Wearing them, he's an expert."

Joe 90 ran for one series of 30 episodes, covering Joe's tenth year (he turns ten in the final episode). Shooting wrapped in August 1968 when Leo Eaton shot the downright bizarre *See You Down There* in which W.I.N. convince a crooked businessman that he's hallucinating, in order to trick him into compensating companies that he ruthlessly destroyed. Eaton also completed the linking segments for the 'flashback' episode *The Birthday*, while Peter Anderson filmed *Viva Cordova*, featuring a guest voice from *Captain Scarlet* actress Elizabeth Morgan. She comments on her solo *Joe 90* appearance: "You know how it is. They needed a voice, they called around and everybody else was out shopping. So they called me in."

As with *Captain Scarlet and the Mysterons*, *Joe 90* had not been unsuccessful, but it had not been *Thunderbirds*. Sylvia reflects on this saying, "Strangely enough kids don't want to see other kids on screen. We found that out by trial and error. Kids don't want to see someone like themselves. They're far more interested in seeing someone who's a role model."

By September 29th when the series premiered on television, it was becoming slowly evident that the audience was losing interest

in the sophisticated puppets, although this didn't stop the launch of a comic especially devoted to the series. "Because of our previous success we were strong enough to launch a *Joe 90* comic which did OK," says Keith Shackleton. "From a standing start it would never have been launched, but it was launched on the back of the success of *TV21* and *Lady Penelope*. Nevertheless it did OK and didn't dent the profit and loss account so everybody was happy!"

Within the studio there was a definite feeling that things were starting to wind down. "I think *Joe 90* turned out very well," says David Lane. "But I think the team themselves were starting to get a little tired."

It was therefore unsurprising to the crew when they learned that the next series was to be the end of the line for Supermarionation…

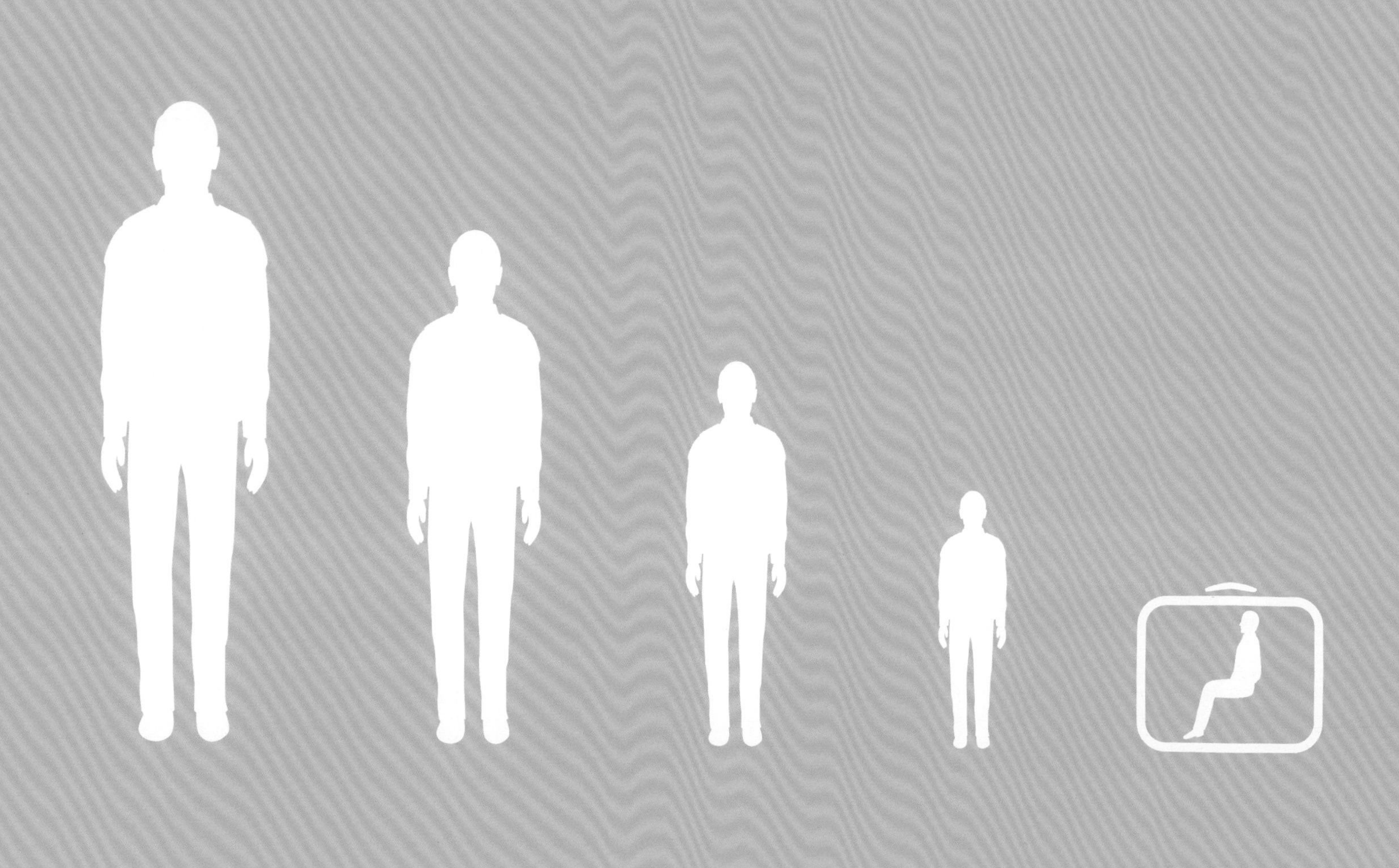

THE SECRET SERVICE

•1968•

11 A CASE FOR THE BISHOP

The Secret Service

Ever since *Thunderbirds Are Go* had entered production, Gerry and Sylvia Anderson had increasingly reduced their involvement with the television side of the operation. The long-held ambition to produce big movies was finally bearing fruit, and so they left the television production to their colleagues, safe in the knowledge that all would be well. For *Joe 90,* Reg Hill, David Lane and Desmond Saunders took control of the day to day running as Executive Producer, Producer and Production Controller respectively. Gerry says: “Knowing me, if the left-hand side of the studio is working on a television series and the right-hand side is devoted to the big screen, with the big sound and the 70-piece orchestra, then that’s where my heart would have been.”[1] However, when it is put to Gerry that he was less hands-on with the later Supermarionation series, he replies defensively, “I have never taken a back seat on any of my productions.”

There is no suggestion that Gerry wasn’t hard working. Indeed, work appeared in many ways to be his whole life. Nevertheless, he was rarely present at the Century 21 studios in the later Supermarionation years, something that did not go unnoticed by the crew. Model maker Alan Shubrook, who joined the company in 1966, comments: “When I started working at the studio, I expected Gerry Anderson - which was a name that flashed up on the front of every single programme - to be there on the set, directing, commanding and telling everybody the magic of his ways. So I was fairly shocked that as the months and months went by that I never saw Gerry Anderson. I used to comment to people, ‘What does Gerry Anderson do because he’s never at the studios?’ Of course he had roles that were in post production, he was into selling the company abroad etc. He was in a much more executive position having sold the company off to ATV.”

Effects Director Shaun Whittacker-Cook feels that Gerry’s lack of presence was bad for morale. “Gerry Anderson, when I first met him, I was very taken. He was another person that was very passionate about the film industry and making films. Sadly, after a few TV series, he took an office suite at Pinewood, there was a

1. From *What Made Thunderbirds Go - The Official Gerry Anderson Biography* by Simon Archer and Marcus Hearn (2002).

SLOW
M TRIM 68.

separation, and we found ourselves the poor relatives over on the Slough Trading Estate."

"He'd kind of mentally left the show," says David Lane. "He was now on another mission – to get this live-action film underway."

The puppets had always been a means to an end for Gerry, and no matter how successful they became, he still had his eye on the elusive treasure of working with real actors. Finally, in 1967, his wish was granted when *Doppelgänger* was greenlit.

Jay Kanter, an executive from Universal Pictures, was on a visit to London in the summer of that year. After reading this in a newspaper, Anderson quickly organised a meeting with Kanter and met him in town, armed with ideas and a script that he and Sylvia had written previously with a view to having it produced as an ATV play. The upshot of this was *Doppelgänger*, the company's first major commission with live actors (*Crossroads to Crime* must be discounted in this context – "The less said about it the better," said Sylvia in 1966!)[2].

After the initial screenplay for *Doppelgänger* – written by the Andersons in collaboration with Tony Williamson – failed to light Universal's enthusiasm, the pair called in writer Donald James (who would also contribute to both *Joe 90* and *The Secret Service*) to scrutinise and revise their work. It was in this updated form that the project entered production at Pinewood Studios in July 1968, when tail-end episodes of *Joe 90* were still being shot.

Starring Ian Hendry and Roy Thinnes (or vice-versa, depending on which side of the Atlantic you were watching, as the billing was reversed for each territory) the film concerns the discovery of a new planet which occupies the same orbit as Earth, but is hidden from view by being positioned exactly opposite us, on the other side of the sun. Colonel Glenn Ross and Dr John Kane are sent by EUROSEC (EUROpean Space Exploration Council) to investigate. An electrical storm causes their space craft to crash and when Ross recovers consciousness he discovers that Kane is in a critical condition. His surroundings lead him to assume that he and his partner are back on Earth. Slowly he begins to suspect that all is not as it should be, and realises that instead of returning home he has crash-landed on the new planet which, it transpires, is a complete mirror image of our own…

Century 21's first foray into large scale live-action movies was not an entirely smooth ride. Despite Gerry wanting David Lane to helm the picture, as he had done with *Thunderbirds Are Go* and *Thunderbird 6*, Universal insisted on what they referred to as a 'bankable' director. This director was found in the form of Robert Parrish, whose career highlights included being one of the many directors credited for the production nightmare that was *Casino*

---

2. Studio publicity material for *Thunderbirds Are Go* charting the history of A.P. Films.

Opposite: Mike Trim's painting of the vehicle assembly building from *Doppelgänger*.

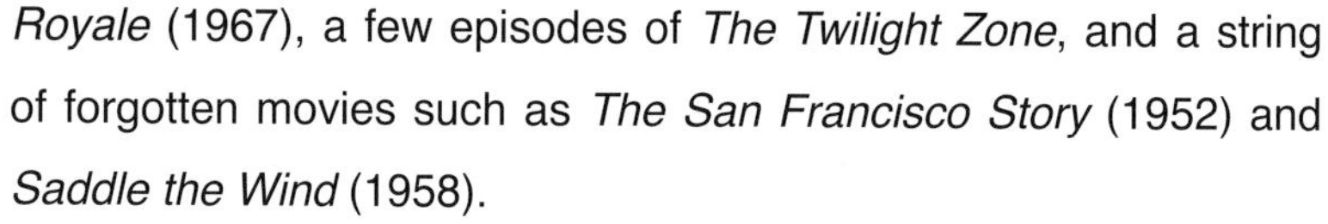

Royale (1967), a few episodes of *The Twilight Zone*, and a string of forgotten movies such as *The San Francisco Story* (1952) and *Saddle the Wind* (1958).

Parrish proved to be a nightmare to work with, generally trying to avoid following any instructions from the directors of Century 21; in one instance, he attempted to delete a number of scenes without reference to anyone else, simply because he, personally, felt they were unnecessary. It was pointed out to him that by doing so, he would be in breach of contract and he reluctantly relented. However, the problems were not to end there and the eventual outcome was a major acrimonious dispute between the four company directors.

As with any contentious moment involving more than one person, the specific details are mangled by time, fading memories and of course the point of view of the person recounting the tale. What can be certain is that John Read, acting as Director of Photography on *Doppelgänger*, had shot a scene in the way that he had been directed to by Parrish. Sylvia remembers the conflict arising from a sequence showing actress Loni von Friedl in the shower, and a dispute about the lighting (Robert wanted a silhouette whereas Gerry wanted to see the full nude image). The upshot was that Gerry asked John to re-shoot the scene according to *his* directions. John refused, arguing that he had to follow the instructions of the film's official director. Gerry, however, felt that John had a duty as a director of the company to act with the firm rather than against it. Whatever the precise situation, the result was that John was forced to resign from the company. Gerry argues that he had the support of Reg Hill and Sylvia, whereas Sylvia is quite keen to place the ball firmly in Gerry's court and distance herself from the decision. Ultimately, however serious it may have seemed at the time, the dispute was not big enough to justify the loss of one of the most important contributors to the company's success. John Read was a brilliant technician who had worked on all aspects of production from pushing the development of the video-assist, right down to the painting of gun flashes onto the negatives for *Four Feather Falls*. Without John, it is difficult to see how the company could have developed so successfully, and his remarkable talent is indelibly marked on every production he participated in.

Doppelgänger failed to impress the executives at Universal and was not released until October 1969. However, the film did convince Lew Grade that the Andersons were capable of transferring their unique style of film-making to productions involving live actors, and made it clear that he'd be willing to set Century 21 free from their puppet constraints.

Whilst Century 21 continued to develop ideas for a new live-action venture, the stages at Slough were well under way with the next series: a series half-way between live action and Supermarionation.

During production of *Doppelgänger*, Gerry discovered that entertainer Stanley Unwin was also on-site at Pinewood, doing the post-syncing[3] for his role in *Chitty Chitty Bang Bang*. Unwin was famous for his trademark 'Unwinese', a corrupted form of English, that had its own internal logic, meaning that it was possible to follow what was being said, despite it breaking many grammatical rules. Unwin attributed the beginnings of this strange dialect back to a conversation he had had one night with his mother: "I said to my mother, 'Why are you in such a distraught, mother?' So she said, 'Well, I fallolloped in front of a tram and grazed my knee-clapper.'"[4]

From there, Unwin developed this special language for his children: "I found they enjoyed the stories even more when I used double talk. I was also interested in speaking like this because I had always been intrigued by the lack of communication between people when talking to each other, and I realised that they listened far more attentively if you said something strangely."[5] Unwin got his break while working as a radio engineer at the BBC in the 1940s, when he used his 'Unwinese' on a test recording. This was played to BBC producers who encouraged Stanley to enter show business in addition to his work as an engineer. By 1960, he was so much in demand that he abandoned his job as an engineer to pursue a full-time career in entertainment.

Gerry Anderson loved Stanley Unwin and his gobbledygook language, so he dreamt up a format around him, as he explains: "I thought it would be a great idea if I cast him in the role of a secret agent; he played the part of a priest and he had his own church, hence the title – the double meaning – *The Secret Service*. If he ever got into a difficult spot, say the police had stopped him, he would talk to them in his Unwinese and that would fox the police totally.

---

3. Post-syncing is where dialogue is re-recorded in a studio with the actor making sure that their new attempt at their lines matches perfectly with their mouth movements on-screen. It is often necessary for scenes that are recorded on location, where there may be background noise that has rendered the original soundtrack unusable.

4. Interview with Kevin Jon Davies (1995)

5. From the ITC publicity booklet.

They'd have to be polite – 'I'm sorry, I didn't quite get that,' because they're writing it down. He says, 'I'll repeat that,' then he repeats the whole lot and, of course, the guy is saying 'I didn't understand that'. Eventually, the police would say, 'Yes, yes, I quite understand, Sir. Sorry to trouble you, off you go.' So that was the gimmick."

Although it seems extremely unlikely that any official would let someone go simply because they couldn't understand their bizarre speech, Stanley Unwin did find himself in a not dissimilar situation when he was in the Army and had to get past a military policeman, as he recounted in 1995: "We had to have a password (to enter). He asked me for the password, and I gave him the right one, but he was still using the previous one and wouldn't let me in. I wanted to get in because it was a briefing by General Patton, so I said, 'Look, credit of on the shoulders whom either side for these, you see, and furthermore this is important – the V.I.P.s that I get this message through.' 'Oh,' he said, 'Why didn't you say so?' and he opened the gate and let me in. I rather expected to get put in jail for that. I think I was very lucky on that occasion."

Unwin also discussed meeting Gerry Anderson: "On *Chitty Chitty Bang-Bang* we were doing the post-syncing, because a lot of it was recorded in the open, out in the Mediterranean. It wasn't easy to do my Unwinese, which I did off the top of my head, largely. So I had to listen to a recording of my voice, learn it and do it all over again. While I was there, my agent happened to be up there and he said, 'I want you to meet Gerry Anderson.' He was there at the time and we had a chat and he explained that he wanted me to appear in long-shot live and be a parson – how did I like the idea? I said, 'It sounds great,' and he said, 'We'll make a puppet that looks like you.'"

The idea of filming on location for effects shots had started with *Thunderbird 6*, and was extended to include giving the puppet-unit an outing in an episode of *Joe 90*. This happened when Director, Ken Turner, took a crew to a church in Harefield (St. David's, parish church of the Reverend Joseph Shepherd) to film certain sequences for the Christmas episode *The Unorthodox Shepherd*. A full-sized dummy, representing the episode's villain, Mason, accompanied the team and was used in various shots at the church. It was felt that the effect was convincing, so Anderson extended the idea further for *The Secret Service*.

Anderson's idea was to conquer the age-old curse of Supermarionation once and for all – by getting humans to take on those tasks that revealed puppets to be just that: puppets. "Again it was the problem that we couldn't make the puppets walk," says Gerry. "I came up with the idea of getting Stanley Unwin to do all the walking shots, and driving shots in this Model T Ford that he had. If, for example, you had a sequence where Stanley Unwin would arrive at a building in his Model T, he would drive it down the street, up to the curb, turn the engine off, get out, walk down the path, and as he opened the door, you'd cut to the reverse angle and that would be the *puppet* of Stanley Unwin. So, in the same way that I used (real) hands to enable a puppet to pick things up, I used Stanley Unwin, married to his own puppet to enable him to do all the things that the puppet couldn't do."

On the 20th August 1968 Unwin was sent a contract confirming the terms of his employment. The contract stipulated that Unwin must "[...] *render such services in such studios as may be required of you in accordance with the provisions of the two attached engagement forms by way of recording dialogue for sound tracks and appearing before the cameras to perform the part of Father Unwin all in respect of the series.*" He also agreed to, "*attend such sittings and to assist in such processes as we may reasonably require to enable a puppet with a facsimile of your face in the make-up and pose of Father Unwin as portrayed by you to be made for use in the series,*" and that "*You [...] acknowledge that any copyright and all other rights in both the said puppet and the character Father Unwin (including your portrayal of the character) belong to us absolutely.*" Unwin was engaged for an initial run of 13 episodes, with Century 21 having the right to extend for a further 13 instalments. For each picture Unwin received £250.

The initial idea was fleshed out into a full format which was detailed thus in the publicity guides:

Opposite, above: Onlookers can't quite believe Century 21's latest piece of hardware.

Below: Matthew is chased up a tree in *The Feathered Spies.*

A country priest and his gardener are hardly likely to be suspected of being secret agents, but they become one of the most efficient and versatile teams of operators in the British Intelligence.

Father Unwin lives in the Vicarage next to his beautiful country church. It's a quiet and peaceful setting, with Mrs Appleby attending to the housework and Matthew Harding helping out in the garden. Nothing could be more natural...

Father Unwin, like most priests, is directly responsible to his Bishop, but in this case, the Bishop stands for British Intelligence Service Headquarters Operation Priest, and the Bishop sits not in the midst of a diocese but in Whitehall. Only he knows of Father Unwin's service activities and, when duty calls, he can contact him at any time via a cleverly camouflaged inter-communication system incorporated into Father Unwin's hearing aid.

And when duty calls, Matthew drops his slow-thinking yokel act and becomes the alert, athletic, intelligent counter-agent, embarking with Father Unwin on the next case, with the aid of their unique scientific equipment which enables Father Unwin to reduce Matthew in size until he is only about two feet high. Matthew can then be transported in a specially converted suitcase.

The electronic controls of the miniaturisation process are concealed in what seems like an ordinary book, which Father Unwin keeps in his study.

Inside the book is an elaborate instrument panel, and when he manipulates the controls, a series of electronic sounds are heard, increasing in pitch, and a small periscope rises from the control panel and focuses a beam of light on Matthew's chest. The light flashes brilliantly and then the periscope recedes, leaving Matthew a third of his normal size, dwarfed by surrounding objects.

The case he travels in is equipped with a chair and a periscope so that he can watch the world go by in comfort and see what is happening outside. There are also drawers and compartments to house the miniature tools and instruments he may need on a mission.

He can open and close the case himself by means of controls, and if he wants to communicate with Father Unwin he has only to speak and Father Unwin can hear him through his hearing aid. In turn, Matthew himself can receive messages by donning a hearing aid when on a mission.

They work independently but in very close association towards the same goal. Father Unwin takes the travelling case, with Matthew inside, to a strategical point, or as near as possible to the assignment, and leaves it there. Matthew is thus able to gain entry and operate at the heart of the crime or as an inside link-man. In one episode, for example, he has to cause a 'plane to make a forced landing and to do this Father Unwin takes him to the hangar where the 'plane is kept.

In his reduced size, Matthew is able to avoid detection when it would be difficult for a full-sized man to do so. He can also take advantage of conditions where there is limited space to manoeuvre.

The entire success of their undercover work depends on their being able to operate anonymously, and Father Unwin and Matthew have an excellent front for their activities. Not even Mrs, Appleby, Father Unwin's housekeeper, suspects what they are doing.

And Father Unwin is as conscious of his spiritual responsibilities as any other priest. If his experiences can provide him with any material for his sermons, he conveys it to his congregation in symbolic and well-disguised terms.

"*The Secret Service* was just a bit weird!" says director Leo Eaton bluntly. "All of us, even at the time said, "What!?" He is not alone in his negative assessment, as Production Controller Desmond Saunders attests: "*The Secret Service* was an experience that I suppose I never really felt happy about. It was strange. I suppose it was the gobbledygook and the mixture of live action with puppets. It never seemed to me to be a very good idea."

"When we moved on to *The Secret Service*, not only did I feel that something wasn't right, but I think the team around me felt the same," says model maker Alan Shubrook. "We were going into a series which was a mixture of live-action, a mixture of puppets, a mixture of special effects and all that with a leading character that talked gobbledygook that you couldn't understand. We'd gone through *Thunderbirds*, *Captain Scarlet* and *Joe 90* and surely we were looking now for something that would be so *special*. So when *The Secret Service* scripts were put in front of us they didn't really excite anybody at all. I think there was an air of almost depression in the effects studio because the effects were fairly boring for us. It certainly wasn't a direction that I thought the studio should be going in. *The Secret Service* was the alarm bells ringing for the beginning of the end."

"He was a funny old stick," says Leo of Stanley Unwin. "I never thought he was funny. I remember him coming in once and Mary (Turner) showing him the head, and he was really impressed that he had a puppet head." Fellow voice artist Gary Files remembers Stanley more fondly: "He was always such a gentleman and a gentle man as well. How many people can you say that about? He also made me feel that it was a real partnership between us. He wore his stardom with genuine surprise. So many people would recognise him in the street and it always surprised him. If they got lost remembering who he was, he would take devilish pleasure in admitting to being that uncle of someone in the family, or whoever else they came up with...'because they really did know him.'

"But always, more than anything, he was the consummate professional. He did some terrific stuff for the show, and it was an education for me to watch him at work and learn by it. He had some wonderful stories – but unlike many, chose the right time to tell them. We all loved working with him. How could you be otherwise with a man who answered his phone with, 'Who calls?' and when you said who you were replied, 'Deep joy.'"

When it came to making the miniature Unwin, he was in the safe hands of Mary Turner, who apart from being the second longest serving puppeteer / sculptor, had also sculpted the John Rostill puppet for the dream sequence in *Thunderbirds Are Go,* and so was well-versed in capturing true likenesses. Following a photographic session at the Century 21 studios, Mary was given the pictures of Unwin and she began sculpting the head; the result is one of the most impressive artistic feats accomplished by the puppet workshop, as it is an uncanny likeness.

The remaining characters were all drawn from the repertory company, with the exception of Mrs Appleby (sculpted by Christine Glanville to look like her mother) and The Bishop.

Similarly, with the exception of Stanley Unwin, the supporting voice cast were drawn from the same pool of supporting regular actors that had featured in *Captain Scarlet* and *Joe 90*: Keith Alexander (Sam Loover – *Joe 90*); Jeremy Wilkin (Virgil Tracy – *Thunderbirds*, Captain Ochre – *Captain Scarlet and the Mysterons*); and David Healy (Shane Weston – *Joe 90*). The three regular supporting roles of Mrs Appleby, Matthew and The Bishop were assigned to Sylvia Anderson, Gary Files and Jeremy Wilkin respectively.

Derek Meddings and his team found themselves sidelined, as there were no major vehicles to be constructed, apart from a miniature yellow Model T Ford that was required to match a genuine

Right: Conventional, everyday things in miniature – the station from *Last Train to Bufflers Halt* and, below, the Gabriel miniature.

version that the studios managed to acquire for filming. With the present day setting (at that time the 1960s) way-out vehicles were a thing of the past (or should that be future?). Most of the effects focussed on making conventional, everyday things realistic in miniature (such as the railway in *Last Train to Bufflers Halt*).

A lot of what would have traditionally been the provenance of the effects team, such as cars speeding along or landscape shots, now fell to the location unit headed by Ken Turner. When filming each episode, they would go out and shoot the location sequences first. This would include anything more easily performed 'live' than with puppets and models. Subsequently, these shots would often be intercut with the puppet / model work, such as in this sequence from *May-Day, May-Day.*[6]

CUT TO:

121. EXT. POLICE STATION – DAY *(Puppet set)*
To establish
CUT TO:

122. MS – TOOLMAKER *(Puppet set)*
On the steps of the Police Station. He turns to the sound of skidding tyres.

123. EXT. CAR – DAY *(Location)*
ARAB with a gun. Roaring fast along the road.

6. Taken from the original script (working title: *Bombs Away).* Notes in italics have been added by the author.

CUT TO:

124. INT. CAR – DAY *(Deleted)*
Shoot across ARAB aiming his gun out of window.
CUT TO:

125. EXT. CAR – DAY *(Location)*
Gun is fired as it roars past.
CUT TO:

126. MCS – TOOLMAKER *(Puppet set)*
He is hit.
CUT TO:

127. EXT. ROAD – DAY *(Location)*
Rear view of car speeding away

Curiously, the use made of the puppet stars in *The Secret Service* is effectively the reverse of conventional filmmaking. Normally, it is usual to have the live actors in the close-up shots while using models for the distance shots. In this instance, it is the models (puppets) in all the close-ups and the live actors in all the long-shots!

It is understandable that Gerry wanted to get away from puppets, and it can be seen why he wanted to reduce the amount of time spent trying to get puppets to do things that they simply weren't capable of doing; however, intercutting the live-action and puppet shots simply doesn't work. It requires more than the audience can give in terms of acceptance. The puppets and special effects had always worked well together because they existed in the same artificial universe. The lighting was consistent and, because the puppets were *clearly* artificial (no matter how hard they tried to hide it), this allowed the audience to believe in the effects shots, even when they didn't pull off absolute realism. There was the bonus that if an effects shot looked real, everyone loved it, but if it didn't, there was a large amount of forgiveness from the predominantly child audience, because the effect was that of your favourite toys coming to life and doing all the things you really wanted them to do. By contrast, no such forgiveness is extended when you see a puppet in a car, then cut to a human getting out of the vehicle and walking across the road. The viewers simply find themselves removed from the storytelling, as the brain knows that the shots do not match. It is one thing to ask the viewer to believe in an aircraft doing incredible things; it is quite another to try to pass off a human and a puppet as the same person. Ken Turner comments: "From my own point of view I didn't feel you could get away with it. But who was I to say? Everything in the past had been so successful."

Projectionist Tony Stacey has fond memories of *The Secret Service* though. "It was a favourite of mine," he reveals. "Mainly because of the other hat I used to wear, running errands and stuff, because I actually taught Stanley Unwin to drive the Model T Ford. I went with John Read to Theydon Bois in Essex to buy the thing. I think we paid £1200; it'd be about £25,000 now I should think!

"Theydon Bois was a town in Epping Forest and this bloke restored classic cars. It was a little 2 seater Model T, 1917 or 18

Reduced to the ranks – Captain Scarlet and Colonel White, amongst the supporting players in *The Secret Service*.

model. It hadn't got an electric starter and of course the crew soon started having problems with that, so they actually modified it to have an electric starter which the later Model Ts did.

"I used to go up to Farnham Road to the shops, park out in the front in this Model T, and do the shopping for the studios!"[7]

Among the live-action sequences filmed for the series was a selection of shots of The Church of St Michael and All Angels in High Wycombe, doubling for Father Unwin's parish in the opening and closing titles. Once back in the cutting room, these shots were assembled and matched to Barry Gray's music. In 1979, Barry discussed the music: "It was Gerry's idea for me to write something in the style of Bach and get the Swingle Singers to do it. To cut a long story short, I went to France to see Wolf Swingle and try and get it set up, but their fee was so exorbitant it just wasn't on. So I came back and we did it with the Mike Sammes Singers. In fact, I wrote the idea for my three-part fugue that I did on the plane coming back."[8]

The title theme was recorded in October, and by December, Gerry was ready for the all-important screening for Lew Grade. The screening proceeded smoothly until halfway through the episode. Father Unwin is speeding to Oakington Airfield, near Oxford, in the Model T, on his way to rendezvous with his miniaturised accomplice, Matthew, who is on-board an aircraft about to make a forced landing. Suddenly, he sees flashing lights and pulls over.

POLICEMAN:	Did you realise, sir, that you were exceeding the speed limit?
UNWIN:	I'm afraid I didn't, officer.
POLICEMAN:	Well you will be reported for the question to be considered of prosecuting you for exceeding the speed limit.
UNWIN:	Quite so.
POLICEMAN:	You're not obliged to say anything unless you wish to do so, but what you say may be put into writing and used in evidence.
UNWIN:	Ah yes. Writey scribbley in your bookery. All uttery words speed of your penciload must deceive my eyebold.
POLICEMAN:	I, er… I didn't quite catch that, sir.
UNWIN:	Ah pardlow, I'll explaidy. Now Matthew my gardener is deep joy with green fingers in the garbage, you understabe?

"Cut! Cut! Cut! Stop! Put the lights up!" cried out Lew Grade, leaping to his feet. Gerry Anderson was startled by this outburst, just as he had been by Lew's reaction to *Thunderbirds* four years before. However, this time Lew's response was vastly different, as

7. Tony Stacey talking to Richard Farrell for *Andersonic* Magazine.

8. Barry Gray speaking to Ralph Titterton for *Viking Radio* in 1979.

133 CS - POLICEMAN

He is now armed with notebook and pencil but is obviously bewildered.

POLICEMAN: I er didn't quite catch that, sir.

CUT TO:

134 CU - FATHER UNWIN

FATHER UNWIN: I'm so sorry, let me explain. Matthew my gardener, he's been very good; dig it and plant with the green fingerload you understand. Well Matthew and I are on an urgent mission for the Bishop. Unforturnode, Matthew in the engine terrible noise, bang crash vibrating with the ear drum, and the plane is about to crash. I must arrive before it's too late. A matter of life and death.

During this dialogue we have cut to the POLICEMAN several times looking up from his notebook, completely bewildered and unable to follow what is being said. Desperately trying to make sense of it all.

CUT TO:

135 CU - POLICEMAN

POLICEMAN: A matter of life and death, you say, sir.

Gerry explains: "'Cancel the show, Gerry. Just finish off the first thirteen.' I said, 'Why?' and he said, 'They'll never understand him in America!' I said, 'But, Lew! That's the whole point, they're not *supposed* to understand.' He said, 'No, no, no, no!'"

It seemed Lew had failed to understand the central premise of the series. In retrospect, Gerry is amused by Lew's reaction: "That was the end of that one!" he says with a broad grin.

It is unlikely that Grade cancelled the series solely because he objected to the Unwinese. Holding the position he did in the entertainment industry, it is hard to believe that Grade was unaware of Stanley's trademark language, and even if he had been, Gerry would surely have explained the inclusion of 'gobbledygook' when he outlined the premise to him. No one knows what was running through Grade's mind the day the first episode was laced up in

Above, left: "Writey scribbley in your bookery." Father Unwin and a real-life security guard.

Right: "Cut! Cut!" The scene that pulled the plug on Father Unwin's adventures, from the original script.

the projector for him, but given the ease with which the 'Unwinese' element could have been removed from the series, it seems probable that he simply didn't like a lot of what he was seeing.

There was also a financial consideration. "We were told that the reason they cancelled making any more of *The Secret Service* was the cost," says Tony Stacey. "There was a comparison that Lew Grade had made with Gerry that they could actually make an episode of *The Avengers* cheaper than they could make a half hour episode of *Secret Service*, which was the beginning of the end for the puppets."

"I think you'd better switch permanently to live action," `Lew Grade told Gerry in one of their frequent early-morning meetings.

Ultimately, Gerry had got his wish and would soon be freed from the manacles of Supermarionation. A number of factors are likely to have prompted Lew's decision. Firstly, whether or not he liked what he was seeing, Lew may have had doubts about who exactly *The Secret Service* was aimed at: the children were hardly going to identify with a priest in a Model T Ford, and the adults were unlikely to be interested in puppets deployed in such a traditional espionage format (no matter how off-beat the implementation was). Secondly, *Doppelgänger* had given him an insight into how a live-action concept might be worked out and *UFO* was now underway. Thirdly, and perhaps most importantly, ITV was at maximum saturation with this specialised form of filmmaking and, even in 1968, it was still possible to see *The Adventures of Twizzle* and *Four Feather Falls*. In fact, the whole of APF / Century 21's back catalogue was on a loop throughout the 1960s and, as with anything that is phenomenally popular, the time must come when the audience is satiated and drifts away to something else.

The harsh reality was reflected in the declining sales of the comic, *TV21*, which limped on a little longer under new ownership, before finally expiring.

The empire was dead.

"I think we'd seen the writing on the wall," says Sylvia Anderson. "It wasn't going to go on forever. It was a novelty that had lost its novelty." She also comments that Lew, who had always provided so much help, was now preoccupied with his own battles. "Lew Grade had a more and more difficult job on with ATV, so it's all beginning to fade a bit." Keith Shackleton agrees: "I opted out at the end of the '60s because I was disenchanted with a number of things. They were losing their way, ATV."

The news that the puppet studios were to close filtered through to an unsurprised crew. "It was a big blow when Gerry said we're closing down and just selling everything," says David Lane.

"I remember none of us thinking it would last," says Leo Eaton. "I don't think any of us were surprised when it was cancelled. I seem to remember Gerry softening the blow to me by saying that I was going on to *UFO* as an Assistant Director."

"It seemed to me that things were winding down a bit because the main crew had gone off to make the live-action film," says Mary Turner. "Which was obviously much more exciting to Gerry because it was live-action instead of puppets which he never really wanted to do." Sylvia feels the end of the puppet era was inevitable. "I think we were just about out of ideas (about what to do with the puppets). It was a natural progression. We were going onto something we'd wanted to do for quite some time."

For a large number of the crew, there was the excitement of moving on to *UFO* as directors, set designers, scriptwriters, effects technicians, etc. In the world of live action though, there was no room for puppeteers. "I think there was a slight sense of betrayal; that Gerry had left behind the people who built his fame. He left them a bit in the lurch," says Eaton. "I do remember a sense of sadness. I particularly remember sadness from Rowena White (puppeteer). I remember her being really sad and sitting on the rail one day and talking about it coming to an end." Mary Turner says: "The puppets had been so successful it seemed silly not to go on and do more."

"Quite a few of us got together," says Ken Turner. "We tried to talk the powers that be into that, 'OK, you go off and do the live-action series and we can make this work. We can still make this a success. There's no reason to give it up.' We really tried hard to keep it going. It was a loss as far as we were concerned."

Keith Shackleton reflects on the situation and feels that the demise of the puppets need not have come as soon as it did. He is critical of Gerry's decision to let ATV buy the company. "We sold out to Lew Grade in the mid 60s and I would characterise the relationship by saying the honeymoon was most enjoyable but the marriage was not so. I wish I'd been able to influence Gerry in the direction of the company. I remember saying to Gerry, 'Why are we selling out to Lew Grade?' His response: 'I want a Rolls Royce.' I said, 'Gerry, hang on a moment and you can have two Rolls Royces.' We could have been another Disney."

Gerry was unmoved to see his puppet days behind him. As a leader of a group of pioneers, he looked to the future and enjoyed his new association with actors: "I started to think: 'It's amazing! They speak! Their mouths are in sync with their words! And they can walk! And they can pick up things! Boy – this is going to be absolutely fabulous!' That was my first impression…"

Production on the final episodes of *The Secret Service* continued throughout January 1969, and filming on the last Supermarionation production concluded on a high, with a glorious episode entitled *More Haste, Less Speed*. Whilst the episode is free from the fare that had made the studios so famous – dramatic action and exciting visuals – it does hark back to the gentler, earlier days of *Supercar* with a story about hunting down plates for printing counterfeit money. In the story, Lord Hazelwell and his sister Martha have inherited one side of a dollar plate from their "late, lamented father." The other plate, as they explain to another crook, Spiker, is in the possession of their father's accomplice, Mullins, who is about to be released from prison. Upon his release, Mullins explains that he knows where the other plate is. The rest of the story concerns the four crooks double-crossing each other in order to escape with both plates. It is a wonderfully quirky story with some nice comedy from scriptwriter

Tony Barwick, enhanced by the excellent vocal performances of the cast, including Keith Alexander as Lady Martha(!), and David Graham making a farewell visit to Supermarionation as Lord Hazelwell. The episode also includes one unintentionally hilarious moment that illustrates beautifully why the live-action inserts didn't work. This occurs when the puppet of Lady Martha creeps out from behind the bushes, before cutting to a shot of a man in drag (Lady Martha again) tip-toeing across the screen and zooming away on a motorbike!

When the concluding episode of *The Secret Service* was complete, Supermarionation died.

"A company reaches its peak. And I think our peak was *Thunderbirds*," says David Lane, who by this time was exhausted by the punishing schedule. "I don't know whether I was relieved, pleased or disappointed. I can't remember. I think I was all three. Because it was 12 years of pure enjoyment really.

"You have great moments in time and I think it was time to close the shop."

On January 24th 1969, the puppet studios closed.

Although the special effects team would remain for *UFO*, gradually the entire studio was dismantled and the building was prepared for a new company to take on the lease. Mike Trim reflects on this time: "One of my great regrets was when Century 21 finally folded and you looked around the place and you saw this wealth of talent that had been assembled slowly over the years, where people had developed their own skills and it all built up into this quite slick machine that could handle these stories. Whatever the writer threw at us it would come out at the end of the day looking reasonably close to what they asked for. And then suddenly here was this whole thing being broken up at a time when the film industry had collapsed and there wasn't the work out there. They couldn't just skip off and work on another *Cleopatra* or whatever it was. They were sort of disappearing into the outer world, trying to employ these techniques and skills that they had developed in some way or another to earn a living. It seemed a very sad time to me.

"I always look back on it with quite a degree of emotion because, for me, it was nearly six and a half years I was there, and I look back with huge affection at the whole thing, really. It was tough. I nearly had a nervous breakdown in the middle of it at one stage. But you know, I'd do it all again. For sure."

The break-up of the studio had a particularly profound effect on Alan Shubrook: "A company had been called in to demolish everything within the studios. It was an outside team, they delivered half a dozen skips, and we had guys with sledgehammers coming in and dragging all the sets out into the field at the back of the studio and smashing them up and putting them into skips. And we had to stand there and watch this happening. We had no idea in those that days that the sets, the models, the puppets would obviously linger in so many people's memories for so many years and become such iconic figures. But the fact that everything we'd been doing for the past so many years was being destroyed in front of our eyes certainly brought tears to my eyes. The shock of it happening, and the shock that you walked away from the studio on that final day with a pile of skips behind you that was your last four years' work crushed into rubble, was a pretty hard thing to swallow. And it left quite a mark on me."

It had all begun with an advert in a newspaper long ago. A two-line notice had shaped the future both in the real world and the puppet world. From humble beginnings in a toyshop where a little girl set her sights on a 'Twizzle' toy, APF / Century 21 had gone on to become one of the most prolific studios in the country and true pioneers in their field. They had struggled with methods now taken for granted, from video-assist through to filming in colour, pushing television production to rival feature films. With the passage of time, it is now clear that the tiny film studio in Slough changed the industry as we know it, and its place in media history is assured.

No one has described the moment when the last lovingly-constructed puppet sets were torn apart, and the small silent characters, each with its personal array of heads, were evicted from their home. Did they perhaps blink sadly?

On that final day, puppeteer Rowena White wrote in her diary:

Last day. All had champagne. Cried.

A picture of the team, alleged to have been taken on the final day.

CODA

The surviving Century 21 crew quickly abandoned their puppet past for the chance to explore more adult film-making with their new live-action series *UFO*. Twenty-six episodes were produced, first at MGM British Studios at Borehamwood, and then, when they closed, at Pinewood Studios in Buckinghamshire. The special effects unit shed no tears for the loss of the puppet unit and quickly expanded to fill the gap left behind, producing some of their most spectacular work yet. Despite inconsistent scheduling across the ITV regions, the show picked up a following and, more importantly, was doing the business in America. Not long after production finished on the first twenty-six episodes, the Stirling Road premises were gutted of any sign of their brief film-making past and handed over to a new company for more conventional use.

With Gerry, Sylvia and Reg's contracts at Century 21 soon to expire, they decided to form a new independent production company called Group Three, that would receive commissions from Lew Grade just as A.P. Films had in the past. Its first commission was a giant step away from the world of space, and took the form of the action series *The Protectors*. In 1972, Grade finally took total control of Century 21. However, its glory days were over and the company was dissolved.

UFO was as susceptible to the whims of the Americans as the marionettes had been, and when ratings in the USA suddenly plummeted, the second series, currently in pre-production, was brought to a halt. With lightning speed, the Andersons pulled together to turn the situation around and revised the concept into a brand new series, *Space: 1999*.

Space: 1999 was a ground-breaking series in many ways and was a success overseas. However, Gerry and Sylvia's marriage was unable to take the phenomenal strain any longer and, after years of increasing tension, finally collapsed on the night of the wrap party for the first series in 1975.

A second series went into production in 1976, with the loss of Sylvia and the gain of unprecedented interference from the

Americans, which robbed the series of its dramatic undertones and replaced them with more comic-book action. When filming concluded in December that year, Gerry Anderson's long association with Lew Grade came to an end.

With the end of *Space: 1999* the last surviving fragments from Century 21 finally dissolved. Yet it is not a sad ending; many creative forces rose phoenix-like from the ashes of Century 21 and went on to new beginnings. After a hiatus, Gerry returned to film-making (and various forms of animation), delighting new generations of children once again; Sylvia carved a new, successful career for herself working at HBO; John Read and Mary Turner enjoyed their own puppet successes, creating the beautifully crafted *Rupert the Bear* series; Derek Meddings won an Oscar for his special effects work on *Superman*. This is merely a sample of the valuable contributions that the many ex-APF / Century 21 staff made to the film industry. However, many of them agree that those little studios in Slough were an incredible launch platform towards their own, personal, future.

Fifty years on: the old crew reunite at Ipswich Road to remember those halcyon days. On the bridge, Mary Turner and Roger Woodburn; down below, Judith Shutt, Desmond Saunders and David Elliott.

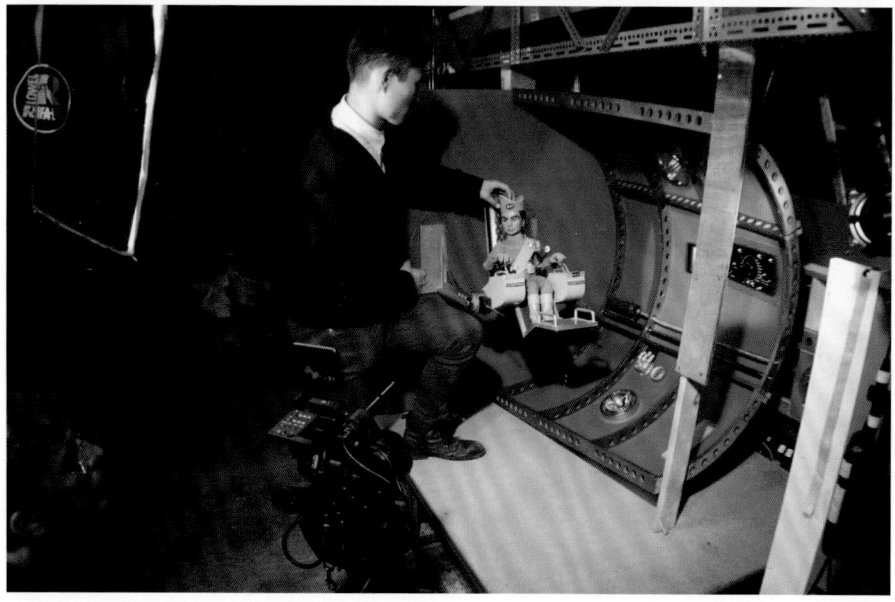

TB1

AFTERWORD

Filming in Supermarionation

As soon as it was suggested that I turn *Filmed in Supermarionation* into a documentary-film, I knew that I wanted to do puppet and special effects recreations. Since the 60s, there have been many great attempts to recapture the spirit of the shows, albeit it in a very modern way. For me, though, the key was to make something that looked like it could have been shot in the '60s. Having written a book on the subject, I felt well-equipped to deal with the challenges we might encounter: broken wires, wonky eyes, twisted arms etc. and on the first day, I walked into our miniature A.P. Films so excited at the prospect of working with the marionette stars of my childhood (albeit these were replicas). That excitement soon turned into a slight feeling of nausea and I rapidly came to understand why Gerry Anderson called them 'little bastards'. It's not that things go wrong - things go wrong on any film set - it's that every time something malfunctions it takes forever to fix it. On the final day of shooting, Parker's solenoid packed up resulting in a three hour break in shooting when it was already 9pm. Over five days, we had to work insane hours - just as they had done in the old days - to film a frighteningly small amount of material, with endless, interminable waits in between each set-up. It's not just a case of sticking these things in front of the camera - the reason why the original shows looked so amazing is that each and every scene was filmed with lavish care. The original crew was made up of people who were masters of their game - lighting cameramen who understood how important getting the lighting and depth of field right was to making these characters look 'non-puppety'; floor puppeteers who knew how to style the hair just right for camera so that you weren't constantly distracted by stray hairs; and puppeteers who honed their stage talents down into a more subtle art form for television. In many ways, the key to good Supermarionation is in what the puppets don't do - movements mustn't be too big and the eyes convey most of the feeling. For us, it was a learning curve I shall never forget.

Opposite: Thunderbirds are Go again – shooting the new material for *Filmed in Supermarionation*.

The special effects were slightly easier as we had a top team of miniature effects experts in to help us. Even so, there were major challenges as, again, we wanted to create effects that felt of the era, and recreation is far more difficult than doing your own thing. The original episodes were studied in mind-numbing detail and, as with the puppets, we sought the help and advice of the pioneering crew that had done it in the first place to make sure that we were using the right lenses, the correct lighting and filming at appropriate frame rates so that our conflagrations looked as impressive as possible. It was a tough experience, but a joyous one as, for a few days, the forgotten art of Supermarionation lived again. We came home from the shoots (a sort of Supermarionation school) burnt out, but full of admiration for the original team. We did it for 12 days, they did it for 12 years, which is probably why the shows still have an audience five decades on. They were made by tenacious, talented technicians, but above all, they were made with love.

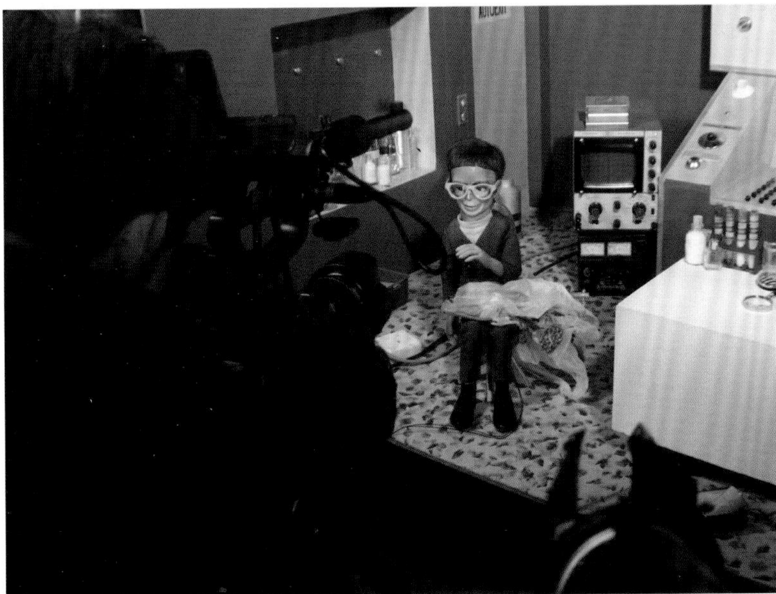

END TITLES

At the time I hated them. But, now, if you asked me, I'd say, 'Yes. I am very proud of them.' They were pioneering days, and they were a *lot* of fun.

Gerry Anderson

(Creator, Producer and Director of A.P. Films / Century 21)

I always remember my first interview with Gerry. He said, 'It's a puppet series we're doing, Julien. It may run for six months, if we're lucky. Possibly, it could go further, but if it runs for six months, then we'll have been very fortunate.' Several years later he was still making them.

Julien Lugrin

(Lighting Cameraman)

One of the great things about working at Slough, was working with a lot of people who had no experience of the film industry. We had quite a few experienced people, we had some moderately experienced people, but we had a lot of people that were introduced to their life in the film industry through us there. It was a marvellous experience.

Desmond Saunders

(Director, Production Manager, Editor and Writer)

They were great days. Great days. Enormous fun, especially in the early days. Everyone pulled together. Marvellous.

David Elliott

(Director, Editor and Production Supervisor)

The thing about APF, was there was nothing at the front door, and a finished product, that was constructed inside, came out the other end. It was all done within.

Alan Perry

(Director and Camera Operator)

It was a sweat-shop, but it was enormous fun!

Brian Johnson

(2nd Unit Special Effects Director)

I would say that A.P. Films was a great opportunity. Gerry was very kind in giving a lot of people their first start. I look back with nostalgia and think, 'Yeah, it wasn't *too* bad!'

Bill Harris

(Director and Editor)

I am pleased to have been creatively associated, with both *Supercar* and *The Avengers*, because I regard them as seminal. There is something different about them that has not happened since.

Martin Woodhouse

(Writer and co-creator of *Supercar*)

I loved being involved. Gerry and Sylvia made the experience so good for all of us, and I hope, (I'm sure) that we responded with good, and at times, inspired, work. The fact that so many Century 21 productions have turned out to be such successful cult programmes so many years after they were made is, for most of us actors involved, bewildering. But then, that's show business.

Gary Files

(Voice of Matthew in *The Secret Service* and many, many others)

The camaraderie and the friendship of all the actors / writers/ technicians, etc., was, I feel, unique to Century 21. They created a family atmosphere which allowed you to always give your best.

Ed Bishop

(Voice of Captain Blue in *Captain Scarlet and the Mysterons*)

I think it's very avant-garde. If you show them now, children do not feel that this is something of another age.

Liz Morgan

(Voice of Destiny, Rhapsody and Harmony Angels in *Captain Scarlet and the Mysterons*)

After about fifteen years, there's a new surge of viewers we've got. Really, it's the children of the viewers who watched it in the first place.

Bob Bell

(Art Director)

I think they'll go on forever. They'll keep coming back, I reckon.

Bill James

(Model maker)

It was a lot of good fun and good laughs and a happy time.

Judith Shutt

(Puppeteer)

We really felt like a family while we were all doing it...at least that is my impression, and I wouldn't change that time for anything.

Matt Zimmerman

(Voice of Alan Tracy in *Thunderbirds*)

It is impossible to imagine what my life would have been like without those incredible years working on over one hundred programmes at the Century 21 studios in Slough.

Alan Shubrook

(Model Maker)

Opposite: An underwater series? A cartoon by Derek Meddings imagining what production on *Stingray* might be like.

A.P. FILMS
GUV
FIRE
DEREK MEDDINGS

ABOUT THE AUTHOR

Born into what Century 21 knew as 'the future' (after *UFO*, but before *Thunderbirds*), Stephen La Rivière led an underprivileged life compared to other youngsters, as he was not allowed to keep a pet monkey, visit Top Secret bases, or bunk off school permanently.

Once his application to join International Rescue as Lady Penelope's cook was declined, Stephen decided to enter the media as a writer / producer / director.

Following two decades of watching television growing up, Stephen has spent an unhealthy amount of time stalking octogenarian actors and filmmakers forcing them to reveal the secrets of their past successes for documentaries on series such as *Upstairs Downstairs*, *The Champions*, *The Persuaders!* and *Danger UXB*.

A life-long love of the Supermarionation shows has resulted in a string of related publications and documentaries including *Full Boost Vertical: The Supercar Story*, *The Genius of Gerry Anderson* comic strip, *Gerry Anderson - A Life in Pictures*, and the book you hold in your hands now. Oh, and a film of the same name.

Stephen's other interests include the Japanese language, procrastinating and Judo. Between 2010 and 2012 he spent time at the Kodokan Institute in Tokyo trying to become Emma Peel. Unfortunately, the catsuit didn't fit.

Stephen hopes that sales of this book will fund his brain-washing experiments on 9-year-old children (for the good of mankind - obviously…)

ROLLS
RR
ROYCE